W9-DGM-771

THE LIFE

OF

RICHARD STEELE

1713. ÆTAT 40.

From Vertue's Engraving of the Portrait by Thornhill.

THE LIFE

OF

RICHARD STEELE

BY

GEORGE A. AITKEN

IN TWO VOLUMES

VOL I.

HASKELL HOUSE PUBLISHERS LTD.
Publishers of Scarce Scholarly Books
NEW YORK, N. Y. 10012
1968

First Published 1889

HASKELL HOUSE PUBLISHERS LTD.
Publishers of Scarce Scholarly Books
280 LAFAYETTE STREET
NEW YORK, N. Y. 10012

Library of Congress Catalog Card Number: 68-24893

Haskell House Catalogue Item # 152

Printed in the United States of America

TO

HENRY MORLEY, LL.D.,

LATE PROFESSOR OF ENGLISH LITERATURE AT UNIVERSITY COLLEGE, LONDON,

FROM

AN OLD STUDENT AND FRIEND.

PREFACE.

More than a century and a half have passed since Richard Steele died, and much that is of value has been written about him; but it is only recently that any accurate study of the facts of his life has been attempted, and the present work is the first in which an endeavour has been made to treat the subject exhaustively.

Throughout the eighteenth century the more important of Steele's works were widely read, and passed through numerous editions; but it was not until 1786 that John Nichols published an edition of the *Tatler* in six volumes, with adequate notes. Nichols and those who assisted him wrote while persons who had known Steele were yet living or had only recently died, and many details were thus preserved which might otherwise have been lost. But Nichols did not attempt any systematic life of Steele. In 1789 an edition of the *Spectator* was published, but it was only slightly annotated. Between 1789 and 1791 Nichols again rendered service by issuing several volumes containing many of Steele's less known works, which, apart from their intrinsic worth, possess much interest to the biographer. Steele's Letters were published for the first time in

1787, and they throw a light, unique in its kind, upon his private life. Bisset and Chalmers added little to our knowledge in their editions of the *Spectator*, and Dr. Drake, while making many sensible remarks upon the Periodical Essayists, confined himself in his account of Steele to putting into connected form facts that were already known.

It was reserved for Lord Macaulay, in his essay on Addison, to make a bitter attack on Steele's character and genius, from which, thanks to the great and well-merited popularity of Macaulay's writings, Steele's reputation has hardly yet recovered. Macaulay was writing of Addison, and with his love of antithesis, he seems to have considered that he must, in order to magnify Addison, sneer at Steele; and, indeed, from the time of Tickell, Addison's first editor, downwards, Addison's admirers have too often endeavoured to exalt their hero by debasing his greatest friend. To quote Hazlitt's words, "I am far from wishing to depreciate Addison's talents, but I am anxious to do justice to Steele." After Macaulay came Thackeray, with the *Lectures on English Humourists*, published in 1853. In the lecture on Steele, Thackeray showed that he looked upon him with quite other eyes than Macaulay's, but along with the love which he felt for his subject, and which he endeavoured to make his hearers share, he lavished more pity than was necessary upon "poor Dick;" and it is easier to rebut Macaulay's misstatements than to remove the false impressions about Steele caused by Thackeray's somewhat condescending though affectionate compassion.

In 1855 John Forster published in the *Quarterly Review* an essay on Steele, of which the declared aim was to answer Macaulay, and Forster's essay remains to this day the noblest vindication of Steele that we have, both as regards his character and his position as a writer. Landor wrote to Forster: "Dear good faulty Steele! The *Quarterly* was not sent to me before nine last night. I would not, I could not, go to bed until I had read it through. My eyes are the weaker for it this morning." But for the facts of the life, so far as it was necessary to refer to them, Forster relied chiefly upon previous biographers. Ten years later, in 1865, Mr. H. R. Montgomery published a Life, the intention of which was good, but the result unsatisfactory. There was nothing new about Steele, and the book was filled up with digressions in the shape of sketches of the lives of all the famous people of the day. Mr. W. H. Wills purposed writing Steele's biography, but unfortunately he was prevented by death from carrying out his plans. He printed nothing on the subject except a paper in *All the Year Round*, in 1868, embodying the results of an examination which he made of the manuscripts at Kilkenny Castle. Mrs. Wills most generously placed at my disposal the materials collected by her husband, together with a few notes by her brother, Robert Chambers, and I have freely used such as were new to me, with due acknowledgment of my indebtedness in each case. Mr. Wills had not, however, gone very far in his labours, and he had not begun to form from his memoranda a connected narrative.

Mr. Austin Dobson has recently published two books about Steele, from which I have derived great assistance; the one, Selections from Steele, for the Clarendon Press, with an Introduction and a number of useful notes; the other, a Life of Steele, in the series of "English Worthies," a very interesting monograph, charmingly written, and containing many new facts, as well as others set in a fresh light.

In preparing the present work I have made every inquiry which seemed at all likely to lead to fresh information. As an illustration of what was yet to be done, I need only mention that no previous search appears to have been made for references to Steele among the treasures of the Public Record Office, and I have gathered more information from the various collections there deposited than from any other place. First in importance are the details of the various law-suits in which Steele was involved; they throw great light upon his connection with the theatre, and upon his pecuniary affairs, and afford valuable illustrations to the correspondence. I am glad to be able to acknowledge in this place the assistance which has been rendered me by the officials of the Record Office, and more especially by the late Mr. W. D. Selby, Mr. E. Salisbury, and Mr. Hubert Hall, whose suggestions have done so much to make my researches fruitful. Rivalling the Record Office in importance is the Probate Registry at Somerset House, where, among many other things, I found the clue to the name of Steele's first wife. My heartiest thanks are due to Mr. J. Challenor Smith and Mr. G. H. Rodman for the interest they have taken in my work and the help they have given me. Mr. Rodman was a friend of the late Mr. John Trevor Scurlock, the last known survivor of the family to which Lady Steele belonged, and he has been able to give me many fresh particulars of the Scurlocks. At the College of Arms, Mr. Alfred Scott Gatty, York Herald, has in the kindest manner given me the benefit of his knowledge in my efforts to solve questions of family history, and Mr. G. E. Cokayne, Norroy King of Arms, was good enough to examine for me several of the transcripts of Church Registers made by Colonel Chester. I must also acknowledge the courtesy of Mr. Watts, of the Vicar General's Office, Doctors' Commons; Mr. T. C. March, of the Board of Green Cloth, who examined the books of the Lord Steward's Office for notices of Henry Gascoigne; and Mr. G. T. Hertslet, of the Lord Chamberlain's Department, who placed at my disposal an Index or Calendar of the notices of theatrical matters among the Lord Chamberlain's records. This Index enabled me to examine readily the original documents, which are deposited at the Record Office.

Next in importance to London are the collections preserved in Dublin. Mr. J. J. Digges La Touche, of the Public Record Office, Dublin, and Sir Bernard Burke, Keeper of the Records in the Birmingham Tower, have very courteously answered my inquiries. I regret that, owing to his recent death, I cannot thank as I intended Mr. R. E. Lyne, of the Royal Dublin Society, who was untiring in the assistance he gave me by examining public records in Dublin, and by suggesting various sources of information. Among others who kindly examined Irish records for me are the Rev. W. Ball Wright and the late Rev. W. G. Carroll. Mrs. W. E. Steele, of Kingstown, and Mr. Lawrence E. Steele have aided me in many ways. The late Dr. W. E. Steele belonged to the family of the Steeles of Rathbride, a branch of the Steeles of Weston, Cheshire, and his interest in all that relates to the family history is shared by Mrs. Steele and her sons.

Several letters of Steele's and various papers relating to him in the British Museum, the Bodleian, and other Libraries are now printed for the first time. I am glad to acknowledge the courteous assistance I have received from the authorities at the British Museum ; the Bodleian ; Trinity College Library, Cambridge ; the Advocates' Library, Edinburgh ; Trinity College Library, Dublin ; Lambeth Palace Library, and the library at the South Kensington Museum. Dr. E. Regel and Prof. A. Beljame have kindly sent me notes upon books in the libraries at Berlin, Munich, and Paris.

The Hon. G. C. Brodrick, Warden of Merton College, and Dr. H. G. Liddell, Dean of Christ Church, have been good enough to examine the College books for records of Steele's life at Oxford.

In preparing my account of the family of Mary Scurlock, Steele's second wife, I had the kind assistance of Mr. W. G. Stedman Thomas, who made a very diligent search among the Wills in the District Registry at Carmarthen, and of the Rev. A. G. Edwards (now Bishop of St. Asaph), who supplied me with copies of entries relating to the family in the Registers of St. Peter's, Carmarthen.

My inquiries as to Steele's first wife led me to apply to the Colonial Secretary's Office in Barbados, and I am indebted to Mr. E. G. Sinckler for the careful examination he has made of the Wills and other records preserved in the office, and for various suggestions.

I am able to print a large number of letters and manuscripts by Steele, as yet unpublished, for which I have to thank their respective owners. The Duke of Marlborough very kindly placed in my hands for my greater convenience the papers relating to Steele in the Blenheim collection. These papers, about one hundred in number, are chiefly in Steele's writing, and consist of letters, drafts, verses, and memoranda of all descriptions. They have been briefly reported on by the Historical Manuscripts Commission, and Mr. Dobson made use of them in his work; but the great majority have not been published, and very few have been printed at length. The Marquis of Ormonde was good enough to allow an examination of the muniments at Kilkenny, and I have to thank Mr. J. G. Robertson, who kindly copied for me certain letters, &c., relating to the Gascoignes. The Earl of Egmont courteously afforded me access to the letters in his possession, including those by Bishop Berkeley, which give an interesting account of his friendship with Steele. Many gentlemen have allowed me to see documents relating to Steele in their collections, or have furnished me with copies. Among those I have to thank are Mr. Alfred Morrison, Mr. F. Locker-Lampson, Mr. Baker, of Bayfordbury, the Rev. J. C. Jackson, and the late Mr. A. Preston, of Norwich.

Mr. D Yeo Bruton made many useful suggestions, and lent me, besides a number of scarce pamphlets, the note-book of Addison's, containing in an early form certain of his *Spectator* essays, which Mr. J. Dykes Campbell printed in 1864.

Colonel F. Grant and the late Mr. Edward Solly aided me with their knowledge of eighteenth century literature, and at the sale of Mr. Solly's library I was able to secure almost all the pamphlets relating to Steele in his extraordinary collection which I did not already possess. An examination of these tracts and of the newspapers of the time has enabled me to give many fresh particulars.

The very interesting portraits of Lady Steele and her mother, Mrs. Scurlock, now published for the first time, are taken from original paintings. The fine portrait of Lady Steele is in the possession of Mrs. Thomas, of Moreb, Llandilo; it was painted by Sir Godfrey Kneller, probably in the early years of her married life. The portrait of Mrs. Scurlock, which is very characteristic, belongs to Mrs. Rae. I have also reproduced portraits of Steele and his children, Eugene, Mary, and Elizabeth, from paintings on ivory in the possession of Miss Mills. They are all interesting, and the expression which the artist has caught in painting Steele is particularly happy. All these pictures were mentioned by Nichols as forming part of the collection of family portraits belonging to Lady Trevor, Steele's eldest daughter. Upon her death in 1782 they passed to her heir-at-law, the Rev. David Scurlock, and from him to his son, Mr. John Trevor Scurlock.

That gentleman left them to his adopted daughter, Miss Mills, and the portrait of Mrs. Scurlock subsequently came into the possession of Mr. Rae, the co-executor, while Kneller's painting was sold to Mr. Rees, from whom it passed to Mrs. Thomas. The present owners of these pictures all very kindly allowed me to have them photographed for the purpose of this work, and Miss Mills gave me access to some interesting documents, which will be noticed in their place.

I shall have opportunities of thanking others from whom I have received assistance and sympathy, including some, personal strangers to me, who have shown their interest in the subject by writing from many parts of the world.

I have noted where the original, if it exists, of every letter printed is deposited, and I have given the authority for each statement made to an extent which may seem unnecessary; but every student who wishes to examine for himself knows how much labour is wasted through the habit, which is too common even among writers of a high class, of alluding only vaguely to the sources of their information.

The rules of spelling were to an unusual degree unsettled at the beginning of the eighteenth century, and in reprinting passages from Steele's works I have adopted modern conventions. To preserve the spelling of the early-printed copies would serve no useful purpose, for the spelling is not Steele's, but the printer's, and the peculiarities of the printers of that time, which include a great superabundance of capital letters, and commas where there should be an "e" in verbs, are trying to the eye of the reader. But where we have Steele's own manuscript the case is different, and I have printed all the letters and other papers which I have been able to collate with the originals exactly as they were written. I have also given notes showing in all cases of any importance the words cancelled while writing; in this way, especially in the case of draft letters, we are able to follow the writer as he is composing, and obtain glimpses of the ideas which passed through his mind, but which were rejected in favour of others.

I have endeavoured to show Steele as he was; the work has been one of love, but I have aimed at setting everything forth impartially. I have at any rate not knowingly withheld or misrepresented any facts, and I am confident that the result of the fuller study of his life which is now rendered practicable will be the conviction that, in spite of weaknesses which are among the most apparent of all those to which mortals are liable, Steele's character is more attractive and essentially nobler than, perhaps, that of any of the greatest of his contemporaries in the world of letters.

G. A. A.

CONTENTS.

VOL. I.

BOOK FIRST.

EARLY YEARS.

1672–1694. ÆT. 1–22.

BOOK SECOND.

SOLDIER AND DRAMATIST.

1694–1705, 1707–1710. ÆT. 22–33, 35–38.

BOOK THIRD.

FIRST AND SECOND MARRIAGES.

1705–1709. ÆT. 33–37.

BOOK FOURTH.

THE LUCUBRATIONS OF ISAAC BICKERSTAFF.

1709–1711. ÆT. 37–38.

BOOK FIFTH.

"THE SPECTATOR" AND "THE GUARDIAN."

1711–1713. ÆT. 38–41.

BOOK SIXTH.

POLITICS. STEELE AS ENGLISHMAN.

1713. ÆT. 41.

LIST OF ILLUSTRATIONS.

VOL. I.

BOOK FIRST.

EARLY YEARS.

1672–1694. ÆT. 1–22.

I.

PARENTAGE AND EARLY CHILDHOOD.

1672–1684. ÆT. 1–12.

RICHARD STEELE was born in Dublin in March 1672 (new style). His baptism is thus recorded in the Register of St. Bridget's:—"1671. March ye 12. Richard the Sonn of Richard Steele baptised." The evidence necessary for identification is furnished by an entry in the Registers of the Charter House for November 17, 1684:—"Richard Steel admitted for the Duke of Ormond, in the room of Philip Burrell—aged 13 years 12th March next." From this it would appear either that Steele, like Addison, was baptized on the day of his birth, or that the exact date of the birthday was forgotten, and the date of baptism given in its place.

Little is known respecting the parents of Richard Steele. It has been frequently stated that his father was a barrister, and private secretary to James Butler, first Duke of Ormond; but no one named Steele appears in the lists of counsel in the Four Courts about that time. A Richard Steele was, however, admitted a member of the King's Inns as an attorney:—"Richard Steele, admitted attorney, 11 June 1667," as it is put in Lodge's List, preserved among the records in the Birmingham Tower. The entry in the books of the King's Inns reads as follows:—"Trinity Tearme 1667. Memorand, that on the eleventh day of June 1667 Richard Steele (   ) was admitted into the society of this house & has paid for his admission the Sum of £2. 13s. 4d." The word after the name has been so carefully erased that there is almost a hole in the paper, but "gent." is just perceptible; if Richard Steele had been a barrister he would have been called "esquire." Duhigg, quoting inaccurately from the records of the King's Inns, gives the following:—"Richard Steele, Esquire, was admitted of the society, and paid an admission fee of £2. 13s. 4d." Duhigg goes on to say that the fee paid is an undoubted proof that Richard Steele was a barrister; and it is the fact that the usual fee paid upon admission as an attorney was 13s. 4d. only.[1] Thus, as the same writer records (but again inaccurately), the entry relating to the admission of Swift's father as an attorney and member was in the following terms:—"Memorandum that on the 26th day of January 1665 Jonathan Swift Gent. was admitted into the Society of this house and hath paid for his admission 00 : 13 : 04." But however the difference in the fee is to be accounted for, it is certain that Steele's father, like Swift's, was an attorney, and this receives corroboration from the fact that the elder Steele was afterwards sub-sheriff of Tipperary, a post which would not be occupied by a barrister. Mr. Wills, who searched the papers at Kilkenny Castle for references to Steele's father, stated that neither in the records at the Castle nor in the papers which Carte deposited in the Bodleian Library was the name mentioned in any official matter, except in one case, that of a lawyer's clerk named Steele, who was paid a small sum of money on account of his master.[2] We shall see, however, that further search has brought to light official papers relating to the elder Steele, both in the Bodleian Library and at Kilkenny Castle. The statement that Steele's father was secretary to the Duke of Ormond no doubt had its origin in the fact that Steele had an uncle (by marriage), Henry Gascoigne, who succeeded Sir George Lane[3] as secretary to the Duke in 1674, and became Steele's guardian not very long afterwards.

We know really nothing about the family of Steele's father. According to one theory, a family tradition of long standing, Richard Steele, the lawyer, was the son of William Steele, who was successively Recorder of London, Lord Chief Baron of the

[1] *History of the King's Inns*, 1806, pp. 220–21.

[2] *All the Year Round*, December 5, 1868.

[3] Sir George Lane was the second baronet, and was made Viscount Lanesborough, Co. Longford, 31st July 1676. His son died without issue, when all the honours became extinct.

Exchequer, and Lord Chancellor of Ireland during Cromwell's rule. William Steele, who was of the family of the Steeles of Weston, Cheshire, married, in 1638, Elizabeth, eldest daughter of Richard Godfrey of Wye, Kent, M.P. for New Romney, and had by her one son, Richard. Fuller particulars of these families of Steele and Godfrey will be given in an Appendix; it will be sufficient here to state what is known about Richard, the son of the Lord Chancellor. In his will, dated 18th August 1641, Richard Godfrey mentioned his eldest daughter, married to William Steele, and "my grandchild, Richard." Nine years later, on the 21st October 1650, Richard Steele, of Gray's Inn, eldest son of William Steele, Recorder of London, was admitted to Gray's Inn, but there is nothing to show that he was ever called to the Bar.[1] It was not until seventeen years later, it will be noted, that Richard Steele, of Dublin, was admitted as an attorney at the King's Inns. In 1658 Richard Steele was overseer to the will of Edward Harris, of St. Giles, Cripplegate.[2] From the State Papers in the Record Office we learn that in May 1657, the *Kinsale* was, by order of Lord Henry Cromwell, in readiness "to transport over Lord Steele, the Lord Chancellor of Ireland's son, and other persons of quality" to Ireland,[3] and in June 1658 William Steele was appointed one of the Commissioners to administer the government in Ireland;[4] but at the Restoration the Lord Chancellor and his family fled to Holland, and on October 24, 1662, information was given of an intended rising before the 28th—"Lord Steele would head the horse, and Col. Ludlow the foot."[5] On November 26, 1662, a William Cullen, of Dover, being examined, said that a stranger, finding he knew the family of the late Lord Chancellor, gave him a note, requesting aid for two kinsmen who wished to get into a vessel coming into the Downs, without having their names discovered; William Cullen understood that the persons

[1] Harl. MS. 1912, and Registers of Gray's Inn, p. 1057, kindly examined for me by Mr. Douthwaite, the Librarian.

[2] Prerog. Court of Cant., 244 Wootton.

[3] Calendar of State Papers (Domestic Series), 1656-7, pp. 557-559.

[4] Ibid., 1658-9, p. 367; 1659-60, pp. 19, 24, 502.

[5] Ibid., 1661-2, p. 526. See, too, the Fourth Report of the Historical MSS. Commission, p. 279.

who were to pass were William Steele and William Harvey.[1] On February 27, 1664, five ships arrived at Holehaven, and among the passengers were "Anne, wife of Col. Desborough, and Mary, wife of Recorder Steele."[2] On March 4, 1664, the ex-Chancellor was still at Rotterdam, conversant with the "fanatics"; and on March 5 a warrant was issued to search vessels at Holehaven, newly arrived from Holland, for papers belonging to Mrs. Steele.[3] In March 1666 a list was drawn up of those who were to be warned home by proclamation, in pursuance of the Act; the list includes Col. Desborough, Algernon Sydney, Richard Steele, and Richard Cromwell; and on April 9 a proclamation was issued recalling Richard Steele and others who had served in wars against their country, for trial, under pain of attainder and forfeiture.[4] After this we lose sight for some years of Richard Steele; but the ex-Lord Chancellor mentions his son Richard in his will, which was drawn up in 1680; and an Ann Mary Godfrey, of Woodford, widow of Michael Godfrey, of London, who was first cousin of William Steele's wife, by her will, made in 1707 and proved in 1708, left £20 to "my cousin Richard Steel." It is not improbable that the Chancellor's son is to be identified with the Richard Steel, late of St. Margaret's, Westminster, whose relict, Sarah, took out letters of administration on August 20, 1712.[5] But be this as it may, the fact that he was alive in 1707, when he must have been nearly seventy years of age, is alone sufficient proof that he was a different person from the Dublin attorney of the same name; for there is no doubt that the attorney's son was left an orphan at an early age, probably about 1677. But I have been unable to find any will or administration proving exactly when Steele's father died, and the coincidences in the case have made it possible to hold that the Richard Steele who was in exile in 1666 was pardoned through the intercession of the Duke of Ormond, the successor

[1] Calendar of State Papers (Domestic Series), 1661–2, p. 575. The Lord Chancellor's second wife was Mary, widow of Michael Harvey, who was brother of Dr. Harvey, the discoverer of the circulation of the blood.

[2] Ibid., 1663–4, p. 498.

[3] Ibid., 1663–4, pp. 505, 507.

[4] Ibid., 1665–6, pp. 318, 342.

[5] Court of the Dean and Chapter of Westminster.

of Henry Cromwell in Ireland, and allowed to settle there. The son of the late Lord Chancellor did study for the law; and the Duke of Ormond thought highly of Henry Cromwell, under whom Steele, the Chancellor, had served, and was willing to render him a favour. It is, however, not necessary to adopt this view in order to account for the presence of Steeles in Ireland; the name was by no means uncommon in England during the seventeenth century, and members of several of the English families resorted to Ireland.[1]

In after years political opponents did not hesitate to sneer at the obscurity which surrounded Steele's early years. Dennis proclaimed that Steele was "descended from a Trooper's horse;"[2] Wagstaff said that he was ashamed of his name; and

[1] William Steele, gent., and his wife Susan, of the Callough, Co. Longford, were among those who suffered in the Rebellion of 1641. Their property was seized in November, and in May 1642 William Steele was hung by the rebels. William and Susan Steele were both English (*Ireland in the Seventeenth Century*, by Mary Hickson, i. 353–4, 358, Depositions of Susan Steele and Dame Mary Browne). Henry Steele, curate of Clontubbrid, Monaghan, and James Steile, cooper, County Antrim, also made depositions respecting the outrages (ibid., i. 212, 286). In a list of the names and subscriptions of the adventurers for lands in Ireland, as also of those who subscribed for the sea service, between 1642 and 1646, we find John Steele, of London, salter, £50 (Prendergast's *Cromwellian Settlement of Ireland*, 2nd ed., 1870, p. 415. See, too, O'Hart's *Irish Pedigrees*, 3rd ed., 1881, p. 710). The will of a Fabian Steele, gent., of Dublin, was proved in 1699, and the will of a Henry Steele, buried in the parish church of St. Michan, Dublin, in 1667. The property of a Richard Steele, of Ballinakill, Queen's County, was administered to by his son John, in 1658. An Elizabeth Steele, with two children, appears in a MS. list of Protestants who fled from Ireland to Chester in 1688 (Trinity College, Dublin, MS. F. 4. 3). There are numerous Steele wills throughout the eighteenth century at Dublin. In the will of Hannah, widow of James Standish (Vice-Treasurer of Ireland, 1649–1661), proved 1693, Benjamin Steele is left the reversion of Germanstown, Co. Meath, for 99 years. A licence for the marriage of John Steel, of St. Andrew's, Dublin, gent., and Mary Hearne, of St. Bridget's, Dublin, spinster, was granted on Dec. 4, 1704 (Prerog. Dublin, "Special"). Several Steeles were parties to actions in the Chancery and other Courts in Dublin in the latter half of the seventeenth century, including Lawrence Steele, Dublin, gent.; Joseph Steele, Dublin, gent.; Henry Steele, Dublin, yeoman; and Samuel Steele, Ballyduff, King's County, gent. There was a family of Steeles living in the parish of St. Catherine, Dublin, at the close of the seventeenth century, and the Rev. W. B. Wright informs me that in the Registers of that parish there are entries of the burial in 1698 of George Steele and Mrs. Steele, and, on the 25th August, of Richard Steele. John and Martha, children of John Steele, were baptized in 1699.

[2] *Characters and Conduct of Sir John Edgar*, First Letter, 1720.

others hinted that he was born at Carrickfergus.[1] To this Steele only replied, that "whoever talks with me is speaking to a gentleman born."[2] In another place he said, "I am an Englishman born in the City of Dublin."[3] Dennis afterwards scoffed at Steele's statement that he was a gentleman born, saying that he was certainly of a very ancient family, "for his ancestors flourished in Tipperary long before the English ever set foot in Ireland," and he added that Steele's native country was stamped upon his face, his writings, his actions, his passions, and, above all, his vanity.[4] Steele answered quietly that "he was born in Dublin."[5] Of course it is not impossible that he was connected with some branch of the Chancellor's family; in after years he used, but without authority, the arms of the Steeles of Sandbach. Of any such connection there is, however, no proof whatever. It is tolerably certain that if his grandfather had been a Lord Chancellor, Steele would have said so.

Papers recently printed in Mr. Gilbert's last report upon the Ormonde MSS.[6] afford us a second glimpse of the life of Steele's father before Steele was born. Upon the passing of the Irish Act of Settlement (14 & 15 Charles II., cap. 2), a Court of Claims was set up in Dublin in February 1663. It sat for three months, to settle the differences between the dispossessed Royalists and the soldiers and adventurers who were in possession; but in 1665 it was found necessary, in consequence of the favour shown by the juries to the native Catholics, to pass another Act (17 & 18 Charles II., cap. 3), which was expressly ordered to be construed beneficially to the Protestants.[7] Richard Steele was, it appears, one of the Clerks of the Registry of the Court of Claims, and at the beginning of 1669 he and other Clerks appealed to the Lord Deputy against the Registrars of the late Court, who would not give them satis-

[1] *Examiner*, vol. iv. No. 37, Oct. 9–12, 1713; *A Second Letter from a Country Whig, to his Friend in London*, 1715.

[2] *Englishman*, No. 57.

[3] Ibid., No. 46.

[4] *Characters and Conduct of Sir John Edgar*, Fourth Letter, 1720.

[5] *Theatre*, No. 11.

[6] Historical MSS. Commission, Tenth Report, Part V., pp. 85, 88.

[7] Froude's *The English in Ireland*, 1881, i. 164–8; C. G. Walpole's *Short History of the Kingdom of Ireland*, 1882, pp. 289, 290.

faction for their three years' service. Legal proceedings could not be taken against Jeffryes, one of the Registrars, without licence first obtained, because he was an officer in the army. Henry Echlin, whose name comes first in the list of petitioners, subsequently became a knight and a baronet, a Baron of the Exchequer, and a Justice of the King's Bench.[1] I cannot identify the "Walter Rawleigh" whose name follows Steele's. This was the petition:—

Henry Echline, Richard Steele, Walter Rawleigh, Edward Jukes, George Houghton, James Halsey, John Fletcher, Daniel Hignett, William Hanaway, and Charles Norwood, gentlemen—"That your petitioners were admitted and sworn clarkes of the Registry of the late Court of Claymes sitting at Dublin, and constantly attended and faithfully and honestly discharged that employment for the space of three yeares last past. That George Phillips and John Jeffryes, Esquires, late Registers of the said Court, doe refuse to give any reasonable satisfaction to the petitioners for their said service, but doe leave them to take their remedy against them in law. And for as much as the said Jeffryes is an officer and member of the army here in Ireland and cannot be sued at Common Law without your Lordship's lycence first had, the petitioners therefore humbly pray your Lordship to grant unto them your licence to sue the said John Jeffryes either at Common Law or in Equity, as the petitioners shall be advised. And they shall pray, &c."

Jeffryes was then required to show cause why the petitioners should not have their legal remedy against him, and this he failed to do. The licence asked for was therefore granted to the petitioners.

[1] *Liber Munerum Pub. Hiberniæ*, Part II. pp. 34, 52. Sir Henry Echlin died in 1725. His great-grandfather, Robert Echline, Bishop of Down, was son of Henry Echline, of Pittadro, Fifeshire. Sir Henry's great-uncle, Hugh Echlin, was murdered in the rebellion of 1641 (*Ireland in the Seventeenth Century*, by Mary Hickson, i. 335). Swift mentions several persons of the name; a Lieut.-General Echlin, in Ireland in 1708; a Dr. John Echlin, "an ingenious gentleman of Ireland," who set to music a burlesque cantata by Swift, &c. (Scott's *Swift*, 2nd ed., i. 400, iv. 25, xvii. 395, xix. 262). The present (seventh) baronet is Sir Thomas Echlin. Full particulars of the family will be found in *Genealogical Memoirs of the Echlin Family*, by the Rev. J. R. Echlin, printed for private distribution. I am indebted to the author for a copy of the second and revised edition.

DUBLIN CASTLE, 11 February 1668[-9].

John Jeffryes, Esquire, is required, within tenn dayes after sight or notice hereof, to show us cause in writing (if any he can) why the petitioners should not be at liberty to take their legal remedy against him for the matter above mentioned, notwithstanding his military capacity.

OSSORY.

An affidavit follows, to the effect that the Lord Deputy's order was duly shown to Jeffryes; and then the licence required was given.

DUBLIN CASTLE, 16 March 1668[-9].

It appearing, by the within affidavit, that our order therein mentioned was on the 18th day of February last shewed to the defendant, John Jeffryes, Esquire, and he not haveing shewed any sufficient cause to induce us to forbeare haveing him to be sued at law, we are pleased hereby to grant the plaintiffs Henry Echline, and the rest in the said affidavit named, our lycence to take their remedy by due course of law against the said defendant, notwithstanding his military capacitie.

OSSORY.

It is probable that after this decision Jeffryes came to a settlement with the petitioners.

The maiden name of Steele's mother was Elinor Sheyles. I have not been able to trace her family, but the name may be a variation of "Sheile" or "Shiell," and the wills of several persons of that name, of good position and living in various parts of Ireland, were proved between 1649 and 1676.[1] The first we hear of Elinor Sheyles is in a licence granted on the 15th August 1663 by the Consistorial Court, Dublin, for the marriage of Thomas Symes of Dublin, Esquire, and Elinor Sheyles of the same, spinster.[2] Their first child, John, was baptized at St.

[1] Calendar of Wills (Dublin), Prerog., 1536–1810. John Sheal was living in Cork Street in 1685 (Hearth Tax Book, City of Dublin). Mary Sheills, daughter of Robert and Elizabeth Sheills, of Wanslin, Co. Meath, was buried, 28th October 1670, at St. Michan's, Dublin (MS. in Trinity College Library). The O'Sheills were an ancient clan in Antrim; and there were Shiells in Westmeath. Several Shiells were in King James's army in 1689, and one, Captain Luke Sheil, of Ballinderry, Mullingar, was attainted in 1691 (D'Alton's *Illustrations, Historical and Genealogical, of King James's Irish Army List*, 2nd edition, 1860, II. 759).

[2] The following is the entry in the Will and Grant Book, Diocese of Dublin, 1661–5, p. 18:—"Liã ad solemnizand' matrimoniu' inter Thomam Symes de Cĩte Dubl' ar' et Elinor' Sheyles de ead' sp̃r concessa fuit ꝑ Rssimu' in Xp̃o

Bridget's Church, April 26, 1664, but he did not live long, for there is an entry of his burial on June 3, 1664.[1] He was buried in the church, not in the churchyard, and this shows that the family occupied a good position in the parish. Thomas Symes made his will[2] on March 28, 1667, and he did not live long after that date, for the will was proved in the Prerogative Court by his widow on the 13th June 1667. Three years later, a licence of marriage was granted to Richard Steele, of Mountain, Diocese of Dublin, gent., and Elinor Symes (or Sims) of St. Bridget's, Dublin, widow, in the following terms:[3]—

"Liã ad solemnizand' mr̃õniū inter Richr̃d' Steele ꝑoch' de Mountaine & dioc' Dubl' gen^t & Elinor Sims ꝑoch' S^tae Bridgittae Dubl' vid' Concess' fuit ꝑ Rs̃s̃m̃ū Archiepū Dubl' primo die menss' Junii 1670 Direct' Tho: Ward Clĩco Curat' de Mountaine subsignat' & sigillat' ut pr̃d'."

I have ascertained that "Mountaine" is the present Monkstown, from the fact that in the Monkstown Registers, which begin in 1669, Thomas Ward is mentioned as minister in the entry of the one marriage recorded for the year 1671. Canon Peacocke informs me that commencing with 1670 the Monkstown Registers appear for a few years to be incomplete, and are perhaps copies from an older book. They contain no mention of Steeles. The name "Mountaine" nowhere occurs in the Registers, but there are to this day two groups of houses called Mountown about half a mile from the church. It is a

patrem ac Dñu' Dnu' Jacobu' providen' diã Dubl' Archiepu' Hibñiæq͡ Primatem et Metro^nu' 15° die Augusti Anno Dñi 1663 direct' Thomæ Rigbey Vicar' Eccliar' parõl' S^tae Catherinæ et Jacobi esq͡ absen' vel recusan' alii cuicunq͡ ministro infra Citem et Dioc' Dubl' et sigillat' cu' sigillo Cur' Cons̃s̃ Dubl'/."

[1] Registers of St. Bridget's, Dublin.

[2] "Thomas Symes, Esquire, of cittie of Dublin," left to his wife Ellinor £300; to his daughter Abbagell £200, to be paid when she came of age or married with her mother's consent; to the child which was not yet born, if a son, £300, if a daughter, £200, to be paid on the same conditions; to his daughter Mary, now in England, £10, to be paid in gold upon her marriage or coming to age; to his loving friend, Mrs. Eliz. Allen, £5; to his trusty and well-beloved friend, James Catlin, gent., £5; to Robert Paine, gent., £5; to his faithful servant, Ann Duxbury, £5; to his well-beloved kinsman, Perrian Poole, gent., the executor, £10. A debt of his brother's, Arthur Symes, of £20 and two years' lodging, was freely forgiven.

[3] Grant Book, Diocese of Dublin, 1665–1706.

curious coincidence that Edmund Ludlow, who often speaks in his "Memoirs" of his house at Monkstown, was a friend of William Steele, the Lord Chancellor. Richard Steele appears to have left the beautiful neighbourhood of Monkstown upon his marriage with Mrs. Symes, whose first husband had probably left her a comfortable house in St. Bridget's parish.

Steele says that his mother was "a very beautiful woman, of a noble spirit,"[1] and this, with what has been already said, is all that has come down to us about her, save the fact that she had two children by her second husband,—Richard, and Katherine, who was baptized at St. Bridget's on March 28, 1671.[2] It is certain, however, that she died while her children were very young, and probably not long after her husband. Her maiden name has almost always been said to be either Gascoigne or Devereux.[3] The statement that she was a Miss Gascoigne probably arose through the name of Steele's uncle being Gascoigne; I do not know what was the origin of the statement that she was a Miss Devereux, of County Wexford. It is true that Steele says he lost "the succession to a very good estate in the county of Wexford"[4] by entering the army, and that persons of the name of Devereux are still living in Wexford, but there appears to be nothing to connect them with Steele.[5] The question is now set at rest by the licences which have been quoted.

[1] *Tatler*, No. 181.

[2] Registers of St. Bridget's, Dublin. Katherine Steele in later life became mad. There is a letter extant about "my poor sister" written by Steele in 1721.

[3] Mr. R. S. Boddington, in *Miscellanea Genealogica et Heraldica* for June 1874, mentioned the name Sheyles, saying that Steele's mother was either a Miss Gascoigne, or a Miss Devereux, or a Miss Eleanor Sheyles. In the will of John Steele of Hampton-upon-Thames, late of Dover, Esq., which was proved on April 13, 1678, there is mention of a sister of the testator, Eleanor Steele; but Steele was here, of course, the lady's maiden name.

[4] *Theatre*, No. 11.

[5] Among the wills, &c., of the Diocese of Ferns, which includes Co. Wexford, are those of Nicholas Devereux, The Huggent, 1629; Lawrence, Duncormich, 1638; John, 1665; and Nicholas, of Ballynabarny, Kilrush, gent., 1698. In the Church Registers at Wexford, kindly examined for me by the Rev. J. K. Lathom, it is recorded that Nicholas Devereux married Elizabeth (?) Devereux, May 23, 1681; that Catherine Devereux was buried Nov. 9, 1681, and Lawrence on March 20, 1681[-2]. On May 7, 1683, William Synnot married Margaret Devereux; on April 19, 1701, John Devereux was married; and on Feb. 17, 1704[-5] "Mr. Devereux of Carrigmannon buried a child."

The parish of St. Bride, in which Steele was born, was at that time a fashionable part of Dublin, though it is difficult to realise, looking at its present poverty-stricken condition, that it was once a favourite place of abode with the rich. The population of Dublin was then probably less than 50,000, gathered round the Castle and the cathedrals. New streets on the north side of the Liffey were only just beginning to appear. The parish of St. Bride lies to the south of the Castle, being bounded on the north by St. Werburgh's parish, which reaches northwards to the river Liffey; on the west is St. Patrick's Cathedral, and to the south-east is St. Stephen's Green. The boundary on the west is principally Bride Street, which, under the name Werburgh Street, stretches in a northerly direction to the river. It is interesting to note that Jonathan Swift was born on November 30, 1667, less than five years before Steele's birth, in an adjoining, or perhaps in the same parish.[1] It is generally said that Swift was born at 7 Hoey's Court, Werburgh Street, either at his uncle Godwin's—which Forster strongly denies—or at his parents' house, still occupied by the widowed mother. The Burial Register and Vestry Accounts of St. Bride's show that about this time and for years afterwards Counsellor Godwin Swift lived in Bull Alley, Bride Street;[2] and there is no contemporary evidence that he lived in Hoey's Court. No. 7 Hoey's Court was the dwelling-place of Swift's parents, and if he was born in Hoey's Court he was not born at his uncle Goldwin's; but if, as Deane Swift and others held, Godwin Swift did receive the Dean's mother into his house, then the Dean was born in Bull Alley. It is to be noted that when Swift entered college he was described as "born in the county of Dublin" (Forster's *Life*, p. 28); now Bull Alley and Bride Street were then *extra muros*, but Hoey's Court was inside the walls, and if Swift had been born there he would have been "natus Dublinii." The matter is not certain one way or the

[1] I am indebted to the late Rev. W. S. Carroll for many hints about his parish and church of St. Bride's. Mr. Carroll claimed that Swift was born in St. Bride's. The Rev. S. C. Hughes, of St. Werburgh's, has also kindly examined the Registers of St. Bride's for me.

[2] Nichols (*Illustrations*, v. 381) gives a letter, which shows that Deane Swift regarded the house in Bull Alley as his grandfather Godwin's abode.

other, but the birthplaces of the two men who in after years came so much in contact were, in any case, almost within a stone's throw of each other.[1]

Swift was born after his father's death; Steele's father lived till his son was about five. Of the occurrences of those five years I am able to give one or two glimpses, which, though slight, are not without interest. In 1674 "Rich'us Steele de Dublin, gen.," was plaintiff in an action against Robt. Ford, gen., for the recovery of a small sum of money.[2] We shall see that thirty years later Richard Steele, son of the plaintiff in this case, was, by a curious coincidence, to marry a lady whose brother was a Robert Ford, of Barbados. A Robt. Foord, gent., was plaintiff in a case Foord *v.* Fitzgerald, in the Court of Exchequer, Dublin, 1674–6, and a Sir Robert fford was living in the parish of St. Nicholas Within, Dublin, in 1666–7.[3]

From a petition among the Carte Papers at the Bodleian it appears that Richard Steele was sub-sheriff of Tipperary in 1672 and 1673, and as the Duke of Ormond was Lord of the palatinate of Tipperary, and appointed his sheriffs, &c., in the same manner as the King did in other parts, there can be little doubt that the Richard Steele who here petitions the Duke was Steele's father. The position of sub-sheriff was perhaps obtained by Henry Gascoigne's influence, or possibly through Godwin Swift, whose first wife was a cousin of the old Marchioness of Ormond, and who was Attorney-General for Tipperary. Richard Steele was probably acquainted with Dean Swift's father, Jonathan,

[1] There are constant entries of the Swift family in the books of St. Bride's from 1681 to 1793. Dean Swift's uncles, Godwin and Adam, lived in Bull Alley, and his uncle William in Bride Street; Godwin and Adam were vestrymen at St. Bride's. The only mention of Dean Swift in the books of the church is when the Dean and Chapter of St. Patrick's sent £12 towards the restoration of the Round Tower of St. Michael's le Pole. Swift, while Dean of St. Patrick's, appointed three incumbents to St. Bride's. It was the incumbent of St. Bride's who applied for the writ *de lunatico*, and the curate assistant was Swift's guardian under the commission.

[2] Judgment Books, Common Pleas, Hilary 25 & 26 Charles II. (Public Record Office, Dublin).

[3] Hearth Money Roll, City of Dublin. From the same source we learn that a Martyn ffoord lived in St. Patrick's Close Yard. Mathew Ford, Esq., was M.P. for the County of Wexford in the Parliament which met at Dublin in August 1695.

though the latter, who was Steward of the King's Inns, died shortly before Steele was admitted a member; and he may have had some intercourse with the Uncle Godwin to whom Swift's mother had to look for help in her widowhood. This is Steele's petition:[1]—

THE HUMBLE PETICŌN OF RICHARD STEELE

To his Grace ye Duke of Ormonde.

Shewing—That yor Petr served as subsheriff to Bartholomew Fowke, Esqr, yor Graces late sheriff in ye sd County of Tipperary, for ye yeares 1672, 1673.

That in Respect of his sd office there were Committed to him Sevll Rolls of Greenwax of fines & forfeited Recognizances &c. to be collected to yor Grace's use, ye most of wch rolls had been in ye hands of former sheriffs, who had allready been opposed by ym.

That yor Petr being opposed upon all such Rolls as Came to his hands before yor Grace's Comrs appointed to receive ye Sheriffes accounts, he being a stranger at yt time in ye Country was Surprized in Totting or chargeing himselfe with many Sums he could never collect, The Persons from whome they became due being at yt time Insolvent, & haveing since so with Drawne, or absconded themselves yt yor Petr could never meete with their prsons nor find out any Substance to answer ye Charges:

That notwithstanding all such sums though Insolvent do still Remaine upon yor Petrs acct & are allowed unto him for monys by him disbursed to yor Graces use & for his Charges in ye Entertainment of yor Grace's Justices at ye Sevll Quarter sessions held for ye sd County of Tipperary, During ye time yor Petr served as aforesd what-

[1] Carte Papers, clx. p. 95. A copy of this document is among the materials collected by Mr. W. H. Wills. His attention was drawn to it by the late Rev. J. Graves of Stoneyford. The Rev. W. B. Wright informs me that in the old Corporation books—now in the possession of Mr. R. Langrish—of the borough of Knocktopher, of which the Ormondes were patrons, it is recorded that on the 16th October 1676 Thomas Steele was admitted freeman, and on April 21, 1707, Richd Steel, gent., was admitted freeman and burgess, on the ground of birth. On May 1, 1707, this Richard Steele was present at a meeting of the Corporation; and that is all we know. Whether these Steeles of Knocktopher were at all connected with Sir Richard's family—and Knocktopher is not very far from Kilkenny, where Henry Gascoigne lived—cannot be told; Steele himself was, of course, in London at the beginning of May 1707, commencing his duties as gazetteer.

soever Remaines upon y^{r} Pet^{rs} account, wch is Solvent, being required of yor Pet^{r} or his high Sheriff, whome yor Pet^{r} is bound to Indemnifie, wch will tend to yor Pet^{rs} great losse, unlesse Releived by yor Grace herein, he being much Impoverished by Divers losses & much sicknesse having alsoe a great Charge of Children to ꝑvide for:

Humbly prays yor Grace's order to yor Com^{rs} to allow yor Pet^{r} to apply such Charges as doe Remaine upon his acc^{t} being Solvent to answer his Disbursments, as afores^{d} & to discharge yor Pet^{r} of all such Sums of mony soe as afores^{d} Totted or charged upon him, wch he shall declare upon Oath y^{t} he hath not nor Could Receive, & y^{t} ye s^{d} Sumes soe to be taken of youre Pet^{rs} account, may be yet Continued in *ꝑ esse*, & transferred to ye Collection of yor Graces succeeding Sheriffe, to yor Graces use as hath been granted to all his Maties Sheriffes, in this Kingdome, who desired y^{e} same & particularly to yor Petr^{r} in his acc^{ts} in y^{e} King's Excheq^{r} by order of [the] Barrons of his Maties Court of Excheq^{r} & by y^{e} Consent of y^{e} Com^{rs} of his Ma$^{tie's}$ Treasury:

And he shall Pray.

In this petition, it will be noticed, Richard Steele speaks of a "great charge of children;" and it would seem that he held the position of sheriff in some other county, under the Court of Exchequer. The petition was thus endorsed by the Duke of Ormond:—

KILKENNY, 5 Feby 1674[-5].

I desire ye Judge of ye Court of ye Regalityes & Libertyes of ye County of Tiperary together with ye Com^{rs} of Reducem^{t} to Consider of ye above Peticōn, and to take such course for ye Pet^{rs} Reliefe as is used in his Maties Courts at Dublin to such Sherifs, as have made their application on ye like Occasion. ORMONDE.

The result of the inquiry does not appear, and we know nothing of the remaining years of Richard Steele's life. But in a paper in the *Tatler* (No. 181) his son has left an account which, while not necessarily describing his own history in every detail, yet certainly is based upon the recollections of his childhood.[1]

[1] In No. 22 of the *Tatler* (octavo edition), Steele says, speaking of the actor, Cave Underhill: "My father admired him extremely when he was a boy;" but this is not autobiographical, because the passage originally ran, in the folio issue, "my grandfather."

"The first sense of sorrow I ever knew was upon the death of my father, at which time I was not quite five years of age; but was rather amazed at what all the house meant than possessed with a real understanding why nobody was willing to play with me. I remember I went into the room where his body lay, and my mother sat weeping alône by it. I had my battledore in my hand, and fell a-beating the coffin, and calling Papa; for, I know not how, I had some slight idea that he was locked up there. My mother catched me in her arms, and, transported beyond all patience of the silent grief she was before in, she almost smothered me in her embraces; and told me in a flood of tears Papa could not hear me, and would play with me no more, for they were going to put him under ground, whence he could never come to us again. She was a very beautiful woman, of a noble spirit, and there was a dignity in her grief amidst all the wildness of her transport; which, methought, struck me with an instinct of sorrow that, before I was sensible what it was to grieve, seized my very soul, and has made pity the weakness of my heart ever since."

Steele was now fatherless, and, probably at no long interval, motherless.[1] But he had a kind uncle, Henry Gascoigne, who

[1] In a letter to his wife's mother, Mrs. Scurlock, June 15, 1708, Steele says: "Divested as I am of all relations that might enjoy anything after me." Henry Gascoigne died in 1707. In a scarce tract, published in 1714, containing a coarse and scurrilous attack on Steele, *The Ecclesiastical and Political History of Whigland of Late Years*, by John Lacy, Esq. (probably a pseudonym), there is a circumstantial account of Steele's parents, which contains a grain of truth, but which, when we take into account the nature of the other charges in the pamphlet, is absolutely worthless as an authority. The pamphleteer says that Steele's father was an honest farmer, a man of honour and integrity. The goodness of his father made him *indeed* a gentleman. He lived rich in poverty, and respected by all his superior neighbours. When he died he left a wife, two sons, and a daughter to battle with the world as well as they were able. But he had a sister [? Mrs. Gascoigne], a waiting-woman to an honourable lady, and she every now and then supplied the widow, and took charge of the children, sending her nephews to school, and having her niece well educated under her own eye. She distributed her savings, "as I have been credibly informed by one of that very family where she lived," as follows:—£600 for her niece's portion, and the remaining £900 equally between her nephews. The poor widow, their mother, was at length left to the hardest shifts; and in the most flourishing part of Steele's life his mother was starving, and washed for her bread, and caught her death through exposure to hardships. Steele, amid all his grandeur, was so mean that, though often importuned by his mother, he never sent over so much as ten guineas. And here the pamphleteer leaves him and the blackest imputations to go together

was, as we have seen, private secretary and confidential adviser to the Duke of Ormond; and Uncle Gascoigne became a real guardian to his nephew. Steele often spoke afterwards of Henry Gascoigne in warm terms of gratitude as "the author of all my advancement," "to whose bounty I owe a liberal education."[1] I am able to give here and in a subsequent book many fresh particulars of the Gascoignes. A Captain, afterwards Major, Thomas Gascoigne was in command of a company of one hundred men in Colonel Crafford's regiment in 1641;[2] and for the services which he rendered to the Royalists in Ireland before the 5th June 1649 there was a very considerable arrear due at the Restoration. Accordingly, by a warrant dated the 6th February 1662, the Duke of Ormond, Lord Lieutenant of Ireland, ordered His Majesty's Vice-Treasurer and Treasurer-at-Wars in Ireland, out of such sums as by His Majesty's declaration of the 30th November 1660 were appliable to the payment of such commissioned officers as received no satisfaction in lands or money for their services, to pay to Ellen Gascoigne, the disconsolate relict of Major Thomas Gascoigne, or her assigns, the sum of £40 sterling towards the relief of herself and her great charge of children, which sum was to be deducted from the satisfaction to be given for the arrears due to Thomas Gascoigne. Afterwards Ellen Gascoigne, by petition to the Lord Deputy, stated that this warrant was casually lost, and prayed that it might be renewed; and Lord Ossory, by a warrant dated April 12, 1665, directed that Ellen Gascoigne was to be paid £40, provided that the same had not been paid nor should hereafter be paid on the former warrant.[3] There can be little doubt that Major Thomas and Ellen Gascoigne were related to Henry Gascoigne. On the 25th April 1660, £10 was paid by

as the fittest companions. We shall have to notice this pamphlet again, and we shall see that during the political warfare of 1713–14 no charge was too gross for Steele's opponents to use against him. Perhaps I should apologise for disentombing this passage, but it will serve as a type of others. It will be seen that Steele is credited with a brother, of whom we hear nothing elsewhere.

[1] Letter of introduction addressed to Mr. Keally, April 2, 1711.

[2] *History of the Irish Confederation and the War in Ireland*, ed. by J. T. Gilbert, 1882, i. 230.

[3] Carte MSS., Bodleian Library, vol. 165, f. 323.

Thos. Parry, Treasurer for the contingencies of the Council of State, to Henry Gascoigne, for bringing a letter from the Committee of Co. Notts.[1] In 1665 we have the first evidence of Henry Gascoigne's employment by the Duke of Ormond, in the shape of a letter to Gascoigne from his "affectionate friend and humble servant, Ja. Buck," dated Moore Park, May the 7th, 1665, in which the writer says he has "delivered the inclosed you sent to my Lady Dutchess wch was prudently done on you by sending, consideringe from whome itt came, and the welcome newes it brought. . . . I have byn allway very confident of yor Honour & must thanke you for this last."[2] The earliest of Henry Gascoigne's letters at Kilkenny Castle is dated Dublin Castle, 9th October 1666, and relates to bonds respecting certain estates in Co. Longford.

In January 1668, Henry Gascoigne was appointed Chief Chamberlain of the Exchequer in Ireland. The warrant ran thus:[3]—

CHARLES R.

Right trusty and right Entirely beloued Cousin & Councelo^r Wee greet you well. These are of our especiall Grace & princely Favour to will and require you to cause Effectuall Letters patents to be passed under the great Seale of that Our Kingdome of Ireland unto Our welbeloued Subject Henry Gascoigne Gent. of the Office of chiefe Chamberlaine of Our Exchequer in that Our Kingdome of Ireland together with all Salaryes fees benefitts proffits & advantages to the said Office belonging or in any wise appertaining in as large & ample manner as ye same was granted by Our Royall father of euer blessed Memory unto Roger Moore the present Patentee thereof, To haue and to hold the said Office with all the Salaryes fees benefitts proffits and advantages to the same any way belonging or appertaining unto the said Henry Gascoigne during his naturall life from and im̄ediately after the death surrender avoydance forfeiture or other determination of the Letters Patents formerly granted of the s^d Office to the said Roger Moore in as large ample and beneficiall manner to all intents & purposes as the s^d Roger Moore or any other

[1] State Papers (Domestic), 1659–60, i. 108, p. 66 (Calendar, p. 599). The warrant is signed by Fairfax, Evelyn, and John Trevor, among others.

[2] Ormonde MSS.

[3] Carte MSS., vol. 43, fol. 643 (*olim* 383).

person or persons formerly executing the s^{d} Office held or enjoyed or of Right ought to haue held or enjoyed the same. The said Office to be exercised & executed by the said Henry Gascoigne or his sufficient deputy or deputyes. And these Our Letters notwithstanding the Statute made in the tenth yeare of the Reigne of King Henry the seventh in force in that Our Kingdome which doth prohibit the Grant of all Offices Accomptants for any longer time than during pleasure and notwithstanding any misrecitall or misnaming of the said Office or other cause whatsoeuer shall be unto you a sufficient Warrant. Given at Our Court at Whitehall the twenty fourth day of January in ye 19th yeare of Our Reigne 1668.

By His Maties Com̄and

ARLINGTON.

This Warrant, addressed to James, Duke of Ormond, "Our Leiveten^{t} Generall & Generall Gouerno^{r} of Our Kingdome of Ireland," was "Entred at y^{e} Signett Office the 25th of January 1667," and endorsed, upon its receipt in Ireland: "His Maties P^{ts} Dat. 24 / Rec. 31 } January 166$\frac{7}{8}$, concerning Harry Gascoigne." The patent was dated Dublin, April 9, 1668.[1]

In the following year Arthur Padmore and Henry Gascoigne, gent., were appointed, upon the surrender of the office by Sir George Lane, keepers of the records in the Birmingham Tower. The tenure of office was during good behaviour, and Gascoigne held the post until his death. The patent was dated August 21, 1669.[2] In 1674 Henry Gascoigne became secretary to the Duke of Ormond in the place of Sir George Lane, and in 1679 he and Edward Bagaley, Esq., were appointed Clerks and Keepers of the Hanaper, and of the Crown, in reversion after Richard Domvile, now deceased, and Thomas Domvile's patent. But this office appears to have been retained only for a few months, for in May 1680, William Domvile, Esq., son, and William Hartpole, Esq., grandson of Sir William Domvile, Attorney-General, were appointed in reversion after all the said patents.[3] In 1681 Gascoigne was made Doctor of Laws of

[1] *Liber Munerum Publicorum Hiberniæ*, 1824, &c., Part II. 61 (Lodge's Patentee Officers).

[2] Ibid., Part II. 78. Addison was appointed to this office in December 1709.

[3] Ibid., Part II. 25.

Trinity College, Dublin. There are two letters among the Ormonde MSS. addressed to Henry Gascoigne by his "affectionate cousin," James Gascoyne, who was in the army. In the first of these, dated Dublin, 10th February 1682[–3], James asked his cousin to get the Duke of Ormond to write to Lord Darnly in his behalf, either to advance him or to move him, as he was at so great a distance from his wife and family that the expenses of travelling were heavy, and his allowance was so small that he was capable of giving his wife and children little or no assistance towards their support. In the second letter, dated Dublin, February 23, 1683[–4], James, understanding that the army here was to be modelled and augmented, entreated his cousin to put his Grace in mind of him, in order that he might be preferred either in the Dragoons or Grenadiers, which it was reported were speedily to be raised. In a postscript James added, "My most humble Service to yor Lady." Gascoigne's wife was a sister of one of Steele's parents; he had married before 1671, for in a letter to Captain George Mathew, Dublin, dated Whitehall, 18th March 1670[–1], Gascoigne speaks of having made inquiries of his wife upon some point. James Gascoyne was in all probability the Ensign Gascoign who was living in Cook Street, Dublin, in 1685.[1] There are two letters among the Ormond MSS., dated April 30 and May 15, 1689, from E. Gascoigne, probably another cousin, to Henry Gascoigne. This was the Edward Gascoyne, gent., whose son, Thomas Gascoyne, born in the county of Kilkenny, matriculated at Trinity College, Dublin, on the 18th May 1698, at the age of nineteen. Thomas had been educated under Edward Hinton of Kilkenny; his tutor at Trinity College was Gratan, and he took his B.A. degree in 1703.[2] The letters at Kilkenny

[1] Hearth Tax Book, City of Dublin (Public Record Office, Dublin).

[2] Registers of Trinity College, Dublin; and Calendar of Graduates. The name Gascoigne occurs in the list of principal families in Ireland at the end of the seventeenth century, given in MS. vols. F. 3. 23, F. 3. 27, F. 4. 2, and F. 4. 18 in Trinity College Library (O'Hart's *Irish Pedigrees*, 1881, p. 699). Edward Gascogne of Dublin, gen., Alderman, and Edward Gascogne of Cappagh, Co. Kilkenny, gen., were, with others, summoned in 1674 to answer Val. Smith of the city of Kilkenny as to a money recovery (Judgment Books, Common Pleas, Dublin, Trinity, 26 Charles II.).

addressed to George Gascoigne, Esq. (July 17, 1682), and Fra. Gascoigne, Esq. (Sept. 16, 1689, and May 16, 1690), are business letters intended for Henry Gascoigne, whose Christian name was mistaken by the writers.

In January 1685–6 Henry Gascoigne was appointed Clerk of the King's Scullery, doubtless through the Duke of Ormond, who was Lord Steward of the Household. This was the Royal letter to the Duke, addressed "To Our Right Trusty and Right Intirely Beloved Cousin & Councellour James Duke of Ormond Lord Steward of Our Household."[1]

JAMES R.

Our Will and Pleasure is

That you give Order for the swearing and admitting of Henry Gascoigne Esq. Supernumerary Clerk of our Scullery in Ordinary and that you settle upon him the stipend allowed him by the present Establishment of our Household and all other the profits, Perquisites, priviledges and Advantages to the place of Clerk of our Scullery in Ordinary belonging untill a vacancy happen in the succession of the Clerks of Our House and then he is from time to time to rise and take place according to the ancient established Custome of Succession in our Household. Given at Our Court at Whitehall the 29th day of January 1685 In the first yeare of our Reigne.

The Lord Steward's warrant ran thus: "Whereas I have received a Warrant from his Matie in these words, vizt.," &c., "These are to will and require you to sweare and admitt the said Henry Gascoigne into the said Place of Supernumary Clerk of Our Scullery in Ordinary according to the contents of his Maties Warrant and for soe doeing this shalbe your Warrant. St. James Square the first day of February 1685.—ORMOND. To my very Loving Friend the Clerke of his Maties Greencloth attending."[2]

On the 25th January 1686[–7], Gascoigne was appointed Tail-

[1] Ormonde MSS.

[2] Lord Steward's books.

Cart-taker to the Board of Green Cloth,[1] and he kept that position at anyrate until 1704, and probably until a short time before his death.[2] There were four Tail-Cart-takers, each of whom received £2. 13s. 4d. wages, and £37. 6s. 8d. board wages, making £40 in all. Gascoigne was subsequently Clerk of the Woodyard in Ordinary,[3] and Clerk of the Bakehouse in Ordinary. The warrant to the Lord Steward, directing his appointment to the latter post, dated May 1, 1690, invested him with "the Wages, Boardwages, Fees, Profitts, Perquisites, and advantages thereunto belonging, in as large and ample manner as any in ye like Place have formerly held and injoyed the same." The Lord Steward's warrant to the Clerk of their Majesties' Greencloth is dated June 22, 1690.[4] By 1693 Gascoigne was Joint-Clerk of the Accatry in Ordinary, and he held this post, which carried with it wages of £6. 13s. 4d., and board wages of £113. 6s. 8d., or £120 in all, until his death.[5]

At this point we may leave for a time the story of Henry Gascoigne's life, and turn back to 1684. Steele, who had then reached his twelfth year, was placed upon the foundation of the Charter House through his uncle's influence with the Duke of Ormond, who was one of the governors. I have already quoted the entry in the Registers of the school for November 17, 1684:

[1] Ormonde MSS. (Mr. Wills' notes). The warrant from the Earl of Devonshire to the Clerk of their Majesties' Greencloth, preserved in the Lord Steward's books, is, however, dated July the 1st, 1689. Possibly there was a fresh warrant upon the change of sovereign.

[2] Miege's *New State of England*, 2nd ed. (1693), p. 389; 5th ed. (1703), p. 479. By 1707, when the 6th ed. was published, Gascoigne had, it would appear, ceased to be Tail-Cart-taker; but in the 22nd edition of Chamberlayne's *Angliæ Notitia* (1707), p. 540, he still appears as Tail-Cart-taker.

[3] The warrant appointing John Thompson, Esq., Clerk of Our Woodyard, "the same being vacant by the removall of Henry Gascoigne Esqr," is dated May 1, 1690.

[4] Lord Steward's books.

[5] Miege's *New State of England*, 2nd ed. (1693), p. 388; 5th ed. (1703), p. 477; 6th ed. (1707), Part III. p. 172; Chamberlayne's *Angliæ Notitia*, 18th to 22nd editions (1694–1707). In the Lord Steward's books there is a warrant, dated June 30, 1702, directing the swearing and admitting of Henry Gascoigne, and John Jackson, Esqr., in the Place of joint Clerks of Our Accatry in Ordinary, from which it would appear probable that a fresh warrant had to be obtained on a change of sovereign.

—"Richard Steele admitted for the Duke of Ormond, in the room of Phillip Burrell—aged 13 years 12th March next."[1] Steele afterwards called the Duke of Ormond "the memorable and illustrious patron of my infancy."[2]

[1] Mr. Lee, Registrar of the Charter House, has kindly verified this extract for me. One previous writer printed "last" for "next," destroying the corroboration as to the date of Steele's birth which the entry affords.

[2] Dedication to *The Lying Lover*. The first Duke of Ormond was Lord-Lieutenant of Ireland in 1661, and from 1677 to 1685.

II.

SCHOOL LIFE.

1684–1689. ÆT. 12–17.

IN the absence of personal details of Steele's school life, a few notes from a contemporary book upon the Charterhouse —*Domus Carthusiana*, by Samuel Herne, 1677—will be of interest. "They shall keep the accustomed hours of six in summer, and seven in winter, for their coming to school, and eight and three in the forenoon and afternoon for their collations, and of six in summer and winter, if the time of meals will permit, for their leaving off; not failing both morning and evening to begin and end their studies with the Latin prayers and collects now used." Boys in the highest form did special Greek and Latin verses for public inspection on Sunday; and they read the chapters and said grace. The schoolmaster and usher could not go into the country without leave from the master; and there were not to be more than sixty pupils besides those on the foundation—forty-four at that time—unless an additional usher was provided. "In correction they shall be moderate; in instruction diligent." Twenty-nine scholars were maintained at the universities. The form used by a governor in nominating a boy to the school is given in Herne's book. The limits of age for admission were ten and fourteen. The Charterhouse estate is devoted to the maintenance of "decayed soldiers and English gentlemen;" "likewise it is laid out on the maintenance of decayed gentlemen's children, who have a chamber to two of them, wholesome diet, admirable conveniences, and all accommodations imaginable; so that they are no burthen at all to their parents, after their first year's admission to the House."

In 1686 Joseph Addison, who was born on May 1, 1672, and was thus a few weeks younger than Steele, entered the famous school as a private pupil, and Richard Steele and Joseph Addison formed the friendship of which the chief monument was to be the *Spectator*.

Addison's father was a dean; his grandfather was a poor clergyman of Westmoreland. The name of each was Lancelot. The future dean was born in 1632, and was sent to the Grammar School at Appleby, and afterwards to Queen's College, Oxford, where he made his way in spite of poverty, and became successively Bachelor and Master of Arts. But he was an avowed Royalist, and he was obliged to humbly apologise for the speech which he made as one of the *Terræ filii* in 1658. At the Restoration he was made chaplain at Dunkirk, and afterwards at Tangier, where he remained for eight years, and then visited England; but during his absence the chaplaincy was given to another. In this emergency a Wiltshire gentleman, Mr. Joseph Williamson, gave him the living of Milston, Wiltshire, which was worth £120 a year. Lancelot Addison thereupon married Jane Gulston, whose brother was afterwards a bishop. They had six children, the eldest of whom, Joseph, was named after their friend Mr.—afterwards Sir—Joseph Williamson. In the meantime Lancelot Addison wrote skilful books upon West Barbary, Mahomet, the State of the Jews, and he was made one of the King's Chaplains in Ordinary, Archdeacon of Salisbury, and lastly, in 1683, Dean of Lichfield. His son Joseph was sent to a school in Lichfield from 1683 to 1685, previous to his proceeding to the celebrated Charterhouse.

Thackeray, who has, from his own recollections, described the Charterhouse and the Carthusians so lovingly, under the names of Grey Friars and Cistercians, in *The Newcomes*, and as Slaughterhouse, in *Pendennis* and *Vanity Fair*, has given in the *English Humourists* a fancy sketch of Steele's life at school; but as he says, "I have no sort of authority for the statements here made of Steele's early life," and as he bases his theories upon a mistaken notion that Addison was Steele's senior by three years, it is not necessary to repeat his statements of Steele's laziness and subsequent punishments, of his debts to the tart-woman and to his school-mates, or of the way in which he fagged for Addison and blacked his boots. It is rather hard when a biographer chooses to form a conception of what the person whom he is describing was as a man—a conception which may be, and in this case was, to a large extent erroneous—and then says, "If the child is father to the man, then Steele the schoolboy must have been what I have represented." It is certain that Steele obtained a fair knowledge of the classics at school, but it may to some extent have been beaten into him, after the fashion of that day. "In my twelfth year," says Mr. Bickerstaff, "I suffered very much for two or three false concords."[1] Afterwards, in the *Spectator* (No. 157), Steele attacked the brutal system of flogging, speaking, with the experience of "one who has gone through what they call a great school," of the irreparable injury often caused to the characters of the children who were punished.

Addison's friend was an orphan, and the good Dean of Lichfield welcomed young Steele to the Deanery; in later years, after Addison's death, Steele wrote: "Were things of this nature to be exposed to public view, I could show, under the Dean's own hand, in the warmest terms, his blessing on the friendship between his son and me; nor had he a child who did not prefer me in the first place of kindness and esteem, as their father loved me like one of them; and I can with great pleasure say I never omitted any opportunity of showing that zeal for their persons and interests as became a gentleman and a friend."[2] And in the *Tatler* (No. 235) there is a sketch clearly based upon the writer's remembrance of Lancelot Addison:—"I remember, among all my acquaintance, but one man whom I have thought to live with his children with equanimity and a good grace. He had three sons and one daughter[3] whom he bred with all the care imaginable in a liberal and ingenuous way. . . . His method was to make it the only pretension in

[1] *Tatler*, No. 89.

[2] Dedication of the *Drummer* to Congreve, 1722.

[3] Lancelot Addison died in 1703, leaving three sons—Joseph; Gulston, afterwards Governor of Fort George; and Lancelot, who became a Fellow of Magdalen College, Oxford; and one daughter, Dorothy, who married the Rev. Dr. Sartre, and afterwards Mr. Combes. Two other daughters died young.

his children to his favour to be kind to each other. . . . It was an unspeakable pleasure to visit or sit at a meal in that family."

In 1687 Addison entered Queen's College, Oxford, following in the steps of his father; Steele remained at the Charterhouse two years longer. On November 1, 1689, he was, we learn from the Charterhouse Registers, "elected to the University." The head-master of the school during Steele's residence was Thomas Walker, LL.D., who, after being usher for five years, was appointed head-master in 1679, and occupied that post until 1728, when he died, in his eighty-first year. It has been suggested that Addison referred to his old master, when, in No. 488 of the *Spectator*, he said, speaking of the increase in the price of the paper owing to the Stamp Tax: "The ingenious *T. W.* tells me that I have deprived him of the best part of his breakfast, for that since the rise of my paper he is forced every morning to drink his dish of coffee by itself, without the addition of the *Spectator*, that used to be better than lace to it." We shall see, in speaking of the *Spectator*, that Steele maintained his friendship with Mr. Petiver, F.R.S., who was apothecary to the Chartreuse. William Bolton was usher (or second master) from 1679 to 1685, and John Stacey from 1688 to 1695. The school has now been moved to Godalming, and the old Charterhouse buildings have been threatened with destruction, happily averted, for a time at least, by the decision of the House of Commons.[1]

[1] "*Floreat Æternum Carthusiana Domus.*

Blest shades of Addison and Steele
That round the building hover,
The home where wits have knelt and kneel,
Destroy not, but recover!"—*Punch*, January 23, 1886.

It is to be hoped that some at least of the older and more interesting portions of the Charterhouse will never be wilfully removed: such, for example, as the fine old dining-hall, the grand oak staircase, the quaint chapel, the drawing-room with its great fire-place, and the old buildings in Washhouse Court, which keep us in mind of the days when it was the abode of monks, and, after they had been brutally turned out and murdered by Henry VIII., of the Duke of Norfolk. Some good views of the Charterhouse buildings will be found in *Memorials of Charterhouse*, by C. W. Radcliffe, London, 1844, folio.

III.

COLLEGE LIFE.

1689–1694. ÆT. 17–22.

STEELE entered at Christ's Church College, Oxford. In the Dean's Entry Book, under the year 1689, his name occurs as a commoner—"Ricardus Steel, Dec. 21." Every boy who went from the Foundation at Charterhouse to the university had an exhibition;[1] and this exhibition is referred to in the first of the five letters which follow, and which are the earliest productions of Steele's pen that we have. The originals are among the manuscripts of the Marquis of Ormonde, at Kilkenny Castle, and they are in some places injured through damp. These letters were printed by Mr. Wills in *All the Year Round* for December 5, 1868, and by Mr. J. T. Gilbert in his report upon the Marquis of Ormonde's MSS., given in the Seventh Report of the Historical Manuscripts Commission, pp. 753–4. There are a few trifling differences between the two versions.[2]

The first of these letters (not given by Mr. Wills) was written to Uncle Gascoigne before Steele left the Charterhouse. The original is much damaged, and a few words have been conjecturally added in brackets.

[1] Dr. Haig Brown's *Charterhouse, Past and Present*, 1879; Radcliffe's *Memorials of Charterhouse*, 1844. Scholars were elected to the university by a board of governors when they were from seventeen to nineteen years old, after an examination. They could go to any college at Oxford or Cambridge as they chose.

[2] Mr. J. G. Robertson could not find these letters of Steele's during the brief examination which he was able to make of the muniments at Kilkenny Castle, and he could not, therefore, make a fresh collation for me.

SIR,

The advantage [of going] speedily to the un[iversity is that if I am there] before Snt. Thomas's day,[1] I receive 5 p. of my Charter House exhibition, as if I had been resident there this quarter, which I utterly lose if I am not there at that time, for my eight years goe on from the time of my election from hence, and not from my admittance into the University. This, Sir, I conceiv'd would not be impertinent to acquaint you with, since I knew you were told by Mr Pain that we were not to receive pay till the quarter after, but the master, I suppose, either in consideration of our charges at our entrance there, or in furtherance of those that wait for admittance here, who cannot [be admitted until we leave] ordered we . . . which makes . . . I hope you . . . that an inch . . . ting myself . . . [de]mands or th . . . as to be care[less of your expenses] whose benevo[lent inten]sions but . . . and generosity. . . . [No one li]ving can live upon lesse than I, and I would not have mentioned this businesse if I had thought it would not lessen your charges. But I hope, Sir, that my gratitude to you will be always expressed hereafter more by actions and obedience than by all the words and sentences that can be invented by your most obliged and most humble servant, R. STEELE.

As we have seen, Steele was able to enter Christ Church on St. Thomas's Day, December 21st, and would thus secure the £5 of his exhibition respecting which he was anxious. The next letter, which was addressed "For Henry Gascoign, Esq., att Ormond-House, in St. James's Square, London," was written from Oxford.

Jan. 5 [1690].

SIR,

My Tutour has received ye certificate for seven pound, for which I most humbly thank you. I have been wth Dr. Hough[2]

[1] December 21, 1689.

[2] John Hough, born in 1650, was elected a Demy of Magdalen College, Oxford, in 1669; he became a Fellow in 1675, and in the following year was ordained. In 1679 his rooms were searched upon groundless suspicion of his corresponding with a papist. In 1681 he was appointed chaplain to the Duke of Ormond, then Lord Lieutenant of Ireland; he returned in 1682, and a living was subsequently provided for him at Temsford, Bedfordshire. In 1687 he was elected President of his college by the Fellows, who rejected a mandamus from James II. appointing Anthony Farmer president. Dr. Hough's removal from his office by the Ecclesiastical Commissioners was but

who received y^r letter and Enquired very Civilly after Your and my Ladyes health. When I took my leave of him he desired me to inform him, if at any time he could be servicable or assistant to me for he could very readily do it. Dr Aldridge[1] Gives his Service to y^u, and told me he should write to you himself by this post. This is all at present from y^r most humble Servt and ever-obedient nephew, R. STEELE.

Pray, S^r, direct your letters to me myself for 'tis a thing[2] troublesome to my Tutour to receive them. I am and have been very much indisposed by a bile over my left eye; but I think it mends now.

Steele's tutor was Dr. Ellis, mentioned in the preface to the *Christian Hero* as "his Ever-Honour'd Tutor." There is a copy of the second edition of the *Christian Hero* in the Dyce Library, South Kensington, with the following lines written on the fly-leaf:[3]—

To

My Lov'd Tutour Dr Ellis.

With secret impulse thus do streams return
To that Capacious Ocean whence they're born:
Oh would but Fortune come wth bounty fraught
Proportion'd to ye mind wch thou hast taught!
Till then let these unpolish'd leaves impart
The Humble Offering of a Gratefull Heart.

RICH^D STEELE.

temporary, for on October 25, 1688, he was reinstated President by the Bishop of Winchester, commissioned by William of Orange. In 1690 he was made Bishop of Oxford, but he continued to hold the presidentship. He was afterwards Bishop of Lichfield and of Worcester successively, and he lived till 1743. He was greatly attached to his college, and was much interested in deserving young students, whom he often helped by his recommendation.

[1] Henry Aldrich, D.D., was Dean of Christ Church from June 17, 1689, until his death in 1710. He was succeeded by Atterbury. Dr. Aldrich was in every respect an excellent Dean, and was very popular. His *Artis Logicæ Compendium* first appeared in 1691. In 1692 he was made Vice-Chancellor of the University. He was a skilled musician and architect; his famous catch, "Hark! the bonny Christ Church bells," is alluded to in the *Tatler*, No. 34.

[2] "something," according to Mr. Wills' transcript.

[3] A facsimile of these verses is given in the *Handbook to the Dyce and Forster Collections*, p. 23. Years afterwards Steele made use of the first couplet, slightly modified, in his *Prologue to the University of Oxford*.

Welbore Ellis was elected to Christ Church from Westminster in 1680, became M.A. in 1687, and D.D. in 1697. He was chaplain to the second Duke of Ormond when he was made Bishop of Kildare in August 1705, and also chaplain to the 2nd Troop of Guards—the regiment which Steele entered. His elder brother, John, had been secretary to the Duke's father, Lord Ossory. Dr. Ellis was made Bishop of Meath in 1731, and he died in 1734. His portrait is in the hall at Christ Church.[1]

Henry Gascoigne, as secretary to the Duke of Ormond, Chancellor of the University, would have frequent business relations with the authorities at Oxford, and Steele would have the advantage of ample introductions from his uncle. It is, moreover, not at all improbable that Gascoigne visited Oxford during Steele's term of residence. The following pleasant letter was sent to Henry Gascoigne[2] by Dr. Hough, President of Magdalen College—now Addison's college—a few days only after the visit described by Steele in the letter of the 5th January, given above.

MAGD. COLLEGE, OXON,
Jan. ye 15th, 1689 [1690, N.S.]

S^r,

I received yours of ye 7th instant together with ye inclosed for which I return you my hearty thanks, but this post brought me some papers from Sr R^t Southwell so full & satisfactory that I shall not need to give you any farther trouble upon that subject.

I go on Monday to Worcester and shall not return from thence in less than six weeks, but I hope by that time you will thinke of making us a visit in good earnest. All ye heads of houses are your

[1] *Ellis Correspondence*, by the Hon. G. J. W. A. Ellis (1829), Vol. I. xxiii. 218; *Pue's Occurrences*, August 28, 1705; Luttrell's *Diary*, v. 586, 591; Dobson's *Steele*, p. 11. A number of letters from Welbore Ellis to his brother John are preserved in the British Museum (Add. MSS., 28930–28936).

[2] The original is among the Ormonde MSS. It is addressed—

"For
Henry Gascoigne, Esq.,
Secretary to ye Duke of Ormond
at his Grace's house in
St James's Square,
London."

humble servants & you will find tolerable clarett & a hearty welcome from all of them, but the last not more truly and cheerfully from any man than from

S[r]

Y[r] very affectionate

Friend & faithfull Servant

J. HOUGH.

In a letter dated January 30, a fortnight later, Charles Aldworth,[1] of Magdalen College, who was anxious about a History lectureship to which the Duke of Ormond had recommended him, wrote to Henry Gascoigne:[2] "Our worthy president, Dr. Hough, is now gone to Worcester, and intends to write to you from thence on the same account. S[r], be pleased to accept of my hearty thanks for your many favors to my selfe & our whole society." There are also letters to Gascoigne dated January 5 and January 11, from Mr. William Wyatt, of Christ Church,[3] Orator of the University, asking Gascoigne to procure from the Duke of Ormond a letter appointing him Principal of St. Mary Hall, vacant through the death of Dr. Crowther. On the 29th December 1689 Dr. Aldrich had urged Mr. Wyatt's claims in an interesting letter to the Chancellor;[4] and Wyatt was soon afterwards duly appointed.

Steele matriculated on March 13, 1690 (N.S.). The following is the entry in the register of matriculations of the University[5]:—

"Ædes Christi.
Ter[o] S[cti] Hilarii 1689. Mar. 13. Ric. Steele
16. R. S. Dublin Gent,"

which means, On the 13th March, in Hilary Term, 16$\frac{89}{90}$, Richard Steele, of Christ Church, sixteen, son of Richard Steele, of Dublin, gentleman. Steele was really eighteen; and it is probably through this error in the matriculation register that the date of his birth has often been given as about 1675.

[1] Charles Aldworth was B.A., April 22, 1670; M.A., Feb. 4, 1672; and B. and D.C.L., July 12, 1686.

[2] Ormonde MSS.

[3] William Wyat (or Wyatt) was B.A., November 22, 1662, and M.A., June 28, 1665. He was appointed Orator in 1679.

[4] Printed in the *Academy* for May 21, 1887.

[5] *All the Year Round*, December 5, 1868.

The next letter bears the post-mark, "March 31," and is addressed to "Henry Gascoign, Esq., at the Duke of Ormond's house, in St. James's Square, London."

Sr,

I received your letter, and gave Mr. Sherwin[1] his paper from you. Most of the money he had in his hands was before disposed of, therefore he gave me but five pounds, but he will give me the rest next Wednesday, till which time I defer my giving yu A true and particular account how my Tutour and I design to dispose of the whole; the night after I writ my last, Mr. Horne[2] sent for me to the tavern, where he and Mr. Wood,[3] a fellow of that Coll: treated me with Claret and Oysters. I went to give him an account of what you commanded me, but I shall Do at the first Opportunity. Our Dean, whome you expected, Is, I suppose, now at London, the election of[4] students is not very far off now; if you would be pleased to speak with[5] him or purchace from my Lord a word or two; it would perhaps get me the most Creditable preferment for young men in the whole university:[6] there are many here that think of it, but none speak their mind; the places are wholly in the Dean and Cannons dispose without respect to Schollarship; but if you will vouchsafe to use your interest in my behalf there shall be nothing wanting in the endeavours of

Sr, Your most obedient nephew
and most humble servant,
R. Steele.

The Dean has two in his gift. My most humble duty to my lady.

[1] Probably William Sherwin, elected a Fellow of Merton in 1688; he came from St. Edmund Hall. In 1703 he was made a Canon of Chichester.

John Sherwin, of Magdalen Hall, was B.A. February 28, 1659, and M.A., October 16, 1662. William Sherwin, of Magdalen College, was B.A., May 28, 1687; he was of Merton College, when he became M.A., November 13, 1691.

[2] There were several graduates of Oxford of this name towards the close of the seventeenth century.

[3] Presumably Anthony-à-Wood (1632–1695), who became a Postmaster of Merton in 1647. His *Athenæ Oxonienses* appeared in 1691. Wood in describing his life at Oxford says that he loved solitude and retirement, and did not hold communication with any, "unless with some, and those very few, of generous and noble spirits, that have in some measure been promoters of this work" [the *Athen. Oxon.*]

[4] "for" according to Mr. Wills.

[5] "to" (Wills).

[6] A senior student of Christ Church ranks with a Fellow of another college.

In May, Steele again urged his uncle to use his interest for him with the Duke of Ormond.

May 14.

Sr,

I have received the Bundle My Lady sent to me And do most humbly thank ye for that and all the rest of yr favours, but my request to you now is that you would compleat all the rest by sollicit-ing the Dean who is now in London in my behalfe for a student's place here; I am satisfied that I stand very fair in his favour. He saw one of my Exercises in the House and commended it very much and said yt if I went on in me Study he did not question but I should make something more than ordinary. I had this from my Tutour. I have I think a good character through the whole Coll: I speake not this, Sr, out of any vanity or affectation but to let you know that I have not been altogether negligent on my part: these places are not given by merit but are secured[1] by friends, though I question not but so generous a man as our Dean would rather prefer one that was a Scholar before another. I have had so great advantages in being [educated at an[2]] excellent school [that although] my own abilities are so very mean I beleive there are very few of [the] Gown in the Coll: so good scholars as I am. My Tutour before told me that if you should be pleased to use your interest for me, and[3] gt my Lord's letter or word in my behalfe; it would certainly do my businesse. And yr Friend, Dr Hough the new Bishop of Oxon,[4] I beleive may doe much now[5] for Dr Aldrich is, as it were, his Dean. Perhaps, Sir, you may be modest in solliciting him, because you may think others trouble him for the same thing; But pray, Sr, don't let that hinder you for it will be the same case next Election, and if we misse this opportunity 'tis ten to one whether we ever have such another; besides the Dean won't have a place again[6] this three year; therefore I beseech you Sr as you have been always hereto-fore very good to me to use your utmost Endeavour now in my behalfe. And assure yr self that whatever preferment I ever attain

[1] "acquired" (Wills).

[2] This paper is injured in several places.

[3] "or" (Wills).

[4] Dr. Hough was elected Bishop on April 29th, succeeding Dr. Timothy Hall, and was consecrated on May 11th, three days before the date of this letter.

[5] "more" (Wills).

[6] "such a place" (Wills).

to shall never make me ingratefully forget, and not acknowledge the authour of all my advances[1] but I shall ever be proud of writing myself,

Sir,

Your most obliged [nephew] and
Hum: Ser^{vt},
RICH. STEELE.

On a sheet of drafts on various matters, in Gascoigne's writing, one of which is dated May 27, 1690, and begins, "I was on shipboard about three weeks ago, when I sprained my right arm"—which may account for the delay—is the following note: "That your ldship will be pleased to befriend Dick Steele,[2] who is now entered in Ch. Ch., by getting him a student's place there, or something else, to Exse: me of charges beside what is allowed him by the Charter House."

James, second Duke of Ormond—the first duke died in July 1688—was, like his grandfather, Chancellor of the University. Steele did not get the studentship, but in August 1691 he was made a postmaster (*portionista*[3]) of Merton College; he is first mentioned in the postmaster's buttery accounts on August 27th, when he is entered simply as "Ricardus Steele," and afterwards as "Steele" only.[4]

There is one more letter of Steele's in the Ormonde collection; it is addressed to his aunt Dorothy,[5] and has no date.

HONOURED MADAM,

Out of a deep sense of y^{r} la^{sps} Goodnesse Towards me, I could not forbear accusing myselfe of Ingratitude in omitting my duty, by not acknowledging y^{r} Lad$^{ship's}$ favours by frequent letters; but how to excuse myselfe as to that point I know not, but must humbly hope y^{t} as you have been alwaies soe bountifull to me as to encourage my endeavours, soe y^{u} will be soe mercifull to me as to pardon my faults and neglects. But, Madam, should I expresse my gratitude for every benefit y^{t} I receive at y^{r} lad$^{shp's}$ and my good

1 "advancements" (Wills).

2 Several of these letters are endorsed by Gascoigne, "Dick Steele."

3 In 1380 John Wyllott, D.D., invested his estates in Merton College for the maintenance of these *portionistæ*.

4 The bursar's books of Christ Church for some years previous to 1695 are unfortunately missing.

5 Registers of St. Martin's-in-the-Fields.

Vnkle, I should never sit down to meat but I must write a letter when I rise from table; for to his goodnesse I humbly acknowledge my being. But, Mada^{m}, not to be too tedious, I shall only subscribe myselfe Mada^{m}, y^{r} la$^{ship's}$ Humble servant and obedient though unworthy nephew, R. STEELE.

Pray, mad^{m} give my duty to my unkle and my good Ant, and my love to me Ingenious Cousin and humble service to good Mrs Dwight.

There is a notice in the Register of Merton College of Steele having presented the College Library with a copy of the *Tatler* in 1712,[1] and added to the acknowledgment there is the following pleasant recognition of the pride felt by the College at the genius of her pupil:—"In eo tam amico fœdere coeunt seria, jocosa, sensuum (sic) pondus, et sermonis nitor, ut tanti ingenii altrices hæ ædes alumno suo merito exultent, quem universa Britannia jamdudum habuit in deliciis."

Steele always looked back with affection to his college days. In 1706 he published a *Prologue to the University of Oxford;* and in the 34th number of the *Englishman* he wrote, "Some business lately called me to Oxford, and it was with infinite pleasure that I beheld an University of which I had once the honour to be a Member. The sight of that College I am more particularly obliged to filled my heart with unspeakable joy." In his *Apology for Himself and his Writings* Steele quoted this passage in answer to a charge that he had spoken disrespectfully of the Universities, and added, "It appears by these and many other passages in my writings that I have retained the greatest honour and esteem for those learned bodies; in one of which I received a part of my education, and where I can still boast of much personal friendship and acquaintance. . . . Sir, I have reason to esteem the Universities, as I had the happiness to have had a part of my education in one of them."[2]

Steele wrote a comedy while he was at college, but he burned

[1] The entries under "Steele" in the catalogue of the Merton College Library published in 1880 are:—

Spectator, 8 vols., London, 1733.
Tender Husband; Conscious Lovers; Funeral; 8vo, London, 1734-1741.
Tatler, 3 vols., 8vo, London, 1710.
Ibid., 4 vols., 8vo, London, 1737.

[2] See also *Tatler*, No. 39; and *Guardian*, No. 72.

it when he was told by a friend, Mr. Richard Parker, that it was worthless. This college friend was afterwards vicar of Embleton, Northumberland, and Nichols, writing in 1786, says that some twelve years before that time there were several who remembered that Steele spent some time with this learned and hospitable gentleman on his way to or from Edinburgh. Moreover, we are told by the writer of the article "Steele" in the *Biographia Britannica*, that about 1712, when Mr. R. Breton,[1] afterwards Archdeacon of Hereford, was a candidate for a fellowship in Merton College, Steele gave him letters of recommendation to the Warden, Dr. Holland, and to his old friend, Mr. Parker; and it is said that Steele passed through Oxford in one of his last journeys to Wales, and visited his old college.

When Steele went to Oxford, he found Addison a Demy of Magdalen College, and distinguished for his scholarship. No particulars have come down to us of the intercourse of the school friends at the university, but we can picture to ourselves the pleasure they would feel at being again able to be frequently together, and form some idea of the influence they would have upon each other. Addison was sensitive and shy; Steele was full of sympathy for the world around him, and by his frankness drew out the best qualities of his friend. There was the same true foundation in each, but they had been brought up with different experiences; Addison had always had a happy home, and his opinions would be in complete accordance with those which were prevalent at Oxford; but Steele had had a life chequered and lonely, and was inclined rather to acts than refinements of thought.

A few references to contemporary writers will enable us to see a little more clearly what Oxford was like at the close of the seventeenth century.[2] Loggan, in his *Oxonia Illustrata* (1675), gives bird's-eye views of all the colleges as they appeared at that time. The gardens were, as a rule, laid out in a formal, rectangular style; at Christ Church there were several gardens

[1] Probably the Mr. Breton who showed courteous attentions to Addison at Dover in 1699 (Miss Aikin's *Life of Addison*, i. 70).

[2] I am indebted for most of the particulars which follow to C. Wordsworth's *Social Life at the Universities in the Eighteenth Century*, and to J. C. Jeaffreson's *Annals of Oxford*.

of this kind,[1] and in the adjoining meadows we can trace the beginning of the Broad Walk—"Ambulacra, the Walks." But the grounds at the rear of Magdalen College were then more popular, and Addison has left a Latin poem, *Spœristerium*, upon the Magdalen bowling-green. Tickell, in his poem on Oxford, speaks of "Magdalen's peaceful bowers," where "every Muse was fond of Addison." Dr. Ayliffe, speaking of Merton, says, "The garden, which lies to the eastward of the College, is large and pleasant, being encompased on the East and South side thereof with two noble Terrass walks, and shaded in the midst, and on the West and North side with fine grotesques and coverings of trees, in imitation of a wilderness."[2] John Earle, himself of Merton, had celebrated this garden in his poem, *Hortus Mertonensis*—"Hortus blandulus, optimus recessus." Anthony-à-Wood was angry when Lady Clayton—Sir Thomas Clayton was Warden of Merton from 1661 to 1693—induced

[1] Tickell writes, in his poem *Oxford* (1707):—

> "Bear me, some god, to Christ Church, royal seat!
> And lay me softly in the green retreat
> Where Aldrich holds o'er wit the sovereign power,
> And crowns the poets which he taught before.
>
> . . . .
>
> When Codrington and Steele their verse unrein,
> And form an easy, unaffected strain,
> A double wreath of laurel binds their brow,
> As they are poets and are warriors too."

We shall see hereafter that Colonel Christopher Codrington, who left his library and £10,000 to All Souls College, was associated with Steele and others in a pamphlet warfare with Sir Richard Blackmore in 1700; he was a scholar and wit, and a distinguished officer in the Foot Guards. Mr. Dobson has pointed out that as Colonel Codrington belonged to Barbados, where he had property, and where he was born and died, it is possible that Steele's acquaintance with his first wife, who came from that island, may have been in some way connected with Colonel Codrington. There is probably, however, only a coincidence here.

William III. visited Oxford on November 9, 1695. He was met by the Duke of Ormond, the Chancellor, the Vice-Chancellor, and Mayor. "The King alighting, passed directly to the Theatre, where a splendid banquet was provided, with great variety of excellent music. Mr. Codrington of All-Souls expressed the public thanks of the University in a very elegant oration. The Chancellor, on his knees, presented his Majesty with a large English Bible, a large Common Prayer-Book, and the Cuts of the University, all richly bound" (Pointer's *Chronological History of England*, 1714, pp. 417–8).

[2] *Ancient and Present State of the University of Oxford*, i. 276–7.

the authorities to lay out the Warden's garden afresh, and spend £100 on the summer house. In 1707 a new terrace was made in Merton garden, and in 1710 Uffenbach wrote that Merton garden was considered the first in Oxford; but the walks were dark and wanting air. We learn from Dr. Rawlinson's MSS. that on August 14, 1717, "the backdoor to Merton College Garden was shut up, on account of its being too much frequented by young scholars and ladies on Sunday nights;" and "June 17, 1718, for the same reason, the garden was to be kept locked every Sunday."[1] After Merton College garden was closed people went to Magdalen College Walk, which, in 1723, was "just like a fair."

Merton is one of the oldest colleges in Oxford; Christ Church was founded in Henry VIII.'s time. There is a tablet in memory of Anthony-à-Wood, who died in 1695, in Merton Chapel, and the college is distinguished as having been the residence of Catherine of Arragon and Cardinal Wolseley, and of Henrietta Maria during the Civil War.

A coffee-house was opened at Oxford in 1650; and in 1677 Wood attributed the decline of learning to "coffea-houses," taverns, and entertainments in the students' chambers. But of coffee-houses, of the Act, the *Terræ Filius*, and other features of University life, this is not the place to speak fully. It should be added that Dean Prideaux says that about 1675 "£40 per annum for a Commoner and £80 per annum for a Fellow Commoner, was looked on as a sufficient maintenance. . . . But now [1715] scarce £60 per annum for the former and £120 per annum for the latter, will serve for a complete maintenance." Finally, it should be remembered that the journey from Oxford to London occupied two days.[2] A "flying coach" did it in thirteen successive hours, but from Michaelmas to Lady Day it was uniformly a two days' performance.

[1] See *Spectator*, No. 54, and *Guardian*, No. 124; Amherst's *Terræ Filius*, Nos. 28, 33; *Reliquiæ Hearnianæ*, 1857, p. 503; *Merton Walks, or the Oxford Beauties*, 1717; and *Strephon's Revenge*, "a Satire on the Oxford Toasts, inscribed to the author of the *Merton Walks*," 1718. A quarto pamphlet, *Academia*, by Mrs. Alicia D'Anvers [pseud ?], London, 1691, describes in coarse rhymes a young man coming to Oxford, and the mischief he gets into each day.

[2] Hone's *Year Book*, col. 269.

BOOK SECOND.

SOLDIER AND DRAMATIST.

1694–1705; 1707–1710. ÆT. 22–33, 35–38.

I.

IN THE HORSE GUARDS. "THE PROCESSION."

1694–1695. ÆT. 22–23.

STEELE left Oxford without taking a degree, which was not at all unusual at that time; but we are told he took with him the love of "the whole society."[1] His name appears in the Merton postmaster's buttery accounts for the last time on Jan. 12, $169\frac{3}{4}$, and the next thing we know is that he entered the army, early, no doubt, in 1694, enlisting as a private soldier in the Duke of Ormond's regiment of Guards. This is what he himself afterwards said about this important step[2]: "When he mounted a war-horse, with a great sword in his hand, and planted himself behind King William the Third against Lewis the Fourteenth, he lost the succession to a very good estate in the county of Wexford in Ireland,[3] from the same humour which he has pursued ever since, of preferring the state of his mind to that of his fortune. When he cocked his hat, and put on a broad sword, jack-boots, and shoulder-belt, under the command of the unfortunate Duke of Ormond, he was not acquainted with his own parts."

The second Duke of Ormond, who was attainted in 1715, became Colonel of the 2nd Troop[4] of Royal Horse Guards on

[1] *Biographia Britannica*, vi. 3823.

[2] *Theatre*, No. 11. Mr. Bickerstaff did not enter the army on such patriotic grounds: "At fifteen I was sent to the University, and stayed there for some time; but a drum passing by, being a lover of music, I enlisted myself for a soldier" (*Tatler*, No. 89).

[3] It has been often said this good estate belonged to a relative of Steele's mother, but nothing is really known which is more explicit than Steele's own words, quoted in the text.

[4] Not now existing. From Harl. MS., 1308—"A general list of the land forces . . . 1695"—we learn that in 1695 the 2nd troop of Guards comprised

April 18th, 1689, went with William III. to Holland, and was wounded at the battle of Linden in 1693.[1] William was several times defeated, and it was under these circumstances that Steele, always full of patriotism, joined the army under the nobleman who was his uncle's patron and whose grandfather had helped him when he was a child.[2] There has hitherto been some doubt as to what regiment Steele first entered. The terms "Life Guards" and "Horse Guards" were used indiscriminately at first; Charles II. raised two troops of cavalry, in which the privates were gentlemen's sons, and these were the originals of our Life Guards, the troopers of which were known as Gentlemen of the Guard.[3] Steele entered as a cadet, and his position would be practically that of a trooper until he had thoroughly learned his duty; only his next move would be not corporal or non-commissioned officer, but ensign or commissioned officer. At that time young men of all ranks of society entered the army, and especially the Horse Guards, as private soldiers, and they had great privileges and good pay. Indeed, a com-

16 commissioned officers, 5 non-commissioned officers, and 200 private men; the privates received £73 a year each. The total pay of the regiment was £18,517. 13s. 4d. a year, besides £1022, the pay for 14 servants. Steele's name does not appear in any records now in the possession of the Royal Horse Guards.

[1] "The Duke of Ormond, having charged at the head of one of Lumley's squadrons, received several wounds, and had his horse shot under him, was rescued by a gentleman of the French king's guards from the hands of one who was offering to stab him" (*Tindal's Continuation of Rapin's History of England*, ii. 92–3, ed. 1761). The Duke of Ormond was received by the Duc d'Elbœuf with great civility, and was afterwards taken to Namur, where he was treated very kindly by the Count de Guiscard (*The History of the Last Campaign in the Spanish Netherlands, Anno Dom.* 1693, by Edward D'Auvergne, M.A., pp. 76, 101, dedicated to the Duke of Ormond, as is the *History* of the 1695 campaign. The *History* for 1696 is dedicated to Lord Cutts). The Duke of Ormond and others (Life Guards) were quartered at Breda in the winter of 1694 (*History* for 1694, p. 104). Dryden has praised the Duke's generosity to the poor soldiers when he was a prisoner at Namur in the dedication of his *Fables* to the Duke of Ormond.

[2] It may be noted that in December 1693, the Commons resolved to augment the English troops to upwards of 80,000 men, and to add six regiments of English Horse, four of English Dragoons, and fifteen of English Foot (Salmon's *Chronological Historian*).

[3] *The English Army*, by Major A. Griffiths, 1878; Grose's *Military Antiquities*, 1812; Sir C. D. Sibbald Scott's *British Army from the Restoration to the Revolution*, 1880; and an article in *Temple Bar* for 1874, vol. 40, pp. 107–8.

mission could be obtained only by purchase or by favour, accompanied, generally, by a bribe to some great person. It is absurd and unnecessary to invent a fiction that Steele was made an ensign because he was a great favourite with the officers; such a promotion, as the army was then constituted, was by no means unusual.

"I sometimes," said Coleridge to a friend, "compare my own life with that of Steele (yet, oh! how unlike), from having myself also, for a brief time, borne arms, and written 'private' after my name, or, rather, another name."[1] In the *Tatler*, No. 87, Steele has given a letter purporting to come from a Sergeant Hall, at Mons, addressed to a brother sergeant in the Coldstream regiment; and he comments on the gallantry shown by the rank and file of an army; he—Bickerstaff—was a cadet at the battle of Coldstream; "I say, to me, who know very well this part of mankind, I take the gallantry of private soldiers to proceed from the same if not a nobler impulse than that of gentlemen and officers." The bravest man is "a man of great courage and small hopes." In another number of the *Tatler* (164) Steele speaks of the "time that I myself was a cadet in the king's army." We may picture him with the rest, "mounted on black horses, with white feathers in their hats, and scarlet coats richly laced." In November 1699, upon occasion of a march past William III., the *London Post* said, "The Guards had just got their new clothes; they are extraordinary grand, and thought to be the finest body of horse in the world."[2]

And here we may give a few extracts from *Esmond*,[3] in which Thackeray, in his kindliest manner, gives us his idea of Steele as a "trooper." A search had been made for treasonable papers at Castlewood House. Some Latin sermons had been designedly left in a charred state by Father Holt, and these the little boy, Henry Esmond, was directed to read; but after a time the lawyer suggested that the boy might be laughing at them:—

[1] *Letters, Conversations, and Recollections of S. T. Coleridge*, i. 189.

[2] Timbs' *Anecdote Lives of Wits and Humourists.* Steele himself, as we shall see, had left the Horse Guards about 1695.

[3] Book I., chapters vi. and vii.

"Let's have in Dick the Scholar," cried Captain Westbury, laughing; and he called in a trooper out of the window. "Ho, Dick, come in here and construe."

A thick-set soldier, with a square good-humoured face, came in at the summons, saluting his officer.

"Tell us what is this, Dick?" says the lawyer.

"My name is Steele, sir," says the soldier. "I may be Dick for my friends, but I don't name gentlemen of your cloth among them."

"Well, then, Steele."

"Mr. Steele, sir, if you please. When you address a gentleman of His Majesty's Horse Guards, be pleased not to be so familiar."

"I didn't know, sir," says the lawyer.

"How should you? I take it you are not accustomed to meet with gentlemen," says the trooper.

"Hold thy prate, and read this bit of paper," says Westbury.

"'Tis Latin," says Dick, glancing at it, and again saluting his officer, "and from a sermon of Mr. Cudworth's," and he translated the words pretty much as Henry Esmond had rendered them.

. . . .

There must have been something touching in the child's voice, or in the description of his solitude—for the Captain looked at him very good-naturedly, and the trooper, called Steele, put his hand kindly on the lad's head, and said some words in the Latin tongue.

"What does he say?" says the lawyer.

"Faith, ask Dick himself," cries Captain Westbury.

"I said I was not ignorant of misfortune myself, and had learned to succour the miserable, and that's not *your* trade, Mr. Sheepskin," said the trooper.

"You had better leave Dick the Scholar alone, Mr. Corbet," the Captain said.

. . . .

After the departure of the Countess, Dick the Scholar took Harry Esmond under his special protection, and would examine him in his humanities, and talk to him both of French and Latin, in which tongues the lad found, and his new friend was willing enough to acknowledge, that he was even more proficient than Scholar Dick. Hearing that he learned them from a Jesuit, in the praise of whom and whose goodness Harry was never tired of speaking, Dick, rather to the boy's surprise, who began to have an early shrewdness, like many children bred up alone, showed a great deal of theological science, and knowledge of the points at issue between the two churches; so that he and Harry would have hours of controversy together, in which the boy was certainly worsted by the arguments of this singular trooper. "I am no common soldier," Dick would say, and indeed it was easy to see by his learning, breeding, and many accomplishments, that he was not. "I am of one of the most ancient families in the empire; I have had my education at a famous school, and a famous university; I learned my first rudiments of Latin near to Smithfield, in London, where the martyrs were roasted." . . . "'Tis not the dying for a faith that's so hard, Master Harry—every man of every nation has done that—'tis the living up to it that is difficult, as I know to my cost," he added with a sigh. "And oh!" he added, "my poor lad, I am not strong enough to convince thee by my life—though to die for my religion would give me the greatest of joys—but I had a dear friend in Magdalen College in Oxford: I wish Joe Addison were here to convince thee, as he quickly could." . . . That very night at supper in the hall . . . Harry Esmond found Dick the Scholar in a woeful state of drunkenness.

. . . .

During the stay of the soldiers in Castlewood, honest Dick the Scholar was the constant companion of the lonely little orphan lad Harry Esmond: and they read together, and they played bowls together, and when the other troopers or their officers, who were free-spoken over their cups, talked unbecomingly of their amours and gallantries before the child, Dick, who very likely was setting the whole company laughing, would stop their jokes with a "maxima debetur pueris reverentia," and once offered to lug out another trooper called Hulking Tom, who wanted to ask Harry Esmond a ribald question.

This was the view which the large-hearted Thackeray took of Steele's character as a young man of about twenty-three, and it will serve as an excellent specimen of the standpoint from which he pleasantly discoursed upon Steele. As in other passages, he errs somewhat through a misunderstanding as regards the life of the young soldier; and there is more compassion expressed than is necessary. It is difficult to say whether the loving pity which Thackeray felt has not had as much to do with spreading a false conception of Steele as the avowed disdain of Macaulay, which sometimes overreached itself.

Meanwhile the young man was writing verses, some playful,

some full of serious thought. The first that we have are among the Marlborough MSS., and relate to Mrs. Selwyn. Colonel Selwyn[1] commanded an infantry regiment in the campaigns of 1693 and 1694; in the winter of 1694 he was quartered at Dendermond, and in July 1695 he was made a Brigadier-General. He was afterwards Governor of Jamaica, and died in 1702.[2] The following lines may refer to Colonel Selwyn's wife or daughter, with whom Steele may have been made acquainted through the Duke of Ormond. The scrap of paper upon which they are written bears the date 1694, several times repeated.

Verses on Mrs. Selwyn, being Valentine.

Upon having Mrs. Selwyn, by Lot, my Valentine.[3]

One Minute, Fortune, Thou hast let me Live,
I freely all my Life, before, forgive.
Cares did, till now, my rising blisse destroy
And streaks of Sorrow ran through all my Joy.
But,[4] fickle Goddesse, Thou art now sincere
Quite happy now[5] I feel not hope, or fear;
Thy Wealth and Empire on thy slaves bestow,
Slaves[6] who no blisse, but Wealth and Empire know.
Be all thy Power in one great gift display'd,
And to these Arms convey the Lovely Maid,
I never will beseech thy bounty more
But be as rough, and Angry as before.

An event now occurred which stirred the nation, and caused

[1] Salmon's *Chronological Historian*, 1747; D'Auvergne's *History of the Last Campaign in the Spanish Netherlands, Anno Dom.* 1693; and *History . . . Anno Dom.* 1694.

[2] Lord Cutts was offered the post of Governor of Jamaica in 1702, but desired to be excused (*Wentworth Papers*, p. 9).

[3] See *Tatler*, Nos. 137, 141. Hone says (*Year Book*, cols. 196–8) that the earliest poetical valentines are by Charles, Duke of Orleans, who was taken prisoner at Agincourt. The poems, chiefly in English, were written while he was in the Tower of London. As regards presents given to a gentleman's Valentine, see Pepys' *Diary* for Feb. 1667 and Feb. 1668.

[4] This line, as first written, began with the words, "But now, fickle Goddesse," which were then obliterated.

[5] This word was inserted above the line.

[6] "Thy Slaves," first written; "Thy," cancelled.

Steele to write a poem which, though sometimes crude, came from the heart, and is full of patriotic feeling. On December 28, 1694, Queen Mary died of small-pox, at the age of thirty-two, after a week's illness, and on March 5, 1695, her body was conveyed in state from Whitehall and buried in Henry VII.'s Chapel at Westminster. Many writers produced verses upon this subject, and among them Steele, but in his case they were anonymous, and were described only as the work of "a gentleman of the army." This is, it may be noted, the earliest certain evidence we have of Steele being in the army. *The Procession*, as the poem was called, was dedicated to Lord Cutts. John, afterwards Lord Cutts, of the family of Cutts of Matching, Essex, had fought under the Duke of Monmouth, and had been aide-de-camp to the Duke of Lorrain in Hungary. He rendered great services at the capture of Buda in 1686, and his prowess was celebrated by Addison in his *Pax Gulielmi*. In 1690 he was made Baron of Gowran in Ireland; on April 8, 1693, Governor of the Isle of Wight; and on October 14, 1694, Colonel of the Coldstream or 2nd Regiment of Foot Guards. He was wounded at Steinkirk and at Namur, and was famous for reckless bravery. Swift has called him a salamander.[1] But he was at the same time a man of culture, and he published in 1687 a little volume—from which Steele quoted lines, years afterwards, in the fifth number of the *Tatler*—called *Poetical Exercises Written upon Several Occasions*, with a long dedication to Mary, Princess of Orange. And now, in March 1695, Steele dedicated his poem on the late good Queen Mary to Lord Cutts. The piece appeared as a folio pamphlet, with a black border round the title-page. The dedication is here given in full, because it is interesting, and is little known.[2]

[1] In the coarse verses called *The Description of a Salamander. . . . Written in the year* 1706.

[2] The title-page and dedication of this rare pamphlet were printed by Mr. Solly in *Notes and Queries* for March 7, 1885. The poem was reprinted in Steele's *Poetical Miscellanies*, 1714, and in the fourth volume of Nichols' *Select Collection of Poems*, 1780, but in neither case was the dedication to Lord Cutts given.

THE PROCESSION

A

POEM

ON

HER MAJESTIES

FUNERAL

BY A GENTLEMAN OF THE ARMY.

Motto—"Fungar inani Munere."—*Virg.*

London, Printed for Thomas Bennet at the Half-Moon in St. Paul's Churchyard, 1695.

To the Right Honourable The Lord Cutts.

My Lord, compassion which gives us a more sweet and generous touch than any other concern that attends our nature, had at the Funeral Procession so sensible an effect upon even me that I could not forbear being guilty of the paper with which I presume to trouble your Lordship. For what could be a more moving consideration, than that a Lady, who had all that youth, beauty, virtue and power could bestow, should be so suddenly snatched from us? A Lady that was served by the sword and celebrated by the pen of my Lord Cutts. Though, indeed, if we rightly esteemed things, we should lament for our own sakes, not her's; so poor a thing it is to make an evil of that which is certainly the kindest boon of nature, our dissolution. But the men of honour are not so ungrateful to their friend, Death, as to look at him in the ghastly dress the world gives him, of rawbones, shackles, chains, diseases and torments; they know that he is so far from bringing such company that he relieves us from 'em. So little is there in what men make such pother about, and so much is it an irony to call it brave to expire calmly, and resolution to go to rest. This is no news to your Lordship, whom death has so often allured with the glory of dangers and the beauty of wounds; I'll not be so poetical to say, your Muse hovered about you and saved you in spite of the many you have received, but am sure I may say she'll preserve you when you can receive no more; for Apollo is a physician even after death. As to my verses, all, methinks, on the dead Queen ought to be addressed to your Lordship; who, in the dedication of your own works, but adorned her living; if good for your entertainment, bad for your pardon; if when these are thrown aside an eye cast upon 'em introduces the mention of so excellent a Princess where otherwise she had not been spoken of, I have my full end; nor do I think I come late on a subject which all good men will eternally dwell upon; I am sensible how short I have fallen of expressing the graceful concern of some honourable personages whose names I have presumed with; I designed 'em only an oblique commendation, and named 'em for the very reason they walked at the funeral, which was not to show themselves, but to do honour to the Queen. But should it prove any way offensive, I hope to shun their and your Lordship's resentment by the concealment of my name, and borrow the unknown Knight's device, in Sir Philip Sidney, of the Fish Sepia, which when catched in the net, casts a black ink about it and so makes its escape. This thought, my Lord, checks the fervent ambition I have long had of expressing myself, My Lord, Your Lordship's most passionate admirer and most devoted humble servant.

March 19, 169$\frac{4}{5}$.

The poem began with reflections on the pain and strife to which man's life is doomed:—

"No satisfaction is, below, sincere;
Pleasure itself has something that's severe."[1]

The nation, which had long been beguiled into joy by the good fortune of their King, was now filled with universal grief by the Queen's death. The poor, who were ever in her thoughts, were the deepest mourners. Next in the procession came the members of both Houses; but Steele had much more to say of the Lords than of the Commons, because the Commons had for some time shown a disposition to be factious in their relations with King William. Ormond, Somers—in praise of both of whom Addison also wrote—and Baron Villiers, were all specially mentioned. Edward, Baron Villiers of Hoo, and Viscount Villiers of Dartford, afterwards created Earl of Jersey, was Master of the Horse to Queen Mary, and he led her steed, which heaved "into big sighs when he would neigh." Next came the mourning chariot, Death himself; and then the ladies

[1] This line is repeated in the Prologue to *The Lying Lover* (1704).

of the Court, among them being the Countess of Derby, the Duke of Ormond's sister. Who could believe that these were the obsequies of the Queen to whom Heaven so lately gave a crown? But so it was; and now "the dearer part of William" was committed to the dust.

> "In her his vital heart, his glory lies,
> In her the Monarch lived, in her he dies.
> One was their soul; while he secured her rest,
> War's hardships seemed luxurious to his breast:
> And he abroad, no peace repose could yield;
> She felt the distant dangers of the field.
> No form of state makes the great man forego
> The task due to her love, and to his woe;
> Since his kind frame can't the large suffering bear,
> In pity to his people, he's not here:[1]
> For to the mighty loss we now receive,
> The next affliction were to see him grieve."

[1] The King was not present at the ceremony. It is said that he was for some weeks after the Queen's death completely prostrate, partly owing, perhaps, to feelings of remorse.

II.

IN THE COLDSTREAM GUARDS.

1695–1700. ÆT. 23–28.

NOT long after the publication of the *Procession*, Lord Cutts made Steele a member of his household, and obtained for him an ensign's commission in his own regiment of the Coldstream Guards.[1] We have an account of this change of fortune in the writings of a contemporary—Mrs. De La Rivière Manley. But the *New Atalantis*, which was written in 1709, when the author was engaged in serving by violent lampoons the political party opposed by Steele, cannot be taken as a truthful history of those with whom Mrs. Manley had quarrelled; and they were many. A fitter opportunity for giving particulars of her connection with Steele will occur hereafter; the passage which is now quoted may be taken as veracious, because it contains only facts which are corroborated elsewhere. After some severe remarks upon Steele's character, and his face, which portrayed his mind, Mrs. Manley says[2]:—

"He's a Poet too, and was very favourably received by the Town, especially in his first performance, where, if you'll take my opinion, he exhausted most of his stock; for what he has since produced

[1] Steele says explicitly in his *Apology* that he was an "ensign of the Guards;" but his name nowhere appears in the roll of the regiment which is given in the Appendix to MacKinnon's *Origin and Services of the Coldstream Guards* (1833), ii. 458, *seq.* In the British Museum (Add. MS. 17918, f. 10) there is a list of Officers of the Coldstream Regiment, commanded by Lord Cutts, corrected, apparently, up to 1695, but Steele's name is not given. No regimental records of so early a date are preserved by the regiment.

[2] *Secret Memoirs and Manners of several Persons of Quality of both Sexes from the New Atalantis;* 1st ed. 1709, vol. i., 187–8.

seem but faint copies of that agreeable original. Tho' he's a most incorrect writer, he pleases in spite of the faults we see and own. Whether application might not burnish the defect, or if those very defects were brightened, whether the genuine spirit would fly off? are queries not so easily resolved. I remember him almost t'other day but a wretched common Trooper; he had the luck to write a small poem, and dedicates it to a person whom he never saw, a Lord that's since dead,[1] who had a sparkling genius, much of humanity, loved the Muses, and was a very good soldier. He encouraged his performance, took him into his family, and gave him a Standard in his Regiment. The genteel company that he was let into, assisted by his own genius, wiped off the rust of education; he began to polish his manners, to refine his conversation, and, in short, to fit himself for something better than what he had been used."

A Proclamation was issued in 1695, addressed to the Earl of Romney, Lord Cutts, &c., directing, among other things, that "each captain of foot, when he is upon duty, do carry a pike, the lieutenant a partizan, and every ensign a half-pike, when he does not carry his colours."[2] Particulars of the establishment of the Coldstream regiment in 1695 are given in Harl. MS. 1308. Captains had each 14s. a day, and three servants at 10d., coming to £301. 2s. 6d. a year; ensigns had 5s. a day, and one servant at 10d., coming to £106. 9s. 2d. From March 26, 1699, captains had 14s. a day, and 1s. 8d. in lieu of servants (£285. 18s. 4d.); and ensigns as before. The regiment consisted of 44 commissioned officers, 104 non-commissioned officers, and 780 private men. Steele would probably take part in a review held by the King in Hyde Park on the 28th November 1700, of Lord Romney and Lord Cutts' regiments of foot-guards, duly provided with new clothes for the occasion.[3]

Little is known of Steele's life from 1695 to 1700, but he himself afterwards stated that he was an ensign in Lord Cutts' company, and that he was in the highest favour with his Lordship, being employed as secretary when Lord Cutts was Governor of the Isle of Wight, and in many other affairs of importance, in the transaction of which he gave such satis-

[1] Lord Cutts died in 1707.
[2] MacKinnon's *Coldstream Guards*, ii. 304, 389, 392.
[3] Luttrell's *Diary*, iv. 712.

faction that Lord Cutts admitted him into his conversation with great freedom, and treated him like a son or a brother. And besides this introduction into the world, Steele was under the care and support of his relations—Henry Gascoigne, no doubt—who were persons of quality and in good circumstances.[1] This statement is borne out by a series of receipts and other papers relating to the payment of money on behalf of Lord Cutts in 1696 and 1697, from which it appears that Steele was a confidential agent or secretary to Lord Cutts during those years. I give a few of these documents, the originals of which are among the Marlborough MSS., and a facsimile of one, which shows the writing both of Steele and of Lord Cutts. The receipts are in Steele's writing, and are generally endorsed by him on the back.

Jan. 22nd, 1696.

Receiv'd then of Mr Steele, by order of the Lord Cutts, the sum̄ of two pounds, I say, Receiv'd by me

ELLINORE CONIGRAVE.

27th May 1696.[2]

Rent of ye right honble my Lord Cutts upon account The sum of twenty pounds I say recd } 20*l*

Witnesse THO: PERCIVALL.

Richard Steele.

KENSINGTON, June 5, 1696.

Pay Budiani five pounds noting his receipt upon account.

To Mr Steele, &c. CUTTS.

June 6th.

Received then of Richard Steele the sum̄ of five pounds [upon] for the use of the Lord Cutts, I say Receiv'd By Me

NICH. BUDIANI.

June 8th, 1696.

Received then of Richard Steele the sum̄ of three pounds in full of all dues and demands from the Right Honourable the Lord Cutts I say Received By me

C. MICHEL AUMONT.[3]

[1] Answer of Steele in the suit of Sansome *v.* Steele, 1718.

[2] Signature only by Steele.

[3] Another receipt, similar to this one, for £4. 18s. od., is endorsed "Jan. 16th, Chairman."

LONDON, June 24, 1696.

I promise to pay to Mr Arthur Clay or by his order Sixteen guineas at demand. Wittness my hand.[1]

RICHARD STEELE.

Note that I borrowed this for My Lord's Use.

R. STEELE.

KENSINGTON, Oct. 5th, 1696.[2]

Pay budiani three pounds upon account.

To Mr Steel. CUTTS.

Nov. 16th, 1696.

Receiv'd then, of Mr Steele, the sum̄ of ten pounds, by order of my Lord Cutts, I say Receiv'd by me.

SARAH KORSE.

Nobr 21st, 1696.

Received, then, of Mr Steele, by order of the Rt Honourable the Lord Cutts, the sum̄ of five pounds, four shillings, In full of my Wages and Board-wages, I say, Receiv'd By Me

RICHARD GARSTON.

Dec. 7th, 1696.[3]

Receiv'd of Mr Trubshaw	20 : 00 : 00
Paid Decer 7th Mr Abbadie . . .	5 : 00 : 00
Decbr 7th to James	1 : 00 : 00
Decbr 8th to my Lord	3 : 06 : 00
Decbr 9th to my Lord	1 : 02 : 00
Decbr 9th to my Lord	00 : 05 : 00
Debr 9th Dryden's Proposall[4] . .	1 : 2 : 0

[1] Thus far not Steele's writing.

[2] Lord Cutts was in Flanders from July to October 1696 (Luttrell's *Diary*, iv. 79, &c.).

[3] Written on the fly-leaf of a paper containing receipts, in the usual form, for money received for the use of Lord Cutts, signed by Jacob Abbadie and Robert Hampton. These are the names which occur most frequently. Jacob D'Abbadie was surgeon to the Coldstream Guards at the accession of Queen Anne (Mackinnon's *Coldstream Guards*, ii. 453). In a letter to Mr. Ellis, dated Westminster, April 28th, 1698, Lord Cutts wrote: "I desire you'll give a passport to Mr Jacob Abbadie (my Gentleman of the Horse) to goe to Loo, to fetch two Horses from thence, and to repass with them into England, and you'll oblige Sr your most humble servant, Cutts" (Brit. Mus. Add. MS. 28901, f. 93). Jacob Abbadie was, like Henry Gascoigne, a Tail-Cart-taker in the Board of Green Cloth in 1703 (Miege's *New State of England*, 5th ed. 1703, p. 479).

[4] Dryden's translation of Virgil was published by subscription in July 1697. Addison wrote the arguments of the books, and an Essay on the Georgics.

Kensington Jan: 9th 1696/7.

Pay the bearer three Pounds sterling.

To Mr Steel, &c. Cutts

Received Jan: 15th 1696/7 then of Mr Steele by my Lord Cutts's order the sum of three pounds
Jacob Abbadie

De^{br} 10th to Major Hampton . .	5 : 00 : 0
Dece^{br} 10th to my Lord . . .	1 : 00 : 0
De^{br} 10th Coach-hire	00 : 01 : 00
De^{br} 11th to my Lord	00 : 10 : 00
Note. My Lord owes me . . .	1 : 00 : 00[1]

Jan. 16th, 169$\frac{6}{7}$.[2]

Received then, for the Use of My Lord Cutts of Richard Steele the sum̄ of six pounds, I say; Receiv'd by me

JACOB ABBADIE.

Feb. 8th.

Received then, of Richard Steele by order of my Lord Cutts the sum̄ of seventy seven pounds, I say, Receivd By me

THEODOSIA BROWN.

The last of these receipts is dated March 16th, 169$\frac{6}{7}$.

We catch another glimpse of Steele in August 1697, from a letter, now published for the first time, from Henry Gascoigne to "John Ellis Esqr at the R^{t} Honble Mr Secretary Trumbull's Office, Whitehall." This letter shows that Steele was already acquainted with John Ellis, probably through Dr. Welbore Ellis, who had been his tutor, and afterwards chaplain of the regiment in which he first served.

S^{r},

I returne you my hearty thanks for the freedome you are pleased to give me of sending my Lres to my wife under yor Cover as my Nephew Steele informes mee; so I give you the trouble of the inclosed: I writt to you a month ago by my Lady Dutchesses[3] com̄and to desire you to send her the printed flying posts & post-

[1] On the back is:—

"WHITEHALL, Dec^{br} 7th, 1696.

I do hereby, certifie, that the Bearer hereof Mr Abbadie is my Steward, and . . .

I certify by this that . . ."

[2] Written on the back of part of a letter of Steele's, "Whitehall, Jan. 5th, 1696."

[3] The second wife of the second Duke of Ormond, Lady Mary Somerset, daughter of the Duke of Beaufort. She went over to Ireland in 1697, in advance of the Duke of Ormond, "and from benighted Britain bore the day," as Dryden put it in the fine Address to the Duchess of Ormond, which he prefixed to the version of "Palamon and Arcite," in his *Fables*.

man, &c for tho shee does not rely much on the truth of them yet shee finds some diversion in the reading of 'm; she desired they might be directed to the Bp of Ossory; This I repeat because I know not whether that Lr. came to yor Hands. I should be glad I were in a Condition to serve you as I am

S^{r}

Yo^{r} affectionate & most humble Servant

H. Gascoigne.[1]

Royal Hospitall near Dublin[2]
17 Augt 1697.

Of the next three years we have no particulars, and we can only speculate as to Steele's life by noting some of the public events of the time. The beginning of the year 1696 was marked by the discovery of the Assassination Plot. Loyal associations were formed in various parts of the country. The *Post Boy* for March 5 to 7, 1696, says: "The General Officers have subscribed an Association at the Horse Guards, in the nature of that subscribed by the Parliament;" and the *London Gazette* for March 5 to 9 announced that "An Humble Address has been likewise presented to His Majesty signed by His Grace the Duke of Ormond, High Steward, . . . and other inhabitants of the City and Liberties of Westminster." From the same paper for April 9 to 13 we learn that an Address from the Association of the Isle of Wight was presented by Lord Cutts, and one from Oxford by Thomas Felton, Esq. Lord Cutts, as Captain of the Guards, was present during the examination of Prendergrass by the King; and the Duke of Ormond called on Oxford students to enlist in his regiment. Sir John Fenwick and others were executed. Overtures of peace with France were soon afterwards made, and in September 1697 the

[1] Add. MS. 28881, f. 418.

[2] Presumably the recently established Royal Hospital near Dublin, described in a little book published in Dublin in 1713, the title of which I give below. It is not clear why Gascoigne wrote from there, but he may have had some connection with the place in consequence of the interest which the Duke of Ormond took in it:—"An Account of the foundation of the Royal Hospital of King Charles II., near Dublin, for the relief and maintenance of antient and infirm Officers and Soldiers serving in the Army of Ireland. Begun by His Grace James Duke of Ormond, anno 1680, and completed by His Excellency Henry Earl of Clarendon . . . 1686."

Treaty of Ryswick was concluded. But the Commons immediately entered into a contest with William III. as to the strength of the army; and at length the King was obliged to dismiss the Dutch Guards, and to consent to the English troops being reduced to 7000. Another point of contention was the granting of Crown lands; "it was observed that the Duke of Ormond, the Earl of Marlborough, General Douglas, General Talmash, the Lord Cutts, Cunningham, and other British generals and officers who had served in Ireland, and been eminently instrumental in the reduction of that Kingdom, had not a foot of land of all the forfeited estates granted them; only the Dutch, and Lord Galway, a French refugee, tasted the fruits of that conquest, except Mrs. Villiers, the King's mistress."[1] The Commons triumphed, and Parliament was prorogued in April 1700.

By 1700 Steele was a captain in the army, and on friendly terms with the wits who frequented Wills' coffee-house. A paper warfare was at this time being waged between Sir Richard Blackmore and these wits in consequence of a folio poem which Blackmore issued, called *A Satyr against Wit*. Blackmore was a successful physician, who joined in theological controversies, and occupied his leisure by writing epic poems. In 1695 he published *Prince Arthur*, in ten books; in 1697, *King Arthur*, in twelve books. He was made one of the physicians-in-ordinary to the King, and knighted; and in 1700 he produced a *Paraphrase on the Book of Job, and other parts of the Scripture*. The wits, "whom," as Dr. Johnson says, "he provoked more by his virtue than his dulness," rallied round Dryden, who had already attacked Blackmore in the preface to his *Fables*, and in the lines to his kinsman, John Driden, in the same volume, and who now wrote a prologue, which was recited by Colley Cibber at the performance for Dryden's benefit on the 25th March, in ridicule of the *Paraphrase*. Blackmore retaliated with the *Satyr against Wit*. Dryden died on the 1st May, but the other poets and poetasters joined together, under Tom Brown, a dissipated writer of the town, to form a collection of epigrams upon Blackmore. The result was a folio pamphlet, called *Commendatory*

[1] Salmon's *Chronological Historian*, Jan. 18, 1700.

Verses, on the Author of the Two Arthurs, and the Satyr against Wit; by some of his particular Friends. Among the contributors were Sir Charles Sedley, Lord Anglesey, Lady Sandwich, Dennis, Vanbrugh, Garth, Colonel Codrington,[1] and Captain Steele. Many of the verses, including Steele's, were afterwards reprinted, with the author's name, in Brown's *Works*.[2] Steele's verses were occasioned by the following allusion to his friend Addison:—

"But Wit as now 'tis managed would undo
The skill and virtues we admire in you.
In G[arth] the wit the doctor has undone,
In S[malwoo]d the Divine, Heav'ns guard poor Ad[di]son."

This was Steele's retort[3]:—

"To the Mirrour of British Knighthood, the worthy Author of the Satyr against Wit; occasion'd by the Hemistich, p. 8—

'Heav'ns guard poor A——n.'

Must I then passive stand! and can I hear
The man I love abused, and yet forbear?

[1] See page 39, note. Verses by Col. Codrington were prefixed to the *Dispensary*, and Addison wrote the inscription on Codrington's statue in the library of All Souls College, Oxford. He is thus noticed by Weekes in *Barbados, a Poem*, written in 1754 in celebration of the author's native island:—

"And thou, O Coddrington! a native Muse,

Thou, with a Master Hand, the lyre could'st tune,
And shone distinguished in a learned Age.
Garth was thy friend; and Addison, well pleased
To justify to future times his love,
Paid the last tribute that a friend can pay."

Colonel Codrington was Captain-General of the Leeward Islands, where he died on the 7th April 1710, aged 42, leaving the bulk of his estate, upwards of £40,000, to his cousin-german, Colonel William Codrington of Barbados. He bequeathed £20,000 to the Society for the Propagation of the Christian Religion in Foreign Parts (Pointer's *Chronological History*, 1714, p. 675). His will, dated 22nd February 1702–3, is in the Prerogative Court of Canterbury (23 Young), and his name is kept in remembrance in Barbados by Codrington College.

[2] Vol. iv. 67–70 (ed. 1760).

[3] In the copy of this pamphlet in the British Museum the words "Captain Steel" are written in a contemporary hand opposite these lines, and similarly in my own copy there is written "Cap Steele."

Yet must I thank thy favour to my friend,
'Twas some remorse thou didst not him commend.
Thou dost not all my indignation raise,
For I prefer thy pity to thy praise.
In vain thou would'st thy name, dull pedant, hide,
There's not a line but smells of thy Cheapside.[1]
If Cæsar's bounty for your trash you've shared,
You're not the first assassin he has spared.
His mercy, not his justice, made thee Knight,
Which P—rt—r[2] may demand with equal right.
Well may'st thou think an useless talent Wit,
Thou who without it hast three poems writ;
Impenetrably dull, secure thou'rt found,
And can'st receive no more than give a wound;
Then, scorned by all, to some dark corner fly,
And in lethargic trance expiring lie,
Till thou from injured G—rth[3] thy cure receive,
And S[malwoo]d only absolution give."

Blackmore replied with *Discommendatory Verses, &c.*, among which are some "To the Noble Captain, who was in a damned confounded Pet because the author of the Satyr against Wit was pleased to pray for his Friend." Steele is called a senseless bard, who cannot atone for his rhymes. There were other pamphlets published, as, for example, *A Satyr upon a late Pamphlet Entitled, A Satyr Against Wit*, and *A Satyr Against Satyrs*, &c., in which Brown is called "The little Penny Poet of the Town;" and then there was peace for a time.

But we come to a more serious matter. On June 16 Steele fought a duel with a Captain Kelly. We have three short accounts of the meeting. The *Flying Post* for June 18 to 20 says, "On Sunday night last, Captain Keely and one Mr. Steel, an officer of the Guards, fought a duel in Hide-Park, in which the latter (*sic*) was mortally wounded, and some say he is since Dead." The *London Post*, June 17 to 19, reports, "On Sunday

[1] Blackmore lived in Cheapside, and it was said that he received the honour of knighthood because he wrote *King Arthur*.

[2] Porter conspired against William III. with Fenwick and Charnock in 1695, and in 1696 became an informer against Fenwick.

[3] Garth's *Dispensary* appeared in 1696.

last, Captain Kelly, an Irish gentleman, and Mr. Steell, an officer of the Guards, fought a duel in Hide Park, and were both slightly wounded;" and Luttrell records in his *Diary*,[1] under date Tuesday, 18th June, 1700, "Sunday night, one Mr Kelly and capt. Steele, of the Lord Cuts regiment, fought in Hide Park, and the first dangerously wounded." We shall meet with a Mr. Kelly, of Ireland, again, in 1702; he is possibly the same as the Captain Kelly who fought with Steele. No date has been fixed by previous writers for the one duel which it has been supposed Steele engaged in; but Nichols, upon the authority of Dr. Thomas Amory, has given[2] some particulars of a duel, which may or may not be the same as the one which took place in June 1700. Steele says in his *Apology* that after the appearance of his *Christian Hero*, in 1701, "one or two of his acquaintances thought fit to misuse him, and try their valour upon him;" if this means that he was driven to fight them, it is clear that he fought more than once. At anyrate this is the story narrated by Nichols. A brother officer (his name is not given) told Steele that he intended to challenge a person who had fallen under his displeasure, but was diverted from his purpose by what Steele said to him on the subject. Some of this young officer's companions led him to believe that Steele's counsel was due to his partiality for the offender. This misrepresentation led to a challenge to Steele himself, who was just at the time recovering from a fever. Steele used every means of persuasion to avert the duel, but in vain; and thinking that he could chastise the youth's insolence without endangering his life, he accepted the challenge. When they met, Steele's buckle broke as he tightened his shoe, and he then tried again without success to persuade his adversary to desist. He parried his opponent's thrusts for some time, but at last, in an attempt to disable him, he unfortunately ran the young man through the body. For some time it was doubtful whether the officer would recover, but in the end he did. Lord Cutts took up Steele's cause warmly while the young man's life was in peril. In his later writings Steele constantly remon-

[1] Vol. iv. 657.
[2] *Tatler*, 1786, vol. i. pp. 276-7.

strated against the "barbarous custom of duelling;"[1] this was one of many things respecting which his views were far in advance of his time. In one place[2] he says, "As the matter now stands, it is not to do handsome actions denominates a man of honour; it is enough if he dares to defend ill ones."

In Michaelmas term of this same year, 1700, judgment was given against Steele in what was, alas, to be but the first of a long series of actions for debt. Richard Steele, late of the Parish of St. Martin-in-the-Fields, gentleman, was summoned to the Court of Common Pleas by Henry Jones for a debt of £42. Henry Jones, by his attorney, William Battell, said that whereas Steele on the 23rd October, 1700, at Westminster, borrowed £42 of him to be paid when requested, he had nevertheless not paid, and Jones claimed damages to the extent of £10. Steele was represented by William Leeche, his attorney, but made no answer, and the case was therefore decided in favour of Jones, with damages to the amount of 60s.[3]

[1] *Theatre*, No. 26. [2] *Tatler*, No. 25.
[3] Common Pleas Judgment Roll, Michaelmas, 12 William III., Membrane 525.

III.

"THE CHRISTIAN HERO" AND "THE FUNERAL."

1701–2. ÆT. 29–30.

At the beginning of 1701 we have further evidence of Steele's friendship with distinguished writers of the town, and especially with Congreve—"friendly Congreve, unreproachful man," as Gay called him—who had then written all his famous comedies, though he was Steele's senior by only two years. He lived on, however, until 1729, dying a few months only before Steele. In a letter[1] to Joseph Keally, Esq., Dublin, dated January 28, 1700 (1701, N.S.), Congreve wrote, "Dick Steele is yours;" and soon afterwards there was published *A New Miscellany of Original Poems, on Several Occasions*, "Written by the E. of D., Sir Charles Sidley, Sir Fleetw. Shepheard, Mr. Wolelly, Mr. Granvill, Mr. Dryden, Mr. Stepney, Mr. Rowe, and several other Eminent Hands. Never before Printed. London, Printed for Peter Buck, . . . &c., 1701." On p. 335 of this collection is a poem by Steele addressed to Congreve, which was reprinted in 1714 in Steele's *Poetical Miscellanies.* It was called *Epistle to Mr. Congreve, occasioned by his Comedy called "The Way of the World,"* a play which had been published in the preceding year. After referring to the low tone of the drama, Steele spoke in high praise of Congreve as a writer both of comedy and tragedy, as well as of verses joyous, pathetic, and patriotic.

Steele was now stationed at the Tower, of which Lord Lucas was governor. His frank, hearty nature and his love of com-

[1] Berkeley's *Literary Relics*, 1789, p. 319. Joseph Keally, or Kelly, was admitted a barrister in Trinity term, 1700. (List of Barristers in Record Tower, Dublin Castle.)

panionship led him into temptation; like those around him he sometimes indulged in excesses at the table, and he had a natural daughter by a daughter of Tonson the publisher. He has given us his own account of his life in his *Apology*: "He first became an author when an ensign of the Guards, a way of life exposed to much irregularity; and being thoroughly convinced of many things, of which he often repented, and which he more often repeated, he writ, for his own private use, a little book called the *Christian Hero,* with a design principally to fix upon his own mind a strong impression of virtue and religion, in opposition to a stronger propensity towards unwarrantable pleasures. This secret admonition was too weak; he therefore printed the book with his name, in hopes that a standing testimony against himself, and the eyes of the world (that is to say of his acquaintance) upon him in a new light, might curb his desires, and make him ashamed of understanding and seeming to feel what was virtuous, and living so quite contrary a life." Steele never hesitated in openly confessing his faults, and this passage must not be taken as meaning that his mode of living was exceptionally bad.[1] We must remember that the standard of morality was very low even among those who considered themselves on a much higher level than Steele, and that his ideal was far above that of most of his contemporaries, so that

[1] Mr. Dobson has aptly quoted, as "an instance of the growth of scandal in memoir-writing," the writer of the article on Steele in the *Biographia Britannica,* p. 3823, who thus paraphrases Steele's statement:—"He spared not to indulge his genius in the wildest excesses, prostituting the exquisite charms of his conversation-talents to give his pleasures a daintier and more poignant relish." And Dr. Drake says, "He employed the intervals snatched from the orgies of voluptuousness in composing, for his own private use, a valuable little manual entitled the *Christian Hero.* The effort was, alas! unavailing. . . . The succeeding day saw him minister to the mirth of vice, and protract the revels of debauchery." But the book is not exactly "a valuable little manual" any more than it is a poem, as Schlosser states. This gentleman, in his *History of the Eighteenth Century* (1843, English translation, vol. i. 102), writes:—"Steele began his career as a writer with a poem, his *Christian Heroes,* which justified no great expectations. This poem could have little of soul or of nature in it, because the contents stood in a most surprising contradiction with Steele's scandalous and dissolute course of life." The value of these remarks is somewhat lessened by the fact that the author had clearly never seen the *Christian Hero.* The Rev. J. H. Overton, in his *Life in the English Church,* 1660-1714 (1885), calls the *Christian Hero* "trite and vapid" (p. 288).

he confessed the wrongfulness of acts which others either thought little of, or, through their being less frank and straightforward and humble, concealed as far as possible. In the Preface Steele repeats that the "*Christian Hero* was at first attempted to disengage my own mind from deceiving appearances;" and he wishes that his "fellow-soldiers (to whose service more especially I would direct any thoughts I were capable of) would form to themselves (if any do not) a constant reason of their actions." The dedication of the little book to Lord Cutts is dated "Tower-Guard, March 23, 1701," and in the *Post Man* and *Post Boy* for April 15 to 17 there are advertisements of the publication "this day" of the *Christian Hero*, "Written by Captain Richard Steel."

The book is, as the title-page says, "an argument, proving that no principles but those of religion are sufficient to make a great man." There are four chapters; the first describes the heroism of the ancient world, of Cato, of Brutus; their heroism even had far less strength, and was far less adaptable to man's needs than the heroism described by Christ. The second chapter deals with the story of the Bible—"a certain neglected book . . . called the Scripture"—and the life and death of the Saviour; the third explains the Christian man by the character and work of St. Paul, with applications to the life of Steele's own day; the fourth treats of the passions and interests of men, the common springs of action, which are turned to the best account when joined with religion; and then Steele breaks into expression of his patriotic feelings with a character of William III., a glorious captain, and a sincere and honest man.[1] The idea of the book is admirably worked out, and opinions are expressed on many matters which foreshadow passages which Steele was to write years afterwards. He did not, indeed, hesitate to reprint in the *Spectator*[2] considerable extracts from the book, which, as he says in the Dedication, had been written while he was upon duty, "when the mind was perfectly disengaged and at leisure in the silent watch of the night to run over the busy dream of the day."

[1] In this brief description of the book I have closely followed what is said in Prof. Morley's Introduction to the *Spectator*, 1868.

[2] Nos. 356, 516.

When he wrote, in chapter iii., "It sweetens the pain of the obliged, when he that gives does it with an air that has neither oppression or superiority in it, but had rather have his generosity appear an enlarged self-love than diffusive bounty, and is always a benefactor with the mien of a receiver," he was describing a virtue which he carried to excess throughout his own life, for he constantly ascribed to others what was due to himself. In the same chapter he speaks of women in a tone of reverence familiar in the *Tatler* and *Spectator*, but very different from what was common among his contemporaries. The subject was the absurd and vicious manner in which the fair sex were entertained by the gallants of the day. This was due, he says, partly to want of wit and invention; "for there is in their tender frames native simplicity, groundless fear, and little unaccountable contradictions, upon which there might be built expostulations to divert a good and intelligent young woman, as well as the fulsome raptures, guilty impressions, senseless deifications, and pretended deaths that are every day offered her." [1]

In his *Apology* Steele says that the publication of the *Christian Hero* "had no other good effect, but that from being thought no undelightful companion he was soon reckoned a disagreeable fellow. One or two of his acquaintances thought fit to misuse him and try their valour upon him; and everybody he knew measured the least levity in his words and actions, with the character of a Christian Hero." The particulars which are known of Steele's duel or duels have been already given.[2] It is clear, however, that whatever was the opinion among the soldiers in the Tower, the *Christian Hero* found

[1] "There's not a writer of my time of any note, with the exception of poor Dick Steele, that does not speak of a woman as a slave, and scorn and use her as such. Mr. Pope, Mr. Congreve, Mr. Addison, Mr. Gay, every one of 'em, sing in this key, each according to his nature and politeness, and louder and fouler than all in abuse is Dr. Swift, who spoke of them as he treated them, worst of all" (Thackeray, *Esmond*, Book I., chap. xi.). In Book II., chap. ii., there is an account of a visit made by Captain Steele, secretary to my Lord Cutts, "the bravest and most beloved man of the English army," to Lady Castlewood, "that most beautiful woman, as he said." But Beatrix seemed at first a still greater paragon, and "Faith, the beauty of 'Filia pulchrior,' drove 'pulcram matrem' out of my head," but after calling to mind the dignity and grace of the matron, "I thought her even more noble than the virgin."

[2] Pages 62, 63.

many readers, for in three months a second edition was required, and was duly advertised in the *Post Boy* for July 17 to 19, as published that day, "with large additions." These additions consist chiefly of a new paragraph in the preface, and of eight pages which were placed at the commencement of chapter iv.[1] Many misprints in the first edition were corrected in the second, but a considerable number remained.

Among his own companions, as Steele relates in his *Apology*, "he found himself slighted instead of being encouraged for his declarations as to religion; and it was now incumbent upon him to enliven his character, for which reason he wrote the comedy called *The Funeral*, in which (though full of incidents that move laughter) virtue and vice appear just as they ought to do. Nothing can make the town so fond of a man as a successful play." But before we speak of this play, it will be necessary to briefly consider the state of the drama at that time.

The licentiousness of the plays produced and acted in the theatre while it was supported by Charles II. and his court was perhaps surpassed by the coarseness and shamelessness of the comedies written during the reign of William III. Writers of genius set the example, and their imitators carried the evil fashion to still greater extremes. But on the other side men rose up to protest against this preaching of vice. In 1695 Sir Richard Blackmore, in the preface to *Prince Arthur*, made an ineffectual attempt to rescue "the Muses out of the hands of these Ravishers," in words which Steele long afterwards quoted in the *Spectator*. In June 1697 and in February 1699 William III. issued orders forbidding anything to be acted which was contrary to religion and good manners, and warning the companies at Drury Lane and Lincoln's Inn Fields of the peril incurred by acting passages struck out by the Lord Chamberlain; and the Master of the Revels was ordered not to license any play containing immoral or irreligious expressions, and to report if any such were acted.[2] A proposal to form a Society to combat

[1] Article in *The Antiquary* for December 1885 by Mr. Solly; letter in the same paper for January 1886 by the present writer.

[2] Lord Chamberlain's Records, Warrant Book No. 19, p. 162; *London Gazette*, 27th February 1698-9, and 11th to 14th December 1699.

the growing drunkenness, profaneness and vice was encouraged by Queen Mary; after her death the House of Commons addressed King William on the subject, and in reply he issued a Proclamation in February 1698. The parent Society for the Reformation of Manners gave rise to similar societies in various places and among various classes of the community; Burnet says that those who took up this work had, in many cases, originally joined themselves together before the Revolution in order to enjoy their religious devotions in greater peace than they could otherwise have done. In 1699 there was published, with a portrait of the King, "An Account of the Societies for Reformation of Manners, in London and Westminster, and other parts of the Kingdom. . . . Published with the approbation of a considerable number of the Lords Spiritual and Temporal," among the latter being Lord Cutts.

But in the meantime, in March 1698, Jeremy Collier, a nonjuring clergyman, published *A Short View of the Profaneness and Immorality of the English Stage*, which, though sometimes intemperate—as when he spoke of Shakespeare as too guilty to call as evidence—yet attacked a real evil, and in the most conclusive way possible. The facts and examples which Collier quoted spoke for themselves. The stage was, he said, immodest and profane, and an enemy to all religion, and these charges he substantiated by copious references to the most popular plays of the day.[1] Congreve, Vanbrugh, Dennis and others replied, but they could not shake Collier's conclusions. Dryden noticed the attack only incidentally. Two months before his death he wrote in the Preface to his *Fables*, "I shall say the less because in many things he has taxed me justly; and I have pleaded guilty to all thoughts and expressions of mine which can be truly argued of obscenity, profaneness, or immorality, and retract them. If he be my enemy, let him triumph; if he be my friend, as I have given him no personal occasion to be otherwise, he will be glad of my repentance. It becomes me not to draw my

[1] An excellent criticism of Collier's attack on the stage and of those who answered him will be found in Beljame's suggestive work, *Le Public et les hommes de lettres en Angleterre au dix-huitième siècle*, 1660–1744, Paris, 1881, pp. 244–259. In the earlier portion of the book Beljame gives specimens, perhaps in over-abundance, to show how much the drama needed purifying.

pen in defence of a bad cause, when I have so often drawn it for a good one." In this same Preface, however, Dryden charged Collier with mixing truth with falsehood; and in *Cymon and Iphigenia* he fell back upon coarse abuse. In an epilogue spoken at a performance for Dryden's benefit on March 25, 1700, the poet argued that it was the banished court, and not the stage, which brought with it on its return the seeds of open vice.

Dennis published a pamphlet called *The Usefulness of the Stage, to the Happiness of Mankind, to Government, and to Religion*, in which he said that if Collier had only attacked the corruptions of the stage, and not the stage itself, "I should have been so far from blaming him, that I should have publicly returned him my thanks: For the abuses are so great, that there is a necessity for the reforming them. . . . Besides that Vice is contrary to Virtue, it renders the stage little and contemptible." Other dramatists did not, however, treat the question in this fair spirit; and in November 1698 (with the date 1699 on the title-page), Collier issued *A Defence of the Short View. . . . Being a Reply to Mr. Congreve's Amendments, &c., and to the Vindication of the Author of the Relapse.* The opening address "To the Reader" ends thus: "The Poets are the aggressors, let them lay down their arms first. We have suffered under silence a great while; if we are in any fault, 'tis because we began with them no sooner." The conflict still waged, but little that was fresh remained to be said on either side. Congreve and Vanbrugh wrote their best plays during the reign of William III.; Farquhar's plays were exactly contemporary with Steele's.

In 1700 the grand jury of Middlesex made a presentment, stating that many plays which were frequently acted were "full of profane, irreverent, indecent, and immoral expressions," and that they tended "to the debauching and ruining of youth resorting thereto, and to the breach of the peace." [1]

In the summer of 1701, Steele, who tells us that he was "a great admirer" of Collier's work,[2] wrote his first play, or rather

[1] Fitzgerald's *New History of the English Stage*, i. 231.

[2] *Apology*, 1714.

the first which came before the public, *The Funeral, or Grief-à-la-Mode*, and in or about October took it to Christopher Rich, of the Theatre Royal. On October the 9th an agreement was arrived at that Steele was to receive a certain sum, and the play was to be acted "as soon as they could conveniently."[1] The comedy was soon afterwards brought out. I have not been able to find the exact date of the first performance; but the play was published, as Mr. Dobson has pointed out, on the 20th December, the following advertisement appearing in the *Post Boy* and *Flying Post* for December 18 to 20, 1701:—"This day is publish'd, The Funeral, Or Grief-A-la-Mode, A Comedy. As it is acted at the Theatre Royal in Drury Lane. Written by Mr. Steele. Printed for Jacob Tonson at Gray's Inn Gate in Gray's Inn Lane."[2] The music[3] of the new play had been advertised a week earlier:—"Next week will be published Mr Croft's his new Musick in the Comedy called the Funeral, or Grief-à-la-Mode" (*Post Boy*, Dec. 11 to 13, 1701); and the music "composed by Mr William Croft," appeared on the 18th, "price 1s. 6d. the set" (*Post Boy*, Dec. 16 to 18, 1701). The original quarto edition of the play is dated 1702, in accordance with the frequent practice in the case of books published at the close of the year.

The play is sprightly, and the tone is generous and pure; the earnest satire is directed against undertakers and lawyers, against the mockery of grief and the mockery of justice.[4]

[1] See Rich's answer to Steele's bill of complaint, in the case Steele *v.* Rich.

[2] The next issue of the *Post Boy* (Dec. 20 to 23) has a similar advertisement, "There is now publish'd, The Funeral," &c.

[3] See Appendix IV.

[4] Dibdin (*A Complete History of the Stage*, iv. 307–8) says: "Nothing can establish a better proof of the admirable merit of this play . . . than the diligence with which the critics have attempted, to no purpose, to discover that it is not genuine; for the plot and the style are unquestionably the author's own, and the last is so peculiar, which is indeed the characteristic of Steele's writings, that nothing can be more difficult to get by heart; but when attached to the memory, nothing can be more easy to retain. . . . Everything is perfectly in nature, and the moral is complete." Hermann Hartmann, in his *Sir R. Steele als Dramatiker* (Kneiphöfische Mittelschule, Königsberg, i/P., 1880), has given an elaborate analysis and criticism of *The Funeral* and of *The Tender Husband*, with many sensible remarks. He says that the title, "The Funeral," is misleading, for the play has for its main point the contrast

Cibber, Wilks, Norris, Mrs. Verbruggen, and Mrs. Oldfield were in the cast; and in the prologue Steele said that he knew that his numerous friends who were present would "for the fellow-soldier save the poet," and he did not appeal to his comrades without result, for the play was very successful. Cibber, after complaints that Rich secured first his own profits and paid the actors only what the receipts of the theatre afterwards enabled him to do, says (*Apology*, chap. viii.) that the manager promised to pay arrears of salary, "and that we might not have it always in our power to say he had never intended to keep his word, I remember . . . he once paid us nine days in one week: This happened when the *Funeral*, or *Grief à la Mode* was first acted, with more than expected success." The play was afterwards dedicated to the Countess of Albemarle, who had then recently married Arnold Joost van Keppel, Earl of Albemarle, and Colonel of the first troop of Horse Guards. The Countess was the daughter of Adam Vander Duin, Lord of St. Gravemoer, General of the Forces to the States General.

The opening scene, where Sable, the undertaker, arranges his men for the funeral, has often been quoted, and Thackeray and Sydney Smith have left on record their admiration of its humour. Says Sable, "Let's have no laughing now on any provocation: [*Makes faces*]. Look yonder, that hale, well-looking puppy! You ungrateful scoundrel, did not I pity you, take you out of a great man's service, and show you the pleasure of receiving wages? Did not I give you ten, then fifteen, now twenty shillings a week, to be sorrowful? and the more I give you, I think, the gladder you are." The dialogue between Puzzle, the lawyer, and his clerk is, too, excellent, and Forster has called the character of the widow "a masterpiece of comedy." Her conversation with her lady visitors in the third act was no doubt familiar to Sheridan when he wrote similar scenes in *The School for Scandal*. The manner in which the knot of the play is cut at the end by the introduction of bigamy on the part of Lady

between virtue and vice: the first represented by Hardy, Campley, the orphan ladies, and Trusty; the second by Lady Brumpton and Tattleaid. Hartmann remarks that the characters of the Ladies Charlotte and Harriet are an illustration of the honour in which Steele held the female sex.

Brumpton is, however, as Hartmann has remarked, unnecessary and unæsthetic, for when Lord Brumpton came to life again he could, of course, have executed a second will. The scene with the company of recruits in the fourth act must have much delighted Steele's comrades. Matchlock, who had brought Mr. Campley off at Steinkirk, had been whipped from constable to constable all the way from Cornwall; yet, after all, says Trim, "'tis upon the neck of such scoundrels as these gentlemen that we great Captains build our renown." The tone of the morals in all Steele's plays shows how different his views were from those of many of his contemporaries, and he did not hesitate, in the fifty-first number of the *Spectator*, to himself condemn one passage as printed in the first edition of the *Funeral*, as an offence to delicacy and modesty.[1]

William the Third died on March 8, 1702; and Steele says, in his *Apology*, that his successful play, "with some particulars enlarged upon to his advantage (for princes never hear good or evil in the manner others do) obtained him the notice of the King: and his name, to be provided for, was in the last Table Book ever worn by the glorious and immortal William the Third." We are not told who recommended Steele to the King's notice; it may have been the Duke of Ormond, or the Duke of Albemarle, to whose wife *The Funeral* was dedicated. Both these noblemen were present at King William's death. Or it may have been the Duke of Devonshire, Lord Steward of the Household, who had attended the rehearsal of

[1] An epilogue to *The Funeral* by Thomas Hull, actor, play-writer, and deputy-manager of Covent Garden Theatre, is in my possession. The actress who represented Lady Brumpton describes how a rigid Don might indignantly say the Widow was enough to ruin all his family; how the hypocritic Fair might pretend her modesty was shocked by such a monstrous character; and how the rake might cry—

> "A pretty devil to have made a Wife,
> What think you of her? Ah! Dick Steele knew life!
> Neither uncommon, nor unnatural!
> Egad, there's too much of her in 'em all!"

But the virtuous and the good would find the moral which the bard designed. A prudent bee culls what is useful from the flower, and leaves the bad; each virgin should essay to be the Lady Sharlot, and let the Widow's character remain the object to be shunned, as virtue's bane.

the play.[1] There would be no difficulty in finding expressions in both the *Christian Hero* and *Funeral* to prove to the King the loyal feelings of their author.

Before passing from these works, it will be well to notice here an interesting specimen of contemporary criticism. On April 14, 1702,[2] a little book appeared, called *A Comparison between the two Stages; with . . . some critical remarks on the Funeral . . . and others.* Of the 200 pages in this work, pages 145 to 171 relate to Steele. The book is attributed to Charles Gildon, a man some seven years older than Steele, who, having refused to enter the priesthood of the Romish Church as his father wished, led a life of dissipation, and published, as a free-thinker, *The Oracles of Reason*, a posthumous work by Charles Blount. Afterwards, however, he abandoned his heretical views on religion, and in 1705 wrote *The Deist's Manual.* He died in January 1724. The *Comparison between the two Stages* is in the form of a dialogue between Ramble and Sullen and Chagrin, a critic. When Ramble proposes to speak of *The Funeral*, Sullen says, "'Tis a dangerous matter to talk of this play; the Town has given it such applause, 'twill be an ungrateful undertaking to call their judgments in question." He agrees that it is diverting, and written with noble intentions. Ramble remarks, "I hear the gentleman is a fine companion, and passes for a wit of the first rank;" but Sullen and the Critic agree that *The Funeral* is not a just comedy, the principle being much amiss. They argue that Lord Brumpton could not, as was supposed, have lain dead in the house so long, and no one see him; intrigues and amours going on in the meantime in the house of death. The widow, too, joins in the drollery, though she is represented as a hypocrite. It is farce, not comedy. Look at the manner of Lady Sharlot's escape—a forced situation which was quite unnecessary. Is it likely that a man of Cabinet's wickedness would have been frightened into a confession by a ghost? The undertaker is not adequately punished; for he was paid anyhow. Nevertheless, the satire on some widows, and on undertakers, is happy.

[1] *Funeral*, Preface.

[2] *Flying Post*, April 11 to 14, 1702.

The Critic thinks the language "too concise and stiff" for comedy; see, for example, the scene between Lord Brumpton and Trusty in Act I., and that between Trusty and Cabinet in Act IV. There are difficult lines in the Preface, and long parentheses in the play. Ramble turns round and asks, "Did you ever read *The Christian Hero?*" The Critic says, "Yes; what do you mean by asking me?" Ramble replies, "Pray, don't be angry. Is it not an extraordinary thing?" The answer is, "Look ye, sir—to answer you dogmatically, and in a few words—No." Critic gives reasons: "Thus, then, briefly: 'Tis a chaos, 'tis a confusion of thoughts, rude and indigested; though he had the advice of an ingenious man to put it into method. 'Tis dated from the Tower-guard, as a present to his Colonel, that his Colonel might think him even in time of duty a very contemplative soldier, and I suppose by the roughness of the style, he writ it there, on the butt-end of a musket." Sullen replies, "Hush! no reproaches; the gentleman has done very well, and chose a worthy subject," and Ramble adds, "It bore two editions." The Critic rejoins, "It did not; it was but once printed, nor is all that impression sold; 'tis a trick of the booksellers to get it off." Ramble, however, maintains his good opinion of the author. The discussion of *The Funeral* is then resumed; and Ramble suggests that, in the opening of Act III., Mademoiselle's "promises" is a mistake for "premises." The Critic objects, among other things, to the use of the word "bagatelle." And then Sullen turns to the merits of the play—the characters, the visiting scene, the incidents, all flowing naturally, and the moral, which is the true result of the play. Ramble adds warm praises of the author—who is described as "indued with singular honesty, a noble disposition, and a conformity of good manners"—and his works, and the Critic hopes, if he will divert the town with another play, that it may be more correct. The author does not want understanding.

This "correctness" demanded by the Critic is what the writers of the time all aimed at; and those who talked about writers quoted from the great French writer, Boileau, without fully understanding what he taught, or how to apply rules, which were right as regards the French language, to the requirements of English. There is only one point in the dialogue given above that requires notice, and that is the statement made by the Critic that the second edition of the *Christian Hero* was merely "a trick of the booksellers to get it off." This is not true, for, as we have seen, the second edition was really corrected, and contained eight more pages than the first edition. A third edition was not called for until 1710, when Steele was famous as the editor of *The Tatler;* fourth and fifth editions followed in 1711, and a sixth in 1712, during the publication of *The Spectator*. The appearance of the seventh edition in 1722 was probably due to the popularity of *The Conscious Lovers*, which was first produced in the November of that year.

IV.

LANDGUARD FORT.

1702. ÆT. 30.

SHORTLY before the death of King William, Steele made an important change in his position in the army. The strength of the army was considerably augmented, and among the corps embodied was the Thirty-fourth Regiment of Foot.[1] Its first Colonel was Robert Lord Lucas, from the Lieutenant-Colonelcy of Sir John Jacob's regiment, now the Thirteenth Light Infantry. Lord Lucas was a foremost friend of the Revolution, and was put in charge of the Tower in December 1688, an appointment which was confirmed by William III., who gave him a commission as Governor of the Tower.[2] Lord Lucas served under the King in Flanders, and was made Lieutenant-Colonel. He remained Governor of the Tower until June 1702,[3] when Queen Anne superseded his commission, and appointed the Earl of Abingdon as Constable.

The commission of Lord Lucas to the Colonelcy of the new regiment is dated the 12th February 1702, and by June 24 there was due to him "for pay of his regiment of foot from the dates on which they were raised," £2134. 6s. 2d.[4] The regiment consisted of men from Norfolk, Essex, and the adjoining counties, and was

[1] Cannon's *Historical Records of the Thirty-fourth or Cumberland Regiment of Foot*, 1884, pp. 9, 10, 11, 79. The regiment is now known as "Borderers."

[2] Luttrell's *Diary*, i. 485, 560.

[3] The money for the pay of the soldiers in the Tower was paid to Lord Lucas up to June. It was afterwards due to Lord Abingdon. See Add. MSS. 9756, f. 215, and 9757, ff. 65, 67; and Luttrell's *Diary*, v. 164. Lord Lucas's own pay was at the rate of £1. 18s. 4½d. per diem (Hist. MSS. Commission, 11th Report, Part IV., p. 217).

[4] Add. MS. 9757, f. 61.

raised by Lord Lucas, and, among other officers, Captain Richard Steele. Each officer raised a company; and when the numbers were nearly complete the establishment was increased to twelve companies, each of three officers and sixty-six non-commissioned officers and men. One wing of the regiment had its rendezvous at Colchester, and the other at Norwich. Upon the King's death the soldiers took the oath to Her Majesty; this was shortly followed by the fitting out of an expedition against Cadiz under the Duke of Ormond, and Lord Lucas's regiment was ordered to send five companies to Landguard Fort, Sheerness, and Tilbury, early in May, to relieve the Buffs, who were ordered to embark for the Isle of Wight to join the expedition to Spain. At the same time seven companies of the regiment were ordered to relieve a detachment of the Foot Guards on duty at the Tower of London; and two companies were afterwards sent to Dover Castle. Steele went to Landguard Fort.

It seems then that the common statement that Steele became a captain in Lord Lucas's regiment of Fusileers about 1700 is entirely wrong. Steele himself stated, many years afterwards, that "soon after" (that is, after John Sansome lent him money, which was in January 1702[1]) he "was made Captain of Foot by His Grace the Duke of Marlborough, in pursuance of a list made by King William, in the Lord Lucas's Regiment of Foot."[2] He was still in the Coldstream Guards at the beginning of 1702, for Gildon says that Steele dedicated the *Christian Hero* to "his Colonel," Lord Cutts. He doubtless became known to Lord Lucas while he was quartered at the Tower, and was thus chosen as one of the officers of the new regiment formed in February 1702. He was already Captain Steele in the Coldstream Guards in 1700. There is nothing to show that either Steele or Lord Lucas had anything to do with "Fusileers,"[3] specially so called.

[1] Page 137.

[2] Steele's Answer in the suit of Sansome *v.* Steele, 1718.

[3] This term was originally applied to soldiers who carried a fusil. Thus Cannon says (*Historical Record of the Seventh Regiment, or Royal Fusileers*, 1847, p. 2) that "the regular regiments of foot were composed, in 1685, of Musketeers, Pikemen, and Grenadiers; but in the Ordnance Regiment every man carried a long musket called a fusil, with a sword and bayonet; and thus they were called Fusileers."

Langer, or Landguard, Fort is situated on a point of land, half marsh and half common, which forms the northern and eastern shores of the mouth of the Stour and the Orwell. Harwich lies opposite, to the west, separated by the harbour, or estuary, a mile or more wide. Taylor,[1] writing in 1676, says that "the principal officers of His Majesty's Ordnance in the Tower of London, do still (according to former precedents) continue the writing of Landguard Fort in Essex: and although several now living pretend to the remembrance of the building of it, yet we may find there was an ancienter fort thereabouts and called by the same name as this; south-west of which is the entrance into Harbour;" and the editor added a note in 1730:—"The Landguard Fort mentioned by our author was a handsome square fortification consisting of four bastions. . . . About sixty men used to be here in garrison. This I am told hath been lately much diminished both in buildings and number of men." In 1659[2] the force at Landguard Fort consisted of a governor, marshal, and storekeeper, gunners, two boatmen, and one company of foot, consisting of a captain, at 8s. (who was to be governor); a lieutenant, 4s.; two sergeants, each at 1s. 6d.; two corporals, and one drum, each at 1s.; and sixty soldiers, at 8d. each. Sir Charles Lyttleton was governor in Charles II.'s reign.[3] Upon the new establishment introduced in April 1700 a lieutenant-governor of the Fort was appointed, with a salary of £283 a year.[4] Colonel Jones was governor

[1] *History and Antiquities of Harwich and Dovercourt*, by Silas Taylor, 1730, pp. 15, 16.

[2] Harleian MS. 6844, f. 188.

[3] Lewis's *Topographical Dictionary of England*, "Harwich."

[4] Add. MS. 9759, ff. 49, 63. There is a petition from Captain Francis Hamon (June), 1702, in which he says he was appointed lieutenant-governor of Landguard Fort in 1693, with 4s. a day for his pay, over and above the pension of 4s. a day thereto allowed him. Of this additional allowance £243. 8s. was in arrear on April 25, 1700, and since then only had he been put upon the establishment of pay for the Fort. His pension for 3¼ years—ending June 1702—was also due, amounting to £237. 8s., making £480. 16s. in all. He was already in debt, and could no longer get credit; he was threatened with an execution, and utter ruin. He therefore prayed to be paid. The petition was laid before the Queen in August 1702, but the prayer was not granted, Mr. Blathwait saying that Captain Hamon had 4s. a day on the establishment in lieu of his pension (Treasury Papers, Public Record Office, vol. lxxx. 83).

during Steele's residence at the Fort. At the present day the force at Landguard Fort consists of a battery of garrison artillery—about eighty men—under a major.

A writer, speaking in 1790 of Steele's residence at Landguard Fort, said, "I am well acquainted with his writing and lodging-room in a farm-house at Walton, hard by that garrison."[1] Several letters written by Steele at the Fort are in existence, none of which have been published before. The first, which is in the possession of Mr. Alfred Morrison, is an energetic request that reasonable steps should be taken for the preservation of the health of the soldiers.

LAND-GUARD-FORT, Sept^{br} 28th, 1702.

GENTLEMEN

The Governor of this Garrison, Coll. Jones, before he went to town, where He is at present, directed Mr. Hubbard your officer here, to represent the ill condition, the Barracks and all parts of this Garrison, is in, as to our Windows and Tyling; There are Sick Men of the Company here (whereof I am Captain) lye in their Beds exposed to all the injuries of the Weather; I have at present two Sergeants, two Corporalls, and nine Sentinells so ill that they cannot do Duty; which if I cannot attribute to this cause I am sure I may say, I cannot expect the continuance of other men's health, if the Remedy be defer'd till the Winter advances further upon us: I hope my duty to them has not press'd me beyond rules to you in giving you this trouble:

I am, Gentlemen,

Y^{r} most obedient & most Humble Servant

RICH^{D} STEELE.

Steele was soon afterwards involved in a Chancery suit. The following are, briefly, the facts set forth in the pleadings.[2] The Bill of the complainant, Richard Steele, of St. James's, Westminster, is dated 23rd October 1702. It states that Steele had observed great intimacy between Elizabeth Moore of St. James's aforesaid, widow; William Kelly, of Ireland, now residing in or near Westminster; and Elizabeth Moore, daughter of

[1] *Gentleman's Magazine*, vol. lx., pt. ii. p. 993, letter signed "P. T., Sandgate Bank."

[2] Chancery Pleadings—"Steele *v.* Moore." Public Record Office, Reynardson V. No. 134. See page 62 as to a Captain Kelly with whom Steele fought in 1700.

the said Elizabeth Moore; and that he was informed by Kelly that the daughter was married to him, but without her mother's knowledge, and that the daughter had a great fortune—£1500 or other great value—which was, however, in the power of the mother. Kelly being in need of money and wanting to borrow £100 from the elder Moore, persuaded Steele to become bound with him to her; it would increase their amity, and Steele should not lose a penny. But now Steele found that there was no real marriage, and that Kelly, the Moores, and others were in a conspiracy, saying that Kelly did not get the £100. This bond, made in 1689, was, it was understood, to be paid off by other monies, and it had so been; but now a solicitor, Road, came to Steele, said he had had the bond assigned to him, and demanded the money. Steele prayed the court for relief from this demand, and asked for an answer from the Moores. In any case, the others who entered into the bond should pay their share. They would possibly say that Steele owed money for entertainments, &c., given by the Moores while they were getting him to sign the bond, but they themselves partook of these, and Steele owed nothing.

In the answer put in by the Moores and Road, it was maintained that the bond was honest. Kelly and Pepper—the other person who signed it—were beyond sea, or not to be got at; so Mrs. Moore, hearing that Steele was near Colchester, got a writ from the High Sheriff of Essex. Steele was at Harwich—a Captain of Foot thereabouts—and Road visited him. Steele acknowledged the debt, and said that the defendant had "done him the greatest favour that could well be done him not to cause him to be arrested, and took four guineas or some such sum, alleging it was all he had, and offered this Def[t] to give him part thereof for his civility," but Road refused, and took only one guinea for the other defendants. Steele said he would soon come to London and settle the matter, and sent by Road a letter to Elizabeth Moore, sen., in these or similar words:—

LAND GUARD FORT, June 28, 1702.

The bearer, Mr. Road, came to me to this place (finding it, I suppose, impracticable to obey your directions about my obligation for

Kelly), and demanded the payment of the bond. I told him nakedly my affairs, and shall about fourteen days hence be in town in order, with other business, to do you justice, and hope you'll be ready for an assignment, that the weight of this calamity may fall upon Mr. Pepper as well as, Madam,

Y[r] most humble servant,

RICH[D]. STEELE.

But Mrs. Moore considered that this letter was written merely to cause delay, and assigned the bond to Mr. Road, with power of attorney to get the money. She had the bond in her possession. On February 13th next, £130 would be due, besides law charges. Mrs. Moore had received only £12, and Road £1. 1s. 6d. She denied that there was any conspiracy or pretence of her daughter being married to Kelly.

In November there were several decrees:[1] one, granting an injunction against the action being proceeded with by the defendants, because they had not answered the complainant's Bill, and had shown contempt of Court; another (November 13), saying that this injunction should be absolved in a week if the complainant did not take certain steps; and then on the 20th another, finally absolving the injunction. There is no record of anything further being done in the case. But there is not much room for doubt as to the character of the Moores and of Kelly, "of Ireland," who persuaded Steele in 1689, when he was only seventeen, and had not yet left school for Oxford, to become bound for £100, with the argument that "it would increase their amity," and that Steele could not lose a penny in the matter. The bond is mentioned on a paper containing memoranda of accounts, in the Blenheim collection. The amount is there given as £89.

M[r] Sansome	£248 : 00 : 00
Bound for Kelly	89 : 00 : 00
To M[rs] Phipps	17 : 00 : 00
To M[r] J[n] Foxall	30 : 00 : 00
M[r] Godley assignee of M[r] Clay[2] deceas'd	40 : 00 : 00

[1] Chancery Decrees (Pub. Rec. Office), 1702, B., pp. 93–95.

[2] Mr. Arthur Clay lent Lord Cutts money in 1696; see p. 56.

To Mr Barradell Taylour . . .	6 : 00 : 00
To Mr Fearne Corn-chandler Haymarket .	10 : 00 : 00
To Mr Willis	70 : 00 : 00
	510 : 00 : 00

On the back there is the following significant note upon Mrs. Phipps:—

"Mrs Phips a Midwife in Watling-street at the sign of the Coffin and Cradle—

"Her bond she obtained by threatening to expose the Occasion[1] of the Debt it is [*sic*] 22*l*:—5*l* of it is paid."

Another memorandum among the Blenheim papers refers to the Mr. Willis mentioned above.

"Mr Pye[2] to go to Mr Bentley's at the[3] Queen's Arms Tavern in the Strand and know whether the bill of Seventy pound of Snaggs be well paid, and to demand seeing a Judgement of fifty pounds, and Bond of fifty from Mr Gascoigne[4] and self to Mr Willis, and whether said bill is acknowledg'd and endors'd—

"Mr Willis[5] an Apothecary near the Bear Tavern Piccadilly:

"Note that Mr Walker the Tenant to my Estate was one of the Executors to my Brother—but disclaim'd acting as such—? can He resume that trust."

From the last sentence of this paper it is evident that the memorandum was written after Steele's marriage to his first wife, for George Walker appears as a "loving friend" in the will of Major Ford, Steele's brother-in-law.

1 "reason" first written.

2 Mr. John Pye, of Furnivall's Inn, was one of the securities to the administration of the property of Steele's first wife.

3 "Crosse Key," cancelled.

4 Steele's uncle.

5 Willis is mentioned on another paper among the Blenheim MSS:—

"Mr Nunes—100*l* secur'd by Mr Samuel Shepheard Jun—Time desir'd—

Mr Oldfield in Stanhope-Street.

Attorney for Mr Cardonnell—Sued by Him in sixty pounds paid to sixteen, &c. He has the value of more in his hands.

Dacres has a note of Seventy pounds—

Mr Isaac Ferdinandez Nunes in Mark-lane.

Mr Willis's debt about 47*l* } Not in Steele's
Mr Hopall's Release of Erro*l* } writing.

Of several of the other persons mentioned in these memoranda, we shall hear again in subsequent actions for debt against Steele. In July 1701 Steele borrowed £60 from Mr. John Foxall, and in January 1702 £600 from John Sansome, Esq. Mr. Barradall was Steele's tailor in June 1703; and Mr. Isaac Fernandes-Nunes was a subscriber to the collected edition of the *Tatler*.

V.

"THE LYING LOVER."

1703–4. ÆT. 31.

IN December 1702 or January 1703 Steele entered into an agreement with Rich to sell to him a comedy which he had nearly finished, and which he proposed to call the *Election of Gotham.*[1] The agreement, according to Rich, was signed on or about the 7th January, and the play was to be ready on or about the 20th February. Rich adds that there was a friendship contracted between them; and Steele, being in want of money, and being likely to be arrested, prevailed upon him to advance £72, becoming bound in the sum of £144 for the payment of the £72 on the 8th March following. But when March came Steele did not pay back the £72 or interest, nor did he furnish Rich with the promised play. Indeed, Rich says—omitting all reference to *The Lying Lover*—that he got no play from him until March 1705, when Steele came to Rich and asked him to accept the *Tender Husband* in lieu of the *Election of Gotham.* According to Steele the £72 was paid in order to induce him to write further, and upon condition that he would bring his next comedy to Rich. Steele charged Rich with "minding to oppress" him, "and extort great sums of money from him." The quarrel led to proceedings in Chancery in 1707, which will be described in their place. Nothing more is known of the play called *The Election of Gotham.*[2]

[1] Chancery Pleadings, "Steele *v.* Rich."

[2] A farce, called *The Gotham Election*, by Mrs. Centlivre, who was a friend of Steele's, was published in 1715, but not acted. It was intended, says the writer, to give their Royal Highnesses—the Hanoverians—an idea how our elections were managed.

There is nothing more to record during 1703, until December, except a letter to Carrell, probably John Caryll, by whom it seems likely Pope was afterwards introduced to Steele, and to whom we shall have to refer again when it becomes necessary to allude to the intricacies of Pope's correspondence. When Secretary Caryll, a Roman Catholic of Sussex family (made titular Lord Caryll by James II.), was outlawed, his estate, and the life-interest in the entailed estates, were granted to Lord Cutts.[1] John Caryll, the nephew, was at that time (May 1696) in Horsham Gaol, but when he was liberated he entered into negotiations with Lord Cutts, and purchased his uncle's life-interest. Steele was then secretary to Lord Cutts, and made Caryll's acquaintance. In 1703 Steele was writing to him from Landguard Fort.[2]

LANDGUARD FORT, June 17th, 1703.

DEAR CARRELL

George Wilcocks one of the fellows you brought from Ship-board, a Taylor, whose wife, as he told you in my hearing, keeps a Broker's Shop in Monmouth Street, deserted on Munday-evening: you'll please do what you can to retake him; and sollicit Major Soul [3] to write to me p next, a letter of Advice about Money: You know we are paid but to 24th; and the misfortune twill be to tick: I am

Yr very Affectionate

Humble Sernt

RICHD STEELE.

My Duty to my Lord.

[1] Luttrell's *Diary*, 23rd May 1696, quoted in Dilke's *Papers of a Critic*, i. 250–2; and Luttrell, iv. 303.

[2] The draft of this letter is among the Marlborough MSS. On the back is the following:—

Preface to Generall Lover.

There is no character so sublime as a Lover, which if I may be permitted to aspire to, I leave other all other (*sic*) pursuits to the Humbler world who pretend no higher than to write Æneids, lead Armies, or sit on Thrones:

This passion has left Æternal Monuments of it's Force in the Poems and Actions of the Ancients: Ovid's Corinna, &c.

It is the secondary Motive at least of All the World: Women dared before the Priests of Mars to intimate that most Gallant actions were undertaken through hope of pleasing Women.

[3] See page 106.

Land: Guard: Fort
Dec^r: 28th - 1703

This is to Certifie that the Bearer hereof =
M^r: Oliver Linnacre ~~has~~ Served ~~the Her Majest~~ in that
Company of her Majesties Regiment of Foot Commanded by
the R^t Honourable the Lord Lucas whereof I am Captain
for the Space of Six Months, and that I do hereby Discharge
him from the Same for his better provision and advancement as Witnesse my hand and Seale

Rich^d: Steele

There is a draft of another letter written in 1703 among the Blenheim MSS. It is not certain to whom it was addressed. The first portion is here given in facsimile.

LANDGUARD FORT, Dec[br] 28th, 1703.

This is to certifie that the Bearer hereof M[r] Oliver Linnacre has served in that Company of her Majesties Regiment of Foot commanded by the R[t] Honourable the Lord Lucas whereof I am Captain for the Space of Six Months, and that I do hereby discharge him from the same for his better provision, and advancement. as Witnesse my hand and Seale RICH[D] STEELE.

MY LORD

I some time ago promis'd your Lordship that if Oliver Linnacre's Relations could persuade him to Leave me, I would upon notice from M[r] Coleman, and in obedience to y[r] Lordship send him discharge; which I have enclos'd to you, and am very proud of the opportunity of Subscribing my self, my Lord,

Y[r] Most Obedient and most [1] Humble Serv[nt.]

Steele's second play, *The Lying Lover*, was acted in December 1703; it was written, he says, in the severity required by Collier. It will be convenient here to notice a few facts relating to the condition of the drama in 1702 and 1703, the years which intervened between the production of *The Funeral* and *The Lying Lover.*

In 1702 Queen Anne directed that certain players of Lincoln's Inn Fields should be prosecuted, and they were duly tried and found guilty of "uttering impious, lewd, and immoral expressions." In "A Refutation of the Apology for the Actors," 1703, published in the *Camden Miscellany*, we read: "The English poets and players are still like themselves; they strain to a singularity of coarseness. . . . They labour for perspicuity, and shine out in mire and in scandal. . . . They are proof against reason and punishment, and come over again with the old smut and profanity." [2] Defoe wrote in 1702, in *The Reformation of Manners, a Satyr*—

[1] "Faithfull" cancelled.

[2] Fitzgerald's *New History of the English Stage*, i. 230, 225.

"Let this describe the nation's character:
One man reads Milton, forty Rochester.

The case is plain, the temper of the time,
One wrote the lewd, and t'other the sublime;"

and in answer to his persecutors he published, in 1703, *More Reformation, a Satyr upon Himself*, showing how the world treats the man who attacks crime—

"And he that first reforms a vicious town,
Prevents their ruin, but completes his own."

Collier wrote another pamphlet, *A Dissuasive from the Play House*, which was answered by Dennis with *The Person of Quality's Answer to Mr. Collier's Letter*, reprinted in the second volume of his *Original Letters*. On the 15th January 1704 the Lord Chamberlain issued an order to the Companies at Drury Lane and Little Lincoln's Inn Fields, directing that as there were many indecencies in the plays which were represented, all plays must be licensed by the Master of the Revels, and all prologues, epilogues, and songs submitted to him; and on the 17th January the Lord Chamberlain ordered Charles Killigrew, Esq., Master of the Revels, not to license anything which was not strictly agreeable to religion and good manners. Plays must be submitted before the parts were distributed, and not just before they were brought out.[1] In the *Daily Courant* for January 20, 1704, we find, "This present day is published, A Representation of the Impiety and Immorality of the English Stage . . . Price 3d. Also, Some Thoughts concerning the Stage, in a Letter to a Lady. Price 2d. Also, Mr. Collier's Dissuasive from the Play House . . . Price 2d., or 12s. per hundred," and in the same paper for January 22, "Last Fast Day there were given to the people at all the Church Doors within the Bills of Mortality and Places adjacent, many Thousands of Books of different kinds, setting forth the outrageous Impiety and Immorality of our English plays Acted in the Present Theatres. With some Questions addressed to all persons in general that resort thither; and in particular to

[1] Lord Chamberlain's Records, Warrant Book, No. 21, pp. 433-4.

Parents and Masters of Families, who have the charge of Youth, showing the great danger and evil that attend the frequenting of such places." Farquhar's *The Inconstant* was published in March 1702,[1] Dennis's *Comical Gallant, or the Amours of Sir John Falstaffe* in May,[2] and Farquhar's *Twin Rivals* and Cibber's *She would and she would not* in December.[3] On May 28, 1703, the *Funeral* was acted at Drury Lane, "in which will be performed several new Sonatas by the famous Gasperini; particularly one for a violin and flute composed by him, but the Flute part performed by Mr. Paisible. And entertainments of singing. . . . With several Dances. . . . And a Comical Epilogue spoken by Mr. Pinkeman. To begin at half an hour after five a clock."[4] The hours of performance are well illustrated by this advertisement:—"For the entertainment of several Persons of Great Quality, lately come from beyond the Seas. At the new Theatre, in Little-Lincoln's Inn Fields, tomorrow . . . will be performed, a Consort of all Sorts of Instrumental Musick, as Trumpets, Kettle-Drums, Haut-Boys, and Flutes, &c. Together with several new entertainments of singing by the famous Signiora Francisca Margarita de l'Epine. . . . Also an entertainment of several Dances. . . . Beginning at 5 of the Clock, and to be ended at 8, for the conveniency of the Qualities resorting to the Park after. Boxes 6s. Pit 4s. Gallery 2s."[5]

The *Funeral* was acted on October 26th for the benefit of Mrs. Moore, and again on the 1st November; and then it was advertised in the *Daily Courant* for Monday, November 29, 1703, that on Wednesday (December 1st) at Drury Lane there "will be presented a new Comedy never acted before, called *The Lying Lover*, or the Ladies Friendship, Written by the Author of the Funeral, or Grief-à-la-Mode." But the performance was postponed a day, and the new play was first acted on "this present Thursday, being the 2nd of December." It ran for six nights, December the 8th, the sixth night, being "for the benefit of

[1] *Post Man*, March 10–12, 1702.
[2] *Ibid.*, May 16–19, 1702.
[3] *Daily Courant*, December 9, 1702; *Post Man*, December 15–17, 1702.
[4] *Daily Courant*, May 28, 1703.
[5] *Ibid.*, June 10, 1703.

the Author."[1] There was another performance on the 15th December. An attempt will be made in an Appendix to give a list of the performances of all Steele's plays during his lifetime.

By some curious mistake most writers have stated that the *Tender Husband* was the second of Steele's plays, and that it appeared in 1703, while the *Lying Lover* has been placed in 1704; and they have proceeded to surmise that the failure of the *Lying Lover* caused Steele to abandon play-writing for many years. But in reality the *Tender Husband* was not acted until April 23, 1705, whereas the *Lying Lover* had appeared on December 2, 1703.[2] On the 14th January 1704, "the last new Comedy," the *Lying Lover*, was advertised as about to be published next week; it actually appeared on the 26th January, "as it was acted at the Theatre Royal by Her Majesty's Servants. Written by Mr. Steele. . . . Price 1s. 6d."[3] Nichols (*Literary Anecdotes*, viii. 301) gives a list of "Copies when purchased" from a note-book of the Lintotts. Among these is "1703–4, June 11, Lying Lovers [*sic*], £21. 10s. 0d." No doubt "June" was a misreading for "Jan.," especially as the year is expressed in old and new style, which would not be the case if the month were June.

In his *Apology* Steele afterwards wrote of the *Lying Lover*:—"Mr. Collier had, about the time wherein this was published, written against the immorality of the stage. I was (as far as I durst for fear of witty men, upon whom he had been too severe) a great admirer of his work, and took it into my head to write a comedy in the severity he required. In this play I make the spark or hero kill a man in his drink, and finding himself in prison the next morning, I give him the contrition which he

[1] *Daily Courant*, passim.

[2] See *Steele's Plays*, by the present writer, in the *Athenæum* for September 20, 1884. The correct sequence of these two plays was given by Genest, Ward, and in a MS. by Isaac Reed (Add. MS. 25390); but the *Biog. Dramatica* (1812) reprints the common error. It is to be observed that the wrong dates were already given in 1718, when "A complete Catalogue of all the Plays that were ever yet printed in the English language" was published; and the mistake is repeated in Jacob's *Poetical Register*, 1723; *Theatrical Records*, 1756; *Play House Pocket Companion*, 1779, &c.

[3] *Daily Courant*, passim. On March 2, 1704, the play, "by Captain Steele," was again advertised as "Newly publish'd."

ought to have on that occasion. . . . I can't tell, Sir, what they would have me do to prove me a Churchman; but I think I have appeared one even in so trifling a thing as a comedy; and considering me as a comic poet, I have been a martyr and confessor for the Church; for this play was damned for its piety." In the Dedication of the play to the Duke of Ormond, Steele says, "The design of it is to banish out of conversation all entertainment which does not proceed from simplicity of mind, good nature, friendship, and honour;" and in the Preface he again refers to the manner in which the English stage had offended against the laws of morals and religion; "I thought, therefore, it would be an honest ambition to attempt a comedy which might be no improper entertainment in a Christian commonwealth." He admits that the anguish and sorrow in the prison scene "are, perhaps, an injury to the rules of comedy; but I am sure they are a justice to those of morality." It was to be hoped that wit would now recover from its apostacy, for the Queen had "taken the stage under her consideration."

The plot of the *Lying Lover* was taken from Corneille's *Menteur*, and, at any rate in the first three acts, Steele often directly translated or adapted passages from Corneille. Corneille in his turn had taken the story from the *Verdad Sospechosa* of Ruiz de Alarcon, but which he supposed to be by Lope de Vega. The *Menteur* was translated in 1661 as *The Mistaken Beauty, or the Liar;* and a century later Foote again used the story, which he professed to derive from Lope de Vega; but it is certain that he had read Steele's play.[1] In Alarcon's play the liar is punished by being compelled to marry a girl he does not care for instead of the one he loves; Corneille represents the liar's love as having changed, so that the marriage was really agreeable to him. Steele, in the latter part of his play, sent his liar to prison on a charge of killing the man who was in the end to marry the lady whom the liar loved; the liar being rewarded eventually for his repentance by the promise of the other lady. The last line of the play is,

"There is no gallantry in love but truth."

[1] Genest, iv. 649; Morley, Introduction to the *Spectator*, 1868.

Hazlitt says, "The comedies of Steele were the first that were written expressly with a view not to imitate the manners, but to reform the morals of the age. . . . It is almost a misnomer to call them comedies; they are rather homilies in dialogue."[1] Certainly the *Funeral* does not deserve the attack which Hazlitt has made upon it; but in the *Lying Lover* art is somewhat sacrificed to sentiment. The serious portion of the play, in which blank verse is attempted, is entirely Steele's own, and it is to a great extent unsuited to comedy. Ward has called it "the first instance of Sentimental Comedy proper. It is attempted to produce an effect, not by making vice and folly ridiculous, but by moving compassion."[2] Much of the play, however, is very entertaining, and the adaptation of French scenes to London and Oxford is neatly done. There is a vivid description in Act IV. of the life in Newgate, "with the crowd of jail-birds." As to duelling, the Constable says, "There's a man killed in the garden, and you're a fine gentleman, and it must be you; for good honest people only beat one another." Another characteristic saying occurs in the first scene—"I always judged of men as I observed they judged of women;" and in Act II. there is a charming description of the New Exchange, which is often spoken of in the *Tatler* and *Spectator*, with "the pretty merchants and their dealers."

[1] *Comic Writers*, Lecture VIII.
[2] *English Dramatic Literature*, ii. 602–6.

VI.

STEELE'S CONTEMPORARIES. "THE TENDER HUSBAND."

1704–5. ÆT. 32–3.

THE opening of the year 1704 found the four greatest prose-writers of the reign, Steele and Addison, Swift and Defoe, in London. Addison returned to England about September 1703. Somers and Montague, Addison's patrons, had persuaded him to give up the idea which he once entertained of going into the Church, and they sent him abroad, with a pension of £300, to gain experience in diplomacy. He went to France and Italy; and was at Geneva when William III. died. The pension now ceased, and it is not certain what income Addison possessed; but he continued to travel, visiting Vienna, Dresden, and Hamburg. In September 1703 he was at the Hague, where he heard of his father's death, and returned to England, taking cheap lodgings in the Haymarket. At last his opportunity came; the battle of Blenheim was won in August 1704, and Mr. Boyle, Chancellor of the Exchequer, upon the suggestion of Montague, now Lord Halifax, asked Addison to write a poem on the victory, and at once made him a Commissioner of Appeal in the Excise. *The Campaign* was published on the 14th December 1704,[1] and brought great fame to the author. In 1705 [2] Addison produced his *Remarks on Italy*, with a dedication to Lord Somers; and perhaps the comedy called *The Drummer* was written at this time. The *Remarks on Italy* were not widely popular; the series of illustrations of Latin

[1] *Post Man*, Dec. 12–14, 1704.
[2] Published on the 15th November (*Daily Courant*).

poets by description of the country where they lived gave no token of those powers which Steele afterwards described in a preface to the *Drummer* published after his friend's death: "He was above all men in that talent we call humour, and enjoyed it in such perfection, that I have often reflected, after a night spent with him apart from all the world, that I had had the pleasure of conversing with an intimate acquaintance of Terence and Catullus, who had all their wit and nature, heightened with humour more exquisite and delightful than any other man ever possessed." And in the same preface Steele speaks of the bashfulness and modesty which often concealed Addison's mirth and raillery.

Thackeray has given us a picture of Addison at this period in *Esmond*, Book II. chapter xi. He describes Steele and Esmond walking down Germain Street, when Steele suddenly "left his companion's arm, and ran after a gentleman who was poring over a folio volume at the book-shop near to St. James's Church," and would have kissed him if the other had not stepped back with a flush on his pale face. Esmond was introduced, and was able to quote from one of Addison's charming Latin poems. Addison took them to his lodgings in the Haymarket, and with perfect grace welcomed them to his shabby apartment. He was writing a poem on the campaign, he told them, and Steele read the sheets with unfaltering enthusiasm, until he was brought to a maudlin state of tenderness by the wine, which only unloosed Addison's tongue.[1]

Addison obtained through his friend a ready welcome to the principal places of resort of the town: Will's coffee-house, where Congreve, Prior, and other wits were constantly to be found; the St. James's coffee-house, the meeting-place of the Whigs; and the Kit-Cat Club. A few words may here be said of the last-named

[1] The signatures of Steele and Addison are among those attached to a certificate of character dated December 18, 1704, in Mr. A. Morrison's collection: "We whose names are subscribed haveing often frequented the house of Margery Maplesden, late Sutler at the Tilt Yard Guard, do hereby certifie whome it may concerne that the said Margery Maplesden hath behaved herself justly, modestly, and well, and we do not know of ourselves or have heard or believe that she hath imposed upon any officers or soldiers of either of the Regiments of Guards or others."

and most famous of them all. Little is known for certain of the date or circumstances of its formation, or of the origin of the name. Some writers believe that the club was formed about 1688 by noblemen and gentlemen in favour of the Protestant succession; others, that it was of later origin. The meetings were held at first at a Mutton-pie house in Shire Lane, by Temple Bar, which was kept by Christopher Cat.[1] Shire Lane—re-christened Lower Serle's Place late in the present century—opened into Fleet Street opposite to Child's Bank, and owed its name to the fact that it divided the city from the shire. It long bore a bad name; but Sir Charles Sedley once lived there, and Anthony-à-Wood dined at the house of Elias Ashmole in the lane. The dwellings were afterwards turned into spunging-houses, and Theodore Hook and Dr. Maginn were confined in them. In the summer the Kit-Cat Club met sometimes at the Upper Flask Tavern, on the edge of Hampstead Heath. The object of the meetings was partly political, partly literary; probably it began with suppers given by Tonson the publisher to his literary friends.[2] In a poem on the club, attributed to Sir Richard Blackmore, we read—Jacob Tonson's Christian name being spelt backwards as Bocaj—

> "One night in seven[3] at this convenient seat,
> Indulgent Bocaj did the Muses treat;

[1] I am indebted for many particulars about the Kit-Cat Club to Mr. D. Yeo Bruton, who was the last private owner of the Trumpet Tavern in Shire Lane, prior to its demolition to make way for the new Law Courts. Further particulars about Shire Lane, &c., will be found in Diprose's *Some Account of the Parish of St. Clement Danes*, 1868. In 1720 there was a "Steele's Coffee-house" in Bread Street, Cheapside, which boasted that there only could be obtained in perfection herb-gruel, which was very beneficial when drunk in the morning (*Daily Journal*, Feb. 3, 1720, quoted by Mr. W. Roberts in *Notes and Queries*, 7th S. v. 466).

[2] Morley's *Spectator*, No. 9, note. Jacob Tonson was son of Jacob, a barber-surgeon in Holborn, who died in 1688. Jacob and his brother Richard became booksellers. In 1719-20 Jacob Tonson was made Stationer, Bookseller, Printer, &c., to various Government offices, and he was succeeded by his nephew Jacob, son of Richard Tonson. The nephew, however, died in 1736 (four months before his uncle); and Jacob, senior, then made his great-nephew, Jacob, his executor and residuary legatee. This great-nephew died in 1767, without issue (Nichols' *Literary Anecdotes*, i. 292).

[3] In a contemporary account of Anthony Henley, who was a member of the Kit-Cat Club, we are told that that society met weekly and that every one

Their drink was gen'rous wine, and Kit-Cat's pies their meat.
Hence did the Assembly's title first arise,
And Kit-Cat wits sprang first from Kit-Cat pies."

Addison says, in the 9th number of the *Spectator*, "The Kit-Cat itself is said to have taken its origin from a Mutton-pie." The earlier assemblies led to the formation of a club, with Tonson as secretary, in which the Whig chiefs were associated with the principal wits of the party. George Stepney, writing to Tonson from Vienna, on March 24, 1703, sent his hearty affection to the Kit-Cat Club: "I often wish it were my fortune to make one of you at three in the morning." The members seem to have visited various places in the South of England in 1704—Brighton, Portsmouth, and Southampton—and there were unattached members living on the Continent. In a quarto pamphlet, called *A Kit-Kat C—b described*, printed in 1705, which contains abuse of the club, it is styled "A Club, not for diversion, but for business." Ned Ward says the Club took its name from one Christopher, who lived at the Cat and Fiddle, in Shire Lane. In a prologue to a play written in 1700 we find the line—

"A Kit-Cat is a supper for a lord;"

but Dr. King, in the *Art of Cookery*, speaks of something as—

"Immortal made, as Kit-Cat by his pies."

The Club early became famous for its toasting glasses, for which Halifax, Garth, Maynwaring, and others wrote verses. Hence Arbuthnot playfully suggested another derivation of its name. It is evident from what he says that the question was even then involved in obscurity:—

"Whence deathless Kit-Cat took its name,
Few critics can unriddle;
Some say from pastry-cook it came,
And some from Cat and Fiddle.

in his turn was Master of the Feast (*The Lives and Characters of the most Illustrious Persons, British and Foreign, who died in the year* 1711. London, 1713, p. 535).

From no trim beaus its name it boasts,
Grey statesmen or green wits;
But from this pell-mell pack of toasts,
Of old Cats and young Kits."

Malone, in a note to his edition of Dryden's Prose Works, describes a MS. poem by Settle, addressed to the most renowned the President and the rest of the Knights of the most noble order of the Toast, in which the writer asserts the dignity and antiquity of this illustrious society. This seems to have been written in 1699. The Club patronised literature; and in 1709 the members subscribed 400 guineas for the encouragement of good comedies. It is doubtful for how long after that date the Club was continued. In 1703 Tonson went to Holland to obtain paper and engravings for the edition of *Cæsar's Commentaries* which he published under Dr. Clark's care in 1712; but before he went he acquired a villa at Barn Elms, and built a room for the Club. In a letter, addressed to Tonson at Amsterdam, Vanbrugh says: "In short, the Kitt-Catt wants you, much more than you ever can do them. Those who remain in Town are in great desire of waiting on you at Barnes Elms; not that they have finished their Pictures either: tho', to excuse them (as well as my Self), Sr Godfrey has been most in fault. The Fool has got a Country house near Hampton Court, and is so busy about fitting it up (to receive nobody) that there's no getting him to work. Carpenter Johns too is almost as bad. . . . There's all disorder still, every room is Chips up to your Chin; they han't been at work you must know this fortnight; their's a great deal done however; one week's sticking to't will fit it for the reception of a King."[1] Each member gave his portrait by Kneller, who was himself a member; he died in 1723, leaving more than 500 paintings unfinished. The portraits of the members of the Club were on a new sized canvas—

[1] In 1727, when the Club had gone, Vanbrugh wrote to Tonson: "You may believe me when I tell you, you were often talked of, both during the journey and at home, and our former Kit-Cat days were remembered with pleasure. We were one night reckoning who were left, and both Lord Carlisle and Cobham expressed a great desire of having one meeting next winter if you can come to town; not as a club, but as old friends that *have* been of a club, and the best club that ever met" (*All the Year Round*, July 8, 1871).

36 inches long by 22 wide—suited to the size of the room in which they were hung, and thus the name "kit-cat" has been applied generally to three-quarter length portraits. Engravings of the Kit-Cat portraits, by Faber, were published in 1735 by Tonson, with a dedication to the Duke of Somerset. After the death of Tonson's last surviving great nephew Richard, the original portraits became the property of Mr. W. Baker, whose father, Sir W. Baker, had married Mary Tonson, and they were removed in 1782 from Water Oakley, Richard Tonson's country seat, to Mr. Baker's house in Hill Street, Berkeley Square. They were afterwards taken to the Park House, Hertingfordbury, and in 1812 they were again removed to a room built for their reception at Bayfordbury.[1]

Barn Elms is approached by a private road to the left, towards the river, on the way from Hammersmith to Barnes Common. In the seventeenth century it was the abode of Abraham Cowley, and is mentioned several times by Pepys. We have a description of the place in 1820 by Sir Richard Phillips, in his *A Morning's Walk from London to Kew* (pp. 201–9). Tonson's house had been taken down a few years before; the present house belonged to a Mr. Hoare, who was not at home, and the servants knew nothing of the history of the place. The rooms used by the Club were full of rubbish, and falling to pieces with dry-rot. The names of the members were still visible on the walls, written in chalk as they had been marked for the guidance of the man who hung up the pictures, and the marks made by the pictures were still to be seen. "I involuntarily shed a tear of sympathy for the departed great," says Sir Richard Phillips. The estate has now been taken by the Ranelagh Club,[2] and the old building restored. The largest room,

[1] I owe to the courtesy of Mr. Baker, the present proprietor of Bayfordbury the opportunity of seeing these portraits, and of making use of several letters, including the one from Vanbrugh quoted in the text, the originals of which are in his possession. I have also been able to consult some notes made by Mrs. H. J. Jenkinson, second daughter of Mr. W. Baker, who intended to write a history of the Kit-Cat Club, but gave up the idea when the *Memoirs of the Celebrated Persons composing the Kit-Cat Club* appeared in 1821. Both text and portraits in that work are very poor.

[2] Mr. Barrett, secretary of the Ranelagh Club, has written, for private circulation, a history of the house.

the meeting-place of the Club, had been used as a laundry, and a fire in the adjoining room had damaged the roof. The rooms command a view of the Thames, and the neighbourhood still retains to some extent the peaceful country aspect which made it so dear to Cowley.

And now we may turn to see what writers of another kind were doing in 1704. Jonathan Swift lived at Moor Park until the death of Sir William Temple in 1699, after which he went to Dublin and became chaplain to the Earl of Berkeley, who obtained for him the living of Laracor. But he paid several visits to London, one extending from November 1703 to May 1704, and another being in April 1705. The *Tale of a Tub* and the *Battle of the Books*, which were published in 1704, placed their author in the first rank of writers, and the former of them led to Swift being misunderstood and suspected by the section of the Church which he had served the best. He was doubtless already acquainted with Addison; but in 1705 we have entries in his note-book showing a more intimate intercourse:—"Tav^{rn} Addison 2s. 6d.. Tav^{rn} Addison 1s. Tav^{n} Add^{sn} 1s. 6d. Tav^{rn} Addis^{n} 4s. 9d. Tav^{n} Addis^{n} 2s. 6d." Addison sent Swift a copy of his *Travels in Italy*, with this inscription:—"To Dr Jonathan Swift, The most Agreeable Companion The Truest Friend And the Greatest Genius of his Age This Book is presented by his most Humble Servant the Authour."[1] Swift was well known both at Will's and the St. James's Clubs by 1703, for in that year he wrote verses on Vanbrugh's house.

There is yet another great writer to notice, and he certainly was not a member of the clubs where the wits assembled, yet his work was in the closest way akin to Steele's, and one of his publications was the only real forerunner of the *Tatler*. Daniel Defoe, born in 1661, eleven years before Steele and Addison, was a Dissenter, who had had varied experiences in a business life, and who had found time for writing many pamphlets in the cause of King William. One of these pamphlets, *The True Born Englishman*, issued in 1701, had a sale of many thousands before the end of the year. But with the accession of Queen Anne came an attempt to suppress differences of opinion in religion, and

[1] Forster's *Life of Swift*, 159–161.

Defoe wrote an ironical pamphlet, called *The Shortest Way with the Dissenters.* It was some time before the party opposed to tolerance saw that the book was a satire, but when this was realised a reward was offered for the author's apprehension. Defoe surrendered in order to save the publisher from imprisonment, and he was sentenced to stand thrice in the pillory, and to suffer other penalties. The exposure in the pillory was a popular triumph rather than a disgrace, but Defoe was kept in prison, with occasional intervals of freedom on parole. In 1697 he had published the *Essay on Projects*, in which he made suggestions on many subjects which were far in advance of the ordinary ideas of his day; and in prison he continued to write pamphlet after pamphlet, until, in February 1704, he issued the first number of a paper called *The Review*, which was continued until June 1713, and which had a large share in suggesting to Steele the publication of the *Tatler*. I shall give particulars of *The Review* when I come to discuss Steele's first periodical paper.

The few letters given below, which are now printed for the first time, and the judgment in an action for debt, are all that we have to show respecting Steele's life during 1704. In Hilary term (January 24 to February 12), 1703–4, Richard Steele, late of London, *alias* Richard Steele of Piccadilly, gentleman, was summoned by John Foxall, gentleman, for a debt of £60.[1] Foxall, by John Hargrave, his attorney, said that Steele on the 16th July 1701, at London, in the parish of the Blessed St. Mary of Bow, in the Ward of Cheap, by his bond acknowledged himself bound to him in the sum of £60; but the money had not been paid, and Foxall claimed £20 damages. Steele came *in propriâ personâ,* but said nothing in bar of judgment, which was therefore given against him, with damages to the amount of fifty-six shillings and eightpence.

The five letters following were written to John Ellis, M.P. for Harwich, and elder brother of Steele's tutor at Oxford. John Ellis, born in 1645, was the son of the Rev. John Ellis; he came to Court shortly after the Restoration, and was one of the many lovers of the Duchess of Cleveland. He entered public life as Secretary to Lord Ossory, who was deputy for his father, the Duke

[1] Common Pleas Judgment Roll, Hilary 2 Anne 1504. See page 83.

of Ormond, as Lord Lieutenant of Ireland; and he subsequently became Secretary to the Commissioners of the Irish Revenue, Controller of the Mint (May 1701), and Under Secretary of State (January 1702). He was removed in May 1705, when it was reported that Addison would succeed him; and he died in 1738[1]. In the first of these letters Steele asks for the interest of Mr. Ellis in obtaining for him a troop in a new regiment of dragoons which was being raised by the Duke of Ormond. It does not appear that Steele was successful.

March 25th, 170$\frac{3}{4}$, LAND-GUARD-FORT.[2]

S^{r}

I was order'd hither on a sudden, or had waited on you to receive your commands, but indeed I do not trouble you only to make my apology for that, but also to desire your Friendship, and interest to the Duke of Ormond in my behalfe: What I would pretend to is a Troop in a Regiment of Dragoons which I understand He is going to raise to be commanded by His Grace Himself: This request is the more reasonable for that it is no advancement of my post in the dignity, but the income of it only, since I am already a Captain: If I can be so fortunate as to have any encouragement from you in this Matter, I'le hasten to town; In the mean time any commands from you will be receiv'd as a very great Honour to, S^{r}

Y^{r} Most Obedient

Humble Ser^{nt}

RICH^{D} STEELE.

LAND-GUARD-FORT, Aprill 15th, 1704.[3]

S^{r}

I had yours of the thirteenth this morning, but we are here so forc'd to snatch at opportunities of sending over our letters, that I have at present only just time to thank you, and desire the continuance of your good inclination to me. In the other matter I will as soon as possible give you the best light I can, and go about it with the caution such an affair requires.

I am, S^{r},

Y^{r} most oblig'd Humble Ser^{nt}

RICH^{D} STEELE.

[1] *The Ellis Correspondence*, edited by the Hon. G. Agar Ellis, 1829; Luttrell's *Diary*, v. 48, 127, 555, 569.

[2] Ellis Papers, British Museum, Add. MS. 28927, f. 171.

[3] Add. MS., 28927, f. 173.

The next letters relate to election matters at Harwich. Sir Thomas Davall, Kt., was Member for Harwich from 1695 to 1708, and from 1713 until his death in the following year; Dennis Lyddall, Esq., was elected Member in 1700 and 1701, and John Ellis, Esq., in August 1702 and June 1705.

LAND-GUARD-FORT, May 13th, 1704.[1]

S^{r}

I give you this to acquaint you that Mr Lyddall was at Harwich last Weeke, and did gracious things in paying off a small Vessel or Two there: He told the Mayors [2] Brother that the method of reinstating his Son in the Navy-office, was to have Sr Thomas Davall and you appear both for him at a Generall Board-day, when the Board of Admiralty, and that of the Navy met, which it seems is frequent, and methodicall: It is now beleiv'd Mr Lyddall will himself stand and tis as certain that Sr Thomas has thoughts of putting up his eldest Son; The Mayor is now at London, and not much inclined to you, but you perhaps have opportunity there of reforming Him:

I am, S^{r},
Y^{r} very Humble and
Obedient Ser^{nt}
RICH^{D} STEELE.

HARWICH, July 20th, 1704.[3]

S^{r}

I have the honour of yours of the 18th, and am also to acknowledge another acquainting me that our march would not be so sudden, as I apprehended; It is a very signall Service to this place

[1] Add. MS. 28927, f. 176. This letter is addressed to "John Ellis, Esq., at the Office of the Principall Secretary of State, Whitehall."

[2] Charles Smyth was elected Mayor of Harwich in November 1703; Daniel Smyth was Mayor the following year. Among the Marlborough MSS. there is this memorandum:—

Jan. 2^{d}, 1704.

Sent down to Coulter a bill of twenty pounds payable to Mr Charles Smyth at six days sight.

De^{br} 26th, 1704, a bill of 20^{l} sent Coulter.

Mr Hardy 10 : 15 : 00.

Mr Haugh for Coulter 3 : 00 : 00.

Jan. 9th—10^{l} value receiv'd payable to Mr Smith after three days sight.

Mr Batchelor to speake Ld Cutts.

[3] Add. MS. 28927, f. 178.

what you are doing in relation to the Sick Souldiours, and don't doubt but they will resent[1] it as such; I have the High happinesse of conversing sometimes with the Grandees of the Corporation, and beleive your interest here immoveable, except some Freind of the Navy-office should appear either for himself or against you; Mr Ch. Smith is very anxious about his Son: I'm mightely pleased with the hope of seeing you here, before my Lord Lieutenants departure, and shall take the measures of my application, there, From you;

I am, Sr,
Yr Most Obedient
Humble Sernt,
RICHD STEELE.

I take no notice that I hear of your coming hither: They expect a new Election.

LAND-GUARD-FORT, July 29th, 1704.[2]

Sr

I do not question but you are as good a judge as any man, upon what Views you are to Act in businesse, but I am persuaded, whatever you may think, that Mr Lyddall, and Mr Atkinson are the persons many of the Corporation have their thoughts upon, and that they, either, already have had, an application from them, or grounds to expect one: Your's relating to the Mayor's Nephew has not the effect it deserves, for I find they have not a Just Idea of the matter, nor will conceive it to be the same thing to provide for Him elsewhere: but I give these hints for your own use, and 'would be an ill accident to me to have any correspondence between us known: As to my own private opinion, as far as I can guesse,[3] I believe Sr Tho. Davall aims for Himself, and very coldly for any Colleague, having Thoughts for his Son; and as to the other gentlemen It would be of Use to you, when you come here, if it could be insinuated that Serving you was obliging them, and would have the same effect for the Town's interest: This, or their sollicitation for you I beleive you'll find of almost absolute necessity:

I am, Sr,
Yr most obedient
Humble Sernt
RICHD STEELE.

[1] "Resent," feel. French, "ressentir."
[2] Add. MS., 28927, f. 180.
[3] This clause was afterwards struck out.

There is a draft of another letter of this period among the Blenheim MSS. It does not appear to whom it was addressed—

LAND-GUARD-FORT, May 20th, 1704.

Sr

I had answer'd yours of the 11th instant before now but that I could not give a satisfactory account of the poor old Heron;[1] who is now here, under my care, and disposall having in exchange for him giv'n another Able Man to that Regiment, which cost me two Guinneas; nor shall I insist upon more than having that sum̄ restor'd me, and sending Him about his affairs; There came an Order for Him with other recruits before I had settled the matter, so that he was plunder'd on ship-board, of all the money He had; Our neighbourhood to Holland gives him an opportunity of buying[2] some commodities at a cheaper rate here with which He thinks to help himself after his losses: In order to this He has giv'n me a bill of twenty five pounds drawn in my name upon one Mr Jenks, which He desir'd me to advertise you of, that there might be care taken of paying it; He says Mr Jenks has fifteen pounds of His without interest besides 100*l* on land: If the twenty pounds is paid to the bearer Major Soul[3] of the Tower to whome I have this post sent it I shall[4] immediately pay it Him Here, and give him his own time to go in Peace: I am very much oblig'd to you for your good wishes [to[5]] me, and tho' I have not the Happinesse to be known to you, I hope I shall always [appea]r to men of yr Character a most Obedient

Humble Servant

RICHD STEELE.

Colonel Lord Lucas died on the 31st January 1705, when the title of Baron Lucas of Shenfield, Essex, became extinct. He was succeeded in the colonelcy of the 34th Regiment by Lieutenant-Colonel Hans Hamilton, from the Earl of Derby's regiment, now the 16th Foot.[6] Steele wrote the following

1 "Man" first written.

2 "Trinkets and Paper, &c," cancelled.

3 See page 87. The words "the bearer" were inserted.

4 "give him his own," cancelled.

5 The original paper is torn.

6 Cannon's *Historical Record of the Thirty-fourth or Cumberland Regiment of Foot*, 1844, pp. 11, 79. Luttrell (*Diary*, v. 514), writing on the 1st February, says Lord Lucas was succeeded in command by Lieut.-Colonel Dove.

epitaph on his late Colonel,[1] who "was ever reputed a man of great honour and integrity": [2]—

EPITAPH L^D LUCAS.

H : S : E.

Quicquid in Terris potuit detineri
Roberti Baronis Lucas de Shenfield [3] in Agro Essexiensi [4]
Stemmatis aviti Fortitudine Virtute Generositate,
Inclyti Nobilis, Illustris
Hæres Nequaquam Degener
Qui toto Serenissimi Principis Gulielmi tertii Regno
Arci Londinensi præfuit Regis Locum tenens
Anna deinde Magna Britanniæ Auspiciis
Felicissimis rerum potiunte
Inter fortissimos [5] Libertatis Europæ Vindices
Legionem duxit, . . .

It is not clear when Steele left the army. Dennis, in his fourth letter to Sir John Edgar (1720), attacked Steele for having, in a time of war, taken pay as a soldier for twenty years, without ever having been in action; how could he be a hero, when he had never been present at siege or battle? But of course Dennis's figures are not to be taken seriously. Steele was doubtless often called "Captain Steele" long after he left the army. He must at any rate have sold his commission before his second marriage, for in the detailed account of his means which he gave to Mrs. Scurlock in September 1707, he does not mention any pay from the army. As regards Dennis's charge that Steele never took part in active warfare, it may be mentioned that another hostile critic,[6] writing in 1712, spoke

[1] Blenheim MSS. There is a second copy of this epitaph among these papers, headed "Epitaph—Ld Lucas," which is perhaps in Steele's writing, although it is different from his usual style. The alterations in both copies are the same, and the last few words are illegible.

[2] Pointer's *Chronological History of England*, p. 509.

[3] "Comit" written but cancelled.

[4] Followed, as first written, by "Magni Nominis Gloriæ."

[5] "patriæ," cancelled.

[6] *The British Censor. A Poem*, 1712, 4°, p. 12 (Lambeth Palace Library, 111 D., 13[26]).

"Once a cadet, obscure and little known
(Now such a bright conspicuous wonder grown)

of Steele as having been once a cadet, who exposed himself to bullets and the foe; but it is difficult to say whether this was meant as irony or not. In a letter bearing his own signature, printed in the first number of the *Englishman*, Steele says, "tho' I have marched with fifty thousand valiant men in my life-time." This passage, which does not appear to have been noticed before, certainly implies that he had at least taken some share in the work of a large army.

About the end of March 1705 Steele submitted his third play, *The Tender Husband*, to Rich,[1] and on the 23rd April there was an advertisement in the *Daily Courant*:—"Never acted before. At the Theatre Royal in Drury Lane, this present Monday, being the 23rd of April, will be presented a new Comedy, called The *Tender Husband;* Or, the Accomplished Fools." The play ran for five nights, "with several entertainments of singing by Mrs Tofts; and dancing;" but the profits were, as we shall see, small.[2] On the 9th May the *Tender Husband* was published, "As it was acted at the Theatre Royal in Drury Lane. Written by Mr. Steele." Addison wrote the Prologue and assisted in the play itself, and to Addison it was dedicated, though, as Steele said, his friend would "be surprised, in the midst of a daily and familiar conversation, with an address which bears so distant an air as a public Dedication." "My purpose in this application is only to show the esteem I have for you, and that I look upon my intimacy with you as one of the most valuable enjoyments of my life." And the reception given to the play was such "as to make me think it no improper Memorial of an inviolable friendship." In the 555th number of the *Spec-*

His springing parts he ventures to expose,
To thoughtless bullets, and to blundering foes."

Afterwards, says this pamphleteer, he grew pious for the sake of gain; was poet, and chemist; and finally—such was his presumption—Censor.

[1] See the case "Steele *v.* Rich" given below.

[2] In the address "To the Reader" prefixed to *Ximena*, 1719, Colley Cibber in explaining that a writer's subsequent plays sometimes do not succeed so well as the first, because many take a mean pleasure in praising a new writer in order to rival the reputation of others, but hold that when the new writer is no longer new he must be made to know that they who gave him fame can take it away, remarks, "I am apt to believe that after the success of the *Funeral*, it was the same caprice that deserted the *Tender Husband*."

tator, the last number of the original series, Steele afterwards wrote:—"I remember when I finished the *Tender Husband*, I told him there was nothing I so ardently wished as that we might some time or other publish a work written by us both, which should bear the name of the *Monument*, in memory of our friendship. I heartily wish what I have done here were as honorary to that sacred name, as learning, wit, and humanity render those pieces which I have taught the reader how to distinguish for his. When the play above-mentioned was last acted, there were so many applauded strokes in it which I had from the same hand, that I thought very meanly of myself that I had never publicly acknowledged them."

Isaac Reed states that this play was at first intended to have been called the "City Nymph."[1] The incident of Clerimont disguising himself as a painter is taken from Molière's *Sicilien: ou, l'Amour Peintre;* Professor Ward suggests that the moral of the play was derived from Cibber's *Careless Husband*.[2] Several great writers have borrowed ideas from the *Tender Husband*. The country squire, Sir Harry Gubbin, is the forerunner of Fielding's Squire Western; and his son Humphrey certainly furnished Goldsmith with suggestions towards the creation of Tony Lumpkin.[3] Forster thought that the hand of Addison, who afterwards gave the world the Tory Foxhunter, could be traced in the scenes in Steele's play in which these worthies appear. Sheridan, when creating Lydia Languish, doubtless had in his mind the romance-loving Parthenissa, Biddy Tipkin,[4] a character played by the charming Mrs. Oldfield, who was assisted by Wilks, Norris, and Estcourt. The *Tender Husband*, though not so good as the *Funeral*, contains a great

[1] Brit. Mus. Add. MS. 25390.

[2] *English Dramatic Literature*, ii. 606. The *Careless Husband* was first acted on the 7th December 1704, and printed on the 19th December (*Daily Courant*).

[3] Humphrey told his father that his cousin was akin to him, and he did not think it lawful for a young man to marry his own relations. In the same way Tony Lumpkin "boggled a little" at marrying his cousin; as he says to Miss Neville, "I know what sort of a relation you want to make me, though; but it won't do. I tell you, cousin Con, it won't do; so I beg you'll keep your distance; I want no nearer relationship."

[4] Dennis (*Characters and Conduct of Sir John Edgar*, Letter I., 1720) says that Steele took Biddy Tipkin from Molière's *Les Precieuses Ridicules.*

deal of genuine comedy. The weakness of the play lies in the "moral" scenes in which Clerimont, senior, makes trial of his wife by means of Fainlove. This part of the story, together with Fainlove's marriage with Humphrey Gubbin, is far-fetched and out of place.[1]

[1] Hartmann (*Steele als Dramatiker*, 1880) has some useful remarks on this point. He thinks that Addison's touch is to be found in the scenes between Clerimont, senior, and his wife rather than in the scenes of pure comedy. The comparison which he draws between Sir Anthony and Captain Absolute and Sir Harry Gubbin and Captain Clerimont respectively is rather imaginary.

VII.

CHANCERY SUIT AGAINST RICH.

1707–1710. ÆT. 35–38.

IN 1707 Steele commenced a case in the Court of Chancery against Christopher Rich, to which reference has already been made. As the controversy turned upon the agreement which existed between writer and manager when the *Tender Husband* was produced, and as Steele's fourth and last play was not acted until 1722, it will be best to describe the case with Rich in this place. The pleadings are printed in full, as they give an interesting account of theatrical matters, and of the arrangements made between manager and author; but a brief summary is prefixed for the sake of clearness. It will be observed that there is a curious confusion of dates in Steele's Bill, and that no mention is made of the *Lying Lover*, although that play was acted at Drury Lane in December 1703.

In his bill dated July 3, 1707, Steele complained that about December 1702 Rich paid him £72 upon the understanding that Steele would write for him another play. The £72 was to be deducted from the author's profits, and for Rich's security Steele gave a bond of £144. About April 1704 (*sic*) Steele brought the *Tender Husband* to Rich, and it was acted, on condition that Steele was to have the profits of two days' acting in the autumn. The profits were more than sufficient to cover the £72 which had been advanced, but Rich eventually refused to pay Steele the balance, and commenced an action against him for the £144. Steele now prayed that an injunction might be granted to stay these proceedings, and that Rich might be made to answer this bill.

Rich's reply is dated November 9, 1707. He said that in October 1701 he agreed to produce Steele's *Funeral*. This play was acted, and the terms of the agreement carried out to Steele's satisfaction. In January 1702–3 Steele agreed to hand over to Rich in the following month a new play, *The Election of Goatham*, and the arrangements as regards the author's profits were fully set forth. At the same time Steele told Rich he was in want of money and in danger of arrest, and Rich consented to lend him £72, to be repaid with interest in March. If not repaid Steele was to forfeit £144, for which he became bound. Moreover, if the money was not paid before the acting of the new play, so much as was necessary of Steele's profits was made over to Rich. Steele never paid Rich; nor did he hand over the promised play; but in March 1705 he brought in its stead *The Tender Husband*, and that play was acted in April, but the profits were so small that, by the terms of the previous agreements, £10. 8s. 2d. was all that Rich was required to pay the author as the result of the first four days' acting. Steele thereupon agreed that this sum should go to the use of the company, on the condition that the play should be acted once next winter for his benefit. In due course this performance was announced in November, and the play was acted, though at the last Steele objected on the ground that he did not expect a sufficiently good audience. Baggs, the treasurer, was instructed to pay to Steele the balance of £2. 17s. 6d. that resulted, together with the £10. 8s. 2d. already due to him; but Steele neglected or refused to receive the money. Rich denied that he wished to oppress the complainant, and added that *The Tender Husband* had been several times acted at the Haymarket Theatre without his consent. It was true that he had instituted proceedings against Steele for debt, but this was in accordance with his rights; and he prayed that the present case might be dismissed, with costs.

This was the text of the complainant's Bill:[1]—

[1] Public Record Office, Chancery Pleadings, B. & A. Hamilton, IV. before 1714, No. 642. Steele *v.* Rich.

3° die Julii 1707.

To the right hon^rble William Lord Cowper Baron of Wingham Lord high Chancellor of Great Brittaine

Humbly Complaining, Sheweth unto y^r Lordship your Orator Richard Steele of Westm^er Gent That your Orat^or haveing writt Severall Comedyes & Playes at the request of & for Christopher Rich Esqr for the use of the Theater or Playhouse in or near Bridges Street in Covent Garden in the County of Midd̄x of which playhouse the said Christopher Rich was & is cheife Patentee or has an assignm^t or some other Conveyance of the Patent thereof or otherwise hath the cheife Interest therein and the ꝑfitts ariseing from the acting of Playes there He the said Christopher Rich to induce your Orator to write further for him on or about the Month of December in the year of our Lord one Thousand seaven hundred & two advanced & payd to your Orat^or the Sum̄e of Seaventy & two pounds upon this Agreement then or about that time made between them That your Orator should bring to him the said Christopher Rich & for his use the next Comedy your Orator Should be the Author of and out of the Profitts when the same should come to be acted that belonged to your Orator as the Author according to the Usage and Custome in such Cases he the said Christopher Rich was to deduct & pay himself for the said seaventy & two pounds and Interest thereof and in the meane time for the said Christopher Rich's security your Orator was ꝑvailed with to give and accordingly did give his bond of one hundred forty and four pounds penalty condiconed for the payment of the said seaventy two pounds and alsoe a Warrant of Attorney to enter up Judgment on the said bond to him the said Christopher Rich And afterwards (viz.) sometime in or about the Month of Aprill in the Year of our Lord one thousand seaven hundred & four [1] your Orator being the Author of the Comedy called the Tender Husband he did bring to and deliver into the hands of the said Christopher Rich the said Comedy being the next Comedy your Orator was author of and it being then in an ill season of the Year and your Orator being therefore unwilling to have it then acted the said Christopher Rich promised to & agreed with your Orator that it should not be to your Orator's losse or Detriment but that your

[1] There is a curious mistake in the date of the *Tender Husband* throughout Steele's Bill. As we have seen, it was first produced in April 1705. There are several allusions in the play to the battle of Blenheim, which was not fought until August 1704.

Orator should have assigned to him the profitts of Two Nights made by acting of the said Play the next following Winter in Lieu of his Two dayes Profitts according to the Usage & Custome in such case And the said Christopher Rich did cause the said Comedy or Play to be acted on the said Theatre in or about the Month of Aprill & year one thousand seaven hundred & four aforesaid And severall dayes in the Autumne or Winter following which proved very successefull and the said Christopher Rich made & received great profitt thereby And by the Agreement aforesaid and accordinge to Usage & Custome in the like Cases your Orator was to have the whole profitts of the first third day it was acted in Autumne or Winter aforesaid without any diduccon of Charges of Acting and alsoe of the second third day or Sixth day it was acted on as aforesaid diducting only the charges of Acting Which profitts of the said two dayes came to the hands of & was received by the said Christopher Rich and was more then sufficient to pay & satisfye the said Seaventy two pounds & Interest Whereupon your Orator expected as he had reason that the said Christopher Rich would have delivered up to your Orator the said bond and acknowledged satisfaccon on the Record of the Judgment which the said Christopher Rich had caused to be Entred upon Record against your Orator and would have payd your Orator what was over & above the said seaventy Two pounds & Interest thereof—But now soe it is May it please your Lordship That the said Christopher Rich minding to oppresse your Orator and extort great sumes of Mony from him refuses to allowe your Orator the profitts of the said two dayes Acting in Autumne or Winter following according to his Agreement or any dayes profitts or any other profitt whatsoever in consideracon of the said Comedy or Play but threatens to Sue your Orator on the said Judgment & take your Orator in Execucon for the same and hath caused a Scire facias or some other Suite or accon to be comenced against your Orator on the said Judgment[1] In Tender Consideracon

[1] In Easter term, 1707, the Queen sent her writ to the Sheriff of Middlesex in these words: Whereas Christopher Rich, Esq., in our Court at Westminster by our writ and by judgment of the said Court recovered against Richard Steele, gentleman, *alias* Richard Steele of the parish of St. Martin-in-the-Fields, gentleman, £144 of debt, also 53s. for his damages, whereof Richard is convicted as is manifest to us by the Records: Now on the part of the said Christopher we understand that in spite of the judgment aforesaid the debt and damages still remain unpaid, wherefore Christopher prays us to give him a suitable remedy. We willing to do what is just in the matter command you by honest men of your bailiwick to cause Richard to know that he is to come before us at Westminster on Wednesday next after the Quindene of Easter to

of all which ꝑmisses & for as much as your Orator can have noe releife therein save in a Court of Equity and for that your Orator's witnesses who could prove all & singular the premisses are either dead or in parts beyond the Seas or in other parts remote & to your Orator unknown To the end therefore that the said Christopher Rich may true & perfect answare make to all and singular the premisses as if here againe particularly interrogated and charged and in a more particular manner sett forth & discover what Playes your Orator hath brought & delivered to him & for his use And whither he did not advance & pay your Orator the said sum̄e of seaventy two pounds upon such Agreement as aforesaid or upon what other Termes or Agreement and whither your Orator did not bring and deliver to him for his use the said Comedy or Play called the Tender Husband and when the same was soe given or delivered as aforesaid & whither he & your Orator did not come to such agreement for your Orator's share of the profitts of the said play as aforesaid and what other Agreement was made between him & your Orator about itt and how often the same play was acted in the sum̄er of the said Year one thousand seaven hundred & four & how often in the autumne or Winter of that year and whither your Orator was not to have been allowed all or any and what profitts of any & what days and what & how much he the said Christopher Rich hath received of the said profitts And that the said Christopher Rich may come to an account with your Orator and that the said bond may be delivered up to your Orator and the said Christopher Rich may acknowledge satisfacion of Record on the said Judgment and your Orator may have what is over and above the payment of the said seaventy two pounds and Interest payd to him and may be further relieved in all

show if he knows or can say anything in bar of execution why Christopher may not have execution of his debt and damages, according to the force, form, and effect of recovery, if he shall think proper, and further to do and receive what the Court shall consider to be just in the matter.—On the 12th February, 5 Anne (170$\frac{6}{7}$), at Westminster, Christopher came, and the Sheriff acknowledged that Richard has nothing in his bailiwick by which he could cause him to know, &c. [*i.e.*, he had no property to which he could affix the notice]. Richard did not come; therefore it was commanded to the Sheriff to make known to him that he was to be before the Queen at Westminster on Wednesday next after the month of Easter, to show if, &c., and further, &c. The same day was given to Christopher, whereupon he came, and the Sheriff again acknowledged that Richard had nothing, &c., but Richard did not come. It was therefore considered that Christopher might have execution against him of debts and damages, according to the form and effect of the recovery aforesaid (Queen's Bench Judgment Roll, Easter 6 Anne, 375). I have not been able to find the original judgment here referred to.

& singular the premisses according to Equity & good Conscience & that in the Meantime all his vexatious proceedings att Law against your Orator may be stayed by the Injuncon of this hon[rble] Court May it please your Lordship to grant unto your Orator her Maj[tyes] most gracious writt of Spa to the said Christopher Rich directed therein & thereby comanding him personally to be & appeare before your Lordship in this hon[rble] Court at a certaine day & place therein to be limited & appointed to true & perfect answare make to all & singular the premisses and further to stand to abide & obey such Order & Decree as your Lordship shall think fitt to make touching the premisses And your Orator shall ever pray etc.

JN[O] SQUIBB.

Rawling.

This was the defendant's answer:—

Jurat 9 die Novembris 1707 Coram me Jo: Edisbury.

The Answere of Christopher Rich Esq[r] Deft to the bill of Complaynt of Richard Steele gent Complaynant.

This deft now & att all times hereafter saveing & receiving to himselfe all & all manner of Benefitt & advantage of Exeption that may be had or taken to the manyfold Errors untruthes unsuffiencies & Imperfections in the Complaynant's said Bill of Complaynt conteyned ffor answere thereunto or unto as much thereof as this Defend[t] is advised is any wise materiall for him this Deft to make answere unto Hee this Deft answereth and sayth That this Deft being one of the Assignees of the patents of the Theatre or Playhouse in or neare Bridges Street in Covent Garden as the Complt's Bill menconed and of one other Theatre or Playhouse in Dorsett Garden London and owner of part of the shares or profitts arising by acting (if any) To his owne use the Complaynant in or about the month of October in the yeare of our Lord One thousand seaven hundred and one brought a Comedy or play to this Defend[t] which he the Complaynant alleadged he had written and stiled the ffunerall for which he the Complaynant came to an Agreement with this Defend[t] in writing on about the Ninth day of October Anno Dni 1701 and thereby for the Consideracon therein menconed sold the same to this Deft to be acted by the Actors under this Deft's Government as soone as they could conveniently which Comedy was soone after acted in pursueance of the said Agreement and the said Complaynant was paid and satisfyed in full according to the Conditions and the tenor and true Intent of the said Agreement and to the Content and Satisfaccon of him the Complt as he acknowledged and declared And this Deft is informed and believeth that he the Complt gave a Receipt to Mr Zachary Baggs[1] the then and now Treasurer of the said Company for his the Complaynt's profitts arising by acting of the said Comedy by vertue of the Agreement aforesaid And this Defendt further sayth that the Complaynt in or about the month of January Anno Dni 1702[2] inforeming this Defendt that he had neare finished another Comedy which he intended to call the Election of Goatham he proposed to sell the same to this Deft and accordingly in or by a certaine writing or Agreement beareing date on or about the Seaventh of January Anno Dni 170 2/3 signed by the Complaynant in Consideracon of one shilling to him the Complt then paid by this deft and for the Consideracon therein and herein after menconed he the said Complaynant did sell or is therein or thereby menconed to sell unto this Defendt his heires and assignes A Certaine Comedy which he the Complaynt was then writing called the Election of Goatham and which he was to deliver to this Defendt on or about the Twentyeth day of ffebruary then next in order to be acted by the Company of Actors under this Defendt's Governmt assoone as they could conveniently[3] In Consideracon whereof the said Complaynt was to have all the Receipts of the third day on which the said play should be acted Hee the Complt paying out of the same all the Charges of the house both constant and Incident But if the Receipts of the ffourth day should double the Charges thereof then the Charges of the third should be returned to him and he thereby obliged himselfe to make good the Charges of the second day out of the profitts of the third day in case the Charges of the second day should not arise to soe much Item if the Receipts on the ffourth day of acting the said play should amount to fforty pounds or upwards the said Company was to act it the ffifth day and if the ffifth dayes Receipts should be fforty pounds Then they were to act it the sixth day for the Benefitt of the Complaynt Hee paying out of the same the Charges of that day But if att any time there should appeare Reason to doubt whether the play would bring Chardges or not Then the

[1] Baggs commenced an action for debt against Steele in the Court of Queen's Bench in Michaelmas term 1707.

[2] 1703, N. S.

[3] The *Examiner* for October 12, 1713, evidently written by some one well acquainted with Steele's affairs, said, "I and the Upholsterer retired to the bench and parade in the Park, not doubting but your Author would finish his rough draught of the *Election* at *Goatham*, according to agreement with Mr. Rich."

Company should not be obliged to act it the next day unlesse he the Complaynt would oblige himselfe to make good the full charges And lastly the Complaynant was not to print the said play untill a month should be expired from the ffirst day it should be acted and three of the printed Books in Marble paper Covers and Gilt edges were to be delivered into the office for the use of the patentees assoone as the same should bee printed (As in and by the said Agreemt in Writing last menconed under the hand of the said Complaynt and to which this Defendt for more Certainty referreth himselfe ready to be produced to this honoble Court may appeare) And this deft sayth that there being a ffreindship contracted between him the Complt and this Deft and the Complt expressing greate kindnesse to this Deft and telling him of his the Complts want of Money and of his being likely to be arrested for moneys oweing by him prevayled with this Deft to advance lend and pay to him the Complt and to his use the Sume of Seaventy and Two pounds And he the Complaynant in or by one Bond or Obligacon bearinge date on or about the Seaventh day of January Anno Dni 1702 [1] became bound unto this Defent in the penall Sume of One Hundred fforty and ffower pounds Conditioned for the payment of the said Seaventy and two pounds with Interest on the Eighth day of March then next And alsoe he the Complt executed a Warrant of Attorney to confesse a Judgemt upon the said Bond in the Court of Queen's Bench att Westmr which Judgement was Entred up accordingly as by the said Bond Warrant of Attorney and the Record of the said Judgement and to which this Defendt referreth himselfe may appeare And this defendt sayth that he the Complt Steele as an Additional Security for the better payment of the said Debt did by a writing under his hand beareing date the Seaventh day of January Anno Dni 1702 [2] assigne and sett over or is therein menconed to assigne and sett over unto this Deft all the Money and profitts which was or were to come to him the Complt for his play intended to be called the Eleccon of Goatham by the Agreemt therein before written upon this Condition That if the said debt should not be paid unto this Deft before the acting of the said play That then this deft his Executors or assignes might retaine and apply such profitts for or towards paymt of the said debt of Seaventy and two pounds with damages But if such profitts should amount to more moneys then should be due to this Deft or his assignes att the time of acting such play then the Overplus of the moneys and profitts arising due to the Complaynant on his play by the agreemt aforesaid was to goe to the

[1] 1703, N. S. [2] 1703, N. S.

use of the Complt and his assignes after payment of the aforesaid debt with damages to this deft and his assignes as by an Agreement in writing under the hand of the Complt bearing date the said Seaventh day of January Anno Dni 1702[1] ready to be produced to this honoble Court and to which this deft alsoe referreth himselfe may appeare And this deft sayth that the Complt did not pay or cause to be paid unto this deft the said debt of seaventy and two pounds or any part thereof or any Interest for the same according to the Condition of the said recited Bond on the Eighth day of March next after the date thereof nor hath he ever since paid the said debt or any part thereof or any Interest for the same to this deft And this deft sayth that he the Complt did not deliver to this deft the said Comedy sold as aforesaid to this deft by the writing before menconed to beare date the seaventh of January Anno Dni 170$\frac{2}{3}$ on the twentyeth of ffebruary then next as thereby was mentioned nor hath he the Complt ever since that time delivered to this deft any Comedy called the Election of Goatham altho this deft very often requested him the Complt for the same But this deft confesseth that the Complt about the latter end of March Anno Dni 1705 brought a Comedy to this deft which he stiled or called the Tender Husband or the accomplished ffooles & desired and urged this deft and his cheife Actors that the same might be acted by them with all speed which he the Complt said was in leiu and in stead of the said play which he intended to have called the Election of Goatham and the same was the next and onely play or Comedy which the Complt has brought sold and delivered to this deft since the lending of the said Seaventy Two pounds as aforesaid And this deft Beleiveth that his this defts Company of Actors did according to his the Complts desire gett up the said Comedy called the Tender Husband with all the speed they could and acted the same the first time on the three & twentyeth of Aprill 1705 and acted the same the second time the next day after and the third time on Wednesday the five and twentyth of the same month of Aprill for the Benefitt of the Complt the Author according to the same Conditions in the said ffirst and second Agreements menconed and acted the same the ffourth time on the next day after being Thursday the six and twentyeth of Aprill 1705; on which day the Receipts being but Twenty Six pounds and Eleaven shillings as this deft beleives the same was thirteen pounds and Nine shillings short or wanting of fforty pounds the contingent in the said agreement menconed This deft was not obliged by the said Articles or any

[1] 1703, N. S.

Agreement to cause the same to be acted on the Sixth day or any more for the Benefitt of the Complayn[t] save as hereinafter is menconed And this deft sayth that the said M[r] Baggs the Treasurer computing each dayes charge of acting the said play called the Tender Husband to amount to Thirty Eight pounds ffifteen shillings and Ten pence and the Receipts of the third day being Sixty one pounds and six shillings & noe more as this deft beleives out of which the said Sum̄e of Thirty Eight pounds ffifteen shillings and ten pence being deducted there then rested two and twenty pounds ten shillings and two pence as this Deft computes the sume But the Receipts of the second day of acting the same play amounting to but twenty and six pounds and ffourteen shillings being deficient Twelve pounds one shilling and ten pence to make up the charge of that day which twelve pounds one shilling and Ten pence being deducted out of the said two and twenty pounds and ten shillings the Residue of Neate and cleere profitts to come to the Complt pursueant to the Agreement aforesaid amounted to Ten pounds Eight shillings and two pence and noe more as this Deft is informed and beleives with which this deft beleives the Complt was acquainted and that he was well contended and satisfyed with the account given to him the Complt of the Receipts and Charges of and for the said play called the Tender Husband for the ffower ffirst dayes of acting thereof And this Deft sayth that the profitt accrewing due to the Complaynant being soe small the Complaynant applyed himselfe to this deft and alsoe to the principall Actors under this deft's Government That he the Complt would waive his profitt by the said play being Ten pounds Eight shillings and two pence as aforesaid and permitt the same to goe to the use of the Company provided they would act the said play the then next Winter one day for his the said Complt's Benefit instead of the third day aforesaid he paying or allowing out of the Receipts on such day in Winter the constant and incident charge thereof and alsoe what money the Receipts on the said second day of acting the said play wanted to make up the full charge for that day being Twelve pounds one shilling and ten pence as aforesaid which this deft as well as most of the Cheife Actors Consented to or to such effect And thereupon the said Treasurer made the full Receipts on the third day of acting the said play called the Tender Husband to be charged for the use of the Company without chargeing any part thereof paid to the Complaynant in regard the Complaynant refused to receive the profitts due to him for that day But chose to have a day in Winter in Leiu thereof as aforesaid And this deft sayth that in pursueance of such Request made by the Complt to this deft and the Cheife actors as aforesaid a day was appoynted in the winter following according as the Complaynant desired and Bills were sett up the day before it was to have been acted and it was ordered by this deft to be geven out that Night and Bills putt up for the same to be acted the next day for the Author's Benefitt; But a little before it was to have been given out the Complt forbidd the same to be given out on the Stage or putt into the Bills for his Benefitt saying that he did not thinke there would be such an Audience att it as would please him or used words to some such or the like Effect But how ever the same play was acted on the then next day and the whole Receipts that day being Thursday the Twentyeth of November[1] one thousand seaven hundred and ffive amounted to sixty ffower pounds three shillings and Six pence and noe more (as this deft beleives & is informed by the said Treasurer) which was about two pounds seaventeen shillings more then the Receipts came to on the said third day that the same play was acted as aforesaid which two pounds seaventeen shillings and Six pence this deft and the said principal Actors were willing should be paid to the said Complt as well as the sum̄e of Ten pounds Eight shillings and two pence before menconed And this deft sayth that as to the Ten pounds Eight shillings and two pence which was due to the Complt out of the Receipts of the said third day according to the Agreement before menconed this deft never received the same or any part thereof nor the said two pounds seaventeen shillings and six pence But both the said Sumes remaine in the said Treasurers hands for the use of the Complt as this deft beleives And this deft gave order to the said Mr Baggs the Treasurer to pay the same to the Complaynant amounting together to Thirteen pounds ffive shillings and Eight pence as this deft computes the same And this deft beleives that Mr Baggs hath severall times offered to pay the same to the Complt and is still ready to doe the same But that he the Complt hath neglected or refused to receive the same as the said Treasurer has informed this deft And this deft denyeth that the said play called the Tender Husband was acted att any time in the yeare one thousand seaven Hundred and ffower either in the Summer or Winter as in the Complt's Bill is suggested But the first time the same was acted was on the said three & twentyeth of Aprill Anno Dni 1705 as this Deft verily Beleives and as is before sett forth And this deft denyeth that

[1] There is some mistake in this date On November 20, 1705, the *Bassett Table* was acted for the first time.

he this deft ever made any other agreement with the Complt touching or concerning the Comedyes or Playes before menconed or either of them other than as is herein before sett forth And this deft denyeth that he lent the said Seaventy two pounds upon any other agreement then as aforesaid and Sayth that he this deft did never agree to stay for the said debt untill the Complt should bring the said play called the Eleccon of Goatham or any other play to this deft And this deft denyes that he was or is minded to Oppresse the Complt and extort greate Sumes of money from him and not allow the Complt any profitt whatsoever in Consideracon of the said Comedy called the Tender Husband which Comedy as this deft hath been informed and beleives hath been severall times acted in the last yeare by the Company of Actors in the playhouse in the Hay Markett [1] witnout this deft's consent or direccion & in Opposition to this deft's Interest which this deft has reason to beleive was soe done by the Incouragement or att least the Conniveance of the Complt But what Benefitt or profitt the Complt hath had from thence for the same this deft doth not know And this deft Confesseth that the Complt haveing for a long time delayed the payment of the said debt of seaventy two pounds with Interest and Damages to this deft and not keeping his promises touching the same this deft hath caused prosecucon to be made against Complt for Recovery of the said debt with Interest & damages which this deft humbly insists was & is lawfull for him to doe and humbly hopes this honoble Court will not hinder him therein & this deft denyeth all and manner of unlawfull Combinacon & Confederacy for any the ends or purposes in the Complt's Bill menconed without that that there is any other matter or thing Clause Sentence or allegacon in the Complt's said Bill of Complaynt conteyned materiall & effectual in the Law for him this deft to make answere unto and not herein and hereby well and sufficiently answered unto confessed or avoyded traversed or denyed is true to the knowledge of this Deft all which matters & things this Deft is and shall be ready to averre justifye maintaine and prove as this honoble Court shall direct & humbly prayes to be hence dismissed with his Reasonable Costes & Charges in this behalfe most wrongfully susteyned.

TURNER JOHN METCALFE

[1] "Never acted there before. At the desire of severall Ladies of Quality. By her Majesty's Company of Comedians, At the Queen's Theatre in the Haymarket, this presant Saturday being the 7th of December [1706] will be presented a Comedy, called The Tender Husband or the Accomplished Fools." The Play was repeated at the Haymarket Theatre on Monday, Dec. 9th, and on Feb. 25th 1707, "for the benefit of Mrs. Oldfield" (*Daily Courant* passim).

No further action seems to have been taken until the 29th April 1710, when counsel for the defendant showed that his client had submitted his answer to the plaintiff's Bill on Jan. 27, 1708, since when the plaintiff had taken no action; it was therefore prayed that the Bill should be dismissed, with costs; "which is ordered accordingly." The costs of the defendant, however, were to be taxed.[1] Truly, Steele was not fortunate in his lawsuits.

[1] Pub. Rec. Office, Chancery Decrees, 1709 B, p. 320, "Steele *v.* Rich."

BOOK THIRD.

FIRST AND SECOND MARRIAGES.

1705–1709. ÆT. 33–37.

I.

MARRIAGE WITH MARGARET STRETCH.

1705–1707. ÆT. 33–34.

IN the spring of 1705[1] Steele married. There has been a tradition, handed down from writer to writer, that this first wife was, as it is put in the *Biographia Britannica*, "a gentlewoman of Barbadoes, with whom he had a valuable plantation there, on the death of her brother, who was taken by the French, at sea, as he was coming to England, and died in France." As we shall see, this is substantially correct, but it was not known who the lady was. I searched in vain for any entry of the marriage in Church Registers, or for any licence for the marriage; but by great good fortune the records at Somerset House and in Barbados have enabled me to tell fully, so far as essential points are concerned, the whole story of this part of Steele's life.[2]

The maiden name of Steele's first wife was Margaret Ford, but she was a widow—Mrs. Stretch—when she married Steele. Père Labat, the French missionary, who visited Barbados at the beginning of the last century, has left a description of the very prosperous state of the island.[3] There were fine shops and streets in Bridgetown, and the planters' mansions were very handsome; but there were numbers of miserable exiled Irish rebels, and 60,000 slaves. The island was divided, exactly like England, into parishes, each with its church. The Fords were a family

[1] We know the marriage was before June from the fine, which will be found below. See p. 138.

[2] A short account of this discovery was given in the *Athenæum* for May 1, 1886.

[3] *Nouveau Voyage aux Isles de l'Amerique*, 1722, Tom. IV. 386 *seq.*

of good position in Barbados.[1] There is a monumental slab in the churchyard of St. Andrew's, in that island, to "John Foord, Gen[t]," with the date—apparently of birth—1617.[2] There are unfortunately no Registers of St. Andrew's in existence prior to the present century. In a list of inhabitants of St. Michael's, Barbados, in 1680, we find Rich[d] Ford and wife; they had one child, and two slaves; Rose Ford, probably a child of theirs, was buried at St. Michael's in April 1678. In a list of the inhabitants of Christ Church parish in 1680, the name Thomas Ford occurs; he had fifteen acres, and nine negroes. In an Appendix I have given the substance of several wills of a family of Fords in St. Michael's parish; but I do not, for reasons there set forth, believe they were related to the family to which Margaret Ford belonged. What more concerns us is a list of inhabitants of St. Andrew's parish, dated 3rd June 1680; there we find John Foord, Esq[r]., the possessor of 280 acres, 4 men-servants, and 120 negroes. He was the largest landowner but one in the parish, and at the end of the list he signed, perhaps as churchwarden, immediately after the minister.[3] In his will, dated 5th June 1685, he is described as "of the Parish of Saint Andrew Overhills."[4] After directing that his debts were to be paid, he bequeathed to his grandson, Humphrey Waterman, son of Capt. Humphrey Waterman the elder and his daughter Anne, £20, when he was twenty-one; to his two grandchildren, William and John Sandiford, sons of Lieut.-Colonel Wm. Sandiford and Elizabeth, the testator's daughter,

[1] A Thomas Ford, Esq., of the Ridge, Barbados, is stated to have been great-grandfather of Sir Francis Ford, who was created a Baronet in 1793. See Burke's *Peerage and Baronetage*, where it is surmised that the family came from Devonshire originally. A George Ford of Exon was among those who went out to St. Christopher's from Plymouth in February 1633. Several others of the name went to America in 1635, including a Tristram Ford, aged 21, who went to Barbados (Hotten's *Original Lists of Persons . . . who went from Great Britain to the American Plantations*, pp. 62, 85, 103, 105, 128, 143, 152). A Sir Richard Ford, Knight, was a member of the Royal African Company in 1663, and was corresponding with Lord Willoughby, Governor of Barbados (Calendar of State Papers, Colonial Series, 1661–8, pp. 75, 121, 169).

[2] Archer's *Monumental Inscriptions of the British West Indies*, 1875.

[3] Hotten's *Original Lists*, &c., pp. 447, 469, 472, 478.

[4] Record Branch, Col. Sec. Office, Barbados. The St. Andrew Overhills, or Scotland, precinct included St. Andrew's and St. Joseph's parishes. The fol-

£20 each when they attained twenty-one years; to his grand-children, John and William Jeeves, sons of Henry Jeeves and his daughter Mary, £20 each when twenty-one; and to his son-in-law, Wm. Vaudrey, £20 when he was twenty-one. To his son, John Ford, he gave £5; and to his son, Thos. Foord, £50 per annum during his life out of the estate bequeathed to his sons, Samuel and Robert Foord. He gave his three daughters, Sarah, Margaret, and Mary Foord, £1000 a piece when they attained eighteen years or married; but if they died intestate their money was to go to his sons Samuel and Robert. He bequeathed a negro girl to each of his said daughters, and directed that his daughters were to be maintained and educated and provided with horses at the expense of his estate as formerly. He gave his wife, Mary Foord, rings, jewels, and household furniture, and the use of his residence on his plantation and her maintenance therefrom. He bequeathed to his sons, Samuel and Robert Foord, the plantation on which he resided—name not given—and also his plantation called "Sandy Hill," and a plantation lately purchased from Dr. Edward Lammy—perhaps "Lamming's" Estate—his storehouses at Speight's Bay (Speightstown), and all the residue of his estate. He appointed his wife executrix during her widowhood, but if she married again, John

lowing table will make clearer the details that follow. We do not know in what order the children of John Ford should be placed:—

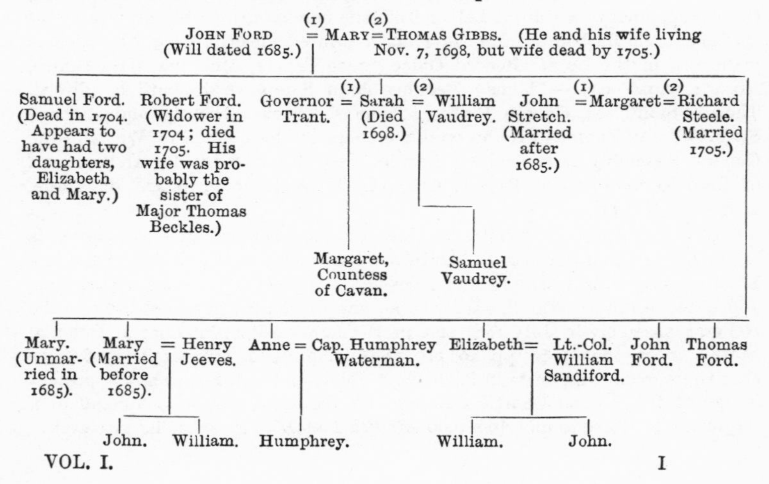

Farmer, Wm. Sandiford, and Humphrey Waterman, senior, were to be his executors; he gave £5 to each of them.

John Foord's son Samuel, who was thus left co-heir with Robert Ford, must have died before 1704, but I have not found the exact date. On the 4th December 1704, Major Robert Ford, enjoying sound and perfect health of body and mind, made his will, which was witnessed by John Perkinson, James Hannay, and John Dymes.[1] After directing that his body was to be buried among his ancestors, Major Ford bequeathed to his brother-in-law, Major Thomas Beckles,[2] £500; to his nephews, John and William Jeeves, £50 each; to his two nieces, Elizabeth and Mary Ford, £100 equally to be divided between them; to John Sandiford,[3] £50; and to his godson, William Sandiford, son of the above, £200. If necessary, these legacies, as well as his debts, were to be paid out of the rents of the real estate. If his niece, the Right Honourable Margaret Countess of Cavan, should survive her present husband, the Earl of Cavan, then, and not otherwise, she was to have during her life yearly £100 out of the real estate. The residue of all his property was to

[1] Prob. Court of Cant. 8 Poley. There is a copy of this will in Barbados.

[2] Robert Beckles and wife appear in the list of inhabitants of St. Michael's Parish, 1680. They had three children, one bought servant, and four slaves. Elizabeth, daughter of Mr. Robert and Susannah Beccles, was baptized at St. Michael's, August 28, 1679 (Hotten's *Original Lists*, 424, 444). The following names, nearly all of which occur in connection with the Fords, are among those appended to a "Joint Letter from the most considerable Proprietors of the Island of Barbados," August 1709, a printed sheet, a copy of which is preserved in the Public Record Office (State Papers, American West Indies, No. 34, paper 60):—Thomas Beckles, John Sandford, Richard Sandiford, Thomas Sandiford, George Walker, Thomas Affleck. Thomas and Richard Sandiford and Thomas Beckles were members of the Council of War and the General Assembly of Barbados. Beckles was Major of the Royal Regiment of Foot Guards (State Papers, Colonial Office Records; Board of Trade, Barbados, No. 15).

[3] Lt John Sandiford, owning 75 acres, one man servant, and 33 negroes, is in the list of inhabitants of St. Andrew's Parish, 1680. In the same list is a Lt Charles Sandiford, who had 15 acres and 4 negroes (Hotten's *Original Lists*, 469, 470). Captain Wm. Sandeford was one of the Burgesses elected to the General Assembly in July 1661 and in December 1662 (Calendar of Colonial State Papers, 1661–1668, pp. 49, 116, 583). Oldmixon, writing in 1708, says that there were five Courts in Barbados; John Sandford, Esq., was the present Judge of the Second Court. Colonel Tho. Sandford was in command of a Regiment of Horse numbering 1000 (*British Empire in America*, ii. 130, 132).

go to his loving sister, Margaret Stretch, and her heirs for ever; and she was to be sole executrix. There were several codicils, all dated 4th December 1704. By one of these it was directed that if Margaret Stretch be out of the island when the testator died, then his brother-in-law, Major Thomas Beckles, and his loving friend George Walker[1] were to act as executors until she could receive notice of his death. His cousin, Mrs. Anne Beckles, and George Walker were each to have £25 for mourning. Immediately upon the testator's death his negro woman, Betty, with all her offspring, were to be set free, as well as the negro man Rich, whom Major Ford's brother, Samuel, bought of Captain John Mead. And, finally, it was directed that if Margaret Stretch was dead when the will was drawn up, or should die before hearing what her brother had left her, then the whole property was to be equally divided between his niece, Margaret, Countess of Cavan, and his brother-in-law, Major Thomas Beckles.

Perhaps it will be best to notice in this place the mistake that has been made about this Countess of Cavan, who has been described as the daughter of a sister of Richard Steele, and thus his niece.[2] She was, in reality, the niece of Steele's wife. Governor Trant, of an ancient Irish family, now represented by the Trants of Dovea, and brother of Sir Patrick Trant, who went with James II. to France, married Sarah,[3] sister of Margaret Ford, and his daughter, Margaret, who was born in 1688, married Richard Lambert, who became fourth Earl of Cavan in December 1702. The Earl of Cavan had previously served in King William's army in Spain, Portugal, and the West Indies, where, it is to be presumed, he formed the acquaintance of Margaret Trant, "a lady endowed with all the virtues which constitute a complete female."[4] She died in

[1] Mr. Walker, however, disclaimed acting as executor. Several persons named Walker were buried at St. Michael's in 1678–9 (Hotten's *Original Lists*, 431, 434–5).

[2] Burke's *Landed Gentry*, 1868, pp. 1532–3; *Peerage and Baronetage*, Art. "Cavan."

[3] See page 134, note 2, upon her will.

[4] Lodge's *Peerage of Ireland*, 1789, i. 1361. Of the Trants it will be sufficient to say that Richard Trant, late of Barbados, made his will during his last illness

1737, aged 49, and her husband was buried by her side, at Maryboro', in 1741. Their second son, born in 1718, who succeeded to the title, was, it is to be noted, christened Ford.

Major Robert Ford was probably an officer in the Barbados militia; all freeholders and white servants were at that time obliged to enter themselves in the regiment of their own district.[1] It is clear that he made his will upon the eve of his setting out on his ill-fated voyage for England,[2] for only three months later, on March 27, 1705, commission was granted to Margaret Stretch, widow, and sister and next of kin to Robert Ford, to administer to his property. The deceased is described[3] as Major Robert Ford, late of the Island of Barbados, widower, and without parents or children; but dying on a French privateer (*super nave privata Bellica Gallica*) on the high sea, *captivum*, in the month last past or thereabouts.[4] His sister

in July 1684, leaving his kinsman, Patrick Trant, Esq., London, sole executor, and guardian of his son John. On the 26th January 1699–1700, a grant was given to Thomas Trant, principal creditor to Sir Richard, to administer to goods not administered to by Patrick Trant, Esq., now also deceased; on the 3rd October, 1701, the property of this Thomas Trant, of Richmond, Surrey, was administered to, and on the 20th October a grant was made to his widow Anne, to administer to the goods of Richard Trant. The will of Lady Helena Trant, relict of Sir Patrick Trant, Bart., is dated 26th Oct. 1721, and was proved in 1728 (P.C.C. 58 Abbott).

[1] Oldmixon's *British Empire in America*, ii. 113 (1708).

[2] No one could leave Barbados without putting up his name in the secretary's office twenty-one days beforehand, or giving security to the secretary's office to answer all demands that should be brought against him in twenty-one days after his departure. If no one underwrote him for debt "he hath a ticket sign'd by the Governor and Secretary that any ship may take him on board" (Letters from Captain Walduck to James Petiver, F.R.S.; Sloane MS. 2302, fol. 3). Walduck also says that estates in Barbados were very precarious, "ill-gott and maintained by charge and violence."

[3] Long Act Book, 1705 (Somerset House).

[4] Among the Barbados State Papers in the Public Record Office, there is an abstract of a letter from Sir Bevill Granville, April 8, 1705, stating that a sloop of Barbados had brought in a French Privateer of 4 guns and 50 men, of which number four were Her Majesty's subjects, and that he was informed many more were on board of the Privateers. In a subsequent letter, dated Barbados, 16th May 1705, Sir B. Granville inclosed a copy of his letter which was sent with the Packet that was taken by the French (Colonial Office Records: Board of Trade, Barbados, No. 103). In those days of war vessels from the West Indies were often captured by the French. In 1693 the *Diamond*, frigate and fireship, with several Barbados men, was taken to France, "where we had great numbers of prisoners" (Calendar of Treasury

stated that she had heard and believed that the will of the deceased was at Barbados, and she prayed administration until the said will should come into her hands. After her death, probate was granted, on January 4, 1707, to Richard Steele, Esq., widower, lawful husband and administrator of Margaret Steele *alias* Stretch, the sole executrix, to administer to the property of Major Ford, of St. Andrew's Parish, Barbados.

It is evident from Major Ford's will that his sister was not in Barbados in 1704, and in all probability she was living in England or Ireland.[1] There was a family of Stretches in

Papers, 1556-1696, xxiv. 20); in 1695 the *Isaac*, brigantine, was taken while coming from Barbados by a French privateer, recaptured, and then seized by a Dutch privateer (Ib. xxxiv. 71). The newspapers of June 1700 record the capture by pirates in the West Indies of two ships from Barbados and one from Virginia, homeward bound. In *Pue's Impartial Occurrences, Foreign and Domestic*, a quarto paper published in Dublin, of which the earliest known numbers (Vol. I. No. 61 to Vol. II. No. 7; Dec. 26, 1704, to Feb. 9, 1706) are among the uncatalogued Irish newspapers in the British Museum, there are several notices of captures at the very time that Major Robert Ford was taken prisoner. In the number dated Jan. 27, 1705, there is a letter from Cork, Jan. 23, published with all reservations: "Last night a person was examined before the Mayor of this city, who said he did belong to a London Barbadoes ship, bound home, and was taken by a French Privateer, who carried them to Cadiz, where they were confined for some time in that Castle. . . . The same person further added, that he and several more prisoners were put on board a French privateer, in order for St. Maloes. But the privateer meeting with, and taking a vessel bound for Kinsale, who ransomed, he got on board the same vessel, which arrived yesterday in Kinsale." The number for March 10, 1705, stated that French vessels from the West Indies had been captured, with upwards of 400 prisoners, and cargoes worth £100,000. On Aug. 23 there was news from London, Aug. 14, "Our Barbadoes fleet are all safe;" and on Sept. 25, "The Roterdam and Barbadoes Fleet are come safe into the River."

[1] Stretch was the name of an old family in Limerick, and, by a curious coincidence, James Stritch, of Limerick, brought an action for money recovery against William Foord, of the same, merchant, in Hilary Term, 11 Anne (Judgment Book, Common Pleas, Dublin). There are many Stretch or Stritch wills at Dublin, including several from Limerick, and others are to be found in the Index to Wills, Dis. Reg., Limerick. Thomas Stritch was Mayor of Limerick in 1651, and was one of those excepted from quarter upon the surrender of the city in October. There were also many Stretches in Cheshire in the early part of the seventeenth century, as appears from the Calendar of Cheshire Wills. Among the Ormonde MSS. there is a petition, 1678, of Francis Stretch (Historical MSS. Commission, Sixth Report, p. 778). Mr. J. G. Robertson made a copy of this petition for me. Stretch said he had had a proceeding for nine or ten years in the Courts of Ireland, and no effects were issued. He therefore prayed for prompt benefit of the laws; he was so vexed by delays and

Barbados, for in an account of the land in St. James's Parish, in that island, according to the Church books, 20th December 1679, we find the name John Stretch, who was the possessor of one negro.[1] No doubt he was Margaret Ford's first husband.[2] By March 1705 he was dead, and very soon after that date his widow married Steele. In September 1707, in a letter to Mrs. Scurlock, the mother of his second wife, Steele wrote, in explanation of his circumstances: "My late wife had so extreme a value for me that she, by fine, conveyed to me her whole estate situate in Barbados, which, with the stock and slaves (proper securities being given for the payment of the rent), is let for eight hundred and fifty pounds per annum, at half-yearly payments; that is to say, 425 each first of May, and 425 each first of December. This estate came to her incumbered with a debt of three thousand pounds, by legacies and debts of her brother, whose executrix she was as well as heiress."

In the early summer of 1705 it seems that Steele wrote to Lord Cutts asking for some payment in return for the services he had rendered. This was Lord Cutts' reply:[3]

persecution that he prayed the Lord-Lieutenant to grant a pass into France, and order his transportation; "it is so impossible for him to live amongst them here longer." A Captain Stritch was killed in a fight at Cavan in 1690 (Hist. MSS. Commission, Tenth Report, Part V. 289). In the Public Record Office there is a paper (S. P. Dom. Anne, Bdle. 11, No. 50) from a Stephen Stretch to Sir Charles Hedges, dated 1706.

[1] *Original Lists, &c.*, G. C. Hotten, p. 505. Among the subscribers to a *Natural History of Barbados*, by the Rev. Griffiths Hughes, published in 1750, there is the name "Mr. George Stretch," as well as "Francis Ford, Jun., Esq."

[2] We know that the husband's name was John, from the will, dated and proved in London in 1698, of Sarah Vaudrey, sister of Margaret Stretch (PCC. 242 Lort). Sarah Vaudrey, late of Barbados, widow, then sick and infirm, left half her property to her son Samuel when he was 21, and half to her daughter Margaret Trant when 18, or upon her marriage. If either died before reaching those ages, the whole was to go to the survivor; if both died, the whole was to go to her mother Gibbs, her brother Robert Ford, and her two sisters Margaret Stretch and Mary Ford, in equal shares. Her executors were her father-in-law Thomas Gibbs, her mother Mary Gibbs, and her brothers Robert Ford and John Stretch.

[3] This letter and the draft answer by Steele are among the Blenheim MSS. Lord Cutts had been appointed Commander-in-Chief in Ireland, under the Duke of Ormond, on March 23, 1705; he died in Dublin on January 26, 1707.

DUBLIN, July the 3d, 1705.

Sr

I have receiv'd a letter from you, dated—*Lady Mildmay's Bond Street Piccadilly;*[1] but without any mention either of the day of the month, or year of our Lord; so that I can't tell when it was wrote. You mention a former letter, which I never receiv'd, nor heard a word of before; so that I am totally a stranger to the Hardships, you say you suffer by my service; and I am the more surpris'd at this, because I have letters under your hand, that doe implicitly if not expressly declare the contrary with a great deal of Warmth.

You desire me to pay you for your long and chargeable attendance, which, since you demand it peremptorily as a Justice, I must answer as plainly, that if you will make it appear to me, that I promis'd you any Allowance in mony, I shall be ready to take your Demands into consideration. But I dare appeal to your cooler and more deliberate thoughts, whether I did not doe you some services (however forgotten now) which at that time were understood by all the World to ballance the service you had done me. If after quitting a Man's service, and making no manner of demand for so many years, such a claim is to be made; no Man is safe, who at any time employs a supernumerary Aid-de-Camp, or any other Officer in his Household, who may serve without pay in hopes of being introduc'd into the World and advanc'd; and, if I submitted to such a claim so circumstantiated, many as legall,[2] more might come upon me, for which there is no foundation in Law or Equity. As to your being bereft of your hopes of my favour; I assure you, you may command it whenever you act like one, who has made those professions, you have done to me; and in any thing just and practicable upon that foot, I shall always be ready to show my self in reality

Sr

Your affectionate

humble Servant

CUTTS.

The following draft, in Steele's writing, is endorsed on the back, "To Ld Cutts Augst 31st." It contains a reference to the property which had come to him through his wife.

[1] This address is underlined in the original. There is a memorandum of Steele's among the Blenheim papers—"Lady Mildmay is desired to send word what Mr Matthew has answer'd about the Standing of his Lodgings."

[2] "as legall" added above the line.

Aug^st 31st 1705
From my Lodgings, at Mr Keen's
An Apothecarye's in Bennett
street near S^nt James's.

MY LORD

I am very sorry to hear by Mr Trubshaw (?) how highly you resent my late expostulations;[1] but if your Excellency pleases to consider that in the midst of the frankest kindest behaviour which you us'd towards me, you did so unsuitable a thing as to postponed[2] my pretentions to those of a young Gentleman you hardly ever spoke to, ev'n at a crisis in my little affairs, you will think I am under very great temptations to forget my self in points of decorum:[3] My Accounts from the West Indies[4] are such, that I am as certain (as the vicissitudes of Humane things will permit) of a provision for my self and posterity, therefore shall[5] now have no inclination to any methods but relying on your own will to do me any favour if you shall think fit, If not, and that you are resolv'd never more to honour me with any commands from you, I assure y^r Excellency nothing shall ever alienate me from very hearty Wishes for y^r Honour, and Welfare.[6] However I hope y^r Excellency will pardon me that I inclose to you this note of seven pound 10s. which I paid for a Lodging taken by y^r Order in Scotland-Yard, for my more convenient attendance on you when in y^r Service, and that you'll direct me[7] to draw a bill payable in Dublin for that sum at sight.

I have occasion for that sum there,[8] and y^r Lordship's[9] direction on whome to draw it will be a very great favour to——

[1] "expostulations in my behalfe" first written, but last three words erased.

[2] "you postponed," as first written, the other words having been afterwards inserted.

[3] After this came the clauses "but tho' I was at that time out, when I writ those letters quite of the Service," successively erased.

[4] It may be noted that on February 11, 1702–3, an official notice was issued announcing that Queen Anne had arranged for a monthly postal service to Barbados and other West Indian Islands.

[5] The words which follow are in place of these, most of which are cancelled: "not be under the necessity of any recourse to harsh methods to Oblige your methods to any methods but your own will to do any things . . . if it lyes in y^r Way."

[6] After this come the following cancelled words:—"I beleive I shall soon be very Well employ'd."

[7] "me;" "Mons. Budiani" was added over the line, and left uncancelled.

[8] After this comes the cancelled sentence, "and 'twill be a very great favour to send me y^r Orders on whome to draw it, I am, My Lord."

[9] "Excellency's" first written.

In the preceding Trinity term—June 8 to 27—judgment had been given against Steele, with damages of 50s., in an action for debt brought against him by John Sansome, Esq., an old school friend, who relieved Steele in his money difficulties when in the army, and of whom we shall hear more in after years.[1] Sansome, by Charles Salkeld, his attorney, said that Steele—"late of Westminster Esq., alias Richard Steele of London Esq."—on the 3rd of January 1701[-2] at Westminster, acknowledged himself bound in the sum of £600, to be paid when requested. But he refused to pay, and Sansome claimed £10 damages. Steele appeared, but his attorney, William Rolfe, said he was not informed of any answer to be made in the matter.

In this same Trinity term, 1705, part of the estate in Barbados was sold by fine to Joseph Addison, Esquire, for £400. At first it might be thought that this was Steele's friend and fellow worker, but it appears this is not the case, for in the list of subscribers to Hughes' *Natural History of Barbados*, published in 1750, there is the name "Mr Joseph Addison," and Captain Lawrence Archer says that the name Addison occurs in Registers in Barbados in 1708.[2] But Addison, curiously enough, did possess an estate in "the Indies" of £14,000, which, as he told Mr. Wortley in 1711, he had "within this twelvemonth lost." By the fine given below Steele and his wife Margaret conveyed to Joseph Addison, Esq., a messuage and land and other

[1] Common Pleas Judgment Roll. Trinity 4 Anne, 1216.

[2] Brit. Mus., Add. MS. 27969, fol. 33. It is curious, too, among the subscribers to this same book by Mr. Hughes, to find the names "George Gascoigne Esq.," "Mr. John Gascoigne." There were baptisms of children of William and Judith Gascoigne at St. James's, Barbados, in 1695, and 1698; and a Margaret Devereux was married at the same church in 1705 (Add. MS. 27969, f. 35; and Add. MS. 23608). The Gascoignes were a family of good position in Barbados. The Honourable Stephen Gascoigne, in his will dated 28th August 1686, mentions his wife Hester; his brother Walwyne, of London; his only son, Walwyne; his brother-in-law, Sir Edwyn Stede (Lieut.-governor of Barbados), and others. The will of Walwyn Gascoigne is dated 1698 (P. C. Canterbury). He was a merchant, with property in Gloucestershire. A Peter Gascoigne was buried at St. Michael's, Barbados, July 18, 1679; and the Hon. Stephen Gascoigne appears again in a list of inhabitants in and about the town of St. Michael's, Barbados, in 1680 (Hotten's *Original Lists*, 116, 264, 436, 447).

property in Barbados,—"in Islington," as it is curiously expressed. Either Islington was the name of the place in Barbados where the property was situated—though there is no trace of any such name in the island—or we are to understand "in Islington" to refer to the place where the agreement was entered into. We shall see that Steele signed bonds at Islington in February and April 1708. Perhaps the clerk who entered the fines left out some words.[1]

Hec est finalis Concordia facta in curia Domine Regine apud Westmonasterium A die Sancte Trinitatis in tres septimanas Anno regnorum Anne Dei gratia Anglie Scocie Francie & Hibernie Regina fidei defensoris etc. A conquestu quarto. Coram Thoma Trevor[2] Edwardo Nevill Johanne Blencowe & Roberto Tracy Justiciariis & aliis domine Regine fidelibus tunc ibi presentibus Inter Josephum Addison Armigerum querelantem et Ricardum Steele Armigerum & Margaretam uxorem ejus deforciantes de uno mesuagio quingentis acris terre viginti acris prati viginti acris pasture & viginti acris bosci cum pertinentiis in quodam loco vocat̃ content̃ in Insula Barbadoes in Islington unde Placitum Convencionis summonitum fuit inter eos in eadem curia scilicet quod predicti Ricardus & Margareta recognoverunt predicta tenementa cum ptinentiis esse jus ipsius Josephi Ut illa que idem Josephus habet de dono predictorum Ricardi & Margarete Et illi remiserunt & quiet-clamaverunt de ipsis Ricardo & Margareta & heredibus ipsius Margarete predicto Josepho & heredibus suis imppetuum Et preterea iidem Ricardus & Margareta concesserunt pro se & heredibus Margarete quod ipsi Warantizabunt predicto Josepho & heredibus suis predicta tenementa cum ptinenciis contra predictos Ricardum & Margaretam & heredes ipsius Margarete imppetuum Et pro hoc recognitione recognitione (sic) remissione quietclam̃ Warrant̃ fine & concordia idem Josephus dedit predictis Ricardo & Margarete quadringentas libras sterlingorum. MIDD.

[1] Public Record Office; Feet of Fines. Middlesex. Trinity 4 Anne (1705).

[2] Sir Thomas Trevor was made Lord Chief-Justice of the Common Pleas in 1702, and he presided over that Court throughout Queen Anne's reign. He was made 1st Lord Trevor at the close of 1711. He must have seen a good deal of Steele in connection with the numerous cases to which Steele was a party which came before the Court; but he would little dream that his second son, who became 3rd Lord Trevor, would, in after years, marry Steele's daughter. Sir Edward Nevil, John Blencowe, Esq., and Robert Tracy, Esq., were the Justices of the Common Pleas from 1702 to 1705, in the August of which latter year Sir E. Nevil died.

The name "Steel"[1] appears on the map of Barbados in the second volume of Oldmixon's *British Empire in America*, which was published in 1708. The same map was used for the 1741 edition. The name is in the Parish of St. Andrew, to the West of the Church, and it is certain that it indicates the position of the property which came to Steele through his wife, because on the map of Barbados published by Lea about 1695 the name "Forde" appears in the same position as "Steel" occupies in the map of 1708; in the elaborate survey made by Mayo between 1717 and 1721 the estate is shown as belonging to "Sandiford," and a neighbouring plantation "of less note," not separately marked on earlier maps, to "Afflick." From this we may gather that the estate, which is marked by Mayo with a sign meaning "Sugar Works of one Windmill,"[2] was sold by Steele to the Sandifords,[3] one of whom, it will be remembered, was brother-in-law to Margaret Steele. The Sandifords and Walkers had each several other plantations in St. Andrew's parish, and in St. Peter's, which is to the West of St. Andrew's, and which includes Speight's Town, where the Fords had storehouses. Steele's interest in the West Indies, and especially Barbados, was afterwards shown in several papers in the *Spectator*.[4]

There is nothing more to record until January 1707, when a grant was issued to Richard Steele Esqr., lawful husband of Margaret Steele *alias* Stretch, late of the parish of St. Margaret,

[1] "Steele" was not an uncommon name in the West Indies during the seventeenth and eighteenth centuries. A Thomas Steele Esq. was Agent for prizes in Jamaica in 1706 (Calendar of Treasury Papers, 1702–7, xcviii. 69). John Steel married in Jamaica in 1669, and there are wills of Robert Steel, 1745, and Richard Steel, 1750 (List of Wills and Marriages registered in Jamaica.—Herald's College, London). Captain R. Steele of Barbados died May 24, 1769. See also Archer's *Monumental Inscriptions*, p. 112; Jeaffreson's *A Young Squire of the Seventeenth Century*, ii. 69; and Hotten's *Original Lists*, &c., 403, 404, 466, 468.

[2] Froude remarks that there are windmills everywhere in Barbados just as in Labat's time. There are no rivers and no water-power, the chief motive agent being the trade wind (*English in the West Indies*, 1888).

[3] See pages 128–130.

[4] See especially Nos. 11, 80, 394, 493 (*The Spectator's Essays relating to the West Indies*, by W. Darnell Davis, Esq., 1885, reprinted from the *West Indian Quarterly*, Part 3, vol. i.).

Westminster, Middlesex, to administer to his wife's property. The warrant, 4 January 1706–7, says that she had been dead fully fourteen days,—"ad 14 dies plene elapš mortem obiise." The securities were Richard Steel of St. Margaret's Westm. Esq., John Pye of Furnivall's Inn, Gent., and Edward Sanders of St. Botolph Aldersgate, clothmaker. The exact date of Margaret Steele's death, and the place of her burial, are not known; but Miss Scurlock, who was to be Steele's second wife, writing to her mother in August 1707, describes Steele as "the survivor of the person to whose funeral I went to in my illness."

In the absence of better authority we must now turn to Mrs. Manley's *Secret Memoirs . . . from the New Atalantis*, published in 1709. Mrs. Manley was the daughter of Sir Robert Manley, a Royalist, once Governor of Landguard Fort, who died soon after the Revolution. While she was young she was made the victim of a false marriage by a near relation, who afterwards deserted her. In 1705 she was concerned in the forgery of an entry in a Marriage Register, and in 1709 she produced *The New Atalantis*, in which she slandered many people of note, under the guise of admonition, while her own book is remarkable for its immorality. Swift attacked her in the *Tatler* (Nos. 35, 63), and Mrs. Manley—"Rivella," as she was called—attacked Steele on the assumption that he was the author of those papers. It is right to say that in 1717 Mrs. Manley dedicated her play, *Lucius*, to Steele, and expressed great mortification at what she had written years before; and in a book called *The Adventures of Rivella; or the History of the Author of the Atalantis*, 1714,[1] which was published with her sanction, it is candidly admitted that "scandal between Whig and Tory goes for nothing," and of Mrs. Manley herself we are told "Of whom we may say, in relation to love, since she has so peculiar a genius for, and has made such noble discoveries in that passion, that it would have been a fault in her, not to have been faulty." In short, "Rivella's" stories can never be believed, unless they are

[1] A third edition appeared in 1717, under the title *Memoirs of the Life of Mrs. Manley*. It is nominally "From the French. By Sir Charles Lovemore;" but Curll says it was written by Mrs. Manley herself, when she found that Gildon was about to publish a book about her.

fully corroborated; but, on the other hand, she certainly was intimately acquainted with Steele. I will now give what she says about his marriage, and the events preceding it, and afterwards a few remarks upon her statements.[1]

"O let me ease my spleen! I shall burst with laughter; these are prosperous times for vice; d'ye see that black Beau (stuck up in a pert chariot) thick set, his eyes lost in his head, hanging eye-brows, broad face, and tallow complexion; I long to inform myself if it be his own, he cannot yet sure pretend to that. He's called *Monsieur Le Ingrate*, he shapes his manners to his name, and is exquisitely so in all he does; has an inexhaustible fund of dissimulation, and does not bely the country he was born in, which is famed for falsehood and insincerity." He covered his own want of morality or principle by dissimulation with his pen. "The Person[2] who had done so much for him, not doing more, he thought all that he had done for him was below his desert; he wanted to rise faster than he did. There was a Person who pretended to the great Work, and he was so vain as to believe the illiterate fellow could produce the Philosopher's Stone, and would give it him. The Quack found him a bubble to his mind, one that had wit, and was sanguine enough to cheat himself, and save him abundance of words and trouble in the pursuit. Well, a house is taken, and furnished, and furnaces built, and to work they go; the young soldier's little ready money immediately flies off, his credit is next staked, which soon likewise vanishes into smoke. The operator tells him 'twas not from such small sums as those he must expect perfection; what he had hitherto was insignificant." Monsieur was introduced to a gentleman [Mr. Manley] who, though not free from doubt, was willing to join him in finding the money required, and Monsieur became a favourite of that gentleman's wife, who supplied him with money. "Still the furnace burnt on, his credit was stretched to the utmost; demands came quick upon him, and became clamorous; he had neglected his Lord's business, and ev'n left his House, to give himself up to the vain pursuits of Chymistry. . . . There was

[1] *New Atalantis*, 6th ed., i. 205–212, iv. 313–15.
[2] Lord Cutts. See the correspondence on pp. 135–6.

a great City-Hall taken, and furnaces ordered to be built, that they might have room enough to transmute abundantly.[1] The Operator had persuaded the young Chymist to sell his Commission, which he was very busy about, and even repined that he met not a purchaser as soon as he desired; for he thought every hour's delay kept him from his imaginary kingdom." The lady urged her husband to warn Monsieur that the Operator was probably a cheat, and the husband at last consented to his wife speaking. When she did so it fell like a thunderbolt on the Chymist; he was utterly broken down, though just before he had been the life of a party of ladies. "He was already undone, or very near it. . . . Monsieur was forced to abscond; all he could preserve from the Chymical Shipwrack was his Commission." The lady, whom he termed his Guardian Angel, and her husband, helped him. "But Fortune did more for him in his adversity than would have lain in her way in prosperity; she threw him to seek for refuge in a House,[2] where was a lady with very large possessions; he marry'd her, she settled all upon him, and dy'd soon after. He remarry'd to an Heiress, who will be very considerable after her mother's decease, has got a place in the Government, and now, as you see, sparks it on the Prado." The lady who had helped him became a widow, and was in trouble; but Monsieur twice, upon her appealing to him, refused to give her enough money to take her to her friends, pleading that he was incapable. "It is not only to her, but to all that have ever served him, he has showed himself so ungrateful." In another place,[3] in a dialogue between Mrs. Tofts and Don Phœbo (Steele), after an allusion to "your first lady's elderly charms," Mrs. Tofts is made to say, "I have none of those fortunate incidents in wedlock; I am still unmarried; but then it is confess'd, I am guiltless of that anxiety you must have often felt in fetters, especially when after complimenting your first Lady (in the condition she was then in) with a real marriage, how must you be affected and perplexed at the report of her

[1] In Nichols' time there was a tradition that Steele carried on his experiments in a house at Poplar, afterwards turned into a garden-house.

[2] Lady Mildmay's, apparently; see p. 135.

[3] Vol. iv. 302-7.

brother's being yet living, by whose death she was entitled to that wealth, which had made a husband of *Don Phœbo?* Your fame is not quite so clear in reference to that ugly and odd misfortune, which was so fatal to her, occasion'd by your sister; but a younger wife, and a cry'd up beauty, were consolations for a less commodious loss."[1]

To take the last charge first. There is nothing to corroborate Mrs. Manley's statement that Mrs. Steele died under peculiar circumstances; but it is a fact that Katherine, the only sister of Steele that we know of, was mad. On the other hand, it is to be remembered that Mary Scurlock, who knew his first wife, and was present at her funeral, married Steele a few months afterwards, which she would hardly have done if there had been suspicious circumstances or even scandal attaching to her friend's death. It is, however, just possible that if Mrs. Steele was approaching her confinement her death may have been caused by fright occasioned by some act of Katherine Steele's. As regards the charge of ingratitude, Steele wrote to Mrs. Manley in September 1709, "I had not money when you did me the favour to ask a loan of a trifling sum of me. I had the greatest sense imaginable of the kind notice you gave me when I was going on to my ruin." This last sentence would, if there were any doubt on the matter, establish the general truth of Mrs. Manley's statement that Steele tried to find the philosopher's stone. I have not mentioned it before, because the information outside Mrs. Manley's story amounts to so little, and it is so very uncertain when these experiments were made. It seems reasonable to believe that Mrs. Manley's very full account is fairly correct; and according to her version the troubles consequent upon the chemical experiments immedi-

[1] In *The Ecclesiastical and Political History of Whig-Land*, 1714, "John Lacy" says that Steele, by the impudence common in his countrymen, obtained for his wife a West Indian beauty, with "more mines of gold than would have made a plentiful fortune for a worthier mortal than Don Ricardo. Well but she was his till she died, and I wish I could say, he was hers." He might say of his lady, in the words of Dryden:

"Fulvia died,
Pardon, ye gods, by my unkindness died."

I have already remarked on the value that is to be attached to Mr. Lacy's scurrilities, most of which could not be quoted.

ately preceded Steele's first marriage. In the *Guardian*, No. 166, which is attributed to Addison by Tickell, there is an account of an operator cheating his client, who has been seeking for the philosopher's stone; and in another paper (No. 107), by Addison, the Guardian says that he was very fond of projects, and he mentions among those in which he has embarked "that never to be forgotten project, which if it had succeeded to my wishes, would have made gold as plentiful in this nation as tin or copper." And in a prologue by Addison, recited in Steele's presence in 1715, we read—

"Early in youth, his enemies have shewn,
How narrowly he missed the Chemic Stone."

Dennis [1] wrote, "You, Sir John Edgar, have been a squanderer in three elements. Some of your gold has been consumed in Roscicrucian fire; when you and Burnaby, the poet,[2] and Tilly,[3] the late Warden of the Fleet, entered into an indenture tripartite, as Face and Subtle, and Doll Common [4] had done before you; but with this difference, that these last were cheats, whereas you and your brethren were gulls; with an eagerness like that of Sir Epicure Mammon, were you embarked in the search of your *aurum potabile;* when you used to say to one another, over your midnight suppers, 'Drink and be rich.'" Possibly Defoe was referring to Steele when he said that among those who would derive benefit from a certain machine called the Cogitator, or Chair of Reflection, used in China, were those who are always travelling in thought, but never delivered into action: "It would teach 'em to dispatch one thing before they begin another; and therefore is of singular use to honest S——, whose peculiar it was to be always beginning projects,

[1] *Character and Conduct of Sir John Edgar*, Letter I. (1720).

[2] Charles Burnaby's comedies appeared between 1700 and 1703.

[3] There are several broadsides and tracts about Tilly's irregularities in a volume in the British Museum, 816m 15 (14, &c.); in one he is called the real, though not nominal, Warden—Mr. Ford being the nominal Warden. There are various papers in the Public Record Office relating to Tilly (State Papers, Domestic, Anne, Bdle. 7, No. 95; Bdle. 9, Nos. 10, 11, 63; Bdle. 10, No. 12). He married Margaret, daughter of Sir John Reresby, Bart., of Tribergh.

[4] Jonson's *Alchemist*.

but never finish any."[1] Steele had his own life in mind when he wrote, in the character of Isaac Bickerstaff, Esq., in the *Tatler* (No. 89), "As years came on I began to examine things, and grew discontented at the times. This made me quit the sword and take to the study of the occult sciences, in which I was so wrapped up that Oliver Cromwell had been buried and taken up again five years before I heard that he was dead. This gave me first the reputation of a conjurer." The passages, too, in the *Lying Lover*, in which Charcoal appears, seem to have been written—whether they contain personal allusions or not—at the very time when Steele was involved in his alchemist's experiments.

[1] *The Consolidator* (1705), p. 105. In another place, where Prior and Addison are mentioned (page 27), Defoe may be referring to Captain Steele when he says, "There C—— S—— may be informed how he comes to be very witty, and a madman all at once."

II.

GENTLEMAN WAITER AND GAZETTEER.

1705–1707. ÆT. 33–35.

In a prologue to Vanbrugh's play, *The Mistake,* which was first acted at Vanbrugh's new theatre on the 27th December 1705, Steele took the opportunity to again satirise the taste for the shows and dances which were taking the place of the real drama. The prologue was spoken by Booth.

Our Author's wit and raillery to-night
Perhaps might please, but that your stage-delight
No more is in your minds, but ears and sight.
With audiences composed of belles and beaux,
The first dramatic rule is, have good clothes.
To charm the gay spectator's gentle breast
In lace and feather tragedy's expressed,
And heroes die unpitied if ill dressed.
The other style you full as well advance;
If 'tis a comedy, you ask—Who dance?[1]
For oh! what dire convulsions have of late
Torn and distracted each dramatic state,
On this great question, which house first should sell
The new French steps imported by Ruel?

[1] The dancing was not confined to comedies. The following advertisements from the *Daily Courant* for April 1706 show in what fashion Shakespeare was studied and acted at the Queen's Theatre in the Haymarket:—"April 26 . . . will be reviv'd a play (never acted there before) called Measure for Measure, written by the famous Beaumont and Fletcher" (!), with a masque, comic dances and songs. "April 30 . . . will be reviv'd the True and Ancient History of King Lear, to which will be added most of the comical songs and dialogues that were performed in the last new opera, called, Wonders in the Sun."

Desbarques can't rise so high, we must agree,
They've half a foot in height more wit than we.
But though the genius of our learned age
Thinks fit to dance and sing quite off the stage
True action, comic mirth and tragic rage;
Yet as your taste now stands, our author draws
Some hopes of your indulgence and applause.

For that great end Vanbrugh had built the new and more commodious theatre.

Thus all must own, our author has done more
For your delight than ever bard before.
His thoughts are still to raise your pleasures filled,
To write, translate, to blazon, or to build.[1]
Then take him in the lump, nor nicely pry
Into small faults that scape a busy eye,
But kindly, sirs, consider, he to-day
Finds you the house, the actors and the play:
So, though we stage-mechanic rules omit,
You must allow it is a wholesale wit.

In July 1706 Steele published a *Prologue to the University of Oxford*. The lines were afterwards printed in the *Muses Mercury* for September 1707, as "By Capt. S——l." This was the advertisement in the *Daily Courant* for July 4, 1706:—"This day is published, A Prologue to the University of Oxford, spoken by Mr Wilks at the opening of the Theatre there: Written by Mr Steele. Printed for Bernard Lintott at the Cross Keys next Nando's Coffee House, Temple Bar. Price 2d." I have not seen this leaflet, and it has not hitherto been noticed that the verses had appeared in a separate form before their publication in the *Muses Mercury*, or that it was a special occasion which called them forth.

These performances at Oxford were held in Burnham's Tennis-Court, probably, as the Hon. G. C. Brodrick suggests, the small tennis-court opposite to Oriel. Christopher Rich seized the

[1] *The Mistake* was one of three plays which Vanbrugh adapted from the French for the Haymarket Theatre. Vanbrugh was Clarenceux King of Arms, as well as a famous architect.

opportunity of bringing actions for breach of covenant against several of the actors who took part in these performances at a theatre or playhouse not governed by him.[1]

PROLOGUE TO THE UNIVERSITY OF OXFORD.

As wandering streams by secret force return
To that capacious ocean whence they're born,[2]
So for their doom their toils our poets bring
To the famed Oxford where they learned to sing;
These happy seats would rudest minds inspire,
And all that see must feel poetic fire;
Aspiring columns here, here beauteous fields,
Here all that Art, here all that Nature yields,
Groves, Theatres, high Domes, and humble shades,
Bright palaces, and intermingled glades,
Make the admiring traveller debate
Whether they're formed for solitude or state;
While empty pomp the inhabitants despise,
With whom alone 'tis greatness to be wise;
Oh happy! and your happiness who see!
Where innocence and knowledge can agree!
Ye calm spectators of a guilty age,
Pity the follies of the world and stage,
Free from what either act, or represent,
Weigh both the character and the intent,
And know, men as they are our authors drew,
But what they should be, we must learn from you.

In August Defoe wrote very strongly respecting the licence to act plays at Oxford which had been granted by the Vice-Chancellor to a set of players of both companies, "than whom I need not describe greater patterns of vice," "engines of the devil." He asked the University authorities if they did not blush at permitting those "who prompt the vanity of our youth, to be set openly to work before your faces, and within your

[1] *Athenæum*, August 11 and 25, 1888, papers by the present writer on "Actors and Managers under Queen Anne."

[2] These two first lines, in an earlier form, had already, as we have seen, served as the commencement of some verses in the copy of the *Christian Hero* which Steele presented to Dr. Ellis.

jurisdiction!" He tells us how the Vice-Chancellor, with the heads of houses, in their formalities, went in procession, followed by the students, inhabitants, and ladies, to the play-house; and he rejoiced that an attempt to introduce the players into Cambridge had been unsuccessful.[1]

In Hilary term, 1706, Henry Barradall commenced an action for debt against Steele in the Court of Queen's Bench. He complained that whereas on the 1st June 1703, in the parish of St. Clement Danes, Steele was indebted to him and to a certain Edward Barradall and Abraham Defflamar, now deceased, in £20 for tailor's work and labour in making divers vestments for him at his special request, and also for divers sums of money paid by Henry Barradall, &c., for him, he acknowledged himself bound to them, and promised faithfully to pay the money. And afterwards, on the 1st June 1703, in consideration that Henry Barradall, &c., made him other garments, and at their own charge found and provided divers goods used in the making of the said garments, Steele promised to pay them what was right both for the making and the materials. They said they ought to be paid £20 for the making and £20 for the materials, whereof Steele had notice. And whereas on the 1st June 1703, in consideration that Henry Barradall, &c., at the special request of Steele, sold and delivered unto him other goods, Steele promised to pay what the goods were worth. Their value, they said, was £20, of which Steele had notice; nevertheless he had not paid, and refused to pay, and Henry Barradall, &c., claimed damages of £60. On the Friday next after the morrow of Trinity (May 24, 1706), Barradall came into court, but Steele neither came nor said anything in bar of judgment; which accordingly was given against him, the Court commanding that enquiries should be made as to the damages sustained by Barradall.[2] This case, of which I have not found any further record, affords a good specimen of the objectionable proceeding known as a "declaration in assumpsit." The debt was in reality only £20, but as the Court rarely awarded the full damages claimed, the complainants repeated the sum owing

[1] *Review*, iii. 377-9, 383.
[2] Queen's Bench Judgment Roll, Trinity 5 Anne 329. See page 84.
*

several times in their Bill, as if for separate services, in order to swell up the damages, and thereby to make the portion of the sum claimed which might be awarded them equal to the whole debt.

In the following term—Michaelmas (October 23 to November 28)—Richard Steele, late of the parish of St. James, Westminster, Esq., was summoned to answer to a plea of Charles Thorold, Knt., and Samuel Stainer, Knt., Sheriffs of Middlesex, who stated that Steele, on the 26th April 1706, at Westminster, acknowledged himself bound to them in the sum of £180, to be paid when required; but he had not paid and refused to do so, wherefore the Sheriffs claimed £20 damages. The bond was brought into Court to bear witness of the debt, and was dated the day and year aforesaid. Steele, by his attorney, Richard Arnold, appeared, but made no defence, and judgment was therefore given against him, and damages to the amount of 70s. awarded.[1]

In August 1706 Steele was made a gentleman-waiter to Prince George of Denmark, "with a salary of one hundred pounds a year, not subject to taxes."[2] As Mr. Dobson has shown, the generally accepted date of this appointment—May 1707—is wrong. In Luttrell's *Diary*,[3] under Thursday, 15th August 1706, there is the following entry: "Charles Nicholas Eyre, and Richard Steele, esqs., are made gentlemen-waiters to the prince, in the room of coll. Durell and Mr. Beverley; the first being made query in the room of coll. Bringfeild, killed at Ramelies; and the latter gent. usher to his royal highness in the room of coll. Webb, sen., deceased." Meanwhile, Addison had been appointed Under-Secretary of State to Sir Charles Hedges, who in a few months was succeeded by the Earl of Sunderland, a Whig, and son-in-law to the Duke of Marlborough. Addison retained his post, and complimented the Duke of Marlborough in the words which he wrote for Clayton's *Rosamond*, an opera, "humbly inscribed to Her Grace the Duchess of Marlborough."[4]

[1] Common Pleas Judgment Roll, Mich. 5 Anne 502.
[2] Letter from Steele to Mrs. Scurlock, September 3, 1707.
[3] Vol. vi. 77. See also Pointer's *Chronological History*, p. 559.
[4] *Daily Courant* for March 6 and 11, 1707.

During 1707 a monthly periodical in quarto, following on the lines of a similar paper called *The Gentleman's Journal*, which appeared in the years 1692–4, was published under the name of *The Muses Mercury*. The full title was "The Muses Mercury or the Monthly Miscellany. Consisting of Poems, Prologues, Songs, Sonnets, Translations, and other Curious Pieces, Never before Printed. By

The Earl of Roscommon,	Mr. Dennis,
Mr. Dryden,	Dr. N——n,
Dr. G——th,	Capt. Steel,
N. Tate, Esquire,	Mr. Manning, &c.

To which is added, An account of the Stage, of the New Operas and Plays that have been acted, or are to be acted this Season; And of the New Books relating to Poetry, Criticism, &c., lately Publish'd." The Dedication, addressed to the Duke of Devonshire, is signed "J. O.," that is, John Oldmixon; and the journal lasted until January 1708. The first number, though dated January 1707, did not appear, as we are told in the December number, until the middle of February.[1] It contained this note: "Mr Farquhar, who wrote the Recruiting Officer, has a Comedy ready for representation; and had not the death of a dear friend hindered Capt. Steel from finishing a Comedy of his, it would also have been acted this Season." Thus the recent death of Steele's wife is noticed. In the same number appeared some verses "To a Young Lady who had married an Old Man. By Capt. Steel." Farquhar's *Recruiting Officer* had been the most popular play of the year 1706. First acted on April 8, there was a performance for the benefit of the author on the 19th, and on the 25th the play was published.[2] A second edition appeared on May 23, and a third on December 6. Farquhar's new play, the *Beaux Stratagem*, was acted for the first time, at the Queen's Theatre, Haymarket, on the 8th March

[1] It was announced as "Just published," price 6d., in the *Daily Courant* for March 4.

[2] *Daily Courant*, passim. See, too, the same paper for October 22 for a notice of a performance of the play on October 24 at Dorset Gardens, "by the deserted company of Comedians of the Theatre Royal."

1707, and was published on the 27th March.[1] It was written during his last illness, and he died in April, before the run of the play was over. Borne down with trouble and debts, he secured his place among the greatest of writers of English comedy in a life which did not reach to thirty years.

The note in this paper about Farquhar and Steele furnishes one of many proofs that Steele was only hindered from producing a new play in the long interval between 1705 and 1722, when the *Conscious Lovers* appeared, by the many other occupations which filled up his time. Berkeley, we shall see, understood that Steele was writing a play in 1713, and Swift alluded in 1714 to the plot with which Steele had "long threatened the town."

In the next number of the *Muses Mercury*, which is dated February 1707, but which did not appear until the 28th March,[2] there was the following

SONG. BY CAPT. STEEL.

Me Cupid made a happy slave,
  A merry wretched man;
I slight the nymphs I cannot have,
  Nor doat on those I can.

This constant maxim still I hold,
  To baffle all despair;
The absent ugly are and old,
  The present young and fair.

In April Steele wrote a petition for Charles Gildon,[3] who had been tried at the Guildhall on the 14th February for publishing a political pamphlet. He was found guilty of libel, and was sentenced on the 17th May to pay a fine of £100.

At the end of April or the beginning of May, Steele was appointed Gazetteer, with a salary of £300 a year, but paying a tax of £45.[4] Thomas Hearne notes in his Diary for May 14 that

[1] *Daily Courant.*

[2] *Ibid.*, March 28, 1707.

[3] See p. 75. The original of this petition is in the British Museum, Add. MSS. 5145 B. Gildon died in January 1724, but was not forgotten by Pope who introduced him into the *Dunciad.*

[4] Letter to Mrs. Scurlock, 3rd Sept. 1707.

"The writer of the Gazette now is captain Steele, who is the author of several romantick things, and is accounted an ingenious man."[1] Swift says in his *Journal to Stella* (October 22, 1710) that Harley gave Steele the post of Gazetteer, and raised the salary from £60 to £300; and in *The Importancé of the Guardian Considered* (1713) he adds that the appointment was made at the recommendation of Arthur Maynwaring, and that when Steele was about to thank Harley, the Secretary of State said, "Pray, Sir, do not thank me, but thank Mr. Maynwaring." Afterwards, in his *Apology*, Steele spoke thus of his new occupation:—"His next appearance as a writer was in the quality of the lowest Minister of State—to wit, in the office of Gazetteer; where he worked faithfully according to order, without ever erring against the rule observed by all Ministries, to keep that paper very innocent and very insipid.[2] It is believed it was to the reproaches he heard every Gazette day against the writer of it that the defendant owes the fortitude of being remarkably negligent of what people say, which he does not deserve." The following letter[3] to "My Lord the Secretary," Lord Sunderland, dated May 10th, shows that the reproaches commenced very soon:—

May 10th, 1707.

My Lord

I presume to Acquaint Your Lordship that Mr Burchet[4] inform'd me he had Orders from the Prince[5] to attend your Lordship with a complaint against the Article from Ostend in the

[1] *Reliquiæ Hearnianæ*, 1857, p. 122.

[2] "No Gazetteer more innocent than I" (Pope's *Dunciad*, i. 215, quoted by Mr. Dobson). There is a fragment of a letter, without date, perhaps addressed to Lord Halifax, in which Steele speaks of the efforts he has made to increase the esteem of the *Gazette*.

My Lord,

I have for some time, according to the duty of my station, taken very particular notice of what reception the Gazettes and other papers have among the readers of those weekly histories, in order to raise the value of the paper written by authority, and lessen the esteem of the rest among the generality of the people; which I am almost confident to effect, if I may presume upon the following assistances: . . . .

[3] Blenheim MSS.

[4] Josias Burchet, Secretary to the Admiralty.

[5] Prince George of Denmark, Lord High Admiral.

last Gazette, where 'tis said a Fleet arriv'd to the Great Satisfaction and Advantage of the People there.[1]

This Article, it seems, is interpreted as an insinuation y^t^ they had not a Convoy in due time, and that their having a Safe One at last look'd like a matter of Extraordinary Good Fortune. All that I can say for myself is that I was directed to take notice of that Circumstance by Mr Addison at Your Lordship's Order and us'd Mr Stepny's[2] very Words tho' I made no such Apology when I was urg'd to know whence I had my Order or Advice, only in Generall acknowledg'd it a Great Misfortune to offend His Royal Highnesse, but said that as to the words Themselves I thought I should rather have gained approbation than displeasure.

There is a dissatisfaction also about ye late Sea-fight;[3] Mr Burchet indeed told me I had better stay till a further account but such as there was I might have at the Office, but it being Mr Hopkins's[4] and Mr Addison's Opinion that I had before stay'd too long, and that 'twould look as if the Government had a mind to stifle the Account, I went to the Admiralty and made a Relation from their Letters.

Your Lordship will please to pardon my taking this liberty of acquainting you with the matter before the Gentleman comes to you from His Royal Highnesse, tho' I beleive the Offence is taken much Lower. I shall look at such Impotent cavills with a great deal of Indifference while I beleive you think I have done my Duty, and promise my self your Lordship's protection in matters where an ill intention is forc'd upon expressions from an ill inclination in the Reader to, My Lord

Y^r^ Lordship's most devoted
Most obedient and
Most Humble Servant
RICH^D^ STEELE.

[1] *London Gazette*, May 5 to 8, 1707. "Ostende, May 12 [N. S.]. A Fleet of Merchant-ships that lay five Months in the Downes, consisting of Fifty-five Sail, arrived at Ostende this Evening, to the great Advantage and Satisfaction of this Place," &c. May the 1st was Thanksgiving Day for the Union between England and Scotland, and the *Gazette* for May 1 to 5, and following numbers, were chiefly filled with loyal addresses.

[2] George Stepney, poet and minister to Holland.

[3] In the *London Gazette*, May 5 to 8, 1707, there was an account of a fight off Beachy Head between H.M. ships *Royal Oak*, *Grafton*, and *Hampton Court*, with a large convoy, and a French squadron of nine men-of-war of the line, and many privateers. The result was disastrous to the English.

[4] Under Secretary of State with Addison.

Another instance of the reproaches of which Steele speaks is given in a letter from Henry Boyle to the Duke of Marlborough, dated December 14th, 1708;[1] "I am sorry that those passages were put into our Gazette that your Grace complains of in your letter of the 17th; whatever Mr Cardonnel has wrote to Mr Tilson against Mr Steel putting anything in the public news relating to the operations of your Grace's army except what came directly from your Grace's camp, was showed to him, and 'tis very strange that it has not had a better effect. . . . Now I hope there is care taken that the same error shall not be repeated." Two letters to Mr. Dawson show how Steele endeavoured to obtain news for the *Gazette*—news which would "make for the dignity or service of the Government."[2]

July 15th, 1707.
LD SUNDERLAND'S OFFICE,
WHITEHALL.

Sr

Having for some time since been appointed by the Secretaries of State to write the Gazette I have authority to use their names in desiring such intelligence as may be usefull or necessary to be inserted in that Paper. Tis upon this foundation that I take the liberty to desire you'de please to give me such notices from time to time of what passes in Ireland which may make for the dignity or service of the Government to be publish'd. If you have any commands of yr own to lay upon me which may entitle me to yr Friendship & correspondence you'le find me Sr

Yr most obedient Servant
RICHD STEELE.

Mr Dawson.

July 31st, 1707.
LD SUNDERLAND'S OFFICE,
WHITEHALL.

Sr

I acknowledge the honour of yours of the 24th instant, and shall be very glad of any occasion you will give me of improving

[1] Blenheim MSS.

[2] State Papers, Dublin, Queen Anne. Joshua Dawson was Secretary to the Lords Justices of Ireland. Swift mentions Dawson's office at the Castle in the *Journal to Stella*, October 14, 1710. Dawson provided largely for his relations out of his official patronage; and the Dawson MSS., including his correspondence with every member of his family, which he carefully registered and preserved, are still preserved at Dublin.

our correspondence so far as to give me opportunityes of doing anything agreeable to you Here, which you think may be within my power or sollicitation. When any thing offers immediately for the Gazette I hope you will write to me by the first. Our Eyes here are wholly turn'd on Toulon, we talk assuredly of it, but I beleive the whole depends on marching, and by our last Advices The Duke of Savoy and an Advance party of the Enemy were Equi distant from the place.

Yr Most Obedient Servt
RICHD STEELE.

Mr Dawson.

In Easter term, 1707—April 30 to May 26—the decision was given against Steele in two actions for debt in the Court of Common Pleas.[1] In the one case, Richard Steele, late of the Parish of St. Margaret, Westminster, Esq., was summoned to answer a plea put in by John Lund, who stated, by Charles Salkeld his attorney, that Steele borrowed of him on the 1st January 1707, at Westminster, £100 to be paid when requested; but he now refused to pay, and Lund claimed £10 damages. Steele appeared by his attorney, William Rolfe, but made no answer, and the Court awarded Lund 50s. damages. In the other case the complainant was Elizabeth Kelson, spinster, who stated, through her counsel, Charles Salkeld, that on the 16th May 1707, at Westminster, Steele acknowledged himself bound to her in the sum of £40; but he had not paid, and she claimed £10 damages. Steele's attorney, William Rolfe, had nothing to say in bar of the action, and Elizabeth Kelson was allowed 60s. damages. In this same term, also, Steele was, as we have seen, involved in an action brought against him by Christopher Rich.

On June 8th,[2] a month after Steele was made Gazetteer, his uncle Gascoigne died. A few particulars may be given of the life of Henry Gascoigne since we last heard of him in 1697. From the Overseers' Rate Books of the parish of St. Martin-in-the-Fields, it appears that from 1698 until his death Gascoigne lived in Bond Street, in the "Suffolk Street and outwards"

[1] Common Pleas Judgment Roll, Easter 6 Anne, 527. In the first case the attornies' names are reversed in the Roll, evidently by a clerical error.

[2] Warrant, Probate Court of Canterbury.

Ward. In the Books for 1698 and 1699 he is described as "Henry Gascoyne Esq[r]" and "Henry Gascogne Esq[r]," respectively, in the Books for 1700, 1701, 1702, 1703, and 1704, as "Henry Gaskin Esq[r]"—misspelt "Baskin" in 1702—and in the Books for 1705, 1706, and 1707, as "Esq[r] Gascoyne." The rate was 12d. in the pound in 1707, and the amount collected on the house varied from 16s. 8d. in 1698 to £1. 10s. 0d. in 1707; but in that year only 7s. 6d. was received, and there is a note "em. [? empty] 3 q[rs]." Gascoigne's next-door neighbour was Captain Chumley, and among the other fashionable inhabitants of what was then "a fine new street, mostly inhabited by Nobility and Gentry,"[1] were Captain Moor, Lord Coningsby, the Hon. Mr. Moor, Sir John Wentworth, Lady Clifford, Captain Pulteney, the Duke of Southampton, Lady Christian Geary, the Earl of Abingdon, and the Countess of Cleveland. A son and a daughter were born to Henry Gascoigne in 1700 and 1701 respectively, and from the entries of their baptisms in the Registers of St. Martin's-in-the-Fields we learn that the name of Gascoigne's wife, the sister of one of Steele's parents, was Dorothy.

> 1700. Apr. 28. Robert son of Henry and Dorothy Gascoigne. born 11th.
>
> 1701. March 30. Katherine daughter of Henry and Dorothy Gascoigne. born 28th.

Of these children we hear no more; they must have died before their father, but there is no mention of their burial in the St. Martin's Registers, or of the burial of their mother, which also must have been before 1707. The name Gascoigne is of frequent occurrence in the Registers throughout the seventeenth century and the first half of the eighteenth century, and notices of Gascoignes are also to be found in the Registers of St. Giles-in-the-Fields.[2]

[1] Hatton's *New View of London*, 1708, p. 10.

[2] I have taken the following from Colonel Chester's transcript of the Registers of St. Martin's-in-the-Fields. *Burials.*—1672, Apr. 11, —— Gascoine, Pu[er]; 167⅔, March 10, James Gascoigne, puer; 1673, May 30, Henry Gascoigne, puer;

Henry Gascoigne appears to have given up his position as secretary to the Duke of Ormond about 1701, when he was succeeded by Sir Henry Walker, son of Sir Edward Walker, Garter King-at-arms.[1] The following letter, now first published, shows that in 1703 Gascoigne was in distress, owing to his pension not having been paid for seven quarters. The letter is addressed "For the Rt Honble Mr Secry Southwell" (Principal Secretary of State in Ireland) "From Mr Gascoigne."[2]

Hd Sr

I am hartily sorry I am forced to give you such frequent trouble for want of money which I was in hopes to have before now out of the pension of 50l which his Grace gave me two yeares ago & of which there are seven quarters unpayd. If his Grace should go his progresse without ordering mee some during his Absence I shalbe in a most Miserable condition the Money I borrowed for my Journey hither being spent & the hope I had of im̃ediate Imployment on my

$16\frac{79}{80}$, March 14, James Gasquin; $168\frac{5}{6}$, Feb. 10, Joel Gascoin, child; 1689, May 15, Margaret Gascoin, a maid; $171\frac{0}{1}$, March 24, John Gascoyn, C[hild]; $171\frac{7}{8}$, Feb. 5, Robert Gascoyne, man; $171\frac{7}{8}$, Feb. 7, Ambrose Gascoyne, man; $172\frac{4}{5}$, Feb. 4, Anne Gascoigne, woman; 1728, Sep. 5, Joseph Gascoigne, Esq., man; 1731, Apr. 3, Mary Gascoigne, woman. *Marriages.*—1621, Sep. 16, Humphrey Goring and Elizabeth Gascoine, Banns; $162\frac{6}{7}$, March 3, William Speede Gent. and Jane Gaskin widow, Lic[ence]. *Baptisms.*—1670, Apr. 5, John, son of John and Dorothy Gascoine, born 25 March; 1672, May 1, Mary, daughter of do., born 28 April; 1674, Oct. 9, William, son of Richard and Alice Gascoigne, born 8th; 1684, Nov. 23, Joel, son of James and Hanna Gasgoin, born 13th; 1703, June 12, William, son of William and Anne Gascoigne, born 10th; 1719, Aug. 22, Anne, daughter of Henry and Anne Gascoigne, born 18th. A Robert Gascoyn was living (Overseers' Rate Books) in Neathouses, Knightsbridge, in 1705, 1706, and 1707. The following are among the Burials at St. Giles-in-the-Fields:—$169\frac{8}{9}$, Feb. 9, Sir Thomas Gascoyne, card away; 1721, Dec. 20, Madam Gascoigne; $172\frac{1}{2}$, Jan. 15, Margaret, daughter of Oliver Gascoigne. This Sir Thomas Gascoyne Bart. was, it appears from his Will (P.C.C. 201 Pett), of Parlington, Yorkshire. A pedigree of the Gascoignes of Gawthorpe and Parlington will be found in Foster's *Pedigrees of County Families of Yorkshire*, vol. i. Worsley and Bateman—the names of the cousins who administered to Henry Gascoigne's goods—are also well-known names in the south-west of Yorkshire, and it is probable that the Irish branch of the Gascoignes came originally from that county.

[1] In November 1886 a quantity of correspondence written by and addressed to Sir Henry Walker as secretary to the Duke of Ormond was sold at Messrs. Sotheby's rooms. The earliest letters were dated 1702.

[2] Add. MS. 21137, f. 9.

Arrivall here diverted another way. I pray be pleased to consider my Condition at present & be instant with his Grace for a speed Recruit for H^d S^r

Y^r unfortunate & most humble Servt

H. GASCOIGNE.

25 June 1703.

The Duke of Ormond, as Lord-Lieutenant, left Dublin on the 28th June to review the forces in Ireland in their several quarters; he returned from his progress on the 20th July, "great respect having been paid him in all the places thro' which he passed."[1] Whatever arrears of pension were owing to Gascoigne, he must have had good means to enable him to keep up the house in Bond Street. He retained his position as Keeper of the Records in the Birmingham Tower, Dublin Castle, Chief Chamberlain of the Irish Exchequer, and Joint Clerk of the Accatry until his death.[2] We know nothing more of the interval between 1703 and 1707. For the following entry from the Register of burials of St. Martin's I am indebted to the Rev. F. C. Paul:—"June 11, 1707. Henry Gascoigne Esq. M." On the 23rd June commission was granted to John Bateman and Blanch Worsley, wife of Evan Worsley, cousins on the mother's side of Henry Gascoigne, late of the parish of St. Martin-in-the-Fields, Co. Middlesex, widower, to administer to his goods; Jane Edwards, aunt on the father's side (*amita*), and nearest of blood to Henry Gascoigne, having, as we learn from the warrant, renounced;[3] and on the 10th September a similar commission was granted in Dublin to administer to the goods of Henry Gascoigne, Esqre.[4] In the entry of the Dublin grant John Bateman is described as "of the City of London, baker" (*pistori*). Steele

[1] *London Gazette* for June 28 to July 1, and July 29 to August 2, 1703.

[2] John Bourne succeeded "Gascoigne dec^d" on the 17th June 1707, as Chief Chamberlain, and Wm. King, LL.D., succeeded "Gascoigne dec^d" on the 19th June 1707 as Keeper of the Records in the Birmingham Tower (*Liber Mun. Public. Hiberniæ*, Part II. pp. 61, 78). The warrant appointing John Price to the place of Joint Clerk of the Accatry, "vacant by ye death of Henry Gascoigne," is dated 11th June 1707 (Lord Steward's Books).

[3] Probate Court of Canterbury.

[4] Public Record Office, Dublin.

spoke of him, four years later, as a poor man, with a numerous family, "the nearest of blood to my uncle Gascoigne."[1]

In August 1707, Steele, by power of attorney, authorised Thomas Beckles, Esq., brother-in-law of his late wife, to act as his agent in the management of the Barbados estates. The original of the following document is among the Public Records in Barbados. It is marked "Entred this 20th of Novembr 1707:"—

By this Publick Instrument of Procuration or Letter of Attorney Bee it known and manifest unto all people that on the sixteenth day of August Anno Dom. 1707 and in the sixth year of the reign of Anne Queen of England &c. before me William Smyth Notary Publick dwelling in London personally appeared Richard Steel of the parish of St Annes Westminster[2] in the County of Middlesex Esquire and hath lawfully constituted and authorized and by these Presents doth make nominate constitute and authorize Thomas Beckles of Bridgetown in the Island of Barbados Esqre his true and lawfull Attorney for and in the name and to the use of the said constituent to act in all and every his matters and bisiness in the island of Barbados aforesaid that is to say to cultivate order regulate and improve all and every his Plantations and to inspect govern and direct all and every the Agents servants and persons employed or to be employed on the same or in every or in any house outhouses edifices or buildings belonging to the same plantations also for and in the name of the said constituent and to his use to receive all and all manner of debts moneys rents duties and demands whatsoever ariseing due or payable from any person or persons to him in any manner of wise whatsoever in the said Island of Barbados or elsewhere in America and to the ends aforesaid making any distresse or distresses for rent and the same to seize drive or carry away and also sue attach imprison implead and prosecute and out of prison to deliver and generally in and about the premises to do say and accomplish whatsoever shall be further needfull and convenient as fully and effectually as the said Constituent himself might or could do personally Promising to hold for good and vallid whatsoever shall be lawfully done in the premises by virtue of these Presents. Thus done the day witnesses and year aforsd

Dan. Chandler
Wm Brookhouse

RICHARD STEELE (L.S.).

[1] Letters to Mr. Keally, April 2 and July 26, 1711.

[2] It is evident that Steele moved several times in the years 1706, 1707.

In Testimonium veritatis,
J. Smith, Not^{rius} Publicus.

To all that shall see these Presents or hear them read Wee Sir Robert F Bedingfield K^{nt} Lord Major and the Aldermen of the City of London doe hereby make known and certifie that Richard Steel mentioned in the aforewritten Letter of Attorney did now before us in Court sign seal and as his act and deed deliver the said Letter of Attorney to and for the uses intents and purposes therein mentioned. In Faith and testimony whereof we have caused the seal of the Majoralty of this City to be hereunto put and affixed Dated the sixteenth day of August Anno Dom. 1707 and in the sixth year of the Reign of Anne Queen of Great Brittain.

GIBSON.

Lord Mayor Seale.

Barbados.

By His Excellency

I doe allowe of this Instrument of writting and and [*sic*] doe hereby declare my allowance thereof . . .[1] to the end the same may be recorded in the Secry's Office and take it is full force & effect. Given att Pilgrim this 20th day of November 1707.

M CROWE.

[1] Original torn.

III.

MARRIAGE WITH MARY SCURLOCK.

1707–1708. ÆT. 35–36.

IN the summer of 1707 Steele was courting Miss, or Mrs. Scurlock—to use the term given in those days to all grown-up ladies[1]—who was, as we have seen, a friend of his former wife. Miss Mary Scurlock was sole heiress to Jonathan Scurlock, of Carmarthenshire, who died in 1682. Jonathan Scurlock was descended from an ancient and honourable Irish family, and after studying at Trinity College, Cambridge, turned his attention to the law, and became a justice of the peace, an alderman, and, in 1678, sheriff for the borough of Carmarthen. Miss Scurlock's mother, Mrs. Elizabeth Scurlock, was still living at Carmarthen. The estate was worth £400 a year, but as there was a demand of £1400 upon it,[2] the net amount derived from it would be be about £330 a year.

The following inscription to Jonathan Scurlock is on a tablet high on the chancel wall in St. Peter's Church, Carmarthen :[3]—

[1] "Let no woman after the known age of twenty-one presume to admit of her being called Miss, unless she can fairly prove she is not out of her sampler" (C. Lillie's *Original and Genuine Letters sent to the Tatler and Spectator*, 1725, i. 224). "Being arrived at sixteen, I have left the boarding-school, and now having assumed the title of Madam instead of Miss, am come home" (Ib. ii. 156).

[2] See page 190.

[3] "On a pane of black marble, in letters of gold" (*An Account of the Progress of his Grace Henry the first Duke of Beaufort through Wales*, 1684. By T. Dineley. Edited by C. Baker. Privately printed, 1864.) See, too, Spurrell's *Carmarthen and its Neighbourhood*, 2nd edition, 1879, pp. 190–1. Nichols (*Epist. Corr. of Sir R. Steele*, 1809, p. 505) gave a translation of this inscription which is incomplete and inaccurate as regards the dates, and which omits all reference to the Irish origin of the family. He states that it was

"P.S. Juxta conditæ sunt Exuviæ Viri ornatissimi, Jonathanis Scurlock, Armigeri, Hibernica Prosapiâ oriundi, Antiquâ illâ Ac perquàm Honestâ, Qui postquam studijs Academicis in S.S. Trinitatis Collegio, Apud Cantabrigienses, dein Juri Municipali In Hospitio (quod vocant Grayes' Inne[1]) Apud Londinates, Non infælicem navâsset operam, In Comitatu Maridunensi Irenarchæ Provinciā Summa cum laude administravit, Hominis verè Christiani omnes numeros implens, Sive Pietatem in Deum, In Parentes Officium, Amorem in Conjugem, In Egenos Liberalitatem, Sivè deniq. in omnes Benevolentiam Spectes; Fato sibi quidem fælici, suis autem luctuoso præreptus. Pijssimam efflavit Animam XVII Calend. Quintilis Anno Æræ Christianæ CIƆDCLXXXII. Ætatis suæ XXVII." In a Table of the Pious Benefactors to this Corporation,[2] in the Vestry, it is recorded that "Jonathan Scurlock, Esqr gave by his Will, Jvne ye 15th, 1682, 20 Shillgs yearly, 10 Shills for a Sermon vpon St. Peter's Day, & 10 Shills to ye poore in bread ye same day," and in a Table of Pious Benefactors to ys Town (about 1719), in the South Porch, we find "John Scurlock of Blaencorse, Esqr gave 10 shillings for a Sermon on St. John the Evangelist's day, and 8 shillings for bread to be distributed to ye poor on ye same day for ever." The vault of the Scurlocks bears the inscription, on a broken flagstone, under the encaustic tiles, "Jonathan Scurlock, of Blaencorse, 1683, and John, his brother, 1715."[3]

There were Scurlages in Wales in very early times. A Sir Herbert Scurlage, of Norman or Flemish stock, is said to have inherited from his father Scurlage Castle and Kilicura, all in Gowerland, Glamorganshire; and to his great-grandson, William, about 1250, Richard, Earl of Clare, granted a manor, no doubt that known as Scurla' Castle, or Trecastle, near Llantrissant,

Steele who had the tablet erected. The Rev. A. G. Edwards, now Bishop of St. Asaph, was good enough to take considerable trouble in having the monument cleaned, in order to verify for me the inscription, and to correct some misprints in previous versions.

[1] Admitted 29th April 1675 (Harl. MS., 1912). Mr. Douthwaite informs me that in the Register of Gray's Inn (p. 1265) Jonathan Scurlock is described as son and heir-apparent of John Scurlock of Carmarthen, alderman.

[2] Spurrell's *Carmarthen*, 203, 204. [3] *Ibid.* 39, 199.

where the grantee appears to have built a strong house, of which some traces still remain. The grant was made in order that William Scurlage might be in a position to "curb the natives." Passing over three generations we come to Philip Scurlage, who married Mariota, daughter of Sir Richard Stackpole, and had a daughter and heiress, Lucy, who married Richard Mansel of Penrice; through their son, Sir Hugh Mansel, the Castle passed to the Mansel family. William de Scurlog migrated to Ireland in, it is said, 1184, and founded a branch of the family in that country.[1] The arms of the old Welsh family were "argent three bars gules,"[2] and these arms were evidently afterwards used by the Scurlocks, who settled at Carmarthen in the seventeenth century, because Steele adopted them as an escutcheon of pretence.

The name Scurlog became well known in Ireland. In the thirteenth century we find Scurlags in Cork and Kildare. In 1285 Maurice Scurlag or Scurlack was constable of Dublin Castle and Keeper of Randown Castle. In 1302–6 the ecclesiastical taxation of the Church de Scurlog, County Meath, was £7. 5s. 8d.[3] The principal branch of the family appears to have resided in Meath; there is still a parish in that county called Scurlagestown, near Trim; and there is a village of the same name near Kells, in the parish of Burry.[4] There was a principal family of the name in County Dublin between the English invasion of Ireland and the end of Henry VIII.'s reign.[5]

[1] The above statements, taken chiefly from the Golden Grove MSS., are given in *Limbus Patrum Morganiæ et Glamorganiæ*, by George T. Clark, Esq., of Talygarn, 1886, pp. 502–3. Mr. G. T. Clark has kindly furnished me with some particulars not given in his book. See, too, *Annals and Antiquities of the Counties and County Families of Wales*, by Thomas Nicholas, 1875, pp. 513, 571.

[2] Papworth's *Ordinary of British Armorials*, Records in Heralds' College.

[3] Calendar of State Papers, Irish Series (Record Office), 1171–1251, p. 468; 1252–1284, pp. 310, 394, 427–8; 1285–1292, pp. 67, 121, 370; 1293–1301, p. 263; 1302–1307, pp. 256, 265.

[4] See Swift's *Journal to Stella*, February 21, 1710–11.

[5] Trinity College, Dublin, MS. Vols. F. 3. 23, F. 3. 27, F. 4. 18, quoted in O'Hart's *Irish Pedigrees*, 3rd ed., 1881, p. 691. Martin Scurlock, of Rathcridan, Co. Dublin, who was buried in 1599, had issue Patrick, Barnaby, James, Mary, and Rose (Irish Funeral Certificates, in Herald's College). The names Scurlock, Scurlog, are found in a list of principal families in Ireland at the end of the seventeenth century (O'Hart, 699).

Captain Oliver Scurlock served with the Irish at the siege of Boulogne in 1544, and his son, Aristotle Scurlock, was Physician to Queen Mary, and had from her Rosslan Manor, Co. Wexford.[1] In 1553 Gerald Fay conveyed by deed to Barnaby Scurlock of Becktiffe the fee of his estate at Otterstown in Meath, in exchange for Scurlock's lands of Martinstown, &c., and at the same time he gave Scurlock an annuity of £4. 13s. 4d. a year.[2] James, Earl of Desmond, in a letter dated December 15, 1551, appointed Barnaby Scurlock, being well learned, after the holidays to hear, examine, and determine all manner of causes within the liberty of Kerry. Barnaby Scurlock, of Bectiffe, Co. Meath, was appointed Attorney-General in 1554, and held the post until his death in 1559.[3] A few years later, in December 1567, the collection of matters found against the Earl of Desmond and his brother was delivered to Patrick Scurlock, who made a declaration to the Lord Deputy in 1573.[4] In 1577 Patrick Scurlock was among those who represented the County of Kilkenny on the question of cess; and in the following year he was Sheriff of Co. Kilkenny.[5] In 1575 Barnaby Scurlock, who had married a daughter of Mr. Justice Plunket, was temporary Chief Justice in Ireland. In 1576 he was reported to be somewhat aged and sickly; but in the following year he was one of a deputation to the Queen, sent to complain on behalf of the Lords of the Pale of the burden of cess. The members of the deputation were imprisoned in the Fleet for saying that cess was contrary to the ancient law and customs of Ireland, but upon submission they were discharged. We find Barnaby afterwards sending his son without licence to obtain a confirmation or regrant of Scurlockstown and Ifernack.[6] Among the "burgesses taken into protection by Sir William Winter to help building the toune again"—

[1] *Limbus Patrum Morganiæ et Glamorganiæ*, by G. T. Clark, pp. 502–3.

[2] *Illustrations, Historical and Genealogical, of King James's Irish Army List* (1689), by John D'Alton, Esq., 2nd ed., Dublin, 1860, i. 339.

[3] *Liber Mun. Pub. Hiberniæ*, Part II.; Carew MSS., Calendar, 1515–1574, p. 288; 1575–1588, p. 480.

[4] Calendar of State Papers, Irish Series, 1509–1573, pp. 121, 193, 360.

[5] Carew MSS., Calendar, 1575–1588, p. 141.

[6] Calendar of State Papers, Irish Series, 1574–1585, pp. 54, 102, 110, 114, 115, 117, 122, 123, 128, 513; Carew MSS., Calendar, 1575–1588, p. 57, 58, 61, 76, 80, 83, 106.

Dingle, Co. Kerry—in 1580, were Teraunts and Skurlockes; "Governor Trant" was Governor of Dingle.[1] In 1581 a Robert Scurlock, persisting in Romish doctrines, was executed for treason; three years later certain attainted lands were granted to Peter Scurloke.[2] In 1606 Walter Scurlock was His Majesty's attorney in Connaught; in 1609 "Walter Skourlock, of the Frayne," is entered under Meath in the commission of surrenders and sales of land; two years later he was a commissioner for compositions, as well as attorney of Connaught; but in 1613 he was to be removed if he would not sign the oath of supremacy.[3] In April 1622, Barnaby Scurlock surrendered his castle and manor, and a new grant was made.[4] Many Scurlocks are mentioned in inquisitions held in the counties of Dublin, Kildare, Louth, Meath, Westmeath, and Wexford during the reigns of Elizabeth, James I., and Charles I., and of these one, Edmund Scurlock, of Frayne, an Irish papist, forfeited his estates in October 1641.[5] Ludlow tells us that in 1651 "Sir Walter Dungan, Commissary General of the enemy's horse, and Capt. Scurlock, a forward officer, and one who had done us much mischief, with five hundred foot and two hundred and fifty horse, marched into Wexford with a design to plunder that county." But on their return they were routed "after some dispute," 200 being killed, besides divers officers, and the booty was all recovered.[6]

There were several Scurlocks among the forfeiting proprietors

[1] *Misc. Genealogica et Heraldica*, New Series, ii. 260.

[2] State Papers, Irish Series, Calendar, 1574-1585, pp. 126, 324, 329, 353, 355, 370, 510. See, too, Carew MSS., Calendar, 1575–1588, p. 128; 1603–1624, p. 337.

[3] Calendar of State Papers, Irish Series, 1603–1606, p. 432; 1608–1610, p. 324; 1611–1614, pp. 115, 138, 382; Carew MSS., Calendar, 1603–1604, p. 184. Charles O'More, who settled in Kildare, married, in 1600, the daughter of Walter Scurlog of County Meath (D'Alton's *Illustrations of King James's Irish Army List*, 2nd ed., ii. 609).

[4] State Papers, Irish Series, Calendar, 1615–1625, p. 349.

[5] *Inquisitionum in officio Rotulorum Cancellariæ Hiberniæ asservatorum Repertorium*, Vol. I. Printed by command. 1826. Folio.

[6] Ludlow's *Memoirs* (1721), i. 408. In a MS. in Trinity College, Dublin (now printed by Mr. Gilbert), called "Aphorismical Discovery of Treasonable Faction," Book V., chap. i. (1651), 699, we are told that "Captain Scurlage went with his troupe to the enemie," and there is a marginal note, "Captain Scurlage revoulted."

under the Cromwellian Settlement,[1] but if we follow the Golden Grove MSS., we must assume that the founder of the Carmarthenshire family—John Scurlag—went over to Wales some years earlier, and that his grandson was the John Scurlock who bought property in Carmarthenshire about 1653, and had a son Jonathan, who is described as of an ancient and honourable Irish family, and who was father to Mary, afterwards Lady Steele. In a letter to Steele, dated May 25, 1713, John Scurlock, Lady Steele's uncle, says that his father bought "Pibur (an estate of 80*l.* a year)" about sixty years ago. In 1656, when Thomas Lloyd, of Llanllawddog, was High Sheriff for the County, John Scurlock was the principal of the two sheriffs for the county borough of Carmarthen; in 1665 he was Mayor of Carmarthen; in 1668 he was Deputy Mayor under John Vaughan, of Court Derllys, and in 1677 he was High Sheriff for the County. In the following year he died; "Johannes Scurlock, armiger," being buried on the 21st April 1678, at St. Peter's Church.[2] His effects were administered to by his widow, Mary Scurlock, 12th May 1679.[3] The Inventory, taken on the 14th May 1678, amounted to £246. 8s. 8d. Mary Scurlock's bondsmen were (1) Jona. Scurlock (or Jonathan, as it is given in the body of the bond), her eldest son; (2) John Morris, of the town of Cardigan, Attorney-at-law (he had married a Margaret Scurlock, at St. Peter's, on the 9th November 1675); and (3) Martyn Beynon, of the Co. Borough of Carmarthen, Mary Scurlock's son-in-law. The witnesses to the bond were Matt. Davis, Thomas Powell,[4] and Lod. Powell.[5]

[1] O'Hart's *The Irish and Anglo-Irish Landed Gentry when Cromwell came to Ireland*, 1884. A "Remonstrance of the Roman Catholic Nobility and Gentry of Ireland," 1661, was signed by Lieutenant Colonel Thomas Scurlog (D'Alton's *Illustrations of King James's Irish Army List*, 2nd ed., i. 6.

[2] The Registers of St. Peter's Church do not go back beyond 1670, and there is no transcript of earlier Registers in the Diocesan Registry.

[3] This Administration of 1679 appears to be the first reference to the Scurlocks in the Indexes at Carmarthen.

[4] Sir Thomas Powell, Bart., was son of Sir John Powell, Bart., one of the judges at the trial of the seven bishops. Sir John died in 1696. Sir Thomas Powell was M.P. for Carmarthenshire, and married Elizabeth, daughter of Thomas Mansel, of Briton Ferry; she died in 1697; and Sir Thomas died in 1720, aged 56. Copies of the family inscription in Laugharne Church are given in Spurrell's *Carmarthen*, p. 85.

[5] According to the Index at the Carmarthen Office an administration was

Mary Scurlock, widow of John Scurlock, lived until 1699, surviving her eldest son, Jonathan. Her will, which is dated 11th February 1696, was proved the 7th August 1699, before John Bevan, Surrogate; the witnesses were John Ryder, Charles Richards, and Nathaniel Morgan;[1] the trustees, John Scurlock, her eldest surviving son; John Phillipps, her brother-in-law, and James Phillipps, her son-in-law. She mentions her daughters, Mary Scurlock and Elizabeth Beynon; Martyn Beynon,[2] alderman, her son-in-law; Elizabeth Scurlock, widow, her daughter-in-law, and her grand-daughter, Mary Scurlock—afterwards Steele's wife—to whom she left 20s. to buy a ring.[3] By a codicil, dated 23rd January 1698, she left to her daughter Mary, wife of Griffith Williams,[4] Esq., then Mayor of Carmarthen, and High Sheriff for the County—he had taken the place of George Lewis, Esq., who died in office—lands and tenements in Llangunnor parish, called Landye and Amyle-maur, which she had lately purchased, mortgaged, or leased from her daughter-in-law, Elizabeth Scurlock. She also left to her daughter Mary the property called Sanders Hill, or Ventrecill, in the Lower Franchise of the Borough of Carmarthen. The witnesses to the

taken out to a second John Scurlock, "Armigerus," in 1685. But there is no trace of the administration to be found among the papers for that or the following year; and probably the entry in the Index is due to some error.

[1] Mary Scurlock's nephew. Years afterwards an Edward Morgan was a suitor for the hand of Steele's daughter Elizabeth.

[2] A Thomas Beynon was Mayor of Carmarthen as early as 1558. Martyn Beynon's father, Thomas, was Mayor in 1664; his will is dated 1685. Martyn Beynon was made Mayor in 1688, and soon afterwards he was defendant in a suit about land in which Griffith Lloyd and Ann his wife were plaintiffs (Exchequer Depositions, Hilary 3 and 4 William and Mary, 14). For notices of the Beynons see Spurrell's *Carmarthen*, 119, 174–5, 190, 203.

[3] On a Table of Benefactors at St. Peter's Church, we find Mary Scurlock, who gave 20 shillings yearly for two sermons yearly, and 8 shillings to the poor in bread.

[4] The will of Griffith Williams, Esq., was proved 4th April 1699. He left his real estate in the County and in the County Borough of Carmarthen in trust to his brother-in-law, William Beynon, of Castle Gorvod, and his nephew, Rice Thomas, gentleman, to receive the profits and rents for his executrix, Mary Williams, and his son John, until his son was twenty-one. He gave to his brother-in-law, William Beynon, and to his sister, Hister Williams, 10s. each for a ring. The witnesses to the will were Jane Phillipps, Wm. Beynon, and Walter Jones.

codicil were David Meyrick,[1] John Jones, Polly Powell, and Griffith Williams. She left the will in the custody of her brother-in-law, John Phillipps, Esq.,[2] to whom she gave 20s. to buy a ring. On the 10th September 1700, this will had to be exhibited in a law-suit in the Court of Chancery at the suit of William Lloyd and Mary, his wife. This was the Mary whose first husband was Griffith Williams.

We can now turn to Jonathan, son of John and Mary Scurlock, who was born about 1655. On the third August 1677, Jonathan Scurlock and Elizabeth (the surname is not given[3]) were married at St. Peter's Church. In 1678 Jonathan Scurlock was an alderman and sheriff for the Borough of Carmarthen; and in that year his daughter Mary was born. There are two entries in the Church Registers, under "Nomina baptizatorum," as follows:—

Maria filia Jonathan Scurlock, gen. 5 Nob^{bris} 1678.
Maria filia Jonathan Scurlock, 17 Sept. 1680.

Now, we know that Mary was born on the 4th November,[4] and

[1] An Essex Meyricke wanted to marry Elizabeth Steele.

[2] John Phillipps was an attorney-at-law; in 1682 he was Deputy Sheriff for the County, and in 1685 Mayor of Carmarthen. He died in August 1730, aged 85; his wife Anne died in 1720, after having "ye comfortable satisfaction of seeing her 6 children married in ye same order they were born." The eldest son, James Phillipps, of Pentypark, was Mayor in 1708, and M.P. for Carmarthen from 1724 to 1727. He died in 1730, shortly after his father. The inscriptions in St. Peter's Church give full particulars of the family at that time (Spurrell's *Carmarthen*, 120-1, 176, 181-2, 189, 205). The will of John Phillipps (or Phillips, as it is in this case spelt), dated 25th July 1730, was proved at London, 6th November 1730 (PCC. 313 Auber). All his children are mentioned; also his brother James and wife; his uncle James and wife; his cousin, Erasmus Phillips; his nephew, Vaughan Phillips, and wife; his grandson, Robert Bowen; his brother-in law, William Thomas; three sons of Sir John Phillips, Bart., &c. The will of James Phillipps, of Pentypark, Co. Pembroke, was proved 16th February 1731. His property went to his only son James, with the exception of £200 to each of the children of his only daughter Mary (PCC. 43 Isham). The will is dated 19th November 1730 eight days before the testator's death. His son James was a suitor for the hand of Elizabeth Steele.

[3] "Stylt," or "Still," of Worcester, according to the Golden Grove MSS. Neither Mr. H. Sydney Grazebrook nor the Rev. T. P. Wadley, authorities upon questions of Worcestershire genealogy, have been able to give me any information of Stills of Worcestershire; but there were Stills in Gloucestershire soon after the Restoration.

[4] Page 201.

in all probability she was christened on the day after birth, owing to a fear that she would not live, and was then not baptized at church until 1680. Jonathan died, as we have seen, in 1682; his burial is thus recorded in the Register: "Jonathan Scurlock, armiger, 19 Junii 1682." His will is dated 15th June 1682, two days before his death, and for signature there is only a mark, probably meant for "J." By it he charged his lands and tenements in Llangunnor parish with 30s. per annum, for the poor there and for the poor of Carmarthen—10s. each, the remaining 10s. to go to the vicar of St. Peter's annually for preaching a sermon. He appointed his wife executrix, and made her guardian with his brother-in-law, Martyn Beynon, of his beloved daughter, Mary Scurlock. To his brother John he gave his cellar on the Quay in Carmarthen. His inventory of goods and chattels was valued at about £400. The name of his wife, Elizabeth Scurlock, then a widow, is given in the Surrogate's fiat attached to the inventory.

Some light is thrown on the question of the position of the Scurlocks by the proceedings in a Chancery suit of 1685-7, brought by Evan Harries against Elizabeth Scurlock, widow, and executrix of Jonathan Scurlock, who administered to the property of John Scurlock, his father; Mary Scurlock, an infant [afterwards Lady Steele]; Mary Scurlock, widow, relict of John Scurlock; William Davies; Theophilus Bevan, &c.[1] The evidence largely related to the question of the property left by John and Jonathan Scurlock respectively; to money borrowed by John Scurlock, and to efforts made by his son Jonathan to pay off debts owing to Rice Jones, William Lloyd, Griffith Phillipps, and William Davies. Harries said that he had a real estate of £200 a year, and that he had contracted with Sir Ralph Banks, Knt., for the purchase of a manor worth £350 a year, which purchase was taken in the name of John Jefferys, Esq., who paid down part of the purchase money on behalf of John Scurlock, who, however, could redeem the property upon payment of £2000. In 1676 Harries became bound with Scurlock for the repayment of money Scurlock borrowed; and before the

[1] Mitford VI. Depositions, bef. 1714, No. 642; Chancery Decrees, 1686 A. 1153; 1687 A. 1196.

money was repaid John Scurlock died, leaving a real estate of £640 and a personal estate of £1200. The real estate went to Jonathan Scurlock, who paid Jefferys the £2000 redemption money. Martyn Beynon said that Elizabeth Scurlock brought to her husband Jonathan a fortune of £2300, of which £2000 was applied to the redemption of the estate bought from Sir R. Banks; and that estate, together with lands called White House (Tygwyn) and Pibur Lloyd, were settled by Jonathan in jointure upon his wife. When Jonathan died, leaving one child, Mary, aged six, he owed about £1300 (independent of the mortgage of £500 upon Pibur Lloyd), and the inventory of his goods amounted to about £512. Harries said that Elizabeth Scurlock, upon her husband's death, possessed herself of his personal estate of £700, and a real estate of £300. In her reply Elizabeth said that John Scurlock, before his purchase from Sir R. Banks, had a real estate worth about £125. 8s. 4d. a year, and that the lands which he purchased were but of the value of £227. 5s. 10d. a year. Lord Vaughan owed him £200, and he agreed to purchase a tenement of him of £55 a year, called Pibur Lloyd, which, with the £200 debt, cost £900; but Scurlock was forced to mortgage it and other lands. All the personal estate of John Scurlock which came to his son was but £450; and Elizabeth paid off her husband's debts of £522. The judgment was long, and Elizabeth Scurlock does not seem to have shown any readiness to obey the orders of the court.

Jonathan Scurlock had several sisters, and one brother, John, whose children are frequently mentioned in Steele's private correspondence. Of these relatives of Steele's wife fuller particulars can be given when occasion arises; but it will be convenient in this place to insert for ready reference a pedigree of the family, which is now worked out for the first time, and which, from the John Scurlock who died in 1678 downwards, is based wholly upon the authentic information furnished by wills, church registers, monumental inscriptions, and the like. The fact that Jonathan Scurlock was the eldest son of John and Mary Scurlock—established by the entry in the Gray's Inn Register already noticed—is corroborated by the Pleadings in a Chancery suit entered into in 1692 by Elizabeth Scurlock, widow, against Rowland Phillipps, infant, whose mother and guardian was Frances Phillipps.[1] The action was about land called Pibur, with meadows "Morva Rhodwig" and "Morva Mawr," which was said to have belonged to John Scurlock, alderman, from whom it descended to his *eldest* son, Jonathan. In the complainant's Bill it is stated that the Scurlocks had enjoyed this land for *sixty years and upwards,* without interruption from Sir John Stepney, Bart., or his ancestors. In the reply the defendant said his grandfather, Rowland Phillipps, bought the property from Sir John Stepney. The "sixty years and upwards" is evidently an exaggeration, and is no valid argument against the supposition that these Scurlocks came over from Ireland about 1653; as we have seen, John Scurlock, writing in 1713, said his father bought Pibur sixty years before that date.

The earliest letters we have from Steele to Miss Scurlock are supposed to have been written in August 1707, and the marriage seems to have taken place on the 9th September following. Steele's wife treasured up the letters and notes she received from her husband, and for the next eleven years we have a record of events, passing troubles, successes, hopes and fears, such as cannot be paralleled in all literature. Swift's *Journal* is to some extent a similar unfolding of private thoughts and feelings, but Steele was entirely exempt from the limitations imposed upon Swift by his relations towards his correspondents. In judging of these letters it must be remembered that they were meant only for a wife's eye. In one of the earliest in the series Steele said expressly: "I beg of you to show my letters to no one living, but let us be contented with one another's thoughts upon our words and actions without the intervention of other people, who cannot judge of so delicate a circumstance

[1] Chancery Pleadings, Bridges III. B. and A., before 1714, No. 300. The Phillips, Meyrick, Morgan, Griffiths, Bevan, Lloyd, and other families to which allusion has been made, were often involved in litigation at the beginning of the century, and further particulars of their connections and property may be gleaned from the Exchequer Bills and Answers, Anne, Carmarthen, at the Record Office. See, for example, Nos. 1, 4, 14, 28. In 1677 there was a Chancery suit about some water mills between the Lloyds and Scurlocks (Chancery Pleadings, Bridges IV. before 1714, No. 515).

SCURLOCKS OF CARMARTHEN.

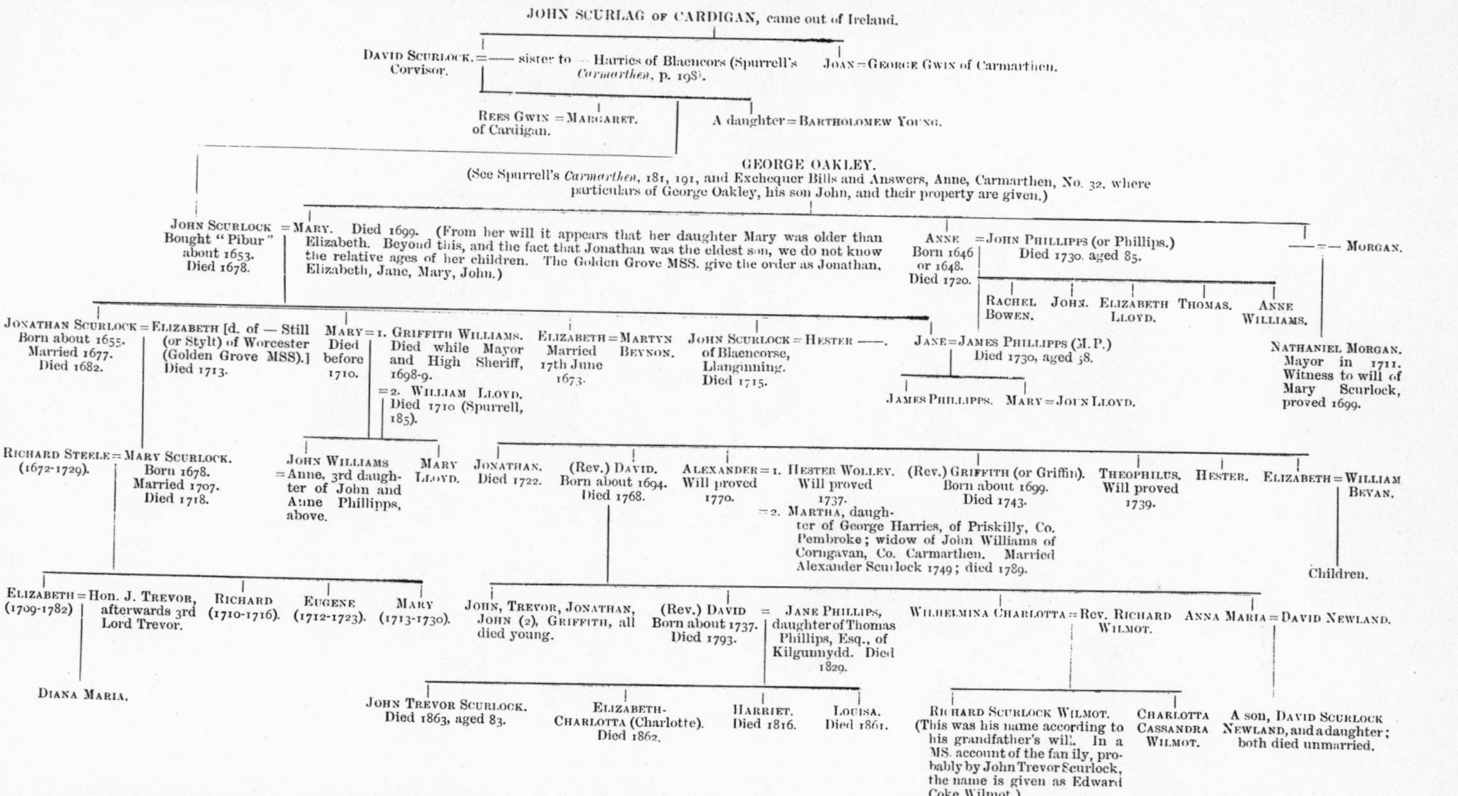

NOTE.—On March 22, 168$\frac{8}{9}$, upon the application of William Thomas, of St. Paul's, Covent Garden, a licence of marriage was granted at the Vicar-General's Office to Ismael Thomas, of Carmarthen, aged about 30, bachelor, and Jane Scurlock, aged 21 and upwards, her father being dead.

The following are mentioned in the Registers of St. Peter's, Carmarthen: Mary Scurlock, died 5th Sept. 1681; David Scurlock, buried 15th June 1682; Mary, daughter of John Scurlock, baptized 3rd Jan. 1688.

In the Golden Grove MSS. (Record Office), which are supposed to have been compiled early in the eighteenth century by Hugh Thomas, Deputy Herald to the Garter King of Arms in 1703, there are two Scurlag pedigrees (Vol. I. C. Glamorgan, 265, and Vol. II. Advenae G, 62–3). In the first of these the marriage of Steele with a daughter of *John* has been erroneously inserted in a later handwriting, believed to be that of Theophilus Jones; no note is added to the "daughter and sole heiress" of *Jonathan*, whom Steele did marry.

To follow page 172, Vol. I.]

as the commerce between man and wife." But, notwithstanding this, the whole series of 400 notes was published in 1787, without any suppressions, by John Nichols, who purchased the originals from Mr. Scurlock, next of kin to Steele's daughter, Lady Trevor, who had received them from her mother.[1] Steele himself, it should be remembered, published some of these letters in the *Tatler* (No. 35) and *Spectator* (No. 142). Few men's character and innermost life have been exposed to anything approaching such a searching scrutiny, and very few could have passed through the ordeal with the honour that attaches to Steele. The marriage was one of affection, and it remained so on both sides until the end. There were, of course, defects of character in each; it would be absurd to contend that Steele was not faulty in many ways, and the faults were such as are seen most easily, especially by those who read to prove to their own satisfaction that the noblest of men fall short even as they; but the great fact remains that during all the years of married life Steele retained his affection for his wife unimpaired. At the end she was still his "dear Prue" and "dear Wife;" and when we remember the expressions of ridicule respecting marriage which were then prevalent, we can only wonder at the perfect frankness and union and purity which pervade these letters.

The series begins with letters conjecturally put down as being written in August; the day of the month has been cut out from several of them. It will be remembered that "Mrs." Scurlock was, according to Mrs. Manley's testimony, a "cried up beauty."

1707.[2]

MADAM

Your wit and Beauty are Suggestions which may easily lead You into the intention of my Writing to You. You may be sure that I cannot be cold to so many Good Qualities as all that See you must

[1] Nichols afterwards presented the MSS. to the British Museum. They now form Add. MSS. 5145 A, B, and C; and whenever in these volumes no special authority is given for a letter, it is to be understood that the original is in this collection. The letters I have printed from this correspondence have been freshly collated with the MSS.

[2] Dated August 9 by Nichols.

observe in You. You are a woman of a very Good Understanding, and will not measure thoughts by any ardour in my expressions, which is the Ordinary Language on these occasions.

I have reasons for hiding from my nearest relation [1] any purpose I may have resolv'd upon of Waiting on You if You permit it, and I hope you have confidence from mine as well as Your own Character that such a condescension should not be ill us'd by, Madam,

Yr Most Obdent Servnt

R: STEELE.

1707.[2]

MADAM [3]

I Writ to You on Saturday by Mrs. Warren, and give you this trouble to Urge the same request I made then, which was that I may be admitted to wait upon You. I should be very far from desiring this if it were a Transgression of the most severe rules to allow it; I know you are very much above the little Arts which are frequent in your sex of giving unnecessary torment to their Admirers; therefore hope you'le do so much Justice to the Generous passion I have for You, as to let me have an opportunity of acquainting yu upon what motives I pretend to your Good opinion. I shall not trouble you with my Sentiments till I know how they will be receiv'd, and as I know no reason why difference of Sex should make our Language to each other differ from the ordinary rules of right reason, I shall affect plainnesse and sincerity in my discourse to you, as much as other Lovers do perplexity and rapture. Instead of saying, I shall die for you, I professe I should be glad to Lead my life with you; you are as Beautifull as Witty as prudent, and as good humour'd as any woman breathing, but I must confesse to you I regard all those excellencies as you will please to direct 'em for my Happinesse or Misery. With Me, Madam, the only

[1] Was this Steele's sister? His uncle Gascoigne was, as we have seen, dead by June 1707.

[2] Dated August 11 by Nichols.

[3] This letter was introduced in the *Tatler*, No. 35, in an article from White's Chocolate-house: "I know no manner of news from this place, but that Cynthio, having been long in despair for the inexorable Clarissa, lately resolved to fall in love the good old way of bargain and sale, and has pitched upon a very agreeable young woman. He will undoubtedly succeed; for he accosts her in a strain of familiarity, without breaking through the deference that is due to a woman whom a man would choose for his life. I have hardly ever heard rough truth spoken with a better grace than in this his letter." *Mrs. Warren* is changed to *Mrs. Lucy* in the *Tatler;* and the same alteration has been made in the margin of the MS.

lasting motive to Love is the hope of It's becoming Mutuall; I begg of you to let Mrs. Warren send me word when I may attend you. I promise you I'le talk of nothing but indifferent things, tho' at the same time I know not how I shall approach you in the tender moment of first seeing you after this declaration which has been made by, Madam,

Y^{r} most Obedient &

Most Faithfull H^{mble} Ser^{vt}

RICH^{D} STEELE.

1707.[1]

MADAM

I came to Your house this night to wait on You, but You have commanded me to expect the happinesse of Seeing You at another time of more Leisure. I am now under Your own Roof while I write, and that imaginary satisfaction of being so near You tho' not in Your presence has in it something that touches me with so tender Ideas that it is impossible for me to describe their Force. All great passion makes us dumb, and the highest happinesse as well as highest Greif seizes us too Violently to be express'd by Our Words.

You Are so Good as to Let me Know I shall have the honour of Seeing You when I next come Here. I will live upon that Expectation, and meditate on y^{r} perfections till that happy Hour. The Vainest Woman upon Earth never saw in her Glasse half the attractions which I veiw in you, your Air, y^{r} Shape, Your Every glance Motion and Gesture have such peculiar Graces that you possesse my whole Soul, and I know no life but in the hopes of your approbation; I know not what to say but that I Love y^{u} with the Sincerest passion that ever enter'd the Heart of Man. I will make it the businesse of my Life to find out means of Convincing You that I prefer y^{u} to All that's pleasing upon earth.

I am, Madam,

Y^{r} Most Obedient, Most Faithful Hum^{ble} Sv^{nt}

RICH^{D} STEELE.

Friday Morning.[2]

MADAM

Hoping You are in good Health as I am at this present Writing I take the liberty of bidding You good Morrow and thanking You for Yesterday's Admission. To Know so much pleasure

[1] August 14, according to Nichols.

[2] Dated August 15 by Nichols.

with so much Innocence is methinks a satisfaction beyond the present condition of Humane life, but the Union of minds in pure affection is renewing the First State of Man.

You cannot Imagine the Gratitude with which I meditate on Y^r^ obliging behaviour to Me, and how much improv'd in Generous Sentiments I return from Y^r^ Company. At the same time that you give me passion for Your self, you inspire Me also with a Love of Virtue.

Mrs. Warren inform'd Me of Your intention[1] on Sunday Morning. I forbear indulging myself in a Stile which my Eager Wishes prompt me to, out of Reverence to that Occasion.

I am, Madam,

Y^r^ Most Oblig'd Most Faithful Ser^vt^

RICH^D^ STEELE.

Aug. 16,[2] 1707.

MADAM,

Before the light this morning dawn'd upon the Earth I awak'd and lay in expectation of its return, not that it could give any new sense of Joy to me, but as I hop'd it would blesse you with It's chearfull face, after a quiet which I wish'd you last night. If my Prayers are heard the day appear'd with all the influence of a merciful Creator upon Your person and Actions. Let others, my Lovely Charmer, talk of a Blind Being that disposes their Hearts, I contemn their low images of Love. I have not a thought which relates to You that I cannot with Confidence beseech the All-seeing Power to bless me in. May He direct You in all Your steps, and reward Your Innocence, Your Sanctity of manners, Your prudent Youth, and becoming piety, with the Continuance of His Grace and Protection. This is an unusuall Language to Ladies, but You have a mind elevated above the Giddy motions of a Sex insnar'd by Flattery, and misled by a False and short adoration into a solid and long contempt. Beauty, my fairest Creature, palls in the possession, but I Love also Your mind; Your Soul is as dear to me

[1] To receive the sacrament. See p. 183.

[2] The date in the original has been twice altered; in the first place, "Aug. 16" is changed to "Aug. 23;" and then, when the letter was prepared for use in the *Spectator* (No. 142), to "Sep^br^ 3^d.^ 1671;" and at the same time Steele added the words: "Tho' I made Him no declarations in His favour You see He had hopes of Me when he writ this in the month following." These words have sometimes been quoted as a comment on Steele by his wife; but they are in Steele's writing, and were clearly added when the letter was prepared for the printer of the *Spectator*.

Mrs. SCURLOCK.

as my Own, And if the Advantages of a Liberall Education, some Knowledge and as much contempt of the world Join'd with the Endeavours towards a life of Strict Vertue and Religion, can qualifie Me to raise new Ideas in a breast so well dispos'd as Yours is, our days will passe away with Joy, and old Age instead of introducing melancholy prospects of decay, give us hope of Eternall Youth in a better life. I have but few minutes from the duty of my Employment to write in, and without time to read over what I have Writ, therefore beseech You to pardon the first hints of my mind which I have express'd in so little order.

I am, Dearest Creature,

Yr Most Obedient Most devoted Sernt

RICHD STEELE.

Coleridge, we are told,[1] "dwelt with much *unction* on the curious and instructive letters of Steele to his wife; and with much approval on the manliness with which, in the first letters, he addressed the lady to whom he was afterwards united."

Next we have a letter from Mrs. Mary Scurlock to her mother, addressed, "This—For Mrs. Scurlock, at her Lodgings in Carmarthen, South Wales," telling of the engagement with Steele. It is evident at once that Mary Scurlock was somewhat imperious and haughty. At the head of the letter some one has written "Aug. 1707," and the letter is endorsed, "Aug. 16, 1707;" the postmark, too, is clearly "16." The cousin Betty[2] was the daughter of Mary Scurlock's uncle John.

DEAR MADAM,

By a Letter I had from Coz. betty Scurlock I find youre resolv'd to Winter in Wales, wch is ye Cause of ys Speed in my Writing having kept a Secret from you through fear yt a Letter might (by ye usual Impertinent Curiosity of people) make a discovery of wt is proper for yr own Ear only & not to divert any in yt tatleing place Where yt wretched impudence H. O. resorts who (Lest wee shou'd think god had not Wholy forsaken him) had ye boldness to send me a Letter wch I had ye very last post. I tore it without once reading it he being beneath my scornfull Laugh.

[1] Allsop's *Letters, Conversations, and Recollections of S. T. Coleridge*, 3rd edition (1864), p. 97.

[2] After her marriage with William Bevan she had to come to her father for money.

But the matter in hand is this. your frequent declarations of y^{r} Earnest Wishes that I might happily please you in oblidging my self by my Choise of a Companion for Life, has Embolden'd me now fate has put it in my power to give so far encouragement as to promise Speedy Marriage upon Condition of y^{r} Consent wch I dont question having W^{n} I tell you I not only make use of ye Most Weighing Consideration I'm Mistress of but also hope my inclination is ye direction of providence, whose guidance in every particular of y^{s} nice affair More perticularly I Cease not to implore Continually. I Cant recomend ye person to y^{u} as having a great Estate, Title, &c., wch are generally a parants Chief Care, but he has a Competency in worldly goods to make easie, wth a mind so richly adorn'd as to Exceed an Equivalent to ye greatest Estate in ye World in my opinion, in short his person is w^{t} I like, his temper is w^{t} I'm sure will make you as well as myself perfectly happy, if ye respect of a Lover wth ye tender fondness of a dutyfull Son can make y^{u} so, & for his understanding & Morals I refer y^{u} to his Christian Hero wch I remember y^{u} seem'd to approve, by this I believe y^{u} know his name, but least memory maint befriend me, tis ye survivour of ye person to Whose funerale I went to in my illness. Enquiries about him any farther y^{n} I've made are altogether needl^{ess} for I am fully satisfi'd & dont question but y^{ul} be so W^{n} business will permitt y^{u} to be an Eye Wittness & pertaker of my happiness. in ye Mean time w^{t} I desire is y^{r} Consent & blessing to my putting it out of my power to delay & so perhaps to Loose my first & only inclination; for I shall never meet wth a prospect of happiness if y^{s} shou'd vanish. You doubtless wonder at ye assurance of my Stile, for realy I do my self but y^{n} if y^{u} Consider ye necessity of it, 'twill paliate ye boldness. for first, ye distance between us is so great y^{t} ye Speediest answar to a letter terminates an Age of days, y^{n} ye Constant Visits, in ye form fitt for a Lover Make a Mighty noise in an idle prying Neiberhood, so will Cause ye uneasiness of an Endless nine-days Wonder as they Call it, but ye main Matter of all, since fate I belive has ordain'd him Mine, is his neglect of business wch his Coming in ye Manner he dose must Cause. these Considerations wth Several More w^{n} known, tho now too tedious to Write, Will I hope Lessen ye Censure this Comprehensive Letter may at first Sight Cause.

theres nothing I shou'd more desire y^{n} y^{r} presence at ye giving my hand wth y^{t} part of my heart you Can Spare, but ye Misfortune of y^{r} Lameness if y^{u} were here Wou'd deny Me y^{t} happiness unless publick doings were intended, wch is w^{t} I abhor, insomuch if y^{u} Consent to my Changing ye Name of Lover for husband, it shant be in ye power of ye town to more y^n^ guess there may be such a thing, until y^r^ Affairs will permitt you to Come & be a witness to our Manner of Living & appearing in y^e^ [world, which God Almig]hty direct us in ye Way of, & also[1] . . . this Letter to your dutyfull Molly . . . there being no room for Long Consideration . . . understood.

I am able to throw very unexpected light upon Mary Scurlock's relations with the "H. O.," of whose addresses she here speaks so indignantly. Mr. Rodman, of Somerset House, has kindly pointed out to me that in 1704 Henry Owen, Esq., of the parish of St. James, Westminster, brought a suit in the Consistorial Court of London against Mary Scurlock for breach of Contract of Marriage. The proceedings began on the 18th February 170$\frac{3}{4}$, when the promoter's proctor returned the mandate to the Court, and an appearance was put in in response. On the 4th March the libel was prayed for by the respondent, and given; and on the 10th March the libel was admitted, and an appointment made for taking the answers; the judge decreeing a compulsory process against persons whose evidence might be required, and who might be unwilling to appear. I give an abstract of the Libel and the Answer.

The Libel[2] stated—(1.) That in 1700, 1701, 1702, and more particularly in 1704, Henry Owen and Mary Scurlock were free from all matrimonial contracts, he being at that time and still being a widower, and she a spinster; and that they often treated of a marriage between them, as is public and notorious. (2.) That in 1703 they, having known each other for several years, became more particularly acquainted, and often frequented each other's company in Wales, at the Bath, &c., and in London. (3.) That he courted her, and she did not refuse, but in divers ways encouraged him. (4.) That while they were lodging in the same house in St. James's parish he became very much indisposed, and made a will, leaving a considerable estate to her; this will he gave sealed to her mother, who gave it to her daughter, who, by opening the cover or otherwise, found what he had be-

[1] The original MS. is here torn.

[2] Consistorial Court of London, "Libels" (1704), 351 (Somerset House).

queathed. On his recovery he renewed his addresses, which were received with favour. (5.) That she accepted presents, some of value, and gave him presents in return; she also admitted him to her bed-chamber at twelve at night and other late hours, and declared to several persons her affection for him, saying that she would let him embrace her, and that they might tell this to another person who was supposed to be courting her. (6.) That in November, December, and January 1703 [O.S.], they, being in the same lodgings, frequently dined and supped together, and visited friends, and were often alone together for hours, early and late. (7.) That she would often resort to his bed-chamber, where they discussed plans for their future married life. (8.) That she freely agreed to enter into a marriage contract in the terms he might think most binding; and that about January 1703[–4] they contracted themselves in marriage, using the words from the Book of Common Prayer, and he put a silver ring on her finger, which she readily accepted, and they embraced. (9.) That she wore the ring for a considerable time, confessing that she received it from him, and the contract they had entered into; but that when it came to her mother's knowledge, Mary, by her mother's direction, threw the ring into the fire, and said that there was an end of the contract. (10.) That she, being sensible that the contract was really valid and obligatory, endeavoured to prevail with him not to insist upon it. (11.) That he was a barrister-at-law and J.P. in County Carmarthen, and had an estate of at least £500 a year, and was 30, 35, or 40 years of age at the most. (12.) That Mary Scurlock was and is within the jurisdiction of this Court.

This was, put briefly, the Personal Answer made by Mary Scurlock.[1] She had known the promoter fourteen or fifteen years, they being of the same country, and she and her mother having several times lodged in the same house with him; they associated together in Bath, &c., and in London, but she had not been in Wales for the last four years. She said that for some years past, and particularly in 1703, Owen made his addresses to her mother in the way of marriage, and that he

[1] Consistorial Court of London, "Answers" (1704), 33.

more than once declared to several persons, as she had heard and believed, that her mother, Elizabeth Scurlock, had promised to marry him. In 1703 he often told the respondent, swearing in an extravagant manner, that she should have nobody but him, and that she should be his wife. It was commonly noticed that he spoke extravagantly, but she gave him no encouragement. He did pretend to be indisposed, and made a will which she, in a jesting manner, took, and opened, according to her best remembrance, in his presence, and found that he had left his estate to "his intended wife," mentioning no name. She looked upon it as a jest, and returned the will to him. She had not received presents this three years past, nor did she believe she made him presents. There having been a long acquaintance, in a manner from her childhood, he had sometimes come into her bedchamber at twelve at night and other late hours, but only as an old and intimate acquaintance. They often dined, supped, and visited together, and he was often in her bedroom at different hours, but only, as above stated, as an old acquaintance. She had sometimes been in his bedroom, which was on the same floor as hers, but the door of his room was, she believed, always open. She denied that she entered into a contract of marriage with him. In the months of November, December, or January last, he had in his hand a piece of silver twisted wire, like a ring, belonging, she believed, to a sword, and she, in a jesting manner, took it out of his hand and played with it on her finger; and some time after, he pleading to a contract on this account, she, knowing that there was no ground for it, and in order to put an end to such pretence or discourse, threw the piece of wire into the fire, saying, That if that was a Contract, there was an end of it, or words to that effect. She had desired him not to make any pretence to her. She believed the greater part of his estate was settled on his eldest son, and that he was much in debt, and upwards of forty years of age. She believed it to be true that she was within the jurisdiction of the Court.

This Answer was signed by Mary Scurlock on the 17th March 1704. On the 5th May 1704, the promoter's proctor alleged that the respondent's answers were not full; but on the 12th the judge decreed that the answer was sufficient, whereupon the promoter alleged a grievance, and on the 20th May an inhibition from the Court of Arches was brought in. Here the matter must end for us; it is not practicable to follow up the case after it went to the Arches Court. There is no mention of the matter in a volume giving a list of cases before the Court in 1704, preserved at Doctors' Commons, and the papers are either lost or are inaccessible. But this is of little consequence; it is evident that Owen lost the day, for Mary Scurlock was able to form a fresh contract of marriage with Steele. Owen was, it would seem, rather fond of litigation. In 1702 he was plaintiff in an action against Bulkley Price, Esq., in the Exchequer Court, to which his father had previously been a party. From the pleadings in that case, which related to family property, we learn that Henry Owen, Esq., of Glassalt, Carmarthenshire, was the eldest son and heir of Morgan Owen, who was the youngest son and devisee of Rice Owen, the brother and heir of Morgan Owen, D.D., the late Lord Bishop of Llandaff.[1] Henry Owen was also plaintiff in an action against Rowland Phillips, Gent., in 1712, in which he eventually obtained an order to dismiss his own bill, with costs to be taxed.[2] He was apparently a gentleman at large, dancing attendance upon Mrs. Scurlock and her daughter; perhaps, as the Answer says, he was in debt, and the Scurlocks' property attracted him. In any case, as we have seen, this "wretched impudence" was still troubling Mary Scurlock with letters in August 1707.

The following lines form the greater part of some verses, the originals of which, in Miss Scurlock's writing, are in Mrs. Wills's possession. If they are the young lady's own composition, they possibly refer to her engagement with Steele.

As free as wanton winds I Lived
that unconcerned do play
no broken faith no fate I grievd
no fortune gave me Joy

[1] Exchequer Bills and Answers, Carmarthenshire, Anne No. 2; Exchequer Depositions, Mich., 13 William III. 36.

[2] Exchequer Q.R. Original Orders, 11 Anne, Mich., No. 152.

A dull content crowned all my hours
my hart no sighs opprest
I calld in vain on no deaf powrs
to ease a torturd breast
the sighing swains regardles pin'd
& stroove in vain to please
with pane I civilly was kind
but could afford no ease
tho wit & flattery did abound
the charm was wanting still
that could inspire the tender wound.
or bend my careless will
till in my heart a kindling flame
your softer sighs had blown
which I with striving Love and shame
too sensibly did own
whatere ye god before could plead
whatere the youths desert
the feeble seige in vain was laid
against my stubborn heart
att first my sighs and blushes spoke
Just when your sighs would rise
and when you gaz'd I wish'd to Look
but durst not meet your Eyes
I trembled when my hand you press'd
nor could my guilt controul
but Love prevail'd and I confest
the secrets of my Soul.[1]

Taking up again the thread of the correspondence, we have next a letter written by Steele to Miss Scurlock on Sunday; the conjectural date is August 17th.

1707.

MADAM

I could not omit writing to You tho' on Sunday-morning when I know I interrupt Your meditation on Higher subjects; There is nothing but Heav'n it self, which I prefer to Your Love, which shall be the pursuit of my Life, and I hope there will not a day appear to our lives end wherein there will not appear some in-

[1] On the same paper are some lines about Jealousy—
"Thou whose sole property is to destroy
Thou opposite to good Antipathy to Joy."

stance of an Affection not to be excell'd but in the Mansions of Eternity to which We may recommend our selves by our behaviour to each other Here.

I am, My Lovely Charmer, Yr Obedient . . . . . . [1]

There is a prayer written by Steele for use before partaking of the Lord's Supper, which may well be given here.

O Almighty Lord God and Saviour, look down with compassion on me, and give me grace to approach the mysterious ordinance of salvation with fear and reverence. O Lord, I love, I adore, I believe in thee. Give me, O Lord, a life suitable to my faith; and let me not cast away, with a soul conscious of, and adoring, thy unspeakable goodness. But wash out my offences; and give me the benefit of this cup, in order to a good mortal, and a glorious immortal, life; through the merits and mediation of Jesus Christ our Lord and Saviour! [2]

The succeeding letters speak for themselves. Some of them are addressed from Smith Street, Westminster; at Lady Day, 1707, Steele had taken a house in St. Martin's Lane,[3] and before the year came to an end he was settled in Bury Street, St. James's.

1707,[4]
LD SUNDERLAND'S OFFICE.

MADAM

With what Language shall I addresse my Lovely Fair to acquaint Her with the Sentiments of an Heart she delights to Torture? I have not a minute's Quiet out of yr sight; and, when I'me with You, You Use me with so much distance, that I am still in a State of Absence heightned with a View of the Charms which I am deny'd to Approach. In a word You must give Me either a Fan, a Mask or a Glove, you have Wore or I cannot Live, otherwise You must expect I'le Kiss Your hand, or when I next sit by You Steal Your Handkerchief. You Your self are too Great a Bounty to be receiv'd at Once therefore I must be prepar'd by degrees least the Mighty Gift distract Me with Joy. Dear Mrs. Scurlock I'me tir'd

[1] The name is cut out.

[2] Copied from the original, in the possession of the late Rev. David Scurlock. [Nichols.] I have not seen the original of this prayer.

[3] Overseers' Rate Books, St. Martin's-in-the-Fields. The entry in the volume for 1707 is as follows (p. 31):—"St. Martin's Lane. Richard Steele. Rated £1. 10. 0. Received £1. 2. 6. Arrears £0. 7. 6.—Ent Lady Day."

[4] Day and month cut out.

with calling You by that name therefore Say the day in which Youle take that of, Madam, Yr Most Obedient Most devoted Hubl Sernt

RICHD STEELE.

SMITH STREET, WESTMINSTER,
1707.[1]

MADAM,

I take up pen and Ink to indulge the sensibility of mind I am under in reflecting upon the Agreeable Company in which I pass'd Yesterday Evening. The Day hangs heavily upon me and the whole businesse of it is an impertinent Guilty Dream in comparison of the happinesse of a few moments of reall Life at yr House which go off in privacy and Innocence. Were it possible the concern I have for You were mutuall, How Tedious would be the moments of each other's absence, How Fleeting the Hours we should be together! How would my Mirth be heightned? how my Sorrow banish'd by the appearance of a Smile in that Countenance where are so charmingly painted Complacency, Good Sense, Innocence, Honour, and Truth? Since this is the figure you bear in my Imagination you cannot blame my desire of having those Good Qualities my Constant Companions and for ever engag'd in my interests. My Heart oreflows with the pleasing prospects which Throng into my mind when I think of You. What shall I say? Prithee, Mrs Scurlock, have pity on, Madam, Yr Most Obedient, Most Faithful Sernt,

RICHD STEELE.

SMITH STREET, WESTMINSTER,
1707.

MADAM

I lay down last night with yr Image in my thoughts,[2] and have awak'd this morning in the same contemplation. The pleasing Transport with which I'me delighted, has a sweetnesse[3] in it attended with a Train of Ten thousand soft desires, anxieties, and cares; The day arises on my hopes with new Brightnesse; Youth Beauty and Innocence are the charming[4] objects that Steal me from myself, and give me Joys above the reach of Ambition pride or Glory. Beleive Me, Fair One, to throw myself at yr Feet is giving my self the highest blisse I know on Earth. Oh hasten Ye Minutes! bring on the happy Morning wherein to be ever her's will make me look down on Thrones! Dear Molly I am tenderly, passionately, faithfully Thine,

RICHD STEELE.

[1] Day and month cut out.
[2] Altered from "imagination."
[3] Altered from "softness."
[4] Altered from "bright."

[Aug. 2]2^{d}, 1707.[1]

MADAM,

If my Vigilance and ten thousand wishes for Your Welfare and repose could have any force You last night slept in security, and had every good Angel in Your attendance. To have my thoughts ever fix'd on You, to Live in constant fear of every accident to which Humane life is liable, and to send up my hourly prayers to avert 'em from You, I say, Madam, thus to think and thus to suffer is what I do for Her who is in pain at my Approach, and calls all my Tender sorrow impertinence. You are now before my Eyes, my Eyes that are ready to flow with Tendernesse, but cannot give releif to my gushing Heart that dictates what I am now saying and yearns to tell you all its Akings. How Art thou, oh my soul, stoln from thy self? How is all thy attention broken? My books are blank paper and my Freinds intruders. I have no hope of Quiet but from your pity. To grant it would make more for Your Triumph. To give pain is the Tyranny, to make happy The True empire of Beauty. If you would consider aright you'de find an agreeable change in dismissing the attendance of a Slave, to receive the Complaisance of a Companion. I bear the former, in hopes of the latter condition; As I live in chains without Murmuring at the Power which inflicts 'em so I could enjoy freedome without forgetting the Mercy that gave it. Dear Mrs. Scurlock, The life which you bestow [on] Me Shall be no more my own. I am Y^{r} most devoted most Obedient Ser^{nt},

RICH^{D} STEELE.

Augst 25, 1707. CHELSEY.

MADAM,

I am observ'd by a freind who is with Me in every gesture and motion I make. I have stole a moment, while He is in next room to tell the Charmer and Inspirer of my Soul I am Her devoted obedient ser^{nt}, RICH^{D} STEELE.

Thursday, Augst 28th, 1707.

MY DEAREST CREATURE,

I begg the favour of you to let me passe this day in your Company. I have contriv'd my businesse so that I have till Eight at night at my own disposall. I can come in a Coach and Mrs.

[1] This date is in part cut out, leaving "2^{d}, 1707," and "Aug. 7, 1671," was afterwards inserted. Over "Madam," at the beginning, is written "Andromache," and "Madam" substituted for "dear Mrs. Scurlock . . . own" at the end. Thus altered, and without the signature, the letter was introduced into the *Spectator*, No. 142.

Warren being in the Way may let me in without observation. My lov'd Creature do not deny this request, nor think I am capable of being allow'd that Liberty without a true sense of Your Goodnesse to me in it. Your Generous condescension in all Your Carriage towards me, shall always give You a powerfull and lasting influence upon the thoughts and Actions of Him who hopes to be, Madam,

Y^r Most Oblig'd and Gratefull Husband,

RICH^D STEELE.

Aug^st 29th, 1707.

MADAM,

I fear it will be an hour later than Usual that I wait upon You to-night for I have an appointment which will detain Me, and which concerns both You and Madam, Y^r Most Oblig'd Most Obedient Humble Ser^nt,

RICH^D STEELE.

Augt 30, 1707.

MADAM,

I begg pardon that my paper is not finer [1] but I am forc'd to write from a Coffee-house where I am attending about businesse. There is a dirty Croud of Busie faces all around me talking of *money;* while all my Ambition, all my wealth is Love! Love, which animates my Heart, sweetens my Humour, enlarges my Soul, and affects every Action of my Life. 'Tis to my Lovely Charmer I owe that many Noble Ideas are continually affix'd to my words and Actions; tis the naturall effect of that Generous passion to create in the Admirer some similitude of the object admir'd. Thus my Dear am I every day to Improve from so sweet a Companion. Look up, My Fair One to that Heav'n which made thee such; and Join with me to Implore Its influence on our Tender Innocent hours and beseech the Author of Love, to blesse the Rights he has ordain'd, and mingle with our happinesse a just sense of our Transient Condition and a resignation to His Will which only can regulate our minds to a steddy endeavour to please Him and each other. I am for ever

Y^r Faithful Ser^nt,

R^D STEELE.

[1] This letter was somewhat altered before it was printed in No. 142 of the *Spectator*. The following words were added at the top by Steele: "He was, when he writ the following letters, as agreeable and pleasant a man as any in England." In the first line Steele originally wrote "guilt"; this was changed to "guilded," and then struck out in favour of "finer." In the fourth line Steele wrote "polities and managing stocks." This is altered to "money." As the letter was first written we find "some similitude in the Admirer of the object," which is changed to "in the admirer some similitude of the object." The date is altered to "Oct^br 20th, 1671."

Saturday Night [Aug. 30, 1707].

DEAR, LOVELY MRS. SCURLOCK,

I have been in very good company, where your Health,[1] under the Character of the Woman I lov'd best has been often drank, So that I may say I am Dead Drunk for Your sake, which is more y^n I die for you. Y^{rs}, R. STEELE.[2]

S^{NT}. JAMES COFFEE-HOUSE,
Sep^{br} 1st, 1707.[3]

MADAM,

It is the hardest thing in the World to be in Love and yet attend businesse. As for Me, all who speake to Me find Me out, and I must Lock my self up, or other people will do it for Me.

A Gentleman ask'd Me this Morning what news from Lisbon,[4] and I answer'd, She's Exquisitly handsome. Another desir'd to know when I had been last at Hampton-Court,[5] I reply'd Twill be on Tuesday come se'nnight.[6] Prithee Allow Me at least to Kisse Your hand before that day,[7] that my mind may be in some Composure. Oh Love ![8]

A thousand Torments dwell about Thee,
Yet who would Live to Live without Thee ?

Methinks I could write a Volume to You, but all the Language on earth would fail in saying how much, and with what disinterested passion, I am Ever Y^{rs}, $RICH^{D}$ STEELE.

Sep^{br} 2^{d}, 1707, between One and Two.

DEAR CREATURE,

Ever since sev'n this morning I have been in Company, but have stole a moment to Pour out the fullnesse of my thoughts, and complain to You of the Interruption that Impertinent amusement

1 Altered from "unknown name."

2 This note is written badly, but Steele was not so far gone as to be unable to be witty; and as Mr. Dobson remarks, he did not conceal his over fondness for "good company" from the lady whom he was courting, and it appears, therefore, as she married him, that she did not consider it a grave error.

3 With the view of publication in the *Spectator*, No. 142, the address was taken out, and the date altered to "Sept. 25, 1671"; and this remark added, "The two next were written after the day for our marriage was fixed."

4 Altered to "Holland."

5 Altered to "Windsor."

6 *I.e.*, September 9th. These words are changed in the original to, "She designs to go with me."

7 Altered to "the appointed day."

8 These two words and the couplet were struck out, as well as the signature, before the letter was reprinted in the *Spectator*.

call'd businesse has giv'n me amidst my Contemplation on the best of Women, and the most Agreeable object that ever Charm'd the Heart of Man. I am, Dearest Lovelyest Creature

Eternally Thine, R. STEELE.

Sep^br^ 3^d^, 1707, Seven in the Morn.[1]

DEAR CREATURE,

Next to the influence of Heav'n I am to thank you that I see the returning day with pleasure. To passe my Evenings in so sweet a Conversation, and have the esteem of a Woman of y^r^ Merit, has in it a particularity of happinesse no more to be express'd than return'd. But I am, My Lovely Creature, contented to be on the oblig'd side, and to employ all my days in new Endeavours to convince you, and all the world of the Sense I have of y^r^ Condescension in chusing, Madam,

Y^r^ Most Faithfull, Most Obedient Humble ser^nt^,

RICH. STEELE.

On the 3rd September Steele wrote the following letter to Mrs. Scurlock, at Carmarthen, giving particulars of his position and means:—

Sep^br^ 3, 1707.[2]
L^D^ SUNDERLAND'S OFFICE,
WHITEHALL.

MADAM,

The Young Lady y^r^ Daughter told me she had a letter from You of 22d instant[3] wherein You gave Her the highest marks of Your Affection and anxiety for Her Welfare in relation to me. The Main prospect on these occasions is that of Fortune; therefore I shall very candidly give you an account of myself as to that particular. My Late Wife had so extreme a Value for Me that she by Fine Convey'd to Me Her whole estate Situate in Barbados, which, with the Stock and Slaves (proper securities being giv'n for the payment of the rent), is Lett for eight hundred and fifty pounds per Annum at Half yearly payments; that is to say, 425 each first of May, and 425 each first of December. This Estate came to her encumber'd with a debt of three thousand pounds by Legacies and debts of Her Brother whose Executrix She was as Well as Heiresse. I must confesse, it has not been in my power to Lessen the incum-

[1] Date changed to "Oct. 23, 1671," and then to "Sep^br^ last 1671." The letter is given in the *Spectator*, No. 142.

[2] The date has been altered from Sept. 3 to Sept. 30, 1707.

[3] Ultimo?

brance, by reason of Chargeable Sicknesses, and not having at that time any Employment of Profitt. But at present and ever since May last I have been appointed by the Secretaries of State to write the Gazette, with a salary of three hundred pounds a Year paying a tax of forty-five pounds. I am also Gentleman-Waiter to his Royall Highnesse the Prince with a sallary of one hundred pounds a Year not Subject to taxes.

Thus My whole income at present per Annum		1250 : 00 : 00
Deduct the interest of 3000*l.*	180 : 00 : 00	225 : 00 : 00
Taxes for my Employment	45 : 00 : 00	
Remains after these deductions . . .		1025 : 00 : 00

This is Madam the present state of my Affairs, and tho' this income is so large I have not taken any regard to lay up any thing further than just what pays the interest abovemention'd. If I may be so happy to Obtain Y[r] favour so as We may Live together with singlenesse of mind, I shall readily go into such Measures as shall be thought most advisable for Our Mutuall interest, and if 'tis thought fitt will sell what I have in the Plantations. Y[r] Daughter acquaints Me there is a demand of fourteen Hundrede upon Y[r] Estate, the Annuall income of which is better than 400*l.* p. Añ. You have now the whole View of both Our Circumstances before You, and You see there is foundation for Our living in an Handsome manner provided We can be of one mind, without which I could not propose to my self any happinesse or Blessing were my circumstances never so plentifull. I am at a present Juncture in my Affairs, and my Freinds are in great power so that it would be highly necessary for Us to be in the figure of Life which We shall think convenient to appear in as soon as may be, that I may prosequte my Expectations in a busie Way while the Wind is for Me, with a Just consideration that about a Court it will not always blow one Way. Your Coming to town is Mightily to be Wish'd. I promise my self the pleasures of an industrious and vertuous life in Studying to do things agreeable to You. But I will not enlarge into professions. I assure You I shall always contend with You who shall lay the Greater obligations on the other, and I can form to my self no Greater satisfaction than having one day y[r] Permission to subscribe my self, Madam,

y[r] Most Obedient Son & Most Humble ser[nt],

RICH[D] STEELE.

It is painful Writing to me.

If you enclose y[r] letters to y[r] Daughter thus they'll come free.

To Rich[d] Steele, Esq[r] at y[e] Secretary's Office Whitehall.

Steele, ever hopeful and sanguine, seems to have always over-estimated his means, and it is to this that we may attribute most of his money difficulties. Mrs. Scurlock's estate was encumbered with debt; and it is evident that there was great trouble in getting any of the money that ought to have come from the West Indian property.

On the 4th, 5th, and 6th September there are three letters to Miss Scurlock, written upon the near approach of the wedding day.

Sep^br 4th, 1707.[1]

DEAR MISSE MOLLY

I am loath to interrupt y^r Prayers or my indispensable businesse with a long Epistle this morning, therefore forgive Me that I only just say

I am ever yours, R. S.

I shall come at night and make all the dispatch here I can not to be wanted.

Sep^br 5th, 1707.

DEAR MADAM

The pleasing hope with which my mind is possess'd is too delicate a touch of[2] Soul to be explain'd, but it is founded on so solid and lasting Motives that I am sure it will actuate the behaviour of my Whole life; For I do not entertain my Imagination with those transports only which are rais'd by Beauty, but fix it also on the satisfactions which flow from the reverence due to Virtue. Thus I am not only allur'd by Your person, but convinc'd by Your Life that You are the most Amiable of Women. Let us go on, My Lovely Creature, to make our regards to each other Mutuall and Unchangeable, that while the world around Us is enchanted with the false satisfactions of Vagrant desires, our Persons may be shrines to each other, and sacred to Conjugall Faith, Unreserv'd Confidence, and Heavenly Society. While We live after this manner Angels will be so far from Being our Superiours that they will be Our Attendants. Every Good Being Guard my Fairest and Conduct Her to that bosome that pants to receive Her, and protect Her from all the cares and Vicissitudes of Life with An Eternall Tendernesse.

I am Ever Most Obligedly y^rs

RICH^D STEELE.

[1] The date is altered in the MS. from Sept. 4 to Sept. 14, 1707.

[2] "man's" erased.

Saturday, Sep^{br} 6th, 1707.

MADAM

I am am at a freinds house where they have giv'n Me, as You see but very Ordinary Instruments to write with However I hope the sincerity of my heart is not to be measur'd by the dresse in which I cloath it. My thoughts hurry upon Me in consideration of the Approach of the moment in which those Fair lips are to give me in one monosallable more than all the Eloquence in the world can expresse, when You say Yes to the accepting of,

Madam,

Y^{r} Most Oblig'd Most Gratefull

Most Obedient Ser^{nt}

RICH^{D} STEELE.

On the 7th September Steele wrote again to Mrs. Scurlock.

Sep^{br} 7$_{th}$, 1707.

MADAM

In Obedience to Your commands by Your Daughter of hearing every post from this Town of Her Health and Welfare I do my self the Honour to inform you of it, and Humbly desire you would accept of my owne Duty.

I hope You have before now receiv'd a letter from Me wherein I Laid before You at large the State of my affairs, and that when We come to be acquainted you will not esteem it a disadvantagious accident that I have the Honour of Being

Madam,

Y^{r} Most Obedient Son & Most Humble ser$^{nt.}$

RICH^{D} STEELE.

The *Muses Mercury* for September, which contained Steele's *Prologue to the University of Oxford*,[1] had also the following paragraph :—"As for comedies, there's no great expectation of anything of that kind since Mr. Farquhar's death. The two Gentlemen, who would probably always succeed in the Comick Vein, Mr Congreve and Capt. Steel, having affairs of much greater importance to take up their time and thoughts. And unless the Players write themselves, the Town must wait for Comedies till another Genius appears."

On the 8th September a licence was granted [2] for the marriage of Richard Steele of the Parish of Saint Margaret, Westminster,

[1] Page 148. [2] Vicar General's Office.

in the County of Middlesex, Esquire, a Widower, with Mary Scurlock of the Parish of St. James, Westminster, in the same County, aged Twenty-four years, a Spinster, the marriage to be in the Parish Church of Saint Margaret's, Westminster. But there is no record of the marriage in the Registers of St. Margaret's, which Archdeacon Farrar has kindly allowed me to examine; and there is no trace of the marriage being performed either at St. James's, Piccadilly, or at St. Martin's-in-the-Fields. It is to be remembered that Steele had said that he had reasons for concealing the engagement from his nearest relation,[1] and that Miss Scurlock had told her mother that she abhorred public doings at the marriage; "insomuch, if you consent to my changing the name of lover for husband, it shan't be in the power of the town to more than guess there may be such a thing."[2] Although the marriage licence named the church at which the service was to be performed, the direction was often not strictly observed, and it would be easy to find means for having the wedding held very privately. There is one rather characteristic point in connection with the licence. Miss Scurlock is there described as aged 24; but according to her monument in Westminster Abbey she died on the 26th December 1718, aged 40, and as her birthday was the 4th November, this would make her age nearly 29 in September 1707. That this is correct is proved by the date of her christening, 5th November 1678. Steele was 35 in 1707.

It seems probable that the marriage took place on the 9th September, the day after the licence was obtained; but it is clear that Mrs. Steele would not have the marriage known, or live with her husband, until her mother's consent had been received. The evidence for this rests upon the following letters, which also show the earnest spirit with which Steele looked forward to his new life:—

Sept^{br} 9th.[3]

MADAM

I hope your denying what I urg'd with so much passion, and which I complain'd of in too vehement a manner, has not been a grief to my tender Companion, for upon reflection this morning I

[1] Page 174. [2] Page 179.

[3] The date is altered in the MS. from Sept. 9 to Sept. 11.

extremely approve Your conduct, and take your behaviour to proceed from an inclination to come to my Arms Hallowed by your parent's blessing. I comply with your Measures in bringing that Happinesse about and shall behave myself as if only in the beginning of a sacred Love made at the Altar. I promise to myself Sincere felicity in a Woman that can Sacrifice all desires to Her Duty, and I assure you whatever appearance of care and disturbance you may observe now and then in my Countenance, it is not the Image of Spleen, ill-nature, or dissatisfaction, but a Strong propensity to make you the happyest of Your Sex which I shall endeavour to do, rather by an industrious ambition to promote Your fortune, than by a meer dallyance of your person only, to show a Greater regard to the Beauty than the Wife. I begg of You to show my letters to no one living, but let Us be contented with one another's Thoughts upon our Words and Actions without the intervention of other people, who cannot Judge of so delicate a circumstance as the commerce between Man and Wife.

I am Eternally y[rs],

RICH[D] STEELE.

Pray write me a line.

Sep[br] 10th, 1707.

MADAM

Being very uneasy when absent from You I desire you'de give Me leave to take Coach and come to your house, in order to which, pray let Warren be in the Way to admit

Y[r] Most Oblig'd Humble Ser[nt], RICH[D] STEELE.

On the 20th September Steele wrote again to Mrs. Scurlock, "at her lodgings in Carmarthen, South Wales," expressing his anxiety as to the reception which his previous letter had met with.

LORD SUNDERLAND'S OFFICE,
WHITEHALL, Sep[br] 20th, 1707.

MADAM

By Tuesday's post I tooke the liberty to write to You on the most Important Occasion, and have been in ten thousand anxieties ever since that time for the reception which that letter is to find. The Circumstance is so tender and my happinesse hangs so much upon it that I could not forbear seconding my first addresse to You with a second, tho I protest to You I sett pen to paper with as much diffidence as if I had the same passion for Your self as for Y[r]

Daughter. I do not entertain y^{u} with an Account of my fortune, and those particulars which will naturally be enquir'd into by a Parent, because I doubt not but you have so good an Opinion of Mrs Scurlock's prudence that You do not beleive she would throw Her self away. As to Your Favour to my pretensions I hope it upon no other foundation than making it appear to You that as to Your Own part in the Affair there is not y^{t} man breathing that could come into Your Alliance, who should in All the Offices of Life and peculiar esteem for y^{r} self Exceed the Gratitude of, Madam,

Y^{r} Most Obedient & Most Humble Ser^{nt}, RICH^{D} STEELE.

The next two notes to Mrs. Steele are addressed, like several of the preceding ones, "To Mrs. Warren." In the second of the two Steele signs himself for the first time "Your most obliged Husband."

Sep^{br} 21st, 1707.

DEAR CREATURE

Y^{r} letter gave me a great deal of Satisfaction. I hasten my businesse to see you early in ye Evening. In the mean time I recommend myself to y^{r} Prayers and kind thoughts, and am

Ever y^{rs}, R. STEELE.

Oct^{br} 6th, 1707.

DEAR CREATURE

I write to tell You before hand that I am not in a very good Humour, but all shall vanish at Her sight whome Providence has giv'n me for the banishment of Care, and the improvement of delight to

Y^{r} Most Oblig'd Husband & Most Humble Ser^{nt},

RICH^{D} STEELE.

On the 7th October Steele wrote twice to his wife, and for the first time addressed the letters "To Mrs. Steele." The second letter was only to bid her good-night. Next morning he wrote again.

Oct^{br} 8th, 1707.

MY DEAR WIFE

You were not I am sure awake so soon as I was for You, and desir'd the blessing of God upon You. After that first duty my next is to let you know I am in health this morning which I know you are sollicitous for. I beleive it would not be amisse if some time this afternoon you tooke a Coach or chair and went to see an house next door to Lady Bulkely's towards S^nt^ James's Street which is to be Lett. I have a solid reason for Quickening my diligence in all affairs of the World, which is that you are my partaker in 'em, and will make me labour more than any incitation of Ambition, or Wealth could do. After I have implor'd the help of Providence I will have no motive to my Actions but ye Love of the best Creature living to whome I am an Obedient Husband,

RICH^D^ STEELE.

As a comment to this last letter we have two prayers, written by Steele soon after marriage for his private use.

Oh Almighty Lord God who hast been pleas'd out of thy Righteous Mercy and carefull Providence, to place us two in the State of Marriage according to thy own institution and Guidance of the first mortalls Grant We beseech Thee that We may live in that State with mutuall Love and endeavour to accommodate our Selves to each others Just desires and satisfactions that We may be a mutuall help [1] in all the Vicissitudes of life through which thou hast design'd us to passe, in such manner as We may contribute to each others Virtue in this World, and Salvation in y^t^ which is to come. Protect us oh Lord most mighty, blesse us oh Mercifull Father and Redeem us oh Holy Saviour. Guard our paths from Errour and keep our Eyes from introducing Wandring desires, but Grant such Peace and Tranquillity of Mind, and such a Steady Course of Virtue and Piety [2] that we may be at Thy Holy Altar never-failing Communicants and by a worthy receipt of the Elements representing thy Meritorious Passion we may through that be partakers of Eternall life which permit us to beseech of Thee in the Words which Thou hast Taught us:

Our Father, &c.

Almighty God, who of thy infinite goodness and mercy didst create, and dost preserve all things both in Heaven and earth; look down with an eye of mercy on us, whom thy good providence has ordained to live together in holy matrimony. Grant, oh God, that no allurement, passion, jealousy, plenty, or want, may so far transport us, as to make us forget a sacred vow, made to each other, and before thee. Let us, Oh Lord, with a lively, cheerful, and habitual sense of such our obligation, check the first motives to anger and

[1] As first written, "that We may be an help to each other through."

[2] "Religion," erased.

distress; and cherish all, and omit none the least instances of tenderness and good-will: so shall we enjoy and pass through this human transient life, in a daily preparation for one that is celestial and eternal; not regarding posterity so as to forget eternity; yet believing it is not displeasing in thy sight, that in our way to a certain and unchangeable being, we neglect not a provision for such, as thou may'st make us instruments to introduce into one that is various and uncertain. This, and whatever else thy omnipresent wisdom sees necessary for us, with relation to ourselves and the whole race of mankind, we beseech thee, Oh Father of all things, bestow upon us. All which we beg in the name, and through the mediation of Jesus Christ, who hath taught us, in a perfect and an unblameable manner to approach thee, saying,

Our Father, &c.[1]

There is a fragment of another prayer by Steele, "copied by the late Rev. D. Scurlock, Lovehill House, Bucks," among the papers in the possession of Mrs. Wills.

O let the mighty power of thy grace strengthen my feeble wishes and endeavours, and enable me to conquer my most inveterate habits. Let the sweet and gentle influence of thy Spirit calm the passions and compose the storms and disorders of my soul, and O do thou save me from the dangers of this troublesome [world].

From a second letter written on the 8th October, it would appear that Steele was already negotiating for the sale of his estate in Barbados. The next is a letter of apology for "every act of rebellion" against his wife.

Monday Morning Oct^br 13th, 1707.

DEAR MADAM

This comes to begg y^r pardon for every Act of Rebellion I have ever committed against You, and to subscribe my self in an errour for being impatient of Your kind concern in interesting Your self with so much affection [in] all which relates to me. I do not Question but y^r prudence will be a lasting honour and advantage to Me in all the occurrences of my Life; the cheif happinesse in it is that I have the honour of being

Y^r Most Oblig'd Husband & Most Humble Serv^nt,

RICH^D STEELE.

[1] I have not seen the original of this prayer, which is printed by Nichols, *Epist. Corr.*, 1809, p. 124.

This letter may suitably be followed by two messages from Mrs. Steele to her husband.

It is but an addition to our uneasiness to be at variance with each other. I beg your pardon if I have offended you. God forgive you for adding to the sorrow of an heavy heart, that is above all sorrow but for your sake.

Ah! Dick Steele that I were but sure
your Love Like mine would stil indure
that time nor absence which destroys
the cares of Lovers and there Joys
may never rob me of that part
which you have given of your heart
others unenvied may possess
what ever they think happines
Grant this O God my great request,
In his dear armes may I for ever rest.

There is a well-known story which illustrates the generosity and sterling worth of character of the wife whom Steele loved so well to the end. Soon after their marriage Steele asked her to accompany him on a visit he intended making in the afternoon. They drove to a boarding-school in the environs of London, and alighted. Presently a young lady appeared, to whom Steele showed the greatest fondness, insomuch that his wife asked him if the child was his. On his acknowledging that she was, the lady said, "Then I beg she may be mine too." The girl was accordingly taken home, and treated as their own; she was called Miss Ousley, and subsequently married a Mr. Aynston.

From the next letter to Mrs. Scurlock, we learn that Steele had taken a house in Bury Street, St. James's,[1] the "third door, right hand, turning out of Germin Street." Swift afterwards lodged in Bury Street, and found it, as he told Stella, "plaguy dear;" but it was near the Palace and the Cockpit, where the office of the Secretaries of State was situated; and it was

[1] The house was taken down in 1830 (*Literary Landmarks of London*, by L. Hutton, 1885, p. 290). Crabbe and Thomas Moore lived in Bury Street.

close to St. James's Church, which was a great point with Mrs. Steele.[1]

Oct^br^ 14th, 1707.

HONOUR'D MOTHER

I am very sorry to find by Mr Scurlock's letter that You keep Your bed, which makes me almost in despair of seeing You so soon as I promis'd my self.

I have taken an House in Berry-street, S^nt^ James's and begg Your Leave to remove Your Goods thither[2] where I hope We shall live all together in the strictest Love and Freindship. Whatever better prospects your daughter might Well have given her self from her great Merit and good Qualities, I shall take care to have it said that she could not have married more advantageously with regard to Her mother who shall always find me

Her Most Obedient Son & Most Humble Serv^nt^,

RICH^D^ STEELE.

Y^r^ Daughter gives Her Duty to You.

Among several notes written in haste to explain absence from home is one from which it appears that Steele had been living with Addison.

Oct^br^ 28th, 1707,
CHARING-CROSSE, Almost Three in ye Afternoon.

MY DEAR

I have been detain'd all this morning sollicting some businesse between the Treasury and Our Office; and My Boy slipping out of the Way I have not had any one to send that you might not stay dinner: Mr Addison does not remove till to-morrow therefore I cannot think of moving my Goods out of His Lodgings. I am come to a Tavern alone to eat a stake, after wch I shall return to the Office, whither I desire you'de send Will. I am, with the most Tender Affection

y^r^ Obedient Husband, R: STEELE.

Send by Will the receipt.

[1] The advantages of Bury Street are thus described in an advertisement in the *Daily Courant* for May 10, 1723: "To be sold, a House in Berry Street, of two rooms and a large closet on a floor, with a wash-house, wood-house, and other conveniences out of doors, in a handsome garden, encompassed with several others, which makes it both airy, healthy, and pleasant, nor is it less valuable for the commodiousness of the situation, being near St. James's Church, Chapel, Park, Palace, Coffee and Chocolate-Houses. Enquire of Mrs. Elliot, at St. James's Coffee-house, at the upper end of the Pall-Mall."

[2] From Mrs. Scurlock's house in Swallow Street.

In Michaelmas term of this year three actions for debt were decided against Steele. Isaac Fernandes Nunes,[1] by his counsel, William Sims, had brought a bill against Steele in the Trinity term last past, stating that on the 7th February $170\frac{5}{6}$, in the parish of the Blessed Mary of Bow in the Ward of Cheap, Steele, by a certain obligatory bond sealed by him, acknowledged himself bound to the said Nunes in the sum of £200, to be paid when requested; but he would not pay, and Nunes claimed £20 damages. And then, on Thursday next after the three weeks of Michaelmas (23rd October 1707), up to which time Steele had licence to examine and answer the said bill, Nunes came, but Steele neither came nor said anything through his attorney, Hezekiah Benson. Nunes was therefore allowed 36s. for damages sustained by the detention of the money, and also for his costs.

At the same Court Elizabeth Smarte, widow, brought a bill against Richard Steele of the parish of St. Margaret, Westminster, Esq., and William Elderton of the parish of St. Clement Danes, gentleman, for debt. Their attorney was Lancelot Tolson; Mrs. Smarte's was John Campion. The bill stated that on the 9th June 1707, in the parish of St. Paul, Covent Garden, by a certain writing or obligation, sealed by them and shown to the Court, Steele and Elderton acknowledged themselves bound to Mrs. Smarte in the sum of £600, to be paid when required. As they would not pay, she claimed £20 damages. Mrs. Smarte prayed them to answer her bill, whereupon their attorney said that he had not been informed of any answer to be given, nor of anything to be said in bar of the action; and Mrs. Smarte was consequently awarded 53s. for her damages.[2]

The third case was tried at the Court of Common Pleas. Richard Steele, late of the parish of St. Margaret, Westminster, gentleman, was summoned to answer to a plea of Robert Towsey, who said, through his attorney, Richard Hastler, that on the 1st October 1707 Steele borrowed £18 from him, to be paid when requested. He would not pay, however; and

[1] Queen's Bench Judgment Roll. Mich. 6 Anne, 342. Isaac Fernandez Nunes lived in Mark Lane. See p. 84.

[2] Queen's Bench Judgment Roll. Mich. 6 Anne, 96.

Towsey claimed £10 damages. Steele's attorney, Richard Arnold, made no answer; and judgment was therefore given against Steele, with 60s. damages.[1]

The next letters are to Mrs. Scurlock. Steele had an attack of the gout, and his wife had been ill.

No^br^ 4th, 1707.

HONOUR'D MADAM

I am sorry your indisposition continues and keeps You in the Countrey, I have my self been under a very severe illnesse for some days but am now almost recover'd: This is my Wife's birthday[2] and I am come down stairs to celebrate it with as much good humour, as my present Health will permit. Your Health is not omitted in Our chearfull moments, and Your Company will extremely improve 'em. I am, Madam,

Y^r^ Most Obedient Son & Most Humble Ser^nt^

RICH^D^ STEELE.

Y^r^ Daughter has been very ill till this day. She gives Her Duty.

No^br^ 13th, 1707.

HONOUR'D MADAM

I am very glad to hear, by my Unkle Scurlock's[3] last letters that you have taken in your horses in Order to Your Journey. Since my last to You I have had an affliction which was perfectly

[1] Common Pleas Judgment Roll. Mich. 6 Anne, 510.

[2] She was then 29.

[3] John Scurlock, of Blaencorse, Llanginning, a mercer at Carmarthen. In 1701 he was complainant in a Chancery suit respecting property called "Blaencorse" left in 1978 by Evan Harris. (Chancery Pleadings. Bridges III. B. and A., No. 325.) In 1702 he was Mayor of Carmarthen, and in 1710 Deputy Mayor. He died in 1715. By his will, dated 11th December 1702, and proved at Carmarthen, 17th May 1715, he directed that his body should be buried decently but not expensively, and he gave to his three younger sons, Alexander, Griffith, and Theophilus, £200 each, when they respectively attained the age of 21; if one died, his share was to be divided equally between the others. His daughter Hester was to have £300 when she was 21, or when she married, if it was with the consent of his beloved wife Hester, whom he left sole executrix, so long as she remained his widow, to manage everything with the approval of the following trustees:—Henry Lloyd, Esq., of Llanllawddog, Co. Carmarthen, and of the Inner Temple, London, Serjeant-at-law, and M.P. for Cardigan Boroughs; John Vaughan, Esq., of Court Derllys, near Carmarthen; his brother-in-law, James Phillipps; his cousin, Richard Phillipps; and his cousin, Nathaniel Morgan. If his wife married again all authority was to go over to these trustees, whom, together with his

New to Me, a fitt of the Gout. I am a little awkard at my Crutches, and have been not so patient as longer experience of this sort of evill usually makes Us. Our new house will be ready for Our Goods next Week and as soon as it is so We will remove to it. I am out of pain, though I can't stirr, in the mean while your Daughter is dancing at t' other end of the roome. She gives Her Duty to You. I am extremely oblig'd to my Unkle Scurlock for His kind present, which will be in town tomorrow-night.

I am, Madam, Y^r Most Obedient Son & Most Humble Ser^nt

RICH^D STEELE.

No^br 20th, 1707,
L^D SUNDERLAND'S OFFICE.

HONOUR'D MADAM

My Wife show'd Me a letter of the 15th from Mrs Pugh, wherein there are the Generall complaints under which every body at present is Sighing, whose concerns are wholly in Land. Chearfull and Ingenuous Tempers may agree so well and concert their affairs in such a manner as to make all things easy. I extremely long to see You, and hope to be on my leggs to receive You, when I first do my self the honour of Kneeling to You, and telling How much I am, Madam,

Y^r Most Obedient Son & Most Humble Ser^nt,

RICH^D STEELE.

My absolute Governess gives her duty to you.

dearly beloved wife, he appointed tutors and governors of his children. He left no bequest to his eldest son, Jonathan, because he had been at a considerable expense with regard to Jonathan's apprenticeship. His second son, David, was to be brought up as a scholar at Oxford until he took one of the degrees in Arts, so as to enable him to provide for himself. All debts, &c., were to be paid out of the estate. The estate real was strictly entailed; it was given to the trustees on behalf, first, of the testator's eldest son, Jonathan, and his lawful issue male in succession according to seniority; in default of such issue male the estate was to go to his second son, David, and his issue male; and so on to his third, fourth, and fifth sons, Alexander, Griffith, and Theophilus; if these all died without male issue the estate was to revert to the daughter or daughters of his eldest son and heir, Jonathan. To his son-in-law, William Bevan, and his wife Elizabeth the testator only gave 10s. each to buy a ring, because they had been a considerable expense to him for their support and maintenance, with their servants, and had had large sums of money from him. In his *Descriptive Excursions through South Wales* (1805, vol. ii. 180), Donovan, quoting what purports to be an inscription in St. Peter's Church, Carmarthen, says that John Scurlock died 22nd Oct. 1715, aged 47; but it is evident, as his will was proved in May, that he died in the spring of the year.

In a few days Mrs. Scurlock reached town, for in the next letter Steele sends his duty to her. There are renewed apologies for being absent from home, occasioned in part by troubles with the Barbados property. In the letter of the 3rd January Steele twice calls his wife "Dear Prue;" this is the first letter in which the name is used.

Debr 8th, 1707.

DEAR RULER

I can't Wait upon you to-day to Hampton-Court. I have the West-Indian businesse on my hands and find very much to be done before Thursday's post. I shall dine at Our Table at Court where the Bearer knows how to come to me with any Orders for

Yr Obedient Husband & Most Humble Sernt

RICHD STEELE.

My duty to my Mother.

Jan. 3d, 1708,
DEVIL TAVERN, TEMPLE-BAR.

DEAR PRUE

I have partly succeeded in my businesse to-day & enclose two Guinneas as earnest of more. Dear Prue I can't come home to dinner. I languish for yr Welfare and will never be a moment carelesse more.

Yr Faithfull Husband R: STEELE.

Send me word you have received this.

Eleven at Night, Jan. 5th, 1708.

DEAR PRUE,

I was going home two hours ago, but was met by Mr Griffith who has kept me ever since meeting me as he came from Mr Lambert's. I'le come within a Pint of Wine. R: S:

We drink yr health, and Mr Griffith is yr Sernt.

Jan. 14th, 1708.

DEAR WIFE

Mr Edgecomb, Ned Ash,[1] and Mr Lumley[2] have desir'd Me to sitt an hour with them at the George in Pall-Mall for which I desire your patience till twelve of clock and that you will go to bed.

I am Ever Thine, RICHD STEELE.

[1] Edward Ash, Esq., M.P. for Heytesbury, was made storekeeper of the ordnance in April 1710 (Luttrell's Diary, vi. 566).

[2] Perhaps Lieut.-General Lumley, who, like "R. Edgecomb, Esq.," was a subscriber to the collected edition of the *Tatler*.

Feb. 3^{d}, 1708, GREY'S INN.

DEAR PRUE

If the man who has my shoemaker's bill calls let Him be answer'd that I shall call on Him as I come home. I stay Here in Order to get Tonson [1] to discount a Bill for Me and shall dine with Him for that end. He is expected at home every minute.

Y^{r} Most Humble Obedient Husband

RICH^{D} STEELE. [2]

Feb. 11th, 1708.

DEAR WIFE

Having your absolute commands to make an end to day, I stay to dine with Mr Tryon in Order thereunto. [3] I will be at home early, and desire you would make much of y^{r} self which is the great favour you can do

Y^{r} Affectionate Husband & Dutyfull Serv^{nt}

RICH^{D} STEELE. [4]

The Mr. Tryon here mentioned, and whose name frequently occurs in this correspondence, has not hitherto been identified. Rowland Tryon, merchant, was a subscriber to the first octavo edition of the *Tatler;* and Oldmixon, in his account of Barbados, [5] says, "The people of the Island have agents in England, to take care of their affairs, to whom they allow £250 a year." There were three of these agents, and in 1708 one of them was Rowland Tryon, merchant, the others being William Bridges, Esq., and Sir John Stanley. This fully explains the allusions to the "effects" which Steele was often expecting to receive from Tryon, and which he sometimes could not get. Rowland Tryon was nephew to a remarkable man, Thomas Tryon, who died in August 1703. Thomas Tryon was born in Gloucestershire in 1634; he came to London in 1651,

[1] The bookseller in Gray's-Inn.

[2] "To Mrs. Steele, third door, right-hand, Berry-street."

[3] This relates to the property in Barbados. In the earlier days of Barbados, property changed hands like chattels by transfer of possession, and not always by deed, and it is therefore difficult to trace property by means of the Public Records.

[4] "To Mrs. Steele, at her house, 3rd door right hand, turning out of Germin Street."

[5] *British Empire in America* (1708), ii. 131. Oldmixon twice quotes from Thomas Tryon's "Letters."

and joined the Baptists in 1654. He studied astrology and physic, and became a mystic in religion, laying down for himself an austere rule of life. In 1661 he married, and then made two visits on business to Barbados, after which he settled down at Hackney, a prosperous City man. He wrote numerous little books, containing his opinions on the eating of flesh, &c., with many wise remarks on diet and cleanliness. Mrs. Aphra Behn wrote laudatory verses upon him. Among his *Letters, Domestic and Foreign* (1700), are several about the production of cotton, sugar, &c., addressed to a gentleman in Barbados. His *Memoirs*, "written by himself," were published in 1705; he also left a manuscript collection of Laws for the Tryonist "Society of Clean and Innocent Livers."[1] In his will[2] mention is made, among other kinsfolk, of his nephew Rowland Tryon, with whom we are more directly concerned. There is a document in the Record Office[3] dated 24th Jan. 1708[-9], bearing testimony to the good character and obliging manner of Mr. Skeen, Secretary of the Island of Barbados, who was known personally or by reputation to those whose signatures were appended, and who all had estates or effects in the Island. Among those who signed this paper were William Tryon, Rowland Tryon, and Richd Steele. Alexander Skeen was, it seems, tried by jury in 1705, for several misdemeanours, but was acquitted.

In Hilary term, 1708, the decision was given in another action for debt. In Michaelmas term last past Zachariah Baggs, treasurer of the theatre, whom we have already heard of in the pleadings in the case of Steele *v.* Rich, which was at this date before the Court of Chancery, had brought in a bill complaining that whereas Steele on the 1st August 1707, at Westminster, was indebted to him in the sum of £4. 6s., which he had lent to Steele before that time, Steele, being so indebted,

[1] It is doubtful if the Tryonists ever formed a sect, such as is described in the not very reliable book, *The Post Boy robb'd of His Mail*, 1706, p. 430. Other particulars of Thomas Tryon may be found in "A Pythagorean of the Seventeenth Century. A paper . . . by A. Gordon, M.A." (1871). Several pamphlets appeared in 1663 describing the trial and execution of "Colonel" James Turner for breaking open the house of Mr. Francis Tryon, of Lime Street, London, "an ancient wealthy merchant."

[2] P.C.C. 176 Degg.

[3] Colonial Office Records; Board of Trade. Barbados, No. 16.

acknowledged it, and promised to pay the money when asked to do so; and whereas afterwards, on the 1st October of the same year, at Westminster, Steele compounded with him for divers sums of money which he owed Baggs, and which were still unpaid and in arrears, and upon this composition was then and there found in arrears in £4. 6s., which sum he promised faithfully to pay when required; nevertheless he had not paid, and refused to do so, wherefore Baggs claimed damages of £15. The case came before the Court of Queen's Bench on Friday next after the Octaves of Hilary, 1708, but Steele neither appeared nor said anything in bar of the action; and the Sheriff of Middlesex was accordingly commanded to inquire what damages Baggs had sustained in this matter.[1] It does not appear what damages were finally awarded.

It is clear from the next letters that other creditors had to be appeased.

Ap. 9th, 1708.

DEAR DEAR PRUE

I have sent Dawson thirty pounds, and will not rest till I have enough to discharge Her. In the mean time I thought fitt to let you know this, that you may see I cannot forbear making You acquainted with any [thing] that concerns Us without yr Asking.

Yrs Ever RICHD STEELE.

TENNIS COURT COFFEE-HOUSE,
May 5th, 1708.

DEAR WIFE

I hope I have done this day what will be pleasing to you; in the mean time shall lye this night at a Barbers, one Legg, over against the Devill Tavern at Charing Crosse. I shall be able to confront the fools who wish me Uneasy and shall have the Satisfaction to see thee Chearfull and at Ease.

If the Printer's boy be at Home send Him hither, and let Mrs Todd send by the Boy my Night-Gown, Slippers & Clean Linnen. You shall Hear from me early in the morning.[2]

[1] Queen's Bench Judgment Roll. Hilary, 6 Anne 204. The language of the Roll is very obscure. Sums of £4. 6s. are mentioned several times, as if they were separate amounts, but I think that to render the matter intelligible we must assume that there was one amount only.

[2] The signature has been removed. The letter is addressed "To Mrs Steele, at her house, the last house but two on the left hand, Berry Street, St. James's."

May 10th, 1708.

DEAR PRUE

I dine at the Gentleman-Usher's Table at S^{nt} James's. I have done a great deal of businesse this morning. Pray send Rich^{d} to me as soon as He has dined. Y^{rs} Ever, RICH^{D} STEELE.

May 19th, 1708,
L^{D} SUNDERLAND'S OFFICE,
11 of Clock.

DEAR PRUE

I desire of You to gett the Coach [1] and y^{r} Self ready as soon as You can conveniently and call for Me here from Whence We will go and Spend some time together in the fresh Air in free Conference. Let my best Periwigg be put in the Coach Box and my New Shoes for 'tis a Comfort to be well dress'd in agreeable Company. You are Vitall Life to

Y^{r} Oblig'd Affectionate Husband & Humble Ser^{nt}

RICH^{D} STEELE.

2 o'clock, May 21, [1708.]

DEAR PRUE,

Mr. Addison being chosen for Lostwithiel [2] in Cornwall; I am obliged, with some persons concerned, to go to him immediately.

Yours ever, RICH^{D} STEELE.

May 25th [1708.]
Almost one of Clock, D. SUNDERLAND'S OFFICE.

DEAR PRUE

I wish Sleeping so long this morning after I came to Work [3] may not do you harm. I design to dine at Court, After which I

[1] Mrs. Steele is said to have been rather given to speaking in company of their *chariot;* and a rather feeble anecdote of how Steele used to call her attention to this habit by saying, "Oysters, my dear"—referring to a story he had told her—will be found in the *Scots Magazine* for 1739 (i. 261–2).

[2] Mr. Addison was at this period returned to Parliament for Lostwithiel, together with James Kendall, Esq. (though they had not the majority of votes), either by the misunderstanding or the partiality of Alexander Johns, the Mayor, who was the Returning Officer. But they were not permitted to take their seats; their opponents (the Hon. Francis Robartes and the Hon. Russel Robartes) having proved that the right of election had been violated. See the Journals of the House of Commons, vol. xvi. p. 14. Mr. Addison was afterwards chosen for Malmesbury. [Nichols.]

[3] "This morning" repeated in original.

shall return to the office and shall be glad of a Visitt there from so Agreeable a Lady as Your self.

I am yrs Unreservedly

RICHD STEELE.

June 4th, [1708.]

DEAR PRUE

I have been earnestly about the Affairs we talk'd of last night, and am to Meet Mr. Foulerton at four in the Afternoon again. Beleive me to be what I really am,

Yr Affectionate Tender

Oblig'd Husband & Lover

RICHD STEELE.

I shall dine abroad & can't go with You to the Park. It would not be amisse if you visited Mrs. Tryon in Lime Street. Be in good Humour if you go.

June 5th, 1708.

DEAR PRUE

What you would have me do I know not. All that my fortune will compasse you shall always enjoy, and have no body near you that You do not like except I am my self disapprovd by You for being devotedly Yr Obedient Husband RICHD STEELE.

I shan't come home till night.

June 7th, 1708.

DEAR PRUE

I enclose to you a Guinnea for yr Pockett. I dine with Ld Hallifax.

I wish I knew how to Court you into Good-Humour, for Two or Three Quarrells more will dispatch Me quite. If you have any Love for Me beleive I am always pursuing our Mutuall Good. Pray consider that all My little fortune is to [be] settled this month and that I have inadvertently made my self Liable to Impatient People who take all advantages. If you have [not] patience I shall transact my businesse rashly and Lose a very great sum to Quicken the time of yr being ridd of all people you don't like.

Yrs Ever RICHD STEELE.

In this month of June judgment was given in an action for debt brought before the Court of Queen's Bench by John Huggins, Esquire, of whom we shall hear further. Huggins was bailiff of the Liberty of the Dean and Chapter of the

Collegiate Church of St. Peter, Westminster. His attorney in this action was Charles Sanderson; Steele's attorney was Henry Benson. In the preceding term—Easter—Huggins brought in a bill for debt against Richard Steele, gentleman, of St. James's, Westminster, in the custody of the Marshal of the Marshalsea. The bill stated that on the 10th January 1706 Steele gave a bond, duly signed and sealed, which was produced in Court, acknowledging that he owed Huggins £60, to be paid when desired; but although the money had often been asked for, Steele neither had paid nor would pay. Huggins, therefore, claimed £10 damages. On the 4th June 1708, up to which date Steele had leave to reply to the bill, both parties appeared; but when Huggins asked for Steele's answer, Steele's attorney said that he was not informed of anything to say in bar of the action, and as there was no defence judgment was given in favour of Huggins.[1]

There is a very interesting letter, written at this time, respecting Mrs. Scurlock's proposals for settling her property. Steele was disinterested—"divested as I am of all relations;" and in urging Mrs. Scurlock to settle everything upon her daughter and her daughter's children, he hints that the plans which his mother-in-law had proposed had been formed during a sudden passion. It is evident that Mrs. Steele was sometimes not on good terms with her mother.

June 15th, 1708.

MADAM

After having been with Mr Owen I chuse this Way of communicating to You my Sense on that occasion rather than by word of mouth in a case wherein I am too nearly concern'd not to be fearfull of letting fall something which might appear too negligent or too carefull of my own interests, which are faults I would Equally Shun.

The Sum̄ of the Orders You have giv'n Your Council I take to be that You would settle an hundred & sixty pound a Year liable to certain Debts upon Us and the Survivor of Us, and to Our Children, and reserve Two hundred and forty in yr self, to be giv'n to whome You shall think fitt after Yr Decease; Adding a very unexpected clause in my behalfe of making the whole estate liable to 2500*l.*

[1] Queen's Bench Judgment Roll. Trinity, 7 Anne, 389.

after My Death in case I outlive my Wife without Issue. After I have thank'd You in the Humblest manner for this very Great instance of Kindnesse to me I begg Leave to represent to You that I sincerely have no regards in this World (Devested as I am of all relations that might enjoy any thing after Me) but what have an immediate prospect towards a Plentifull maintenance of my Wife and Children, and therefore I can say with the strictest Truth that in case I shall live to a time when I shall have neither, I should be very far from desiring to Turn[1] the Current of the Estate out of the Channell it would have been [in] Had I never come into the Family.

Forgive me then If I humbly desire that you would take it into y^r consideration to Settle ev'n lesse if you think fitt on Us during y^r life, but Absolutely fix the whole on[2] y^r Daughter and her posterity, which You'le upon reflection find to be giving lesse out of y^r self (in case you Survive Us both), than if at my Death after that of my Wife I should lay upon You such a Sum as you are inclin'd to Give Me.

I am very confident You have no thoughts of alienating any thing from y^r Child, and however too great a Sensibility of Spirit may sometimes suspend your Kindnesse to each other, You Know Nature does recurr, and all little Bitternesses Vanish into Tendernesse. Now Madam, If you duly Weigh this I beleive you'le be convinc'd that there can be no consequence of y^r reserving a Power of Alienation in y^r self, but laying y^r self open to the Suggestions of sudden passion, to do what you would, in a deliberate Temper, not have it in y^r Power to recall. But if you keep very plentifully for y^r self while living, and bestow the whole after y^r Death, You lay a foundation for y^r being always above fears of any change in Her, or disregard to You, and at the same time secure y^r self against the Temptations which all Mortalls are liable to, that is to say, to other people's designs, or our Own infirmities. I will not trouble You longer at this time, but leave it to y^r own good nature, and good Understanding to determine y^r resolutions towards Me and Mine, which I beseech God to conduct and Reward.

I am, Madam,

Y^r Most Obedient Son,

RICH^D STEELE.

We must now turn back to the beginning of the year to see what was passing in the outer world.

[1] Originally "from turning." [2] Originally "on the posterity of."

IV.

SWIFT IN LONDON.

1708–9. ÆT. 36–37.

SWIFT came over to England in November 1707, and he was in London by the middle of December. In January 1708 he was named for the bishopric of Waterford, but the see was given to another; and then he published, anonymously, two witty but earnest pamphlets, the *Argument to prove the Inconvenience of Abolishing Christianity*, and the *Project for the Advancement of Religion and the Reformation of Manners.*[1] During the summer of 1708 Swift was in constant intercourse with Addison and Steele. In his note-book there are entries of dinners with them, as well as with Halifax and Congreve, and he still oftener met one or other of them separately; as he says to Ambrose Philips, "the truimvirate of Addison, Steele, and me, come together as seldom as the sun, moon, and earth; but I often see each of them, and each of them me and each other." About March he commenced the attack on John Partridge, chief of the astrological almanack makers, who were unprincipled rogues, trading upon the ignorance of the poor.

John Partridge,[2] whose real name appears to have been Hewson, was a cobbler. When he was about 38 he turned his attention to astrology and quack medicine; it was said that he was a pupil of John Gadbury, also a famous almanack maker. Partridge began to publish in 1679, and he seems to have been mixed up in some questionable political transactions. At the

[1] See *Tatler*, No. 5.

[2] Further details about Partridge will be found at the end of the fifth volume of Nichols' edition of the *Tatler* (1786).

accession of James II. he fled to Holland, but returned to London in 1688, when he was sworn physician to the Prince and Princess of Orange, and resumed the publication of his *Merlinus Liberatus.* This continued for some eighteen years, not, however, without various quarrels with rival quacks. After the appearance of Partridge's almanack for 1708, Swift—taking a name from the sign-board of a shoemaker—wrote his *Predictions for the Year* 1708, "wherein the month and day of the month are set down, the persons named, and the great actions and events of next year particularly related, as they will come to pass. Written to prevent the people of England from being further imposed on by vulgar almanack-makers. By Isaac Bickerstaff Esq." Isaac Bickerstaff professed to be a true astrologer, disgusted at the lies told by impostors. He was willing to be hooted at as a cheat if his prophecies were not exactly fulfilled. "My first prediction is but a trifle, yet I will mention it, to show how ignorant these sottish pretenders to astrology are in their own concerns: it relates to Partridge the almanack-maker; I have consulted the star of his nativity by my own rules, and find he will infallibly die upon the 29th of March next, about eleven at night, of a raging fever; therefore I advise him to consider of it, and settle his affairs in time." On the 30th March a second pamphlet was published, *The accomplishment of the first of Mr. Bickerstaff's Predictions . . . in a letter to a Person of Quality*, "in which a detailed account is given of Partridge's death, at five minutes after seven, by which it is clear that Mr. Bickerstaff was mistaken almost four hours in his calculation. . . . Whether he had been the cause of this poor man's death, as well as the predictor, may be very reasonably disputed." Before his death "Partrige"—the spelling of the name was often varied, in order that the astrologer might have no case against his assailants—confessed that he was merely a cheat.

Other pamphlets, such as *An Answer to Bickerstaff*, were written to keep up the pretence that Bickerstaff's *Predictions* were really published at the same time as the other almanacks for 1708. And then Partridge issued his almanack for 1709, protesting that he was still living. "I am still alive and (excepting my age) as well as ever I was in my life, as I was also on the 29th of March. And that paper was said to be done by one *Bickerstaffe*, Esq; but that was a sham name, it was done by an impudent lying fellow." Swift at once replied with *A Vindication of Isaac Bickerstaff Esq.*,[1] in which he complained that Partridge's language towards him was not such as should be used by one gentleman to another differing from him on a point merely speculative. He would prove Partridge was not alive. No one living could write such rubbish as the new almanack. It was true Partridge did not die until the evening of the 29th March; "whether he be since revived I leave the world to judge." The argument that Partridge still published his almanack amounted to nothing; for Gadbury, Poor Robin, and others still issued almanacks, though they had some of them been dead for years.

The jest was now taken up by other wits, including Rowe, Steele, Prior, and Congreve; and in April 1709 Steele began the *Tatler*, under the name of Isaac Bickerstaff. With his usual liberality he gave Swift the highest praise, as having made Mr. Bickerstaff's name famous through all parts of Europe. In August 1710 a pamphlet was announced[2] called *Esquire Bickerstaff detected;* "or, The Astrological Impostor convicted. By John Patridge (*sic*), Student in Physic and Astrology. . . . Pr 1^{d}." Whereupon an advertisement was inserted in the *Tatler* (No. 216): "Whereas an ignorant upstart in Astrology has publicly endeavoured to persuade the World, that he is the late John Partridge, who died the 28th of March, 1708. These are to certify all whom it may concern, that the true John Partridge was not only dead at that time, but continues so to this present day. Beware of counterfeits, for such are abroad." Partridge was silent for some years, and then he published an almanack for 1714 called *Merlinus Redivivus*, "by John Partridge, a Lover of Truth," with an epistle to Isaac Bickerstaff, Esq.

[1] Noticed in *The Works of the Learned* for March 1709, among "Books published during the month."

[2] *Daily Courant*, Aug. 23, 1710. This pamphlet was said to be by Congreve (Addison to Lord Wharton, Aug. 24, 1710).

SIR,

There seems to be a kind of fantastical propriety in a dead man's addressing himself to a person not in being. ISAAC BICKERSTAFF is no more,[1] and I have now nothing to dispute with on the subject of his fictions concerning me,[2] *sed magni nominis umbra*, A shadow only, and a mighty name. I have indeed been some years silent, or, in the language of Mr. BICKERSTAFF, *dead*, yet like many an old man that is reported so by his heirs, I have lived long enough to bury my successor. In short, I am returned to being after you have left it; and since you were once pleased to call yourself my brother astrologer the world may be apt to compare our story to that of the twin stars, *Castor* and *Pollux*, and say, that it was our destiny not to appear together, but, according to the fable, to live and die by turns. Now, Sir, my intention in this epistle is to let you know that I shall behave myself with as much moderation as possible, and that I have no longer any quarrel with you for the accounts you inserted in your writings concerning my death, being sensible that you were no less abused in that particular than myself. The person from whom you took up that report, I know, was your namesake, the author of Bickerstaff's *Predictions*, a notorious cheat. And if you had been, indeed, as much an astrologer as you pretended, you might have known that his word was no more to have been taken than that of an Irish evidence, that not being the only *Tale of a Tub* he had vented. The only satisfaction therefore I expect, is that your bookseller, in the next edition of your works, do strike out my name, and insert his in the room of it. I have some thought of obliging the world with his nativity, but shall defer that to another opportunity. I have nothing to add further, but that when you think fit to return to life again, in whatever shape, of Censor, a Guardian, an Englishman, or any other figure, I shall hope you will do justice to your revived friend and servant,

JOHN PARTRIDGE.

Partridge did not live long after writing this friendly letter. He died in earnest in June 1715, and was buried at Mortlake.[3]

[1] Steele was writing the *Englishman* in 1713.

[2] See *Tatler*, Nos. 7, 11, 56, 59, 67, 99, 216, 228, 240. In the *Post Boy* for Dec. 5 to 7, 1710, it was announced that the almanack published by Benjamin Harris, called *Merlinus Liberatus*, and said to be by J. Partridge, was not by him. "There will not be any almanack written by John Partridge, published for the year 1711."

[3] His tomb is in the S.E. corner of Mortlake Churchyard. It bears the inscription: "Johannes Partridge, Astrologus et Medicinae Doctor, natus est

We must now turn to the position of parties in the country. Sunderland was made Secretary of State in 1706, and at the beginning of 1707 several Whig peers were created; while, on the other hand, Nottingham, Rochester, and Buckingham, all High Tories, were struck off the list of the Privy Council. Marlborough had apparently obtained what he desired—a thoroughly composite Government. But this state of affairs did not last long. Harley intrigued against Marlborough, making use of the Queen's High Church views; his cousin, Mrs. Abigail Hill, was appointed bedchamber-woman, and married Mr. Masham, a gentleman of Prince George's household. Through her Harley represented to the Queen that the Church was endangered. The Whigs were indignant, and in October the composite Ministry broke down. A clerk in Harley's office, named Gregg, was found to be in treasonable communication with France, and the Queen, forced on by a threat of resignation by the Ministers, consented to Harley's dismissal in February 1708. At the same time Boyle, John Smith, and Robert Walpole took the places of St. John, Harcourt, and Mansell. The Whigs seemed for the time triumphant.

When Swift came to London at the close of 1707 he and Addison and Steele were all Whigs together, but Swift was above all a Churchman, after a Conservative fashion. As I have said, this was the time when Swift was on terms of the greatest intimacy with Addison and Steele.[1] We find him dining with Steele at the "George," with Addison as host; and with Addison at the "Fountain," with Steele as host. Addison wrote to Swift on February 29, 1708, "Mr. Steele and Frowde"—Philip Frowde, a great favourite, and the writer of two tragedies—"will dine with us." On September 16, 1708,

apud East-Sheen, in comitatu Surrey, 8° die Januarii, anno 1644, et mortuus est Londini 24° die Junii, anno 1715. Medicum fecit duobus Regibus unaeque Reginae; Carolo scilicet Secundo, Willielmo Tertio, Reginaeque Mariae. Creatus Medicinae Doctor Lugduni Batavorum." (Sir R. Phillips's *A Morning's Walk from London to Kew*, 1820, p. 233.)

[1] Steele and Addison knew many of the prominent men in the Church. Among the Ballard MSS., vol. vii. fol. 9 (Bodleian Library), there is a letter from Dr. Smalridge to Dr. Charlett, dated June 22, 1708, in which Smalridge says, "Since my last I have seen Mr Addison and Mr Steele, but they neither of them know Mr Ward."

Anthony Henley wrote to Swift, "We have had a tedious expectation of the success of the siege of Lisle. . . . I don't know how Steele will get off of it;[1] his veracity is at stake in Hantshire. Pray desire him to take the town, tho' he should leave the citadel for a nest-egg. I han't the honour to know Colonel Hunter, but I never saw him in so good company as you have put him in, Lord Halifax, Mr. Addison, Mr. Congreve, and the Gazetteer." Anthony Henley was son of Sir Robert, whose house, The Grange, in Hampshire, was a frequent meeting-place of the wits. Hunter, who was afterwards Captain-General in Jamaica, was one of Swift's best correspondents. Henley's letter is illustrated by one from Swift to Archbishop King, which shows Swift's influence with Steele:[2] "We are now every day expecting news from abroad of the greatest importance. Nothing less than a battle, a siege, or Lisle taken. . . . Wagers run two to one for the last. In the last *Gazette* it was certainly affirmed that there would be a battle; but the copy coming to the office to be corrected, I prevailed with them to let me soften the phrase a little, so as to leave some room for possibilities; and I do not find the soldiers here are so very positive."

In the meantime Steele had taken or, according to Benjamin Victor,[3] built, a house at Hampton Wick, which he called The Hovel. On December 8, 1707, he told his "dear ruler" that he could not wait upon her that day to Hampton Court. In August 1708 Mrs. Steele was established in the new house, and in the next letters we see the extravagant side of her nature. She had a chariot with two or four horses, a saddle-horse of her own, Richard the footman, the gardener, a boy Will, her own woman Watts, and a boy who could speak Welsh. Steele shows, too, in the letters of this period unmistakable signs of rebellion at the

[1] In the *Gazette*.

[2] Forster's *Life of Swift*, 244.

[3] Victor wrote to Garrick in 1762: "At my last agreeable visit to your delightful villa, one day was charmingly spent at the house of your honourable friend Mr. H——n at Hampton Court; . . . I told you then the enthusiastic pleasure I felt in remembering that house was built, and many years joyously inhabited, by my very worthy friend, Sir Richard Steele." (*Original Letters*, &c., i. 327.)

way in which he was required to account for every minute of his time, and for everything that he did. He did not think his wife should be "his sovereign director."

Augst 11th, 1708.

DEAR WIFE

I have order'd Rich^{d} to take your directions, whether You will have the Chariot with two or four horses to sett you and y^{r} freind down at your house at Hampton-Court. Watts is gone over the Water and says she has your commands to follow in the Stage-Coach. I shall make it the businesse of my life to make you easy and happy: Consult y^{r} cool thoughts & you'le know that 'tis the glory of a Woman to be her husband's Freind and Companion and not his Sovereign Director.

I am with Truth, Sincerity and Tendernesse Ever y^{r} Faithfull Husband,

R. STEELE.

Pray let the Gardner put the place in order.

Aug$_{st}$ 12th, 1708.

MADAM

I have your letter wherein you let me know that the little dispute we have had is far from being a Trouble to you, neverthelesse I assure you any disturbance between Us is the greatest affliction to me imaginable. You talk of the Judgement of the World I shall never govern my Actions by y^{t}, but by the rules of morality and Right reason. I Love you better than the light of my Eyes or the life-blood in my Heart but when I have lett you know that you are also to understand that neither my sight shall be so far inchanted or my affection so much master of me as to make me forgett our Common Interest. To attend my businesse as I ought, and improve my fortune it is necessary that my time and my Will should be under no direction but my own. Pray give my most Humble Service to Mrs Binns. I write all this rather to explain my own thoughts to You than answer Your letter distinctly. I inclose it to You that upon second thoughts you may see the disrespectfull manner in which you Treat

y^{r} Affectionate Faithfull Husband

R. STEELE.

Augst 13th, 1708.

MADAM,

I hope this will find You in good Health as I am at this present Writing thanks be to God for it.

I have not only rebell'd against you but all the rest of my Governours from Y^r Self whome I acknowledge to have the right of Partnership to the Lowest person who had to do with Me. I have a very Just sense of Y^r Merit and think, when I have putt you into the proper methods which You ought to follow I shall be the happiest man living in being

Y^r most Affectionate Husband & Humble Ser^nt

RICH^D STEELE.[1]

Aug^st 13th, 1708,
four in the Afternoon.

DEAR PRUE

I send You some Tea which I doubt not but you will find is very good. I am

Y^r very Affectionate Husband & Most Humble Ser^nt

RICH^D STEELE.

This is my second letter to-day.

Monday Morning, Aug^st 16th, 1708.

DEAR PRUE

I hope you have compos'd Your mind and are convinc'd that the methods I have taken were absolutely necessary for our Mutuall Good. I do assure You there is not that thing on earth except my Honour and that dignity which every man who lives in the world must preserve to Himself, which I am not ready to sacrifice to y^r Will and inclination.

I din'd Yesterday with my Lord Hallifax[2] where the Beauties in the Garden[3] were drank to. I have settled a great deal of businesse within these few days, of all which I will give you an account when We meet. I am with the most sincere affection

y^r Oblig'd Husband R. STEELE.

I sent you some Tea on Friday last. My most Humble Service to Mrs Binns.

Aug^st 18th, 1708.

DEAR PRUE

I have Your letter and all the Great severity you complain of is that you have a Husband Who loves you better than His life who

[1] Directed "To Mrs. Steele, at her house in the Wick, near Hampton Court."

[2] Lord Halifax lived near Hampton Court, and this was perhaps the cause of Steele's extravagance in buying a house there.

[3] Mrs. Steele and her friend Mrs. Binns.

has a great deal of troublesome businesse out of the [fatigue] of which He removes the dearest thing alive.

Y^rs^ Faithfully in spite of y^r^ self RICH^D^ STEELE.

It is to be presumed that Addison lent Steele the £1000 mentioned in the postscript of the next letter to meet the expenses attendant upon the purchase of the house at Hampton Court.

August 20th, 1708.

DEAR PRUE

Yours by penny post came to my hands but Just now. You extremely mistake me in beleiving Me capable of any Cruelty or Unkindnesse to You. I scorn that any man living should have more honour and regard to His Wife than my self. You speak with Heat to me but I will not answer you in that stile but make it my utmost aim to make you easy and happy to which you [*sic*] nothing but doing me the Justice to beleive me with all the affection Imaginable

Yr Faithfull husband RICHD STEELE.

I have paid Mr Addison His whole thousand pound and have settled every man's payment except one which I hope to perfect to-morrow. Desmaiseaux[1] is gone to the Bath for His Health.

I enclose a guinnea and an half & will send more tomorrow or munday if I don't come my self.

I am Mrs Binns' Servant.

Augst 28th, 1708.

DEAR PRUE

The Afternoon Coach shall bring you ten pounds. Your letter shows you are passionately in Love with Me. But We must

[1] Peter Desmaiseaux, Secretary of the Royal Society of London, was the son of a French Protestant minister, and was born at Auvergne in 1666. He retired early, probably as a refugee, into England, and died here in 1745. He had intimate connections with St. Evremond and Bayle. He gave a handsome edition of the works of the former, in 3 vols. 4to, with a life of the author prefixed; and he drew up the life of the latter, which was printed before the edition of his Dictionary in 1730, and separately at the Hague, 1732, 2 vols. 12mo. He published also, the same year, the *Miscellaneous Works of Bayle*, in 4 volumes, folio. He was the editor of other things; and whatever he published, he always accompanied with remarks full of literary anecdotes. He was very exact and curious in his accounts; but somewhat prolix and tedious, by running out into too much detail and minute discussions [Nichols].—In another note, undated, Steele speaks of spending the evening at Desmaiseaux's house.

take our portion of life as it runs without repining and I consider that Good nature added to that Beautifull form God has giv'n you would make an happinesse too great for Humane life.

Y^r^ Most Oblig'd Husband & Most Humble serv^nt^

RICH^D^ STEELE.

Aug^st^ 30th, 1708.

DEAR PRUE

I sent ten pounds by the Afternoon Coach of Saturday and hope you receiv'd it safe. The manner in which you write to Me might perhaps to another look like neglect and want of Love, but I will not understand it so but take it to be only the uneasinesse of a doating fondnesse which cannot bear my Absence without disdain.

I hope We shall never be so long asunder more, for it is not in Your power to make me otherwise than

Y^r^ Affectionate Faithfull & Tender Husband

RICH^D^ STEELE.

Sep^br^ 8th, 1708,
Two Afternoon, SANDY-END.

DEAR PRUE

Having reach'd London about eleven, dispatch'd what was further necessary after what Papers Mr. Addison had before Sent to the Presse, I am Just now arriv'd Here to dinner. You desire me to make submissions in my Epistles which I think is not to be insisted upon, but if acknowledgements will satisfie You I cannot but own to You, what you too well know that you have a power almost Soveraign over Y^r^ Most Enamourd Husband & Humble Ser^nt^

RICH^D^ STEELE.

Mr. Addison is y^r^ Humble Ser^nt^.

Sep^br^ 9th, 1708, Seven in the Morning.

DEAR PRUE

I am going this morning to visitt Mr. Sartre [1] at His Countrey-house to which place Mr. Addison conveys me in Coach and Four.

[1] James Sartre, M.A., formerly a minister at Montpelier, and prebendary of Westminster, from May 17, 1688, till his death, Sept. 5, 1713. Swift, in his Journal to Stella, Oct. 25, 1710, says: "I dined to-day with Mr. Addison and Steele, and a sister of Mr. Addison, who is married to one Mons. Sartre, a Frenchman, prebendary of Westminster, who has a delicious house and gardens; yet I thought it was a sort of monastic life in those cloisters, and I liked Laracor better. Addison's sister is a sort of wit, very like him. I was not fond of her." This lady was afterwards married to Daniel Combes, Esq. [Nichols.]

Mr. Clay[1] who is now at Thistleworth will not be in town till to-morrow and I want to consult Him in some dispatches I am making for the West-Indies. I am Mrs. Binns's Humble Servant and y^r^ most Affectionate Obedient Husband

RICH^D^ STEELE.

My service to Ally.

In a letter of the 13th, to his "peevish beauty," Steele felt it necessary to say, "Good Prue, write me word you shall be overjoyed at my return to you."

Sep^br^ 14th, 1708.

DEAR PRUE

I fear I shall not be so happy as to See You till Thursday having some businesse which Keeps Me in town. I shall, to-day, visit my Mother in Order to discourse about proper methods for paying off, or laying the debt on Y^r^ Estate into one hand. I hope God will blesse my sincere endeavours so as that We may live without the cares of this life, with a Chearfull prospect of a better. 'Tis in no one's power but Prue's to make Me constant in such a Regular course. Therefore will not doubt but you'le be very good humour'd and be a Constant Feast to

y^r^ Affectionate Husband RICH^D^ STEELE.

My obedient service to Mrs Binns.

With the next letter Steele sent seven-pennyworth of walnuts at five a penny, and then he gravely added that since writing the letter there were but twenty-nine walnuts. Mrs. Steele was very thrifty in small matters sometimes.

Sep^br^ 19th, 1708, five in the Evening.

DEAR PRUE

I send you seven-pen'orth of wall nutts at five a penny Which is the greatest proof I can give you at present of my being with my whole Heart

Y^rs^ RICH^D^ STEELE.

The little Horse comes back with the Boy who returns with him for Me on Wednesday evening. In the mean time I beleive it will be well that He run in the Park.

Ime Mrs Binns's Servant.

[1] Afterwards one of Steele's literary coadjutors. See the *Tatler*, No. 83. [Nichols.]

Since I writ this I came to the place where the Boy was order'd with the Horses and not finding him sent this Bearer lest you should be in fears the Boy not returning.

There are but 29 Walnutts.[1]

Sep^{br} 27th, 1708, Monday, se'en at Night.

DEAR PRUE

You See you are obey'd in every thing and that I write over night for the day following; I shall now in earnest by Mr Clay's good conduct manage my businesse with that method as shall make me easy. The news, I am told, you had, last night, of the taking of Lille does not prove true but I hope we shall have it soon. I shall send by to-morrow's Coach.

I am, dear Prue a little in Drink but at all times

Y^{r} Faithfull Husband RICH^{D} STEELE.

Oct^{br} 2^{d}, 1708,
S^{NT} JAMES'S COFFEE-HOUSE,
8 in the Morning.

DEAR PRUE

Mr Gervase[2] going this morning to Hampton Court I desire Him to Throw this over our Wall. I have much difficulty to accomplish every thing necessary to be done here, which makes me fear I cannot come till Tuesday noon. If it pleases God y^{t} I can be so happy as to live chearfully with thee and in thy favour 'tis the Utmost of Good can arrive to, Dear Prue, Eternally Thine,

RICH^{D} STEELE.

Oct^{br} 5th, 1708,
BERRY-STREET, seven at Night.

DEAR WIFE

I send this to begg pardon for not coming to-night, but I have some good Glimpse in my affairs and If I do not fail to morrow we shall be out of difficulties hereafter. I come into Waiting on the Prince to-morrow and am, my Dear Prue

Y^{rs} with the Utmost Kindnesse and Duty

RICH^{D} STEELE.[3]

I hope to see You before twelve tomorrow.

[1] Written outside, below the address.
[2] Jervas, the painter.
[3] "To Mrs Steele, at Mr Hardresse's house, in Kensington Square."

Octbr 7th, 1708.

DEAR PRUE

I send directed to Watts a bottle of Tent. You must not expect Me to night, but I will write by the Penny-post.

I am Yrs Faithfully RICHD STEELE.

Octbr 7th, 1708, Thursday.

DR PRUE

I fear I shall not be able to come out of Town till Saturday Morning. I am, My Dear Creature, Thine for Ever

RICHD STEELE.

On this same 7th October Steele wrote to Joseph Keally, Esq., of Keally Mount, Kilkenny, a great friend of Congreve's.[1] Joseph Keally was the son of a John Keally, Esq., of Kilkenny, whose wife's name was Elizabeth, and who had a daughter named after her mother. Joseph, the son, was, as we have seen, a barrister.[2]

Oct. 7, 1708.

DEAR SIR,

I cannot express to you the sincere pleasure yours of the 30th of last month gave me. I thank you for the kind part you take in my affairs, and understand I am to wish you joy upon the happiness of being an husband, which is at least a snug, if not a rapturous, condition. Harry[3] lives still a knight-errant; by what means it is impossible to tell you. But I now and then meet him, and give him the proper compliment, that I am glad to see him alive. The paragraph you mention was very much censured in the town; but I acted so as to answer it where I am accountable. As to the rest, I take my employment in its very nature to be what is the object of censure, since so many interests are concerned in the matters that I am to relate twice a week: but I am armed *cap-à-pée* with old sentences; among which I prefer that of Horace with 300*l. per annum*[4] salary—

Populus me sibilat; at mihi plaudo
Ipse domi; simul ac nummos contemplor, &c.

[1] This letter is given in Berkeley's *Literary Relics*, 1789, p. 397. The version given by Nichols is very incomplete. Mr. Keally was a near relation of George Monck Berkeley (*Relics*, xi.).

[2] Page 65 (Mr. Wills' MSS.). John Keally's will is dated April 8, 1678.

[3] Harry Keally.

[4] The salary attached to his office of Gazetteer.

You propose a correspondence for what occurs here. I begin it very freely, in desiring you to make up a fine prize suit a little everyway too big for yourself, and direct it to Mr Tyndale at Chester for me. You shall from henceforth have every post from me my circular of what passes with the Gazette. Mr Congreve is at Newmarket. Mr Addison is your servant. The taste for Plays is expired. We are all for Operas, performed by eunuchs every way impotent to please. Lord Manchester is returning from Venice with a singer of great expectation. My way of life should make me capable of entertaining with much politics; but I am not a bit wiser than you knew me. I am, with great truth and esteem, your sincere friend, RICH. STEELE.

Since I writ the within, I hear Mr Congreve is ill of the gout in town.

Next day Steele sent his wife some bohea and green tea.

Octbr 8th, 1708.

DEAR PRUE

This brings you a Quarter of a pound of Bohee, and as much of Green Tea, Both which I hope you will find good. Tomorrow morning Yr Favourite Mr Addison and I shall sett out for Hampton-Court, He to meet some great men there,[1] I to see You, who am but what you make me.

Yrs With the Utmost Fondnesse RICHD STEELE.

Octbr 14th, 1708, Thursday.

DEAR PRUE

I intended to have certainly gone to Hampton Court to-day, but the West Indian post going on Saturday and Mr Clay having leisure but this day I am forced to prepare my letters for His perusall, before night. I am in haste as You see by this scribble.

I am, Yr Faithfull & Most Affectionate Husband

RICHD STEELE.

I shall observe what you desire about James[2] & every thing else.

On the same evening Steele wrote that his business would necessitate his staying in town the whole week. He proposed to arrange with Mrs. Scurlock for a mortgage to enable him to

[1] At Lord Halifax's house.

[2] A man whom Steele proposed to engage as footman. He is described as fit for a thorough servant, and he could speak the Welsh tongue fluently.

pay off the bonds which he had given for money lent to him; but this came to nothing. On the 20th he answered a charge of unkindness.

Octbr 20th, 1708.

DEAR WIFE

I had yours last night, with an enclos'd to My Mother which I do not design to deliver. You accuse me of Unkindnesse for I cannot Imagine what. If you want for any thing it is that you will not supply yr self with it, for I very regularly send you wherewithall. For my Lord Chamberlain is expected this night in town from whome I hope for an Order for a very handsome Apartment in Whitehall. As soon as I receive it I will immediately remove into it where I hope you will [be] pleas'd. I am sure it is the utmost of my Ambition to make you so. I am

Yr Faithfull & Affectionate Husband

RICHD STEELE.

My Mother has alter'd her mind about the Mortgage.

I think to come down to-morrow night to give you an Account of Every thing in the mean time send by your Countryman Two Guinneas.

On the 26th Steele, who was, he says, put to great difficulties, was trying, with all the force he had, to get the post of Gentleman-Usher of the Privy-chamber, worth £200 a year, besides £100 in perquisites. In the postscript of that day's letter he admits that he had been very sick through drinking to excess, a vice of the age which Steele could not withstand. Swift, in his *Project for the Advancement of Religion and the Reformation of Manners*, says: "Any man will tell you he intends to be drunk this evening, or was so last night, with as little ceremony or scruple as he would tell you the time of the day." Elsewhere Swift alludes to Addison as "half-fuddled," and says that he himself was "sick all night" after a supper.

Two days later Prince George died. His illness and death are described in the *London Gazette* for October 28 to November 1. "All orders of men discover an unspeakable grief for the loss of so excellent a Prince." In the *Gazette* for November 11 to 15 there is an account of the private interment of the Prince at 10 P.M. on the 13th. Steele would be among the "gentlemen, servants to his Royal Highness," who were in the procession.

Octbr 28th, 1708,
KENSINGTON, 3 Afternoon.

DEAR WIFE

I came hither according to my [duty] to attend the Prince My Master,[1] by whose Dead Body I sitt while I am writing this. He departed this life half-an-hour after One. I am Order'd to Wait Here and beleive I shall not be releiv'd till Tomorrow-Morning. As soon as I can gett to town I'le dispatch the Coach for You. I am, My Dear Wife, Yr Oblig'd Husband & Humble Servant RICHD STEELE.

Octbr 29th, 1708, KENSINGTON.

DEAR WIFE

I inclose all the cash I can well spare which is four Guinneas. I writ you word by the Penny post last night that I was detained here to sit up with the Prince's Body, and must do so every third night till He is interred.[2] I am still kept bare of money by the Men I have to deal with, but as soon as I can gett to town I will send away the Coach for You. Please to come to Mrs. Hardresse's House in the Square at Kensington, where it will be convenient for You to be till all things are ready for our Greater ease in Town. More I cannot say till We meet. I am with the sincerest Affection

Yr oblig'd Husband & Humble Sernt RICHD STEELE.

Send the Bearer back with an account how you do.
My Service to Mrs Bynns.

Subsequent letters relate to his wife's return to town.

Nobr 13th, 1708.

DEAR PRUE

I send You all the money I have which I hope will bring you to town. Since You have an inclination to See the Funerall I have spoken for a place at the Housekeepers of the House of Lords to place You in till I can gett a more convenient one for seeing the

[1] His Royal Highness Prince George of Denmark, Her British Majesty's consort, died at the time here mentioned, at Kensington, of an asthma. He was born at Copenhagen in April 1653, married the Princess Anne in July 1683, and was an illustrious instance of conjugal affection among the great. On the 11th of November his corpse was brought from Kensington to Westminster; and having lain in state in the Painted Chamber till the 13th of that month, was privately interred in the Abbey. [Nichols.]

[2] After the death of the Prince, the Queen bestowed pensions on all his attendants. Steele received £100 a year, which he some time after gave up. (*Importance of Dunkirk considered.*)

Procession. And I take it that it will be best to be in the Abbey it self for which end you must come soon. I am order'd to stay Here or should come for you.

Y[rs] with all my Soul R. STEELE.

The Fleet is come in.

Another action for debt now came before the Court. Some particulars not given in the record of the judgment are furnished by the following paper. The money was borrowed from George Lewis, goldsmith, for six months. "Whereas Richard Steele, Esq[re], hath borrowed of mee, George Lewis, goldsmith, the sum of one hundred pounds, and for securing the payment thereof, with interest, hath given me his bond, dated herewith payable the second day of August next, and hath assigned to me a bond of one hundred and fifteen pounds, and int: from his mother-in-law, M[rs] Scurlock, as a further security. Now I promise on payment of the said one hundred pounds and interest to mee, according to the said bond, given to me by the said Richard Steele, to deliver up both the said bonds and assignments to the said Richard Steele. Witness my hand this 10th day of February, 1707"[1] (1708, N.S.). The debt was soon increased to £300, and in Michaelmas term Steele—"late of the Parish of St. Margaret, Westminster, Esq."—was summoned to answer the plea of George Lewis, who stated by his attorney, Simon Barwell, that on the 10th February 1708, at Islington, Steele by a certain bond acknowledged himself bound to George Lewis in £200, to be paid when requested; and that on the 20th April 1708, at Islington, Steele by another bond acknowledged himself bound to Lewis in £100, making £300 in all. Steele, however, would not pay, and Lewis claimed £10 damages. Henry Barwell, Steele's attorney, made no defence, and the case therefore went in favour of Lewis, who was awarded 80s. damages.[2]

Arrears of rent were due for the house in Bury Street, and an execution was put in. The Mr. Huggins mentioned in

[1] *Epistolatory Curiosities* (*Series the Second*), edited by Rebecca Warner, 1818, p. 240.

[2] Common Pleas Judgment Roll. Mich. 7 Anne, 419.

the following letters was the bailiff whom we have already met with.[1] He was high bailiff of Westminster, and in September 1710 he was made chief solicitor of the Treasury, a post worth £1500 a year.[2] Some time before 1700 Huggins became Warden of the Fleet Prison, and in 1713 (*Post Boy*, May 23–26) he announced that he had discovered great abuses to have been committed, by his own officers and others, in arresting persons and seizing goods without lawful warrant or power for so doing, and he therefore gave notice that all arrests, &c., without his special warrant were an infringement of his liberty and an abuse to the people, and asked to be informed of such action, in order that the officers might be prosecuted. The committee appointed by the instrumentality of General Oglethorpe to inquire into the state of the gaols of this kingdom reported, in 1729, that John Huggins, Esq., by giving £5000 to the late Lord Clarendon, obtained, by his interest, a grant of the office of Warden for his own and his son's life. During his term of office persons were often allowed to escape; and the Reports contain many charges of atrocious conduct against him. As his son did not wish to continue the office, Huggins, when he was old, procured a new patent in favour of the notorious Bambridge and Cuthbert, in consideration of a large payment to him. Huggins seems, from a passage in Steele's *Letter to Sir Miles Wharton*, 1713, to have taken part in Sacheverell's triumphal march through the country in the summer of 1710.

Nov^{br} 16th, 1708, GARTER-TAVERN.

DEAR PRUE

I am sorry I cannot come to sitt an hour with You to-night being detain'd by businesse with Mr. Huggins which You know off. I have to-day been with Mr. Tryon who does not now deny his having effects, but pretends to Complain of hard Usage in suing Him. Within a day or Two I doubt not but We shall have our Money, which will be the introduction into that life we both pant after with so much earnestnesse.

Y^{r} Oblig'd Husband RICH^{D} STEELE.

[1] Page 208. [2] Luttrell's *Diary*, vi. 385, 630.

Nov^br^ 17th, 1708.

DEAR WIFE

How can You add to my Cares by making so unjust complaints against me as in Y^rs^ of last night. I take all the pains imaginable to bring you home to ease and satisfaction, and made a great step in it yester-night, which I could not had I spent my time elsewhere than where I did. My Dear be chearfull, and expect a good account of things this Evening from, Dear Wife,

Y^r^ Most Affectionate & Most Oblig'd Husband,

RICH^D^ STEELE.[1]

Nov^br^ 18th, 1708.

DEAR WIFE

I am going this morning into the City to make my demand of the money long due to Me. I shall hasten thence to You and am, with the Tenderest Love, Ever Y^rs^ RICH^D^ STEELE.

November 26th, 1708.

DEAR WIFE

I am, by applying to my Adversary[2] prepar'd for ending my present calamity, but was deny'd by my Freind.[3]

I am, Dear Creature, Y^r^ Constant Faithfull Lover & Obliged Husband RICH^D^ STEELE.

I am making it my businesse to find out Mr. Huggins in Order to Withdraw His Officer.

Nov^br^ 28th, 1708.

DEAR WIFE

Take Confidence in that Being who has promis'd protection to all the Good and Virtuous when afflicted. Mr. Glover accommodates me with the money which is to clear this present Sorrow this Evening. I will come to Mrs. Bynns's exactly at Eight.

I am Y^r^ Most Affectionate Husband

& Obedient Ser^nt^ RICH^D^ STEELE.

[1] "To Mrs Steele, to be left at Mrs Scurlock's lodgings, last house left-hand in Brumley-street, Holborn."

[2] Perhaps his landlady.

[3] It has been suggested that this friend was Addison, but this is improbable, because only ten days later Steele writes of "your rival, A——n," in connection with a proposal which "will make me happy at once."

Novembr 30th, 1708.

DEAR WIFE:

Be of Good Chear for I find Freindship among the Lowest when disappointed by the Highest. I have call'd at Mr Elderton's[1] to keep Things at a stand till I come to Him at Ten of Clock.

Dear Creature Be chearfull. God be yr Comfort and yr Protection. While that is so, and you are safe nothing can disturb

RICHD STEELE.

Novbr 30th, 1708, 10 of Clock.

DEAR WIFE

This is to Acquaint you that Honest Glover has effectually Serv'd me. I am now in Search of Mr. Huggins in Westminster-hall. Elderton without my knowledge has also remov'd the other storm to some distance so that We prepare in time to Weather. Be of God Chear; God will blesse Me and make Me a better provider hereafter for my Wife and Dear Child.[2]

Yrs Ever, R: STEELE.[3]

Next week it seemed as if all troubles would be removed. Somers became President of the Council, Addison was appointed Secretary to Lord Wharton, the new Viceroy of Ireland, and Steele's friends set about obtaining for him the post of Under-Secretary vacated by Addison.

Decbr 6th, 1708.

MY DEAR WIFE

I will not defer telling You that there is a thing in Agitation that will make me happy at once. Yr Rivall A——n will be remov'd and if I can succeed Him in His Office It will answer all Purposes. This Will be determin'd before tomorrow at noon. I cannot see Mr Glover till six of Clock. I am Yr Faithfull Loving Husband, RICHD STEELE.[4]

Keep this to Yr Self. I'le come to you as soon as I have din'd.

We have met with this friend of Steele's before in the case Smarte *v.* Steele and Elderton, page 200. In the *Examiner* for Oct. 12, 1713, a paper full of allusions to Steele, there is mention of "Mr. Elderton, late of Tuttle Street, Westminster."

[2] Elizabeth, her first child, was born on the 26th March 1709.

[3] "To Mrs Steele, at her house in Berry-street."

[4] "To Mrs Steele at Mrs Scurlock's lodgings, the last house, left hand, in Bromley-street, Holborn."

Steele was still hoping to obtain Addison's place on the 18th, when he assisted in doing the honours at a farewell banquet given by his friend.

Dec^br 18th, 1708.

DEAR PRUE

Mr Addison has engag'd Me about extraordinary businesse all this day. I hope I have engag'd Him to take Desmaiseaux.[1]

I am oblig'd to go to Supper where He treats to-night to help Him in doing the Honours to His Freinds. Y^rs Tenderly

RICH^D STEELE.

Dec^br 22^d, 1708, COCKPITT.

DEAR PRUE

I desire you to take a Coach and come to this Lodgings. I am oblig'd to wait hereabouts. James will find me at Mr. Delafay's[2] house in Downing-street, or at the Coffee-house.

Y^rs faithfully RICH^D STEELE.

On Thursday the 23rd December Luttrell noted in his *Diary:* "Captain Steele is like to succeed Mr Addison in the secretaries office, who goes secretary to the lieutenant of Ireland;" but on the 28th Peter Wentworth wrote to his brother, Lord Raby: "Mr Addison is certain of going over Secretary to Lord Wharton, and Mr Steel put in for his place, but Lord Sunderland has put him off with a promise to get him the next place he shall ask that may be kept with his Gazette. I hear it is one of the Scotch members that is to come into Mr Addison place, but I don't know his name yet."[3] And so Steele had to wait, hoping that "something additional" would be given him, as he expressed it in a letter to Mr. Keally.[4]

[1] See Steele's letter of the 20th August 1708. Addison took Desmaiseaux with him to Dublin, and there obtained for him an appointment. (Miss Aikin's *Life of Addison*, ii. 19.)

[2] Charles Delafaye, Esq., one of the clerks in the Secretary of State's office, and afterwards himself Under-Secretary of State. [Nichols.]

[3] *Wentworth Papers*, 1883, p. 68. The gentleman who got the post was Robert Pringle, Esq., or, according to Luttrell (*Diary*, vi. 391), John Pringle, Esq., knight of the shire for Selkirk.

[4] Berkeley's *Literary Relics*, 395.

LORD SUNDERLAND'S OFFICE,
Jan. 20, 1708–9.

DEAR SIR,

I have your very kind letter of the 1st instant, and am very sorry you had not intelligence sooner of Mr. Addison's being Secretary of State for Ireland. The same messenger who carried an account of it to the Lords Justices had a letter for you in Dublin, wherein I told you the happiness your old acquaintance proposed to himself in your friendship and conversation. Those letters were dated the 28th of the last month; and I believe mine escaped you by your absence from the town at the arrival of the express.

I have communicated your friendly design to the Secretary, relating to his being chosen a member. He gives you his hearty thanks; and desired me to tell you he believed that matter already provided for.

Since he had the honour to be named himself for this post in Ireland, a brother of his has been chosen by the Directors of the East India Company Governor of Fort St. George, in the room of Mr. Pitt.[1]

I had hopes of succeeding him in this office; but things are ordered otherwise in favour of the North Britons, one of whom is to come into that employment very suddenly. In the mean time, something additional will be given to, dear Sir,

Your most affectionate friend and humble servant,

RICH. STEELE.

The post of Irish Secretary was worth £2000 a year, and Addison also obtained a patent making him Keeper for life of the Records in the Birmingham Tower, Dublin, with a salary of £400 a year.[2]

[1] "On the 20th of December 1709, the Directors of the East-India Company chose Mr. Gulston Addison, an eminent Merchant, residing at Fort St. George, Governor and President of that place, in the room of Thomas Pitt, Esq., who, it is said, has obtained leave to come home." (*Postman*, Jan. 1, $170\frac{8}{9}$.) Mr. Gulston Addison, who was born in August 1673, died at Fort St. George, in the office of Governor and President. [Nichols.] Peter Wentworth wrote to his brother, Lord Raby, about this appointment on Jan. 28, 1709: "It seems Mr Addison's friends can do what they please with the chief of the East India Company, who I think have the liberty of naming their Governor, and by management with them this place is got which they say some years are worth 20,000 pound." (*Wentworth Papers*, pp. 75, 76.)

[2] Treasury Papers, vol. cxx. 22 (Public Record Office; Calendar 1708–1714). Jan. 27, $17\frac{09}{10}$. Report of the Lord Lieutenant of Ireland to the Lord High Treasurer, on a petition of Joseph Addison, Esq., who was Keeper of the

With Hilary term, 1709, came more actions for debt. Richard Steele, late of the Parish of St. James, Westminster, Esq., was attached by a writ of privilege to answer to Charles Salkeld, gentleman, of plea of debt. Salkeld had been attorney for the complainant in two actions against Steele in Easter term, 1707.[1] He now said that Steele had not paid £100, which he borrowed of him at Westminster on the 1st September 1708; and he claimed £20 damages. Steele's attorney, William Rolfe, had nothing to say, and judgment was therefore given in Salkeld's favour, with 50s. damages.[2]

Another case, which had been brought before the Court of Queen's Bench in the preceding Michaelmas term, was also settled at this time. Timothy Fortune, of the Parish of St. Mary-le-Bow, in the Ward of Cheap, complained through his attorney, William Pykarell, that Richard Steele, Esq., in the custody of the Marshal of the Marshalsea, was on the 11th October 1708 indebted to him in the sum of £40 for work done by him as an upholsterer before that time, and for divers necessary materials; and being so indebted, on that same 11th October Steele faithfully promised to pay when required to do so; and at the same time specially requested Timothy Fortune to do

Records in the Birmingham Tower. Addison considered that the Records ought to be arranged and catalogued; this would require several hands, and he asked for a suitable salary. The Lord Lieutenant concurred, and recommended £500 a year, to be continued only during the petitioner's life. This report is minuted, "To be laid before the Queen. 400l a year." The petition covers four pages. The warrant for £400 is in the *Irish Book*, vol. vi. p. 148. In the fourth of the Drapier's Letters Swift wrote: "I will tell you some reasons, why there are so few employments to be disposed of in this kingdom. All considerable offices for life here are possessed by those to whom the reversions were granted; and these have been generally followers of the chief governors, or persons who had interest in the Court of England. . . . Nay, the reversion of several employments during pleasure is granted the same way. This among many others is a circumstance, whereby the kingdom of Ireland is distinguished from all other nations upon earth, and makes it so difficult an affair to get into a civil employ, that Mr. Addison was forced to purchase an old obscure place, called keeper of the records in Birmingham's Tower, of ten pounds a year, and to get a salary of 400*l*. annexed to it, though all the records there are not worth half-a-crown either for curiosity or use." Henry Gascoigne, it will be remembered, was keeper of these records until his death in 1707, when he was succeeded by Dr. William King.

[1] Page 156.

[2] Common Pleas Judgment Roll, Hilary 7 Anne, 1612.

certain other upholsterer's work, for which and for the materials he would pay what was reasonable. Timothy said that for this work other £40 were fairly due to him, and of this Steele had notice. And on the 14th October, Steele, being indebted to Fortune in the sum of another £40 for divers goods, &c., previously sold and delivered to him, faithfully promised to pay the £40 last mentioned, when requested; and specially ordered other goods, for which he promised to pay, amounting in value to £40, of which he received notice. But now, wishing to defraud Fortune, Steele would not pay, although he was requested to do so on the 20th October; Fortune therefore claimed £50 damages. The case came up for judgment on Monday next after the Octave of St. Hilary, but Steele did not appear, and made no defence. Fortune was accordingly allowed damages; but as the Court did not know what loss he had sustained, the Sheriff of London was ordered to inquire diligently by the oath of twelve honest men of his bailiwick respecting the amount of the damages, as well on the occasion of the said premisses as for costs and charges. On Friday next after the Purification of the Blessed Virgin Mary—the 10th February 1709—Fortune came to the Guildhall of the City of London, and the jurors found that the damages sustained were £36. 9s. 10d., and the costs and charges 26s. 8d. The Court thereupon allowed the damages found by the jury against Steele, as well as £6. 3s. 6d. adjudged by the Court for interest; the damages thus amounting in all to £44.[1]

In this way matters went on until March, when Steele's eldest daughter was born. We have the following memorandum in Mrs. Steele's writing: "My daughter Elizabeth was born the 26th of March 1709, on a Saturday evening, half an hour after six, or seven o'clock. She was christened the 6th of April; her godfathers, Mr Wortley Montague and Mr Addison; her godmothers, my Mother and Mrs Vaughan." A week later the *Tatler* was commenced, and we have nothing further to

[1] Queen's Bench Judgment Roll, Hilary 7 Anne, 165. The judgment in the original Latin is very long and involved. The whole amount of the debt was, of course, £40, and the way in which that sum is repeated over and over again in the complainant's Bill is another case of the "declaration in assumpsit," refered to on p. 149.

illustrate the early months of this year except a few notes giving glimpses into the monetary negotiations which Steele was carrying on with Tryon and others.

Feb. 5th, 1708-9.

DEAR PRUE

I was coming home but am indispensably obliged to dine at Tonson's where after dinner some papers are to be read whereof, among others, I am to be a Judge. I have the money for You and the other occasions.

This Absence I hope you will excuse in Yr Affectionate Faithfull

DICK STEELE.

March 11th, 1708-9.

DEAR PRUE

I enclose five guinneas, but can't come home to dinner. Dear Little Woman take care of thy Self, and eat and drink Chearfully.

RICHD STEELE.

March 23d, 1708-9.

DEAR PRUE

Having some doubt about Tilden[1] I dine at Court, and will look into all things between this and six of Clock. The Bearer is a Boy well recommended whose father has been with Me, & whome I approve (as I do all other things) as You like Him.

Yrs Faithfully RICHD STEELE.[2]

In April Steele wrote thus to Mr. Lewis the goldsmith about his debt.[3]

April 13th, 1709.

SIR,

I am in very great pain about the affair between us, having at this time the misfortune of great occasion for dayly expence. You know you are sure, and hope that will prevail upon you not to do a surprising thing to my disadvantage. Care is taking to bring you in your money before the term, and your civility cannot be a prejudice, since that is within the time you could propose by the severest methods.

Your most humble servant,

RICH. STEELE.

[1] In 1710 Tilden sued Steele for debt.

[2] "To Mrs Steele, at her house, last door but two in Berry-street, left hand."

[3] *Epistolatory Curiosities* (*Series the Second*), ed. Rebecca Warner, p. 240.

Swift left London in April to return to Ireland to his congregation of seventeen at Laracor, feeling somewhat sore at the neglect shown him by the Whigs. On the 22nd March he wrote to Colonel Hunter:[1] "I shall go for Ireland some time in summer, being not able to make my friends in the ministry consider my merits, or their promises, enough to keep me here. . . . In the meantime I hold fast my claim to your promise of corresponding with me, and that you will henceforth address your letters for me at Mr. Steele's office at the Cockpit, who has promised his care in conveying them. . . . I am now with Mr. Addison, with whom I have fifty times drunk your health since you left us."

[1] Swift's Works (Scott's 2nd ed.), vol. xv. On January 12, 1709, Swift wrote to Colonel Hunter: "Mr. Steele presents his most humble service to you."

BOOK FOURTH.

THE LUCUBRATIONS OF ISAAC BICKERSTAFF.

1709–1711. ÆT. 37–38.

I.—"THE TATLER."
II.—COMMISSIONER OF THE STAMP OFFICE.
III.—DR. SACHEVERELL'S TRIAL.
IV.—FALL OF THE WHIGS.
V.—IMITATORS OF "THE TATLER."

I.

"THE TATLER."

1709–1711. ÆT. 37–38.

OF the periodicals which preceded the *Tatler* it is not necessary to speak here at any length. Full particulars will be found in Nichols' *Literary Anecdotes* and elsewhere of the occasional pamphlets published at the close of the sixteenth century giving accounts of extraordinary events; of the various "Mercuries" which appeared during the Civil War; and of L'Estrange's *Public Intelligencer*, which was succeeded in 1665 by the *Oxford Gazette*, and in 1666 by the *London Gazette*. The first daily newspaper, the *Daily Courant*, was begun in 1702, and lasted until 1735. All these were simply news-sheets. Other periodicals, such as Tutchin's *Observator* and Lesley's *Rehearsal*, were confined to political controversy.

In 1690 John Dunton commenced the *Athenian Mercury*, in which questions put to the editor by his readers were answered. Richard Sault, Dr. John Norris, Samuel Wesley, and Sir William Temple are said to have contributed to this early precursor of our *Notes and Queries*.[1] Dunton says that the Marquis of Halifax was a constant reader, and that "Mr. Swift, a country gentleman, sent an ode." It is interesting to compare the abusive way in which Swift afterwards spoke of Dunton in the *Public Spirit of the Whigs*, with his letter of the 14th February 1691. In February 1708 another paper of the same nature was started, *The British Apollo*, "or Curious Amusements for the Ingenious. To which are added the most Material Occurrences Foreign and Domestic. Performed by a Society of Gen-

[1] Andrews' *History of British Journalism*, 1859, i. 87.

tlemen." This paper did not expire until May 11, 1711, when No. 20 of the fourth volume appeared.[1] The questions were of a very comprehensive character, embracing theology, natural history, gallantry, and mathematics; and they became so numerous that it was found necessary to issue a monthly and afterwards also a quarterly supernumerary paper. There was, too, a good deal of verse, not always very decent. In 1706 a *Poetical Courant* was published every Saturday, price 1d., to which gentlemen and ladies were invited to contribute verses;[2] and in June 1707[3] there was published *The Diverting Muse, or the Universal Medley*, "Written by a Society of Merry Gentlemen, for the Entertainment of the Town: The 1st Part, price 6d. N.B. Any Gentleman or Lady may have a poem made for them sending any proper Subject or any one of their own to be inserted, paying the Messenger, and directed for Mr George Daggastaff at Hogarth's Coffee House in St. John's Gateway near Clerkenwell." We have already had occasion to notice several times the monthly *Muses Mercury* which appeared throughout 1707.

The only paper, however, which had any real influence over the formation of the *Tatler* was Defoe's *Review*. This wonderful work first appeared on the 19th February 1704, and it was continued until the 11th June 1713. The full title, according to the first number, was, "A Weekly Review of the Affairs of France. Purg'd from the Errors and Partiality of News-Writers and Petty-Statesmen, of all Sides." Defoe says that his object was to set the affairs of Europe in a clearer light; to form a complete history of France; and to pursue Truth, regardless of party. And then he proceeds: "After our serious matters are over, we shall at the end of every paper present you with a little diversion, as anything occurs to make the world merry; and whether friend or foe, one party or another, if anything happens so scandalous as to require an open reproof, the world

[1] I have a complete set of the *British Apollo*. The twenty numbers of the fourth volume are rarely met with; they consist of one leaf only, instead of two. It is tolerably evident that the publication of the *Tatler* and *Spectator* ruined the prospects of the *British Apollo* and other papers which were even more obscure.

[2] *Daily Courant*, Feb. 18, 1706.

[3] *Daily Courant*, June 30, 1707.

will meet with it there." Accordingly, of the eight pages in the first number, one and a half pages consist of "Mercure Scandale; or, Advice from the Scandalous Club, Translated out of French." The censure was to be of the actions of men, not of parties; and the design was to expose not persons but things. The expression "Translated out of French" was not repeated; and in the eighteenth number the "Mercure Scandale" was dropped, and there was left simply "Advice from the Scandalous Club." But the title was still criticised, and in the forty-sixth number Defoe changed it to "Advice from the Scandal. Club," maintaining the sign of contraction after "Scandal" to show that he himself regarded it only as an abbreviation. After the fourth number the paper was reduced to four pages, with smaller type; with the ninth number it began to appear twice a week instead of once only, and eventually it was published three times a week—on Tuesday, Thursday, and Saturday. A monthly supplement of twenty-eight pages was commenced in September, with the title, "A Supplementary Journal, to the Advice from the Scandal. Club; for the month of September 1704. To be continued monthly." The *Review* was very popular; in this September number Defoe protests that he had no idea that he should have all kinds of questions poured in upon him, and that he did not pretend to be able to answer everything, like the *Athenian Mercury*. Defoe's plan embraced both the life of the nation and the life of the individual. He wrote upon political and economical questions in a way quite unknown before his time, and he also made war against the follies and vices which he saw round him in the very spirit in which they were afterwards treated by Steele and Addison. For example, in the twenty-sixth number of the second volume (May 3, 1705) Defoe took the opportunity afforded by the opening of the Haymarket Theatre to speak of the condition of the Drama. "The author has nothing to say to the crime of a Play; nor am I so narrow in my opinion, as to think it an unlawful Action, either in the Player's Acting, or the Person's seeing a Play, if it could be abstracted from all the unhappy circumstances that attend our Theaters. . . . I know 'tis the taste of the town, that will have everything mixed with something vicious, or will not be pleased with it. . . .

Gentlemen and ladies, if you would have a Reformation in the Play House, you must reform your taste of Wit. . . . If you find any foul stuff, tho' wrapped up in never so clean linen, hiss it off the Stage. . . . The errors of the Stage lie all in the Auditory; the Actors and the Poets are their humble Servants, and being good judges of what will please, are forced to write and act with all the aggravations and excesses possible, that they may not be undone and ruined." In the Preface to the first volume Defoe observes that in framing the design of the paper he considered that it would be very historical and long, and that to get over the difficulty of the aversion people felt to anything solemn and tedious he determined "to make some sort of entertainment or amusement at the end of every paper, *upon the immediate subject then on the tongues of the town;* which innocent diversion would hand on the more weighty and serious part of the Design into the heads and thoughts of those to whom it might be useful." On May 15, 1705 (Vol. II. No. 31), Defoe announced that weightier matters prevented his finding room in future for the "Advice from the Scandal Club;" the Society would, however, publish it separately. On March 2, 1710 (Vol. VI. No. 141), he remarked, "When first this paper appeared in the World, I erected a Court of Justice, for the censuring and exposing Vice . . . but tired with the mass of filth, the stench of which was hardly to be endured, I laid aside the Herculean labour for a while, and am glad to see the Society honour'd by the succession (in those just endeavours) of the Venerable Isaac Bickerstaff, Esq.;" but having by long experience found that reformation is a work of time, he proposed a scheme for "a Faculty Office or a License Book for the modern crimes of the Town, upon a price to be paid during the term of their usage among us, so long as, and no longer, than till the laudable endeavour and just authority of Esq. Bickerstaff, aforesaid, has effectually suppressed them." There are several other friendly references in the *Review* to the *Tatler* and the *Spectator*. Of course, as Beljame remarks,[1] the influence of the *Review* was chiefly political; Defoe's style was wanting in art and grace.

[1] *Le Public et les hommes de lettres en Angleterre au dixhuitième siècle*, 1660-1744, p. 275.

Although, therefore, he wrote about duels, swearing, matrimonial fidelity, the theatre, and many other subjects of social interest, he had not the qualifications which would have enabled him to speak most usefully on such matters to the greatest number of his contemporaries.

The first number of the *Tatler* appeared on Tuesday, April 12, 1709, and it was published three times a week—on Tuesday, Thursday, and Saturday, the post days. The ordinary copies, consisting of one folio leaf, were sold at one penny, but after the twenty-fifth number copies were printed with a sheet left blank for correspondence; for these there was a charge of three halfpence. The first four numbers were given away gratuitously. The teaching accomplished by the new paper was to be unobtrusive; the first step was to get at the hearts of the people. In No. 26, after some grave remarks upon duelling, Steele adds: "Pacolet was going on in this strain, when he recovered from it, and told me, it was too soon to give my discourse on this subject so serious a turn; you have chiefly to do with that part of mankind which must be led into reflection by degrees, and you must treat this custom with humour and raillery to get an audience, before you come to pronounce sentence upon it." Steele had the serious end in view from the very beginning, but at first it was not wise to make it too prominent. He called his paper simply *The Tatler*, published, like the rest, "for the use of the good people of England." The tastes of all classes were to be met, and the nature of the topic discussed was indicated by the name of the place from which the article was supposed to have come, which was printed at the head. "All accounts of gallantry, pleasure, and entertainment shall be under the article of White's Coffee House; Poetry, under that of Will's Coffee House; Learning, under the title of Grecian; Foreign and Domestic news you will have from Saint James's Coffee House; and what else I have to offer on any other subject shall be dated from my own Apartment."[1] The earlier numbers contained short papers from all or several of these addresses; but as the periodical progressed it became more and more usual to confine a number to one subject;

[1] *Tatler*, No. 1.

*

and the article of news gradually disappeared entirely.[1] No doubt Steele thought that his position of Gazetteer would enable him to give fresh items of news, which, he says, brought in a multitude of readers, and the idea of increasing his income by a paper above the ordinary may have first led him to turn his thoughts to such an enterprise; but as the *Tatler* grew the support of the paragraphs of news was felt to be unnecessary, and they were practically discontinued after the eightieth number.[2] As early as No. 18, after remarks on the distress which would be caused among the news-writers by the conclusion of a peace, Addison observed, "I cannot be thought to speak this out of an eye to any private interest; for as my chief scenes of action are coffee-houses, playhouses, and my own apartment, I am in no need of camps, fortifications, and fields of battle to support me. . . . I shall still be safe as long as there are men or women, or politicians, or lovers, or poets, or nymphs, or swains, or cits, or courtiers in being."

From the beginning Steele professed that he was writing for the people, and that he expected to be paid by the public for his work. Unlike the mountebank who pretended that he sold his nostrums from purely disinterested motives, "we have," he says, "all along informed the public, that we intend to give them our advice for our own sakes, and are labouring to make our lucubrations come to some price in money, for our more convenient support in the service of the public. It is certain that many other schemes have been proposed to me; as a friend

[1] The motto of the first forty numbers was, "Quicquid agunt homines nostri farrago libelli;" but Nos. 41, 42 had for their motto, "Celebrare domestica facta;" and subsequent numbers generally bore special mottoes, though the original inscription was sometimes resorted to, as in Nos. 56–62.

[2] Macaulay, Forster, and other writers have stated that the character of the *Tatler* changed when Steele lost his Gazetteership, but this, as Mr. Dobson pointed out, is a mistake. Nos. 13, 22, 26, and 34 contained no article from St. James's; many numbers between 39 and 77 were bare of news; and Nos. 78 to 173 contained no items of news, with slight exceptions in Nos. 80, 83, 88, 96, 136, and 137. With the exception of No. 225 (Sept. 16, 1710), No. 175 is the last paper containing news, and this appeared on May 23, 1710, five months before Steele ceased to be Gazetteer. I take these facts, with one or two corrections, from a pamphlet by Wilhelm Ricken, of Elberfeld. This essay "Bemerkungen über Anlage und Erfolg der wichtigsten Zeitschriften Steele's und den Einfluss Addison's auf die Entwicklung derselben," contains many useful remarks.

offered to show me a treatise he had writ, which he called 'The Whole Art of Life; or, The Introduction to Great Men, illustrated in a Pack of Cards.' But, being a novice at all manner of play, I declined the offer."[1] We have here, in brief, a true representation, in his own words, of Steele's relation to the people throughout his life. Addison, on the other hand, played an honest and successful game through the aid of great men, but it was only when he came to work with Steele, and in Steele's fashion, that he wrote the papers by which alone he will always live.

The *dramatis personæ* in the *Tatler* do not hold a position in any way so important as that occupied by their successors in the *Spectator*. Isaac Bickerstaff, Esq., aged sixty-four, "an old man, a philosopher, an humourist, an astrologer, and a Censor,"[2] is alone essential to the plan of the work. For the name Steele was, as we have seen, indebted to Swift, and in various places the combat with Partridge is maintained; the essence of the matter is to be found in the first number, where Steele says that though a man's body still appear, yet if his art is gone the man is gone; and a warning is added that others who are good for nothing may find themselves in the number of the deceased.[3] Besides Isaac Bickerstaff we hear of other members of his family, especially his half-sister, Jenny Distaff,[4] and her husband, and his three nephews,[5] and they are the subjects of some of the most charming sketches. In the last number Steele wrote: "It has been a most exquisite pleasure to me to frame characters of domestic life." There is, too, a familiar named Pacolet. Quite late in the periodical we have a description of some of the members of Isaac Bickerstaff's club, the Trumpet, in Shire Lane;[6] Sir Geoffery Notch, a gentleman of an ancient family, who had run through his estate in his youth, in hounds, horses, and cock-fighting, and called every thriving man a pitiful upstart; Major Matchlock, Dick Reptile, and the Bencher who was always telling stories of Jack Ogle, with whom he pretended to have been intimate in his youth.

[1] *Tatler*, No. 4.
[2] *Tatler*, Nos. 59, 271.
[3] See, too, Nos. 59, 99, 106, &c.
[4] No. 10, &c.
[5] No. 30.
[6] No. 132.

In the Dedication to Maynwaring of the first volume of the collected edition—the subsequent volumes were dedicated to Wortley Montague, Lord Cowper, and Lord Halifax—Steele states in a few words the aim of the *Tatler:* "The general purpose of this paper is to expose the false arts of life, to pull off the disguises of cunning, vanity and affectation, and to recommend a general simplicity in our dress, our discourse, and our behaviour." And in another place,[1] referring to a letter from a country correspondent, he says: "As for my labours, which he is pleased to enquire after, if they but wear one impertinence out of human life, destroy a single vice, or give a morning's cheerfulness to an honest mind; in short, if the world can be but one virtue the better, or in any degree less vicious, or receive from them the smallest addition to their innocent diversions; I shall not think my pains, or indeed my life, to have been spent in vain." At the close, speaking in his own name, Steele says:[2] "The general purpose of the whole has been to recommend truth, innocence, honour, and virtue, as the chief ornaments of life; but I considered, that severity of manners was absolutely necessary to him who would censure others, and for that reason, and that only, chose to talk in a mask. I shall not carry my humility so far as to call myself a vicious man, but at the same time must confess my life is at best but pardonable."

In the Preface to the first collected edition of the *Tatler*, Steele acknowledged with his usual large-hearted generosity the assistance in his work which he received from others, especially Swift and Addison. Of the latter he says: "I have only one gentleman, who will be nameless, to thank for any frequent assistance to me, which indeed it would have been barbarous in him to have denied to one with whom he had lived in an intimacy from childhood, considering the great ease with which he is able to

[1] No. 89.

[2] No. 271. In this number, too, Steele described, as he had mentioned before in Nos. 71, 84, 164, &c., how he was often threatened on account of the characters which he drew being taken to be attacks on particular individuals. In No. 61 he said, "We shall therefore take it for a very moral action to find a good appellation for offenders, and to turn them into ridicule under feigned names."

dispatch the most entertaining pieces of this nature. This good office he performed with such force of genius, humour, wit and learning, that I fared like a distressed prince, who calls in a powerful neighbour to his aid; I was undone by my auxiliary; when I had called him in I could not subsist without dependence on him."[1] In the last number of the *Tatler*, Steele repeated that "the most approved pieces in it were written by others," especially by one who "is a person who is too fondly my friend ever to own them; but I should little deserve to be his, if I usurped the glory of them." And years afterwards, still speaking of Addison's share in the *Tatler*, Steele said, in the Preface to the second edition of the *Drummer*, "That paper was advanced indeed! for it was raised to a greater thing than I intended it! For the elegance, purity and correctness which appeared in his writings were not so much my purpose, as (in any intelligible manner, as I could) to rally all those singularities of human life, through the different professions and characters in it, which obstruct anything that was truly good and great." There have always been some admirers of Addison who have seized upon such ungrudging utterances of his friend to aid them in raising Addison's fame at the sacrifice of Steele's. Fielding has satirised their efforts in his *Journey from this World to the next*,[2] in which he represents Virgil as putting Addison a little out of countenance, upon which the critic "turned aside to a very merry spirit, one Dick Steele, who embraced him, and told him he had been the greatest man upon earth; that he readily resigned up all the merit of his own works to him. Upon which Addison gave him a gracious smile, and, clapping him on the back with much solemnity, cried out, 'Well said, Dick!'" Lord Macaulay,[3]

[1] In No. 176 Steele had Addison in his mind when he drew the character of Aristæus—sensible of every passion, but ruffled by none, kind without profession, expeditious without ostentation, benevolent, but impartial, clear in his judgment, but speaking with doubt in complaisance to his company, never showing confidence in argument except to support the sense of another.

[2] Chapter viii.

[3] Schlosser, who, as we have seen, described the "Christian Heroes" (*sic*) as a poem, is out of court. Speaking of the *Tatler* he says: "This paper was written for ladies," and it had "no flash of genius, no kindling fire, no kernel, no strength." (*History of the Eighteenth Century*, English translation, 1843. vol. i. 102.)

than whom no one has done more reckless injustice to Steele's reputation, says that at the close of 1709 the *Tatler* was more popular than any periodical had ever been, and that it was known that Addison was a contributor, but that it was not known that almost everything good in it was his; and adds that his fifty or sixty numbers were the best, so much so that any five of them were of more value than all the two hundred numbers in which he did not assist. It is not necessary, after the noble defence of Steele set up by John Forster in the *Quarterly Review,* to refute Macaulay at length; and in what follows I can do little more than sum up what previous writers have said. Of the whole 271 numbers of the *Tatler*, Steele wrote —approximately—188, Addison 42, and about 36 were written by them jointly. Steele started the paper without consulting his friend, who did not know who was the author until he read some remarks upon Virgil in the sixth number, which were the result of a discussion he had himself had with Steele. Addison's first contribution appeared in No. 18, but it was not until the autumn of 1709 that Steele received any substantial aid from him.[1] Steele was entirely responsible for the paper, and if some numbers are of unequal merit, it must never be forgotten that Steele was compelled to write whenever he had no article by his friends ready to hand, whereas they only wrote when they found some subject which specially interested them. Swift contributed only one entire paper to the *Tatler*, and a few letters and shorter articles; and contributions from other writers are so few that they need not be noticed here. It is fortunately not necessary nowadays to argue as to the comparative merits of the papers by Steele and Addison, and such a discussion would be the last thing that Steele would wish; but this may be said, that Steele was the originator of nearly every new departure in the periodicals which the two friends produced; and if Steele had not furnished Addison with the opportunity for displaying his special power, Addison would in all probability have been known to us only as an accomplished scholar and poet of no great power. The world owes Addison

[1] In No. 31 (June 21, 1709) Steele answered the "unreasonable objection" that his stock was not all his own.

to Steele. "I claim to myself," says Steele, "the merit of having extorted excellent productions from a person of the greatest abilities, who would not have let them appear by any other means."[1] And although many of Addison's papers are so perfect and polished, yet the very care bestowed upon them frequently makes them come home to us with less force than the often hastily composed papers of Steele, who wrote from his heart, full of impulse and kindly feeling.[2] It is just because the *Tatler* is more thoroughly imbued with Steele's spirit than the *Spectator*, that many competent judges have confessed that they found greater pleasure in the earlier periodical than in its more finished and more famous successor. Hazlitt said that the *Tatler*, with half the number of volumes in the *Spectator*, contained "at least an equal quantity of sterling wit and sense."[3]

It is curious how generally the subjects discussed in the *Spectator* had been already made the topics of papers in the *Tatler*. Gamesters and swindlers are unsparingly attacked;[4] brutal pastimes are condemned;[5] the habits of the drunken "roarers," "scourers," and other boon companions of the day are satirised;[6] a constant warfare is maintained against the practice of duelling.[7] Follies and minor evils of all descriptions are ridiculed, but without one touch of malice; as, for example, in Nos. 127 and 186, on pride and vanity; No. 168, on impudence; No. 142, on fops; No. 184, on wags; No. 27, on a coquette; or No. 210, on the lady who censoriously condemns the vices of the age, meaning the only vice she is not guilty of. The lesson is generally instilled unostentatiously by a vivid sketch of some individual, so full of life that a very few words suffice to make the character remain fixed in our memories. In the number and variety of such portraits Steele is unrivalled.

For short stories full of pathos coming straight from the

[1] *Spectator*, No. 532.

[2] Coleridge valued Steele above Addison. "Steele's papers are easily distinguished to this day by their pure humanity, springing from the gentleness the kindness of his heart." (*Letters, Conversations, and Recollections of S. T. Coleridge*, 3rd ed. p. 97.)

[3] *Round Table*,—"On the *Tatler*."

[4] *Tatler*, No. 56, &c. See, too, the close of the Preface first printed in vol. iv. of the octavo edition.

[5] No. 134. [6] Nos. 40, 45. [7] Nos. 25, 26, 29, 31, 38, 39.

heart I cannot do better than refer to Nos. 5, 55, 82, 94, 95, 114, 172, all of which have been dwelt upon by previous writers. The account of his own father's death, in No. 181, has been already quoted. The story in Nos. 95 and 114 illustrates also Steele's love for children, to whom he gave a position in literature which they had never occupied before. The letters he wrote to his own children show how perfectly these papers reflected his real feelings. Steele stands apart from and above all the writers of his time, except Defoe, in the humanity which is everywhere found in his work. "If things were put in a true light, and we would take time to consider that man, in his very nature, is an imperfect being, our sense of this matter would be immediately altered, and the word imperfection would not carry an unkinder idea than the word humanity."[1] And again: "It is to me a great meanness, and something much below a philosopher, which is what I mean by a gentleman, to rank a man among the vulgar for the condition of life he is in, and not according to his behaviour, his thoughts and sentiments in that condition. . . . This sense of mankind is so far from a levelling principle, that it only sets us upon a true basis of distinction, and doubles the merit of such as become their condition."[2] "The appellation of gentleman is never to be affixed to a man's circumstances, but to his behaviour in them."[3]

One way in which Steele strove to raise the tone of his contemporaries was by inculcating a purer and more chivalrous feeling towards women. "As charity is esteemed a conjunction of the good qualities necessary to a virtuous man, so love is the happy composition of all the accomplishments that make a fine gentleman." And in this same paper, No. 49, Steele observes of Lady Elizabeth Hastings what has passed into a proverb: "Though her mien carries much more invitation than command,

[1] *Tatler*, No. 246. With this compare No. 206, on affection and esteem, and No. 186, on vanity, pride, and ambition. "It may be an useful hint in such cases for a man to ask of himself, whether he really is what he has a mind to be thought. If he is, he need not give himself much further anxiety."

[2] No. 69. See, too, No. 34, where others, more important according to fortune or figure, are described at the same time as Don Saltero; "for half the politicians . . . are, by their place in nature, of the class of tooth-drawers."

[3] No. 207.

to behold her is an immediate check to loose behaviour, and to love her is a liberal education."[1] "Wife," he says, "is the most amiable term in human life."[2] But women must be educated in a right fashion if they are to be treated by and to influence men as they should;[3] and Steele constantly urges the need for bestowing true graces on the mind as well as on the body. "Flavia is ever well dressed, and always the genteelest woman you meet, but the make of her mind very much contributes to the ornament of her body. . . . Her distinction is owing to her manner, and not to her habit. . . . Howsoever she is apparelled she is herself the same; for there is so immediate a relation between our thoughts and gestures that a woman must think well to look well."[4]

[1] In 1884 Mr. Swinburne wrote some letters to the *Spectator* arguing that Congreve, and not Steele, was the author of "this most exquisite tribute ever paid to the memory of a noble woman." The unalterable fact of Congreve's authorship could not, he said, be removed by the verdict of a Leigh Hunt, since whose time the passage has been blindly attributed to "the sentimental debauchee" known to modern sympathies as "dear Dick Steele." When asked for proofs, Mr. Swinburne asserted that no one had disputed Congreve's authorship of the paper (No. 42) before Leigh Hunt, and what authority was he against the evidence of more than a century? He subsequently admitted that the evidence for Congreve might be imperfect; but added that there was no evidence at all for Steele. Then Mr. Justin McCarthy wrote to point out that Mr. Swinburne and the editor of the *Spectator* had both fallen into a curious error. The description of Aspasia in No. 42 was, he believed, unquestionably by Congreve; but the beautiful words quoted are not in that paper, but in No. 49, which is unquestionably by Steele. Mr. Swinburne acknowledged this solution to be "more than plausible," but expressed wonder that Hunt had overlooked such an easy way of refuting the claim made on Congreve's behalf. "C. M. B." pointed out that Thackeray recognised Steele as the author, for in *Esmond* he makes St. John chaff Mrs. Steele about "her" portrait in No. 49, quoting the whole passage. (*Spectator*, March 29, April 5, 12, 19, and 26, 1884.) I am inclined to agree with "C. M. B." that it is doubtful whether Congreve wrote even No. 42. See *Notes and Queries*, April 6, 1889.

[2] No. 33. In No. 149 Steele dwelt upon the importance of cultivating good-nature if the married life is to be a happy one, and quoted from Pliny's letters to Calpurnia to show how a husband should feel to his wife.

[3] Nos. 248, 141. Steele attacked slanderers (No. 42), and satirised those who devoted their thoughts to an undue extent to caressing their dogs or other pets (Nos. 40, 47). These and many other failings and weaknesses were the result of an improper training of the mind.

[4] No. 212. "All women especially are bound to be grateful to Steele, as he was the first of our writers who really seemed to admire and respect them." (Thackeray's *English Humorists.*)

Another way in which Steele aimed at raising the minds of his readers was by maintaining a friendly touch with those who provided the popular amusements. Himself a successful dramatist, he always took a keen interest in the fortunes of the stage, and he did his utmost to aid actors who strove to improve its condition.[1] "How often," said Cibber years afterwards, "have we known the most excellent audiences drawn together at a day's warning, by the influence or warrant of a single *Tatler*, in a season when our best endeavours without it could not defray the charge of the performance!"[2] One result of Steele's love for the drama was, that he was acquainted with Shakespeare, and criticised his plays in a way adopted by no other writer of the time. He quotes Shakespeare naturally as a great authority on many topics, without any attempt at subtlety, and he urges that Shakespeare must be followed if the stage and the plays acted are to be reformed.[3] He maintained the same high standard of criticism in speaking of other forms of literature, and it is especially noteworthy how he refers to Milton. As early as the sixth number of the *Tatler* he contrasts the treatment of the same subject by Milton and Dryden, and in subsequent papers he frequently quotes from Milton with reverence and admiration.[4] In this he led the way to Addison's papers on "Paradise Lost" in the *Spectator*, which were infinitely more elaborate, but sometimes not so natural and appreciative.

It remains to say something of the reception met with by the

[1] Nos. 1, 2, 182, &c.

[2] Dedication to *Ximena*, 1719.

[3] *Tatler*, Nos. 8, 47, 68, 90, 106, 111. De Quincey (*Life of Shakespeare*) observes that Addison never quoted or referred to Shakespeare, although it is evident that public interest in Shakespeare was then considerable, judging by the series of editions, commencing with Rowe's in 1709, which rapidly succeeded each other. Addison omitted Shakespeare in his early poem on the principal English poets; of Milton he said that he was "above the critics' nicer laws." In No. 231 Steele repeated the story of Shakespeare's "The Taming of the Shrew."

[4] Nos. 40, 98, 149. "I would rather," said Landor, "have written what is here quoted from Steele than all the criticisms and philosophy of all the Edinburgh Reviewers. What a good critic he was! I doubt if he has ever been surpassed. Somehow I cannot but connect Steele and Goldsmith, as I do Cowper and Southey. Of all our literary men, they interest me the most." (Forster's *Works and Life of Landor*, 1876, i. 500.)

Tatler at the hands of contemporaries. In the Dedication to the first volume Steele speaks of "the sudden acceptance which my labours met with in the world;"[1] and Addison wrote:[2] "My own countrymen . . . have made such generous subscriptions for the Censor of Great Britain, as will give a magnificence to my old age, and which I esteem more than I would any post in Europe of an hundred times the value. I shall only add, that upon looking into my catalogue of subscribers, which I intend to print alphabetically in the front of my Lucubrations, I find the names of the greatest Beauties and Wits in the whole island of Great Britain; which I only mention for the benefit of any of them who have not yet subscribed, it being my design to close the subscription in a very short time." And in another paper (No. 26) Steele says that he expected hush-money for every vice or folly committed in the whole town; servants could only whisper it to their companions, "but I can tell it to all men living, or who are to live. Therefore I desire all my readers to pay their fines, or mend their lives." In *The Present State of Wit*, 1711, Gay, speaking of the sudden discontinuance of the *Tatler*, says: "His disappearing seemed to be bewailed as some general calamity: every one wanted so agreeable an amusement; and the coffee-houses began to be sensible that the Esquire's lucubrations alone had brought them more customers than all their other newspapers put together. It must, indeed, be confessed that never man threw up his pen under stronger temptations to have employed it longer; his reputation was at a greater height than, I believe, ever any living author's was before him. . . . There is this noble difference between him and all the rest of our polite and gallant authors: the latter have endeavoured to please the age by falling in with them, and encouraging them in their fashionable vices and false notions of things. It would have been a jest some time since, for a man to have

[1] Wycherley, in a letter to Pope dated May 19, 1709, thanking him for a volume of Miscellanies—Tonson's sixth volume, published on May 2—wrote: "But hitherto your Miscellanies have safely run the gauntlet, through all the coffee-houses; which are now entertained with a whimsical new newspaper, called the *Tatler*, which I suppose you have seen. This is the newest thing I can tell you of."

[2] *Tatler*, No. 162.

asserted that anything witty could be said in praise of a married state; or that devotion and virtue were any way necessary to the character of a fine gentleman. Bickerstaff ventured to tell the town that they were a parcel of fops, fools, and vain coquettes; but in such a manner as even pleased them, and made them more than half-inclined to believe that he spoke truth. Instead of complying with the false sentiments or vicious tastes of the age, either in morality, criticism, or good breeding, he has boldly assured them that they were altogether in the wrong, and commanded them, with an authority which perfectly well became him, to surrender themselves to his arguments for virtue and good sense.

"It is incredible to conceive the effect his writings have had on the town; how many thousand follies they have either quite banished, or given a very great check to; how much countenance they have added to virtue and religion; how many people they have rendered happy, by showing them it was their own fault if they were not so; and, lastly, how entirely they have convinced our fops and young fellows of the value and advantages of learning.

"He has indeed rescued it out of the hands of pedants and fools, and discovered the true method of making it amiable and lovely to all mankind. In the dress he gives it, it is a most welcome guest at tea-tables and assemblies, and is relished and caressed by the merchants on The Change; accordingly, there is not a lady at court, nor a banker in Lombard Street, who is not verily persuaded that Captain Steele is the greatest scholar and best casuist of any man in England.

"Lastly, his writings have set all our wits and men of letters upon a new way of thinking, of which they had little or no notion before; and though we cannot yet say that any of them have come up to the beauties of the original, I think we may venture to affirm that every one of them writes and thinks much more justly than they did some time since."

In the *Wentworth Papers* there are various allusions to the *Tatler*.[1] Thus, on May 9, 1709, Peter Wentworth, who knew Steele, wrote to his brother, Lord Raby: "Here I have sent you

[1] Pages 85, 89, 91.

two Tatlers by which you'l see the town is very empty of news, for they are writ by a club of wits, who makes it there business to pick up all the merry storys they can; 'tis a new paper for there has been but 12 of them out tho' they come thrice a week. If you like them I can send them all. Three of the authors are guest at, viz. Swift, that writ the tale of the tub, Yalden, fellow of Magdilin Colledge, Oxford, and Steel, the Gazeetier." On May 31 he wrote: "Mr. Steel told me he knew a gentleman that says he can inform you of several things that will be very advantageous to you concerning your post-fines;" and on June 7: "The Tatlers begin to swell to a volume as you see by the number of this last; therefore since you like them I think I had best make collection of the whole and take the first opportunity that presents to send them over, for by the post 'twou'd be too chargeable."

Like other publications of the time, the successive numbers of the *Tatler* were reprinted in Dublin and in Edinburgh, as they came out. The Dublin reprint was in quarto form;[1] the Edinburgh issue was a folio sheet, rather smaller than the original issue, and containing a fresh set of advertisements of interest to local readers. These reprints afford excellent evidence of the widespread interest that was felt in the paper. Of the very rare Scotch issue, "Printed by James Watson, and sold at his shop next door to the Red Lion, opposite to the Lucken-Booths," I have about sixty numbers; it evidently was commenced about the beginning of February 1710, for No. 62 contains the matter in the London paper nnmbered 191, and it was continued regularly until the close of Steele's paper,[2] and, indeed, afterwards, when one of the spurious continuations of the *Tatler* was reprinted for a time. The date of each number of the Scotch paper is five or six days later than that of the original issue; the reprint was evidently worked off directly the London post came in.

[1] A volume, containing Nos. 1 to 69 of this Dublin issue, was in Dr. R. R. Madden's Library, which was sold in Dublin in December 1886. I have seen a similar Dublin reprint of the *Examiner*.

[2] It was not a reprint of select papers, as surmised in the Catalogue of the Hope Collection of Early Newspapers in the Bodleian Library. In that collection there is only one of the Scotch reprints, No. C.

In the accounts of the "Gentlemen's Society at Spalding"[1] we have an example of the way in which the *Tatler* and its successors were received in the country districts. Maurice Johnson, a native of Spalding, and a member of the Inner Temple, was one of a party of antiquarians who began to hold weekly meetings in London in 1707; but Johnson soon afterwards left London for Spalding, where he at once set about forming a Literary Society. This is his account of the commencement of the Society: "In April, 1709, that great genius, Captain Richard Steele, . . . published the Tatlers, which, as they came out in half-sheets, were taken in by a gentleman, who communicated them to his acquaintances at the Coffee house then in the Abbey Yard; and these papers being universally approved as both instructive and entertaining, they ordered them to be sent down thither, with the Gazettes and Votes, for which they paid out of charity to the person who kept the Coffee house, and they were accordingly had and read there every post day, generally aloud, to the company, who would sit and talk over the subject afterwards. This insensibly drew the men of sense and letters into a sociable way of conversing, and continued the next year, 1710, until the publication of these papers desisted, which was in December, to their great regret." They then read poems, &c., and considered how a parochial library could be formed. "In March, 1711, the Spectator came out, which was received and read here as the Tatler had been," and then it was agreed to form a regular Society, which was started in 1712. In a letter to Mr. Birch, 1752, Johnson says that he aimed always at getting young men into improving society. "It was with this view, *by the encouragement of Mr. Secretary Addison, Captain Steele, and others of Button's Club*, I dared to found, and have since supported, our Society here." In 1713 the *Lay Monk*—a continuation of the *Spectator*—was taken in; and then the *Guardian*, *Englishman*, *Entertainer*, and *Lover*, "so long as they meddled not with politics." A regular communication of Minutes took place between the Spalding

[1] W. Moore's *The Gentlemen's Society at Spalding* (1851); Nichols' *Bibliotheca Topographica Britannica*, III. i.–lxi., 1–92, 411 (1790); Nichols' *Literary Anecdotes of the Eighteenth Century*, vi. 2–68 (1812).

Society and the Society of Antiquaries in London. All sciences and arts were discussed, politics alone being excluded. Maurice Johnson died in 1755.

Notes to the *Tatler* were first added in the six-volume edition of 1786, published by John Nichols. In the "Advertisement" we are told that about twenty-five years before "a writer of distinguished taste and talents"—Dr. Percy—commenced, in conjunction with Tonson the publisher, to annotate the periodical Essayists; but other duties prevented him continuing the work. Dr. John Calder—the "worthy coadjutor"—became acquainted with Percy, and continued the task which he found already begun. Dr. Calder left the following Memorandum on the subject: "On my coming to settle in London, about half a century ago, I was engaged to prepare a new edition of the *Tatler*, *Spectator* and *Guardian*, with Notes and Illustrations, by such of the Booksellers as before the last Act of Parliament limiting the property of Copy-right took place, claimed an exclusive right to these books. I had begun this work at Alnwick for Dr. Percy, late Bishop of Dromore, who on my coming to town entirely relinquished his contract for this purpose to me, on whom it devolved with the request and at the consent of the Booksellers above mentioned."[1] Bishop Pearce—the "late very learned and much respected Prelate"—also helped; and their notes were all used in the 1786 edition of the *Tatler*, in which Percy's notes are signed "P," and Calder's "A," or "Annotator." The *Tatler* was fully illustrated, but the notes were very discursive. All subsequent editions have contained little or nothing but extracts, taken without acknowledgment, from the notes in the 1786 edition.

None of the papers in the *Tatler*, as originally issued, bore any indication of their author's name, and it is occasionally difficult and even impossible to determine who wrote a paper or portion of a paper. The reliable information that we have is furnished, firstly, by Steele's Preface to the *Tatler*, in which he announced the authorship of certain papers; and, secondly, by the list of papers by Addison which Steele supplied to Tickell. But that list was not complete, because, as Steele says in the

[1] Nichols' *Literary Anecdotes*, ix. 805.

Preface to the second edition of the *Drummer*, "What I never did declare was Mr. Addison's, I had his direct injunctions to hide." . . . "Many of the writings now published as his, I have been very patiently traduced and calumniated for, as they were pleasantries and oblique strokes upon certain the wittiest men of the age." It is well known, too, that Swift would not confess all he wrote. There are, therefore, a few papers respecting which a doubt remains.

II.

COMMISSIONER OF THE STAMP OFFICE.

1709–10. ÆT. 37.

DIFFICULTIES caused by the want of money did not cease with the commencement of the *Tatler*, as the following notes show :—

Ap : 19th, 1709.

DEAR WIFE :

I have been with Tryon. He owns some effects which will be of service to Me. I call Heav'n to Witnesse I value nothing but as you are partaker of it : Do not cast Yr self down but depend upon it that I shall bring You home what will make things have a Chear-full aspect and will do that may contribute to yr Satisfaction which is all the ambition of Yrs Eternally

RICHD STEELE.

Ap : 23d, 1709.

DEAREST CREATURE :

This matter must be defer'd till some hour in the Evening or to some other day for I cannot have money till after Chappell.

I am,

Yr Faithfull Tender Husband

RICHD STEELE.

On the 2nd May Steele was, it appears, arrested for debt. On the 5th he wrote four times to his wife, sending ten shillings, and asking her to meet him at Westminster after he had had an interview in the Park with Mr. Edward Wortley Montague. He vowed vengeance upon "that insufferable brute" —presumably the landlady of the house in Bury Street—who had affronted his wife. Matters seem then to have brightened somewhat; but, as we shall see afterwards, this was probably only owing to Mr. Compton advancing, before it was due, Steele's pension as Gentleman Waiter to the late Prince.

May 7th, 1709.

DEAR PRUE

I have been with Mr. Compton[1] and have his order to be at the Office with a request to keep it very Secret that He does me this favour for fear of His being importun'd on the same account by others of the Family. I am,

Yr Most Affectionate and Tender Husband,

RICHD STEELE.

May 7th, 1709.

DEAR PRUE

I am just drinking a Pint of Wine and will come home forthwith. I am with Mr. Elliot settling things. Yrs Ever Ever

RICHD STEELE.

On the 27th May, as we shall find, Steele borrowed £140 from Mr. George Tilden, and next day he wrote to his wife that he had received money, but that, owing to an appointment, he could not come home till four o'clock. There are a few other letters which, though they are undated, were probably written about this time. They refer to a hope of receiving some office through the interest of Henry Boyle, Secretary of State; to matters connected with the *Gazette*, and to the West Indian property. I give only one of these notes here.

Half Hour after 9.

DEAR PRUE

I was coming home from the office after having received some money, but am invited to Supper to Mr. Boyle's. God be thanked all will do well, and I rejoice that I had spirit to refuse what has been lately offered Me.

Dear Prue Don't send after Me for I shall be ridiculous. I send you word to put you out of frights.

R. S.

[1] The Hon. Spencer Compton, who was appointed Paymaster to Her Majesty's Pensioners and Treasurer to the Prince in April 1707 (Pointer's *Chronological History of England*, ii. 569; Luttrell's *Diary*, vi. 165, 267). The words "others of the family" apparently refer to other members of the late Prince's household.

Salkeld, the attorney, with whom we have met before,[1] is mentioned in the next note.

June 9th, 1709.

DEAR PRUE

I put my self to the pain of Absence from You at dinner by waiting to speake with Salkeild: therefore I hope You will forgive me for what I am punished in committing.

Dear Prue I am Unreservedly & Faithfully Yrs

R. STEELE.

There is a well-known story, which may be told in connection with the next letter, written from Nutt's. We read in *Addisoniana* that old Richard Nutt, the printer of the *Tatler*, used to say that Steele paid £50 a year to his barber, and that he never rode out (which he did often) but in a black full-bottomed dress periwig, costing nearly £50.

July 25th, 1709, from Mr. Nutts.

DEAR PRUE

I have finished the Gazette at the Office, and am here ending the other businesse[2] in order to have the Evening with my Wife and Mistresse Prue.

Here is next door a fellow that makes old Wiggs new therefore Pray send both mine in the Bed chamber by this boy to

Yr Loving Devoted Obedient Husband

R. STEELE.[3]

July 28th, 1709.

DEAR PRUE

I enclose 2 guinneas and will come home exactly at seven.

Yrs Tenderly

RICHD STEELE.

On September 3rd Steele admitted into the *Tatler* (No. 63) a letter by Swift which consisted chiefly of an attack on Mrs. Manley, who had then published the first volume of her *Secret Memoirs*. Knowing how she had calumniated him, Mrs. Manley assumed that Steele was the author of the paper in the *Tatler*, and wrote taxing him with it. On the 6th September Steele

[1] Pages 156, 233. [2] See *Tatler*, No. 46.

[3] "To Mrs. Steele, at Mr. Sewell's in King-street, near Whitehall Coffee-house."

sent the following disavowal of the authorship; and in dedicating the third volume of her work to Isaac Bickerstaff, Esq., Mrs. Manley printed Steele's letter *verbatim*, as she says. But she made some judicious omissions and alterations, as we see when we compare her version with the undated original, as printed by Nichols. This was Steele's letter; sentences omitted by Mrs. Manley are in square brackets. It will be seen that Steele corroborates the statement of Mrs. Manley, already given, that she helped him when his affairs were in a critical state.

[Sept. 6, 1709.]

MADAM,

I have received a letter from you, wherein you tax me, as if I were Bickerstaff, with falling upon you as author of "Atalantis," and the person who honoured me with a character in that celebrated piece. [What has happened formerly between us can be of no use to either to repeat.] I solemnly assure you, you wrong me in this as much as you know you do in all else you have been pleased to say of me. [I had not money when you did me the favour to ask a loan of a trifling sum of me.] I had the greatest sense imaginable of the kind notice you gave me when I was going on to my ruin; and am so far from retaining an inclination to revenge the inhumanity with which you have treated me, that I give myself a satisfaction in that you have canceled with injuries a friendship, which I should never have been able to return.

This will convince you how little I am an ingrate; for I believe you will allow, no one that is so mean as to be forgetful of kindnesses,[1] ever fails in returning injuries. As for the verses you quote of mine, they are still my opinion;[2] and your sex, as well as your quality of a gentlewoman (a justice you would not do my birth and education), shall always preserve you against the pen of your provoked most humble servant,

RICH. STEELE.

In her Dedication Mrs. Manley says that though Bickerstaff had, in the *Tatler* for November 10, 1709, called a Patron the filthiest creature in the street, yet she observed he was so delighted with Dedications as even to make them to himself.

[1] Mrs. Manley substituted the word "services."

[2] Mrs. Manley adds—"*i.e.*,

'Against a woman's wit 'tis full as low,
Your malice as your bravery to shew.'"

"I am ravished at the thought of *living a thousand years hence* in your indelible lines, though *to give offence*. . . . I shall be proud of furnishing matter towards your inexhaustible *Tatler*, and of being a perpetual monument of Mr. Bickerstaff's gallantry and morality." Steele is mentioned several times in this third volume of the *New Atalantis*;[1] he is rebuked for having commended for his religion a tyrant—the Earl of Wharton—famed for his cruelty; and under the name of Stelico he is spoken of as a useful hireling, who "cants admirably, and pretends to virtue, but is as ungrateful and unfair as one could desire." Cataline has rewarded him for his services, but not too much, lest he grow too great for business, or "indulge too far his native genius to laziness and being governed by his wife." I do not want to return to the *New Atalantis*, and I will therefore add here that in the fourth volume there was another attack upon Steele, which took the form of a dialogue[2] between Mrs. Tofts and "Don Phœbo," as Mrs. Manley called Steele. Mrs. Tofts says that there is a sort of parity in their destinies. "If my birth was not elevated, yours was not exalted." Each got into debt; each squandered, but Steele unaccountably; each was thankless to benefactors; but Mrs. Tofts was no rival in "the feint you make of virtue and religion." Steele, says Mrs. Tofts, made friends in difficulties lend him their wits; "If every one should have a fancy to his own ray, your worship would be very near shorn of your beams, or those that remain be found with but an indifferent degree of lustre. . . . My excellencies were all my own." "How is it that a man of your sense suffers himself to be governed by the women? The Town have been let into the secret; we know so well from your writing when you have had any matrimonial discontents. . . . How can a person of your fire wait, after midnight, for four hours together, imploring the obdurate beauty to break

[1] 6th edition, pp. 24, 215–6.

[2] Vol. iv. pp. 302–7, 313–5 (6th edition). Three fictitious letters, purporting to be written by Steele, but really "specimens of her wit," as the Preface says (and very poor specimens they are), are to be found on pp. 201–4 of a book called *Court Intrigues*, "in a Collection of Original Letters, from the Island of the New Atalantis. By the Author of the Memoirs." London, 1711.

her killing silence?" He had attacked his Timon—the second Duke of Ormond—who had particularly obliged him, not to speak of what he owed to the Duke's father. "Rivella's" statements count for very little, but it is nevertheless pleasant to remember that in after years she made an ample apology for the charges which she had brought against Steele.

We may now turn back to September 1709. On the 9th of that month the Lord Lieutenant, accompanied by Addison, reached England, after proroguing the Irish Parliament. On Wednesday the 5th October, Addison and Steele dined at Lord Halifax's, and on the 8th Steele wrote to Swift, who was still in Ireland, forwarding a letter written by Lord Halifax two days earlier, assuring Swift of continued efforts in his behalf. Steele adds: "I assure you, no man could say more in praise of another than he [Addison] did in your behalf at that noble Lord's table. . . . No opportunity is omitted among powerful men, to upbraid them for your stay in Ireland." In this letter Steele also laughingly refers to Ambrose Philips and his "Pastorals,"[1] and to the intimacy with the Bishop of Clogher, of which he had heard from his friend. We lea from Swift's note-books that he and Addison had passed several summer days at the bishop's houses in Clogher and Finglas, and that, both there and at Laracor, Esther Johnson was with them. Of Esther Johnson, Swift afterwards wrote: "People of all sorts were never more easy than in her company. Mr. Addison, when he was in Ireland, being introduced to her, immediately found her out; and if he had not soon after left the kingdom, assured me he would have used all endeavours to cultivate her

[1] Swift, writing to Philips in this same month—on the 30th October 1709—says: "I was surprised to find in a letter from Mr. Steele that you are now in London, and am at a loss whether public or private business has brought you over. . . . You have the best friend in the world, Mr. Addison, who is never at ease while any men of worth are not so; and Mr. Steele is *alter ab illo*. . . . I reckon no man is thoroughly miserable, unless he be condemned to live in Ireland; and yet I have not the spleen, for I was not born to it. . . . Pray write to me, and remember me, and drink my health sometimes with our friends." There are letters from Addison to Philips, dated 1708 and 1709, in Mr. A. Morrison's collection, praising Philips' poems, but advising him to imitate Spenser only in his beauties. "Dick Steele and I remember you once a day," wrote Addison to Philips on the 25th April 1710.

friendship."[1] Steele's letter ends with an expression of his admiration of Swift's powers.

LORD SUNDERLAND'S OFFICE,
Oct. 8, 1709.

DEAR SIR,

Mr. Secretary Addison went this morning out of town, and left behind him an agreeable command for me, viz. to forward the inclosed, which Lord Halifax sent him for you. I assure you no man could say more in praise of another than he did in your behalf at that noble Lord's table on Wednesday last. I know not but you will find by the inclosed the effect it had upon him. No opportunity is omitted among powerful men, to upbraid them for your stay in Ireland. The company that day at dinner were lord Edward Russel, lord Essex, Mr. Maynwaring, Mr. Addison, and myself.

I have heard such things said of that same Bishop of Clogher[2] with you, that I have often said that he must be entered *ad eundem* in our House of Lords.

Mr. Philips dined with me yesterday; he is still a shepherd, and walks very lonely through this unthinking crowd in London. I wonder you do not write sometimes to me.[3]

The Town is in great expectation from Bickerstaff: what passed at the election for his first table[4] being to be published this day sevennight. I have not seen Ben Tooke[5] a great while, but long to usher you and yours into the world. Not that there can be any thing added by me to your fame, but to walk bare-headed before you.

I am, Sir,
Your most obedient and most humble servant,

RICH. STEELE.

[1] Forster's *Life of Swift*, p. 265.

[2] Dr. St. George Ashe, formerly a Fellow of Trinity College, Dublin (where he was tutor to Swift); afterward Bishop of Clogher, 1697. In 1710–11 he preserved his seat at the Council Board by the interest of Swift. He was translated to Derry in 1716–17, and died in 1717. Both the Bishop and his brothers, Tom Ashe and the Rev. Dillon Ashe, were celebrated punsters, and in that character occur frequently in Swift's works. In the *Tatler*, No. 230, written by Swift, the Bishop is alluded to. [Nichols.]

[3] Swift, according to his account-books for 1709, wrote to Steele on June 13 and October 20. Steele's letter of the 8th October appears to have reached Swift on the 23rd.

[4] *Tatler*, No. 81.

[5] Swift's bookseller. In June 1710 Swift wrote to Tooke: "If you are in such haste, how came you to forget the Miscellanies? I would not have you think of Steele for a publisher [*i.e.*, editor]: he is too busy." In 1708 Swift had drawn up a list of miscellaneous short pieces which he proposed as "Subjects for a Volume."

On the 6th October, the day immediately after that on which he dined at Lord Halifax's, as described in the above letter, Steele wrote to the Earl asking for the loan of £150.

Ocbr 6th, 1709, Berry Street.

MY LORD,

Nothing but the most Afflicting Circumstance could make me break through so much confusion as I am in when I give this Trouble. My little affairs are in such distraction till I can come to an hearing in Chancery (upon Articles for sale of my Estate), that I am at this time in danger of being torn to pieces for £150.

If your Lordship could be so good as to forgive me this trespass upon the Great Humanity and condescension with which you have ever treated me, and please to accommodate me with this sum̄, it should be return'd in a short time with great thankfullnesse, and your Lordship have ever the veneration of me and my little (*sic*) for the most seasonable good office in a time of solid distresse.

I am, my Lord, your Lordships most oblig'd,
most devoted humble servnt

RICHD STEELE.[1]

The notes from Steele to his wife during September and October are few in number and of little importance. From one of them, dated September 25, and addressed to "Mrs. Steele, at her lodging, over against the King's Head, in Downing Street," we learn that a Mr. Margate had done Steele some friendly turn.

In this Michaelmas term there was another action for debt. Stephen Creagh, assignee of Charles Hapson, Esq., and Richard Guy, Esq., Sheriffs of Middlesex, was the plaintiff. Steele's attorney was Hezekiah Benson. In Trinity term last past Creagh brought a bill against Richard Steele, of Westminster, Gent., praying for the payment of £120 which Steele owed him. On the 2nd May 1709, in the parish of St. Martin-in-the-Fields, Steele was taken, arrested, and imprisoned at the suit of Stephen Creagh, by virtue of a bill emanating from the Queen's Court, directed to the Sheriffs of Middlesex, and to be returned to the Court on the 11th May, the first day of Easter

[1] Add. MS. 7121, fol. 67. This letter is printed in Ellis's *Original Letters of Eminent Literary Men* (Camden Society), p. 344.

term. Being so arrested and imprisoned, Steele and a certain William Elderton—whom we have met with several times before—and John Green, mainpernors for him, on the 2nd May, in the parish of the Blessed Mary of Bow in the Ward of Cheap, by a certain writing there made and sealed, acknowledged themselves to be firmly bound in the said £120, to be paid to the Sheriffs or their assignee when required. Conditions were written on the bill to the effect that if Steele appeared at Westminster on the day aforesaid to answer to Creagh for plea of trespass, and also for the bill for £60, the bond would be null and void, but otherwise would remain in full force. On the 17th June the Sheriffs assigned the bond to Creagh. Steele did not appear at Westminster, whereupon the bond became forfeited, and Creagh claimed damages of £10. On the 23rd October Creagh appeared by his attorney, but Steele neither came nor made any answer; judgment was therefore given for Creagh, with 46s. for damages both in the action and in costs.[1] Perhaps it was a hope of being able to pay this debt and so prevent the matter coming into court that led to Steele asking the Earl of Halifax to lend him £150.

The next letter shows that there had been some friction at home, probably the result of the pecuniary troubles.

Nov^br^ 20th, 1709.

DEAR WIFE

I have been in great pain of Body and mind since I came out. You are extremely cruell to a Generous nature which has a Tendernesse for You that renders your least dishumour insupportably afflicting. After short starts of passion not to be inclin'd to reconciliation is what is against All rules of Xstianity and Justice. When I come home I begg to be kindly receiv'd or this will have as ill an effect upon my fortune as well [sic] mind & body.

R. STEELE.

Dec. 23.

MY DEAR,

I shall not come home to dinner, but have fixed every thing; and received money for present uses. I desire, My Dear, that you

[1] Queen's Bench Judgment Roll, Mich. 8 Anne, 337.

have nothing else to do but to be a darling; the way to which is to be always in good humour, and beleive I spend none of my time but to the advantage of you and

Yr Most Obedient Husband

RICHD STEELE.[1]

Before passing on to 1710, some verses by Steele in praise of the Duke of Marlborough, which have hitherto been supposed to have been written in 1710, may here be given.[2] They were written in 1709, if not before, for they appeared in Fenton's collection, *Oxford and Cambridge Miscellany Poems,* the accepted date of which is 1709, though there is no indication of the year on the title-page. The lines end with what may be a pleasant allusion to the *Tatler*, though at first sight his "muse" would be taken to refer to verses by Steele, of which the authorship is not now known.

AN IMITATION OF HORACE'S SIXTH ODE, APPLIED TO THE DUKE OF MARLBOROUGH.

By Captain R. S.

Should Addison's immortal verse
Thy fame in arms, great prince, rehearse,
With Anna's lightning you'd appear
And glitter o'er again in war:
Repeat the proud Bavarian's fall,
And in the Danube plunge the Gaul.
'Tis not for me thy worth to show,
Or lead Achilles to the foe;
Describe stern Diomede in sight,
And put the wounded Gods to flight:

[1] "To Mrs. Steele, at her house, the last door but two on the left-hand in Berry-street, St. James's. With a barrell: porter paid."

[2] The verses are on pp. 319, 320 of Fenton's collection. In the Table they are described as "By Captain Steele." The poem was reprinted by Nichols, in his *Select Collection of Poems* (1780), iv. 13, 14, and in Steele's *Correspondence* (1809), p. 616. Curiously, a book called *Oxford and Cambridge Miscellany Poems, Vol. I.*, was advertised in the *Daily Courant* for Jan. 6, 1708, as "To-morrow will be published," &c., and as "Just published. . . . Written by Mr Fenton, Mr P——r, Mr C. Hopkins, Mr Phillips," &c., in the same paper for Jan. 13. Presumably this was a different volume from the one in which Steele's lines appeared, though I have not seen such a volume.

I dare not, with unequal rage,
On such a mighty theme engage;
Nor sully in a verse like mine
Illustrious Anna's praise, and thine.
Let the laborious epic strain,
In lofty numbers sing the man,
That bears to distant worlds his arms,
And frights the German with alarms:
His courage and his conduct tell,
And on his various virtues dwell;
In trifling cares my humble Muse
A less laborious tract pursues;
Instead of troops in battle mixed,
And Gauls with British spears transfixed,
She paints the soft distress and mien
Of Dames expiring with the spleen.
From the gay noise, affected air,
And little follies of the Fair,
A slender stock of fame I raise,
And draw from others' faults my praise.

In the volume in which these lines first appeared there are also verses "To Captain Steel, on his poetry," by Thomas Bishop, M.A., of Wadham College, Oxford. Mr. Bishop discovered that it is true that there may be a Muse in arms,

"—— since in you
I find the hero and the poet too."

On the 26th January 1710, Steele wrote again to the Earl of Halifax, enclosing Mr. Bickerstaff's proposal for a subscription:—

Jan. 26th, $17\frac{09}{10}$.

My Lord,

I presume to enclose to your lordship Mr. Bickerstaffes proposall for a subscription, and ask your lordship's favour in promoting it, having that Philosopher's interest at heart as much as my own, and am, indeed, confident I am the greatest admirer he has. The best argument I have for this partiality is, that my Lord Halifax has smiled upon his labours. If any whome your Lordship recommends shall think fitt to subscribe more than the sum proposed for a Book, it may be said that it is for so many more books. This will make the favour more gracefull by being confer'd in an oblique way, and at the same time save the confusion of the Squire, whom I know to be naturally proud.

I am, my Lord, your Lordships most obliged,
most obedient humble servant,
RICH^D STEELE.[1]

It is interesting to compare with this letter the letters now bound up with it, addressed to Lord Halifax by all the greatest writers of the time, and to note their different modes of asking favours or returning thanks for those already received. Most of these letters are printed in Ellis's *Letters of Eminent Literary Men*. Swift says (January 13, 1709): "I must take leave to reproach your Lordship for a most inhuman piece of cruelty; for I can call your extream good usage of me no better, since it has taught me to hate the place where I am banished, and raised my thoughts to an imagination, that I might live to be some way usefull or entertaining, if I were permitted to live in Town." On October 6, as we have seen, Halifax wrote to Swift: "I am quite ashamed of myself and my friends, to see you left in a place so incapable of tasting you." On the back of this letter, from "your unalterable friend," Swift wrote: "I kept this Letter as a true original of courtiers and court-promises." Pope wrote to Lord Halifax (December 3, 1714): "While you are doing justice to all the world, I beg you will not forget Homer, if you can spare an hour to attend his cause." Prior wrote ($\frac{20}{30}$th Aug. 1698): "My good Lord and Master, I have written one letter to you to congratulate you on your honours, one to condole with you, another to dunn you, and here is a fourth to thank you. . . . Adieu, Master; nobody respects the Chancellor of the Exchequer more, or loves dear Mr. Montague better, then his old friend and obliged humble servant, MAT." Defoe wrote: "Pardon me, my Lord, If to a man that has seen nothing for some yeares, but the rough face of things, the exceeding goodness of your Lordship's discourse softened me even to a weakness I could not conceal. . . . I am (my Lord) a plain and unpolish'd man, and perfectly unquallified to make formall acknowlegements; and a temper sour'd by a series of

[1] Add. MS. 7121, fol. 69. This letter is reprinted in Ellis's *Original Letters of Eminent Literary Men*, p. 345.

afflictions, renders me still the more awkward in the received method of common gratitude, I mean the ceremony of thanks." And Addison wrote (May 7, 1709): "I have the happiness every day to drink your Lordship's Health in very good wine and with very honest Gentlemen, and am ever with the greatest respect," &c. Of Steele's letter it need only be remarked that Lord Halifax is put down for "5 Books" in the list of subscribers to the octavo edition of the *Tatler*.

At the end of January 1710 Steele was made one of the Commissioners of the Stamp Office.[1] He had hoped, it will be remembered, to take Addison's place when his friend was appointed Secretary to Lord Wharton, and when this was not found practicable Lord Sunderland promised him the next post which was tenable along with the Gazetteership. After two years the promise was now redeemed, and Steele's income was increased by £300 a year, the salary attached to his new office.

About the same time an action was brought against Steele for debt in the Court of Queen's Bench. John Wright prayed that Steele should pay him £18. 15s., which he owed him and unjustly detained. The money, to be paid when required, was borrowed on the 10th October 1709, in the parish of St. Clement Danes; and as Steele would not pay, Wright claimed damages of £10. When Wright prayed that an answer should be made to his narration, Steele's attorney, Hezekiah Benson, said he had no answer to make; and judgment was given in Wright's favour, with 63s. damages.[2]

From the following pleasant letter, the only one we have written at this period, it appears that Mrs. Steele had been ill:—

Feb. 15th, 1709–10.

Dear Wife

I beleive I am the first that ever rejoiced at the flight of one He Loved. After I was done Writing[3] I went up to visit my Sick

[1] "Richard Steele, Esq., is made one of the Commissioners of the Stamp-office" (*Post Boy*, Jan. 28–31, 1709–10; Boyer's *Annals*, 1710, p. 405). The patent appointing Steele one of the "Commissioners for the duties upon stamped vellum, parchment, and paper," is dated June 1, 1710 (Patent Rolls, 3rd Part, 9 Anne).

[2] Queen's Bench Judgment Rolls, Hilary 8 Anne ($17\frac{09}{10}$), 163.

[3] *The Tatler*, No. 134.

Wife, and found she was Her self gone a visiting. I wish you had given me the pleasure of Knowing you were so well it would have giv'n what I was writing a more lively Turn.

I am y[r] Affectionate Tender Observant & indulgent Husband

RICH[D] STEELE.[1]

It will be seen from the following letter, the original of which is among the Blenheim MSS., that Hughes wanted Steele to insert in the *Tatler* his "Epilogue, spoken by Mr. Mills, at the Queen's Theatre, on his benefit night, Feb. 16, 1709, a little before the Duke of Marlborough's going for Holland." In this epilogue Hughes dwelt upon the gathering of valour and beauty in the audience, which by their presence would make actors and poets strive to nobler heights. Two letters by Hughes, designed for the *Tatler*, are printed in his *Correspondence*. The original of one of these is now in Mr. A. Morrison's collection, but attributed wrongly to Steele. In No. 201 of the *Tatler* (July 22, 1710) Steele noticed Mills' benefit on the following Wednesday.

DEAR S[r]

I send you inclos'd the Epilogue I told you of. I hear it is generally spoke of kindly, & I take it rather to have oblig'd than entertain'd which is what I wou'd chuse. My Lord Duke of M. design'd to have been present but was prevented by his preparation for going over.

If you shou'd have a thought of printing it in the Tatler (which indeed I had not when I spoke of it) I desire my name may not be mention'd; The Subject may perhaps make it acceptable and do me no Disfavour; if you think so too, it may not be amiss to date it from *Will's Coffeehouse*, introduc'd with some Thought on Epilogues, that the following was communicated by a Gentleman who is not often seen at this place (viz. at Will's) that it was spoke lately on the occasion of M[r] Mills his Benefit Night. But I am sincere in telling you I wou'd have no Complemt on the Verses, tho you shou'd be so partial and to think they woud bear it, & you will judge how to introduce them much better than I can direct you.

It may be worth your Thought, after it, to pursue the Hint of the Honours of a British Audience, and the noble Emulation a Poet shou'd have to please them regularly. You may perhaps think it

1 "To Mrs. Steele at Mrs. Binns's lodgings in Silver-street, near Golden-square."

proper to observe that the suggesting to them their own worth (in a proper way) has a good Moral Effect, and that to animate them with thoughts on the Glory of their Country is to send them away with a right Impression. This Subject touch'd by Mr Bickerstaff will make amends for printing the verses, yet I do not impose this Trifle, but shall always with great Pleasure allow you the Freedom of a Friend and the Liberty of your own Judgment.

I have some other Hints of Subjects which with Leave shall be yours another time. I am extremely pleas'd wth the two last Tatlers, and think if Mr Bickerstaff unbends at any time it is but as my Ld Roscommon says of Virgil to prepare for some noble Flight. Excuse the Length of this & believe I am

very Sincerely

Dr Sr

Yr most obedient

humble Servt

J. HUGHES.

25 Febr 17$\frac{09}{10}$.

III

DR. SACHEVERELL'S TRIAL.

1710. ÆT. 37–38.

THE opening of the year 1710 found the country in the greatest excitement about the forthcoming trial of Dr. Henry Sacheverell. Dr. Sacheverell had preached two sermons, one at the Assizes at Derby, on the 15th August 1709, and the other at St. Paul's, before the Lord Mayor and Aldermen, on the 5th November, in which he strongly upheld the doctrine of non-resistance, and these sermons were published at the instigation of the Lord Mayor. The Whigs were very angry, and deter mined to resort to the extraordinary measure of impeaching the author. Accordingly, the Commons resolved, on the 13th December, that the sermons were malicious, scandalous, and seditious libels, highly reflecting upon the Queen and her Government, the late happy Revolution, and the Protestant Succession as by law established. On the 15th Sacheverell was impeached at the Bar of the House of high crimes and misdemeanours, and on the 12th January 1710 the articles of impeachment were carried up to the Lords. On the 25th the Doctor put in his answer. The Government demanded a hearing in Westminster Hall, and the question assumed the proportions of a great party contest, the result of which was the overthrow of the Whigs, after a short-lived tenure of office. Before the Sacheverell incident arose, the Whigs had succeeded in making themselves unpopular both with the Queen and with the people. The recent events of the war, terminating with the terrible victory of Malplaquet in September, had brought about a longing for peace; but the negotiations were unsuccessful. Marlborough refused the terms offered by Lewis, and the Government supported the Germans and Dutch in whatever they demanded. The Duke of Marlborough, probably in his desire to secure an independent position, then applied to the Archduke Charles for the office of Governor of the Low Countries, and to Queen Anne for the position of Captain-General for life. In each case he was unsuccessful, and his demands made the Whig party still more unpopular.

The trial of Dr. Sacheverell began on the 27th February and lasted until the 20th March, when Sacheverell was found guilty, and forbidden to preach for three years. The two sermons referred to in the impeachment were ordered to be burnt by the common hangman. This nominal sentence was of course a victory for the Tories. There was much rioting in London. On the 27th February the mob followed the Queen's coach, crying out, "God bless your Majesty and the Church. We hope your Majesty is for Dr. Sacheverell." On the following days the meeting-house of Mr. Daniel Burgess was wrecked. The houses and chapels of other Dissenters were attacked, and the houses of the Lord Chancellor, Lord Wharton, and other Whig leaders were threatened. Among the places in danger were the church and house of Mr., afterwards Bishop, Benjamin Hoadly, who had taken so active a part in the controversy about passive obedience that the House of Commons had represented in an address to the Queen the services he had rendered in justifying the principles of the Revolution.[1] Order was not restored until the Guards were doubled and the Trained Bands ordered to arms. Defoe, describing the times in his *Review*, says:

[1] Among the pamphlets relating to Sacheverell were "A true Character of Don Henrico Furioso de Sacheverellerio, Knight of the Firebrand, in a letter to Isaac Bickerstaff, Esq., Censor of Great Britain. London. Sold by A. Baldwin;" and "A Letter to the Reverend Dr. Henry Sacheverell. By Isaac Bickerstaff, Esq.; with an Order from the said Isaac Bickerstaff Relating to the Doctor. And an Advertisement to Ben Hoadley. London. Printed for Robert Mawson, 1709[-10]." This last is, of course, the work of a friend of Sacheverell's; it comprises a letter, signed Isaac Bickerstaff, and dated Sheerlane, January the 19th, 1709-10; an Order, by the Censor-General of Great Britain, and counter-signed by Charles Lilly, Secretary, respecting those who scurrilously abused the Doctor, and an advertisement to Hoadly, ordering him to show cause why he should not be pronounced a Dead Man.

"The women lay aside their tea, and chocolate, leave off visiting after dinner, and forming themselves into cabals, turn privy councillors, and settle the affairs of state; . . . gallantry and gaiety are now laid aside for business." The attendance in the park, at the theatre, and at church grew thinner. "Nay, the Tatler, the immortal Tatler, the great Bickerstaff himself was fain to leave off talking to the ladies, during the Doctor's trial, and turn his sagacious pen to the dark subject of death, and the next world; though he has not yet decided the ancient debate, whether Pluto's regions were, in point of government, a kingdom or a commonwealth." "Mobs, rabbles, and tumults possess the streets; . . . even the little boys and girls talk politics." "Sacheverell will make all the Ladys turn good huswis, they goe att seven every mornin'," says Lady Wentworth.[1] Addison afterwards wrote a paper in the *Spectator* (No. 57), deprecating the introduction of party rage among ladies, and he took the opportunity, under the guise of an anecdote of the strife which prevailed when Titus Oates made his disclosures, to refer to the bitter feelings called forth by the trial of Sacheverell, who had been a college friend of Addison's. "For my own part, I think a man makes an odious and despicable figure that is violent in a party." Addison himself, in the years following, managed to keep out of the heat of party strife; it would have been well for himself if Steele's sense of duty had enabled him to do the same.

Coming to April, we have another interesting, but mutilated, letter from Steele to his wife, who, it would seem, was not an early riser.

Aprill 7th, 1710.

DEAR PRUE

I enclose to you a receipt for the Saucepan and spoon and a note of 23*l.* of Lewis's [2] which will make up the 50*l.* I promised for yr ensuing occasion.[3]

I know no happinesse in this life in any degree comparable to the pleasure I have in your person and society, I only begg of you to add to yr other charms a fearfulnesse to see a man that Loves you

[1] *Wentworth Papers*, 113. [2] See page 227, 235.
[3] Her approaching confinement.

in pain and uneasinesse, to make me as happy as 'tis possible to be in this life. Rising a little in a morning and being disposed to a chearfullnesse[1] . . . . . . would not be amisse.

I am y^r Most Affectionate Husband & Obedient Serv^nt,

RICH^D STEELE.

There are papers in the parlour window, dated from Hamburgh and other places, wch I want.[2]

On the 11th April Addison wrote to Swift, informing him of the approaching return of Lord Wharton and himself to Dublin. Steele and he, says Addison, had been often drinking Swift's health. On the 13th Addison wrote to Mr. Keally: "We are here in a great puzzle of politics. Little Ben [Hoadly] speaks half sentences, and grows more mysterious than ever. Dick Steele is entirely yours."

A few days later there was another action for a debt, amounting this time to £1000. The case was heard on the 26th April. George Doddington, Esq., stated that Richard Steele of the parish of St. James, Westminster, acknowledged himself bound, by a bond which he sealed on the 2nd August 1709, at Westminster, in the sum of £1000, to be paid when required. But he had not paid, and refused to do so; Doddington, therefore, claimed damages of £100. Steele's attorney, Richard Ashe, said that he had not been informed by Steele of any answer to be made, and judgment was therefore entered for Doddington, with 53s. for the damages which he had sustained as well by the detention of the debt as for the costs.[3]

A week later Steele wrote to his wife that he was making up his accounts with Nutt and Tonson, being resolved to understand his affairs, and communicate them to her from that hour forward. On May 25 a son was born, and named Richard, after his father; but he died when he was six years old. Lord Halifax was one of the sponsors at the baptism. In a memorandum written by Mrs. Steele we read: "My son Richard was born the 25th of May 1710, on a Thursday morning, a little after three o'clock; and was christened the 24th of June; his

[1] Two or three words are here cut out.

[2] See the *Gazette* of Saturday, April 8, 1710.

[3] Queen's Bench Judgment Roll, Easter 9 Anne (1710), 307.

godfathers Lord Halifax and Mr. Hopkins the elder; his godmother was my mother (Mrs. Vaughan stood for her)."

On the 21st June judgment was given in an action for debt brought against Steele—of the parish of St. James, Westminster, Esq.—by George Tilden, who was agent to Mr. Robert Lowther, Governor of Barbados,[1] and to whom allusion was made in a letter to Mrs. Steele in March 1709.[2] In Easter term, 1710, George Tilden brought a bill before the Court of Queen's Bench, stating that on the 27th May 1709, in the parish of St. James, Westminster, Steele signed and sealed a bond acknowledging himself bound to Tilden in the sum of £140, to be paid when required. But Steele, although very often requested to pay the money, had not paid, and still refused to do so, to the damage of Tilden of £20. Accordingly, on the 9th June 1710 both parties appeared. Tilden's attorney was Thomas Willard; Steele's, Edmund Laycon. Steele asked to hear the writing, and it was read; also the condition of the writing, and it was read in these words: "The condition of this obligation is such That if the above bounden Richard Steele, his heirs executors or administrators well and truly pay or cause to be paid unto the above mentioned George Tilden his executors administrators or assigns the full sum of £70 of good and lawful money of Great Britain on the 29th of September next ensuing the date of these presents Then this obligation to be void, Or else to remain in full force." After hearing this, Steele said that Tilden ought not to maintain his action against him, because after the drawing up of that bond, to wit, on the 19th of September 1709, at the parish of St. James, Westminster, at the request of Tilden, by a writing indented made between them, for and in full satisfaction and exoneration of the aforesaid bond, he conveyed and assured to Tilden certain lands and tenements, with the appurtenances, in the Island of Barbados, to have and to hold to Tilden and his heirs for ever. Tilden replied that he ought not to be precluded from bringing his action against Steele by anything the latter had alleged in

[1] Documents, dated 1712, in Record Office (Colonial Office Records,—Board of Trade, Barbados, No. 17).

[2] Page 235.

his plea, because Steele did *not* convey to him the said lands and tenements in Barbados. After several adjournments the parties appeared in court on the 21st June—Wednesday next after the three weeks of Holy Trinity; and on the 8th July judgment was given in Tilden's favour, with damages to the amount of £9.[1] The contradictory statements in this case about the Barbados property do not help us much, and I have not been able to trace the Chancery suit mentioned in Steele's letter to the Earl of Halifax of the 6th October 1709.

With June came the beginning of the end with the Whigs. The Queen, egged on by Harley, had already made the Duke of Shrewsbury, who had voted for Sacheverell's acquittal, Lord Chamberlain, in defiance of the objections urged by Godolphin, and now she dismissed Lord Sunderland, Marlborough's son-in-law, putting in his place Lord Dartmouth. On July 23 Addison wrote to Swift from Dublin Castle: "About two days ago I received the inclosed, that is sealed up; and yesterday that of my friend Steele, which, requiring a speedy answer, I have sent you express. In the meantime I have let him know that you are out of town, and that he may expect your answer by the next post. I fancy he had my Lord Halifax's authority for writing. . . . Our politicians are startled at the breaking off the negociations, and fall of stocks; insomuch that it is thought they will not venture at dissolving the Parliament in such a crisis. Mr. Steele desires me to seal yours before I deliver it; but this you will excuse in one who wishes you as well as he, or anybody living can do." At this time, too, Steele made the most complimentary allusions to Swift in the Dedication to Maynwaring of the first volume of the *Tatler*. Swift afterwards wrote of this period: "I was a sort of bough for drowning men to lay hold of." On the 5th August Addison wrote to Mr. Keally of the state of tension in the city; but he believed the people were recovering their senses, and that the next Parliament would be of the same stamp with the present one in case of a dissolution. Addison had come to town to see after his election at Malmesbury. Swift wrote to Addison from Dublin, on the 22nd August: "The bishop [Clogher] showed

[1] Queen's Bench Judgment Roll, Trinity 9 Anne, 134.

me the first volume of the small edition of the *Tatler*, where there is a very handsome compliment to me; but I can never pardon the printing of the news of every *Tatler*—I think he might as well have printed the advertisements. I knew it was a bookseller's piece of craft, to increase the bulk and price of what he was sure would sell; but I utterly disapprove of it."

We have only two notes written by Steele to his wife in July. In one of them he said he must stay in town that night because he had important business to settle with Mr. Montague, business connected, no doubt, with the dedication to that gentleman of the second volume of the *Tatler*. In a letter, dated August 8, he informed his wife of Godolphin's dismissal that day. On the 10th the office of Lord Treasurer was put into commission, one of the five commissioners being Harley, but Harley also became Chancellor of the Exchequer, and practically Prime Minister, although the Whigs retained office for a time. Here are two letters written on the 9th August.

Half hour after six,
Wednesday Aug^st^ 9th, 1710,
BERRY-STREET.

DEAR PRUE

Thou art such a foolish Tender thing that there is no living with Thee.

I have broke my rest last night because I knew you would be such a fool as not to sleep. Pray come home by this morning's Coach, if you are impatient: but if you are not here before noon I will come down to you in the Evening, but I must make visits this morning to hear what is doing.

Y^s^ Ever, R. S.[1]

Aug^st^ 9th, 1710, COCKPITT.

DEAR PRUE

I cannot possibly come expecting Orders Here which I must overlook, and having not half done my other businesse at the Savoy.[2]

Dear Creature come in the morning Coach and if I can I will return wth you in the Evening. Pray wrap y^r^ self very Warm.

Y^rs^ Ever, R: STEELE.

1 "To Mrs. Steele, at Mrs. Bradshaw's house, at Sandy-end, over-against the Bull Alehouse in Fulham Road."

2 At Mr. Nutt's. See *Tatler*, No. 209.

Steele's position with those now in power would certainly not be improved by the fact that he had admitted into the *Tatler*, at the beginning of July, papers which, there can be little doubt, were intended as satires on Harley. Of one of these papers Steele twice denied the authorship;[1] but he was the editor, and was naturally looked upon with disfavour.

At the end of August we have a group of letters from Steele, from which Nichols surmised that the writer was, owing to pecuniary difficulties, in prison at this time at the Bull Head in Vere Street. But it is evident, from the note of the 29th August, that Steele's movements were unfettered on that day, and that it was only business engagements which kept him at Vere Street on the following day. It is true that Swift says in his *Journal:* "Yes, Steele was a little while in prison, or at least in a spunging-house, some time before I came, but not since." Swift came to London on the 7th September, and although he may here refer to an incident which occurred in the last week of August, it is at least as probable that the temporary confinement to which he alludes should have an earlier date assigned to it. Swift's statement is corroborated by a pamphlet, without date, but published in September 1710, entitled, "A Condoling Letter to The Tattler: On Account of the Misfortunes of Isaac Bickerstaff, Esq.; A Prisoner in the —— On Suspicion of Debt."[2] The writer, "Censor Censorum," dwells upon the need of a self-appointed Censor having a special regard to his own reputation. Retribution had come; "he that imprisoned Partridge in the grave is himself buried in that worst of graves, a jail." Had not Bickerstaff disqualified himself from reproving any man for nonsense, when he himself got into debt through profuse living and want of thought, and, though he had a plentiful income and no great family, had a good profit for Tatling, and had received large bounties from the generous part of mankind, was found in the Gate-House, or

[1] The letter from Downes the prompter in No. 193. See Preface to vol. iv. of the *Tatler*, and the *Guardian*, No. 53.

[2] This tract was advertised in the *Flying Post* for September 19, and was noticed by Addison in the *Tatler* for September 26 (No. 229).

any house, through debt? What honesty could Bickerstaff pretend to, what pity could he expect?

The "Martyn" from whom Steele hoped to obtain assistance was either Richard Martyn—as Nichols conjectured—who was a fellow Commissioner of the Stamp Office, or Henry Martyn, a barrister, who afterwards wrote for the *Spectator*, and was an intimate friend of Steele's. It is not improbable, by the way, that these two Martyns were brothers, for we are told that Henry Martyn was the eldest son of Edward Martyn, Esq., of Upham, Wiltshire, and that that gentleman had three other sons, Edward, *Richard*, and William.[1]

Augst 24th, 1710,
BULL-HEAD, CLARE-MARKETT.

DEAR PRUE

I begg of you to meet y^{r} Brother Whigg Martyn and my self Here. Ask for me.

Y^{rs} Faithfully

RICH^{D} STEELE.

Augst 29th, 1710.

I am doing my businesse and cannot come to dinner, but stay to come home more Chearfully.

Y^{rs} R: STEELE.

Augst 30th, 1710,
VERE-STREET.

MY DEAR PRUE

If you can be so good as to forgive all that is past, you shall [not] hereafter know any Suffering from indiscretion, or negligence. I have taken care of the matter mentioned in the letter you opened yesterday. Pray let me know how Lugger does. I am waiting Here for a third person to go and receive Money. Martyn sent an excuse yesterday y^{t} He was sick, and promises to come at Ten to-day but I shall not wait or depend on that, tho I dare say He would do all he could.

Y^{r} Affectionate & Tender Husband,

RICH^{D} STEELE.

Pray send linnen for I am to meet the parties before nine.

[1] Drake's *Essays illustrative of the Tatler*, &c., iii. 285.

Sept. 29 [1710].

DEAR PRUE,

Go to dinner. I have sent Cave to Martyn, and I wait till he or his brother brings me the money.

Yours ever, R. S.

Upon second thoughts, I will go and dine at the Gentleman-usher's table.

It is now professedly point of party, and I am required to be here because a great man advised it yesterday. But the remainder of the money will be ready, by means of Martyn and Elderton, before two of clock tomorrow. In the mean time I am contented, and desire you not to come hither till early tomorrow morning, between seven and eight, at which time I would have you be with me precisely. I sent young Elderton to the nurse's, and the child is much better.

Yours with great truth now,
and with care hereafter,
RICHD STEELE.

RUMMER TAVERN, COVENT-GARDEN.

DEAR PRUE,

I am just going to Jeffreys's; have settled my matter with Mr. Potter, who lends me the money. [I] desire you would go to bed at home and be of good cheer.

Yours ever, R. STEELE.

Martyn never came near me.

There are other notes, undated, but some of them evidently written while Steele was still Gazetteer. These letters contain, besides obscure allusions to hopes and disappointments, several characteristic passages reproaching Mrs. Steele for being out of humour on account of want of money and other troubles. "Prue, Prue, look a little dressed, and be beautiful." "I go away because you will have it so, but I have been guilty of nothing that ought to exclude me from the happiness of being yours."

Whether I deserve it or not, I humbly desire you will smile upon me when I come into your presence. I wait for your answer, who am,

Yours tenderly, R. S.

4 of Clock.

DEAR PRUE,

Take this boy to sit behind you in the boat, and put on your mask and come to Somerset-stairs. From whence send him to call me from Nutt's, where your servant [waits] for your arrival to visit my grand-daughter.[1]

R. S.

DEAR PRUE,

I desire you to dress yourself decently before you appear before me, for I will [not] be so easily pleased as I have been, being now in a fair way of being a great man.

[1] This was probably Steele's natural daughter.

IV.

FALL OF THE WHIGS.

1710–11. ÆT. 38.

SWIFT'S return to London at the beginning of September 1710 is an important point in our story, for, among other things, it led to the commencement of that correspondence with Esther Johnson and Mrs. Dingley which goes by the name of the *Journal to Stella*, and which gives us such a wonderful view of the state of parties during the ensuing months. The primary object of Swift's visit to London was to push forward the question of First Fruits in the interests of the Irish clergy, but besides this he was seeking, and seeking very naturally, advancement for himself. It was fortunate for the attainment of this latter object that the mission with which he was entrusted by the Archbishop of Dublin required frequent negotiations with the statesmen who had just come into power. Swift reached London on the 7th September, after a five days' journey from Chester.[1] From that city he wrote the first letter that we have addressed to Esther Johnson; it is dated 2nd September, and contains the direction: "Let all who write to me inclose to Richard Steele, Esq., at his office at the Cockpit near Whitehall.

[1] The serious nature of a journey from London to Dublin in Queen Anne's time is illustrated by an advertisement in the *Post Boy*, May 2 to 5, 1713: "For a sure and certain despatch of all manner of business between Great Britain and Ireland, a person intends to set out of London, the 9th of this instant, for Dublin, by way of Holyhead, which he proposes to reach the 18th, and to leave Dublin the 23rd for London the same way, so as to be in London the 3rd of June; and to keep constantly the same stages every month in the year. It is proposed the undertaking will be of a general service to both kingdoms." From subsequent papers it appears that this person really got back on June 15th, and was to start again for Dublin on the 30th.

But not MD. I will pay for their letters at St. James's Coffee House, that I may have them sooner."[1] On Friday and Saturday, the 8th and 9th September, Swift got through an immense amount of business. On Saturday he wrote that the Whigs were ravished to see him, and would lay hold on him as a twig while they were drowning; but he was enraged at the coldness with which Godolphin received him, and was "almost vowing vengeance." "Every Whig in great office will, to a man, be infallibly put out. . . . The *Tatler* expects every day to be turned out of his employment." On the next day, Sunday the 10th, he sat till ten in the evening with Addison and Steele. "Steele," he repeats, "will certainly loose his Gazetteer's place, all the world detesting his engaging in politics. . . . And I am come home, rolling resentments in my mind, and framing schemes of revenge." On the 11th Swift dined alone with Addison, and on the 15th he again dined with Addison at a country-house near Chelsea, where Addison often retired. On the 18th he dined at the same place, but got home early, and began the letter to the *Tatler* which afterwards appeared in No. 230. Then came the expected removals. Somers, the Duke of Devonshire, and Mr. Secretary Boyle were all turned out, being succeeded by the Earl of Rochester, the Duke of Buckingham, and Henry St. John respectively; and numerous other changes followed. "I never remember such bold steps taken by a Court," Swift wrote; "I am almost shocked at it, though I did not care if they were all hanged." He looked forward to a strange winter, but intended to be an indifferent spectator of the struggles ot parties; he was about to move to Bury Street—to a house next door to the Vanhomrighs—where he supposed he would continue during his stay in London. He had the first floor, at a rent of eight shillings a week, a sum which he much begrudged.

On the 21st September Parliament was dissolved. On that day Swift dined with Steele, Addison, and others, and a dinner for the same party was arranged for Sunday. On the 23rd the long letter already referred to was sent to Mr. Bickerstaff, and on the 27th "all our company dined at Will Frankland's"—son

[1] Forster's *Swift*, 410. "MD." stands here for Esther Johnson and her companion Mrs. Dingley.

of the Postmaster-General—"with Steele and Addison too." On the 29th Swift dined at Addison's country place; on the next day he was to go to Harley; the Duke of Ormond, he remarks, would, he believed, "give me something to make me easy; and I have good interest among his best friends. But I don't think of anything further than the business I am upon." Bishops in Ireland, he adds, must not write to him at Mr. Steele's, but direct for Mr. Steele, at his office at the Cockpit; a mistake of this kind had cost him eighteenpence. Swift repeated this request in a letter to Archbishop King of the 10th October. The Whigs now confessed his ill-usage, but he minded them not; he hoped for good usage from Harley. "The Tories dryly tell me, 'I may make my fortune, if I please,' but I do not understand them—or rather, I do understand them." It had cost him but three shillings in meat and drink since he came to town. "I laugh to see myself so disengaged in these revolutions." On the 2nd October he dined with Lord Halifax at Hampton Court, but he refused to drink to a health proposed by his host, "the resurrection of the Whigs," unless he would add their reformation too. On the following evening Halifax sent his servant to desire Swift to dine with him again, but Swift declined, saying that he had business of great importance that hindered him. This was the meeting with Harley, who received him with "the greatest respect and kindness imaginable," and made an appointment for the following Saturday, when Swift was to "open his business" to him. Swift adds that he had sent to the printers a lampoon upon Godolphin, *Sid Hamet*, which he had been for some days preparing, and he contemplated attacks on other Whig statesmen: "I have more mischief in my heart." Yet he was at the same time going to work at another *Tatler*. This he repeats on the 7th October: "And now I am going in charity to send Steele a *Tatler*, who is very low of late." On that same day Harley saw Swift, entered into his business with all kindness, said he must make Mr. St. John and Swift acquainted, and expressed so much esteem that Swift felt inclined half to believe what some friends had told him, that Harley would do everything to bring him over. On the 10th he dined with Harley, and on his return home proceeded with the writing of the "Description of a Shower in London," which was intended for the *Tatler;* on the 12th he had finished the "Shower," all but the beginning, and was going on with his *Tatler*. There was every desire to conciliate writers who were of the Whig party, and Steele among the number. On the 12th Swift dined with Garth and Addison; the Tories were carrying it among the new members six to one, but "Mr. Addison's election has passed easy and undisputed; and I believe if he had a mind to be chosen king he would hardly be refused."

On the 14th October we have the first tidings of Steele's loss of the Gazetteership. On that day Swift wrote, with reference to a letter addressed to him which had been delayed: "I doubt it has lain in Steele's office and he forgot. Well, there is an end of that: he is turned out of his place; and you must desire those who send me packets to enclose them in a paper directed to Mr. Addison, at St. James's Coffee House."[1] On the 17th he wrote: "This day came out the *Tatler*, made up wholly of my 'Shower,' and a preface to it. They say it is the best thing I ever writ, and I think so too." Three days later comes the question, "Do they know anything in Ireland of my greatness among the Tories? Everybody reproaches me of it here; but I value them not." On the 22nd Swift spent two hours with Erasmus Lewis,[2] Under-Secretary to Lord Dartmouth, talking politics, and "contriving to keep Steele in his office of stampt paper: he has lost his place of Gazetteer, three hundred pounds a year, for writing a *Tatler*, some months ago, against Mr. Harley, who gave him the post at first, and raised the salary from sixty to three hundred pounds. This was devilish ungrateful; and Lewis was telling me the particulars: but I had a hint given me, that I might save him in the other employment; and leave was given me to clear matters with Steele." As Forster points out, Swift seems to have treated Harley's "hint" too exclusively as for Steele's benefit. Harley was not acting wholly from unselfish motives; he was very

[1] "Capt Steele, said to be the author of the *Tatler*, is removed from writing the *Gazette*." (Luttrell's *Diary*, vi. 643; October 17, 1710.)

[2] In October 1713 Erasmus Lewis was appointed Provost Marshal General of Barbados, and in that capacity he may have again come in contact with Steele's affairs. (Pub. Record Office, Home Office Docquets, vol. ii., 1711-13.)

anxious to get Steele back, or at least to prevent his becoming an opponent. Swift afterwards clearly stated, in the *Importance of the Guardian Considered,* that Steele himself resigned his post: "Mr. Steele, to avoid being discarded, thought fit to resign his place of Gazetteer;" and we are also told how, when Steele complained of the hardship of being forced to quit his place, although he had never injured Harley nor received any obligation from him, and when the gentleman with whom he spoke reminded him of the libels in the *Tatler*, Steele answered that they were by other hands, and he was only the publisher. Eventually, it is stated, Steele said, "Well, I have libelled him, and he has turned me out, and so we are equal." Steele did not consider he was under an obligation to Harley for the post of Gazetteer, for Harley had told him he must only thank Mr. Maynwaring for that. In the *Journal* for the 22nd October, Swift says that in the evening, after dinner, he went to sit with Addison, "and offer the matter at distance to him, as the discreeter person; but found party had so possessed him, that he talked as if he suspected me, and would not fall in with anything I said. So I stopped short in my overture, and we parted very dryly; and I shall say nothing to Steele, and let them do as they will; but, if things stand as they are, he will certainly lose it; and therefore I will not speak to him, that I may not report to his disadvantage. Is not this vexatious? and is there so much in the proverb of proferred service?" Swift was vexed that even his nearest friends would not understand that he endeavoured to act with the most perfect honour and conscience. On the next day, he says, he met Addison at the coffee-house, and behaved himself coldly enough to him. Yet on the 24th he met Addison at dinner at Sir Matthew Dudley's, and on the 25th he dined with Addison and Steele, and a sister of Addison's married to Mons. Sartre,[1] prebendary of Westminster. "Addison's sister is a sort of a wit, very like him. I am not fond of her."

[1] Dr. Sartre died in 1713, and his widow afterwards married Daniel Combes, Esq., an agent of the army. In telling his wife of this second marriage, Steele wrote: "He is a very handsome fellow, and she has without much reserve given herself wholly to him; without care of a settlement, even of her own, but in very loose words." Mrs. Combes died in 1750.

Among the Marlborough MSS. is a letter from Mr. Steevens to "The Right

During the remaining days of October, Swift dined in company with Addison several times, and made various attempts to see Harley, without success, however, from one cause or another. Then came a certain alarm that Harley might fail. "God knows what will come of it. I should be terribly vexed to see things come round again." On the 3rd November Swift wrote: "We have scurvy *Tatlers* of late, so pray do not suspect me. I have one or two hints I design to send him, and never any more: he does not deserve it. He is governed by his wife most abominably,[1] as bad as [Marlborough]. I never saw her since I came, nor has he ever made me an invitation; either he dares not, or is such a thoughtless Tisdall[2] fellow

Honourable Joseph Addison Esqr in St. James's Place, London," concerning Mr. Sartre. Mr. Steevens was a clergyman. (Letter to Addison, Egerton MS. 1971, fol. 27.)

Mar. 5th, 1709[-10].

HON'D S^R

Having received no satisfactory answer from Mr Nichols to the message I sent him concerning Cous. Lanty's money, I went this day to Lichfield on purpose about that affair, he tells me he do's not question but to procure 40*l.* to satisfy Mr Sartre by Lady day or about that time. That his estate is upon Sale wch he hopes will be accomplish'd in a little time, and then he will pay of the whole bond, or raise money other wayes to do it if that doth not take effect. I believe his security is good, and should not scruple to lay down the money upon it if I had it in my power altho' I am no otherwise concern'd in it than to serve my friends wch I have hitherto done and shall do with the utmost diligence & fidelity. I lately sent you word that Mr. White had been dangerously ill, and now we have a report that he is dead, and that others are design'd for his prebend. Whether it be really so I cannot tell, but if you had been pleas'd to have recommended me to the Bp, whatever the event had been, it would have been a very obliging favour to

S^r

Yo^r humble serv^t

ARTH: STEEVENS.

I must not forgett to return you and Cap: Steele my continued thanks for the tatlers and Gazett wch I have the favour of receiving every post.

[1] It was probably from some such passage as this that Thackeray took the view which he seems to have held of Lady Steele. In *Esmond* (Book II. chap. xv.) there is a description of an entertainment at the Dowager Lady Castlewood's, at which Steele and his wife were present. "Dick was charming, tho' his wife was odious." St. John remarked to her, "How charming the *Tatler* is! We all recognised your portrait in the forty-ninth number, and I have been dying to know you ever since I read it." But Mrs. Steele, who was ignorant and jealous, regarded the *Tatler* as mere rubbish; and Mr. St. John at length yawned in her face, and went his way.

[2] Probably Dr. William Tisdall, of Belfast, a suitor to Esther Johnson.

that he never minds it. So what care I for his wit? for he is the worst company in the world, till he has a bottle of wine in his head." The day before Swift thus expressed his surprise at the lessening of cordiality on Steele's part, Swift's first paper in the *Examiner* had been published. We must now turn back to see how that paper came into existence.

On May 22, 1710, appeared the first number of the *Moderator*, which was far from moderate, and was chiefly occupied in answering and attacking the *Observator* and the *Review*. This paper reached to fifty numbers, the last of which appeared on the 10th November, when Swift had begun to write for the *Examiner*, and the weaker paper was no longer needed. On the 3rd August appeared the first number of the *Examiner, or Remarks upon Papers and Occurrences.* The intention, as was stated in an introductory notice, was to *examine* some of the papers which misled the town. Dr. William King, St. John, Prior, Dr. Atterbury, and Dr. Freind were contributors to the early numbers of the new periodical. In the second number there is a sarcastic allusion to the letters to Lewis XIV. printed in the *Tatler*, and the fifth number consists of an elaborate paper on Steele, in the form of a comparison of the news given in the *Gazette* and *Tatler* of August the 12th. The writer says he admired many of Steele's papers, and from feelings of friendship urged him not to meddle with matters of State. "After all, Isaac, though I have used this freedom with you, I would not have you take me for your enemy; I am one of your two guinea subscribers, and consequently (if I may take your word for it in your Dedication) am a person eminent for wit, beauty, valour, or wisdom, some one or more of 'em." The paper ends with an allusion to the promise in the *Tatler* to be more witty when the town filled. "I believe he will shortly be as good as his word, for his friends, I hear, are coming from Ireland. I expect, too, some of my friends from the same Country." This was on the 31st August. In the sixth number of the *Examiner* there is an allusion to the expulsion from the Kitcat Club of Prior, who was himself the author of this paper, which was chiefly filled with ridicule of Garth's verses "To the Earl of Godolphin." On the 12th October appeared the eleventh number of the

Examiner; it is attributed to Dr. William King, and is full of personal abuse of Steele. Nowhere is vanity more disagreeable than in a writer, and "a meditating lucubrating fop is intolerable." Steele, continues the writer—though he does not actually mention the name—was a vain officer, a Thraso, no poet, a little writer, a weekly retailer of loose ephemeral papers. The *Examiner* proceeds to attack the *Tatler* for the 26th September, No. 229, but that paper, as it happens, was by Addison, and not by Steele. In it Addison spoke of the "numberless vermin that feed upon this paper; . . . the small wits and scribblers, that every day turn a penny by nibbling at my Lucubrations." The *Examiner*, in reply to this, insinuates that, from the mention of vermin, the *Tatler* had been sleeping in a spunging-house. Then, referring to an allusion of Addison's to a great man's equipage, who do honour to the person on whom they feed, the writer retorts with a statement which has become a well-known anecdote in connection with Steele's experiences of bailiffs' officers. "There is an equipage that does no great honour to the person on whom they feed. I have heard of a certain illustrious person, who having a *guard du corps,* that forced their attendance upon him, put them into a livery, and maintained them as his servants: Thus answering that famous question, *Quis custodiet ipsos custodes?* For he, I think, might properly be said to keep his keepers, in English at least, if not in Latin. If you intend, Mr. Tatler, to keep your attendants, you must be a little more punctual in your payments. They complain that they have nothing to feed upon, and are in great danger of starving."[1] All this comes with a bad grace, as it has been pointed out, from Dr. William King, who was never in very good circumstances, and who, although he succeeded Steele as Gazetteer, was, a year later, "poor and starving," according to Swift's own *Journal.* In the *Tatler* for October 19 (No. 239), Addison answered the *Examiner*, whose criticisms, he said, "make a man of sense sick, and a fool merry." As regards the invective upon one who had been imprisoned for

[1] The same story is told in the *Annotations on the Tatler*, 1710, i. 32. "He gives fees as well as wages: and his people at the same time are no less famed for diligence and fidelity, for he is always sure of a very strict and close attendance."

debt, Addison remarks that he heartily pitied him, whoever he was; poverty was never thought a proper subject for ridicule.

Besides these papers in the *Tatler*, however, Addison had, in the middle of September, started a weekly paper, the *Whig Examiner*, the declared object of which was to give all persons a re-hearing who had been unjustly attacked by the *Examiner*. Mr. Bickerstaff the *Examiner* everywhere endeavoured to imitate and abuse. The *Whig Examiner* reached only to five numbers, of which the last appeared on the 12th October; it was, says the author of *The Present State of Wit*, "written with so much fire, and in so excellent a style, as put the Tories in no small pain for their favourite hero: every one cried, Bickerstaff must be the author." A week before Addison's paper came to an end, the first number of the *Medley* was issued, which was to continue the work of answering the *Examiner*. The *Medley* was chiefly written by Oldmixon, under Maynwaring's supervision, and Steele afterwards contributed one paper. Besides these periodicals, St. John published in pamphlet form a *Letter to the Examiner*, attacking the Whigs. Among other things, he said that the wits of the Kitcat had taken great pains to lessen the character of the Queen in the world. To this the ex-Chancellor Cowper replied in a pamphlet, *A Letter to Isaac Bickerstaff, Esq.* Such was the state of the controversy when Swift took up the *Examiner*. His first paper, dated 2nd November, was originally No. 14, but it became No. 13 in the collected edition of the paper, owing to suppression of the original No. 13. During the winter and following spring Swift wrote a series of masterly papers in support of Harley's policy, with a skill such as had never been seen before in political journalism.

On the 4th November Swift dined with Addison and Steele; on the 8th he wrote: "I have written several other things that I hear commended, and nobody suspects me for them; nor you shall not know till I see you again." But although Swift did not tell Esther Johnson, Steele and Addison must soon have known that Swift was now the author of the *Examiner*, the most powerful engine in the hands of the Tories. On the 10th Swift again dined at Addison's, with Garth and Steele; on the 16th he met Addison at dinner, and returned with him. "Mr. Addison and I meet a little seldomer than formerly, although we are still at bottom as good friends as ever, but differ a little about party." Swift and Steele met again on the 19th, at the St. James's Coffee-House. "This evening," writes Swift, "I christened our coffee-man Elliott's child, where the rogue had a most noble supper, and Steele and I sat among some scurvy company over a bowl of punch; so that I am come home late."

On the 25th November the new Parliament met, and Mr. Bromley was chosen Speaker. A few days later Swift wrote that he had given one or two hints for the *Tatler*, especially the *Tatler* of the Shilling (No. 249); but he had other things to mind, and of much greater importance; "and, besides, the ministry hate to think that I should help him, and have made reproaches on it; and I frankly told them, I would do it no more." On the 2nd December he notes how "Steele, the rogue, has done the impudentest thing in the world," in printing in the *Tatler* a letter, signed with their initials, which Rowe, Prior, and he had sent to Steele, in ridicule of the idea that "Great Britain" ought to be used in common conversation instead of "England." On the 14th Swift wrote: "Mr. Addison and I are different as black and white, and I believe our friendship will go off, by this damned business of party: he cannot bear seeing me fall in so with this ministry; but I love him still as well as ever, though we seldom meet." Next day he dined with Lewis and Ford. "Lewis told me a pure thing. I had been hankering with Mr. Harley to save Steele his other employment, and have a little mercy on him; and I had been saying the same thing to Lewis, who is Mr. Harley's chief favourite. Lewis tells Mr. Harley how kindly I should take it if he would be reconciled to Steele, &c. Mr. Harley, on my account, falls in with it, and appoints Steele a time to let him attend him, which Steele accepts with great submission, but never comes, nor sends any excuse. Whether it was blundering, sullenness, insolence, or rancour of party, I cannot tell, but I shall trouble myself no more about him. I believe Addison hindered him out of pure spite, being grated to the soul to think he should ever want my help to save his friend; yet now he is soliciting me to make another of his friends queen's secretary at Geneva; and I will do it if I can; it is poor Pastoral Philips." If, however, Steele failed to keep his appointment on this occasion, he subsequently had an interview with Harley, which seems to have resulted in a satisfactory understanding. The Commissionership was to be retained. This we learn from a letter of Steele's to the Earl of Oxford, dated June 4, 1713, in which he announced his resignation of the office. "When I had the honour of a short conversation with you, you were pleased not only to signify to me that I should remain in this office, but to add, that if I would name to you one of more value, which would be more commodious to me, you would favour me in it. . . . I thank your Lordship for the distinction you have at sundry times showed me." It is clear that Harley was more reluctant than Swift supposed to let Steele become entirely estranged, but Swift's somewhat insolent air of patronage [1] doubtless annoyed both Addison and Steele, and rendered more difficult, rather than easier, an understanding with the new Ministry.

We can only surmise what was the arrangement entered into at the meeting with Harley, but on the 2nd January 1711 the *Tatler* suddenly came to an end. On that day Swift met Addison and "little Harrison, a young poet, whose fortune I am making," at Darteneuf's house. "Steele was to have been there, but came not, nor never did twice, since I knew him, to any appointment. . . . Steele's last *Tatler* came out to-day. You will see it before this comes to you, and how he takes leave of the world. He never told so much as Mr. Addison of it, who was surprised as much as I; but, to say the truth, it was time, for he grew cruel dull, and dry. To my knowledge, he had several good hints to go upon, but he was so lazy and weary of the work that he would not improve them." Steele himself confirms the curious statement that the paper was dropped without Addison's participation.[2] The commencement of the *Spectator* two months later shows that the *Tatler*

[1] Compare the Preface to *The History of the Four Last Years of Queen Anne*: —"I preserved several of the opposite party in their employments, who were persons of wit and learning, particularly Mr. Addison and Mr. Congreve. . . . Mr. Steele might have been safe enough, if his continually repeated indiscretions, and a zeal mingled with scurrilities, had not forfeited all title to lenity."

[2] Preface to the second edition of the *Drummer*, 1722.

was not really abandoned through weariness or want of matter. Steele says in the last number that the work had grown disagreeable to him, and the purpose of it wholly lost owing to his being so long understood as the author; and that a thousand nameless things made it an irksome task to personate Mr. Bickerstaff any longer. But he adds that what he found to be the least excusable part of all the work was, that he had, in some places touched upon matters concerning church and state; he could not, he says, be cold enough to conceal his opinions on these subjects. In the *Spectator* perfect neutrality in politics was promised, unless, indeed, "I shall be forced to declare myself by the hostilities of either side."[1] Gay, in *The Present State of Wit*, says that most people judged the true cause of the cessation of the *Tatler* to be either that Steele was quite spent as regards matter; "or that he laid it down as a sort of submission to, or composition with, the Government, for some past offences;" or, lastly, that he had a mind to appear in a new shape. Gay adds that the Town generally inclined to the first of these opinions, and was therefore the more surprised when the *Spectator* appeared.

[1] *Spectator*, No. 1, by Addison. In No. 10 Addison says: "As I am very sensible my paper would lose its whole effect should it run into the outrages of a party, I shall take care to keep clear of everything which looks that way. If I can any way assuage private inflammations, or allay public ferments, I shall apply myself to it with my utmost endeavours; but will never let my heart reproach me with having done anything towards increasing those feuds and animosities that extinguish religion, deface government, and make a nation miserable."

V.

IMITATORS OF "THE TATLER."

1709–1711. ÆT. 37–38.

ALTHOUGH Steele closed the *Tatler* with No. 271, the title was seized upon by several writers, who continued for some time to issue papers under the popular name. But before we examine these more closely it will be well to speak here very briefly of the periodicals which had been called into existence, more or less directly, by the *Tatler*, in 1709 and 1710.[1] Addison, in the 229th number, enumerates some of his antagonists: "I was threatened to be answered weekly *Tit for Tat;* I was undermined by the *Whisperer;* haunted by *Tom Brown's Ghost;* scolded at by a *Female Tatler;* and slandered by another of the same character, under the title of *Atalantis.* I have been *annotated*, *retattled*, *examined*, and *condoled*, but it being my standing maxim never to speak ill of the dead, I shall let these authors rest in peace, and take great pleasure in thinking that I have sometimes been the means of their getting a belly-full." "For my part," wrote Defoe, "I have always thought that the weakest step the *Tatler* ever took, if that complete author can be said to have done anything weak, was to stoop to take the least notice of the barkings of the animals that have condoled him, examined him, &c. He should have let envy bark and fools rail, and,

[1] The principal authorities on this matter are the Catalogue of the Hope Collection of Newspapers in the Bodleian Library; Nichols' *Literary Anecdotes*, vol. iv. 33 *seq.*, 259 *seq.;* and the papers in Harl. MS. 5958, referred to by Mr. Lee in his paper in *Notes and Queries*, 3rd series, ix. 53, and by Nichols in his note to *Tatler* No. 229. *The Character of the Tatler*, a stupid folio leaf, "printed and sold by J. Bragg," bound up in the Harl. MS., is, of course, not a periodical.

according to his own observation of the fable of the sun, continue to shine on. This I have found to be agreeable to the true notion of contempt. Silence is the utmost slight nature can dictate to a man, and the most insupportable for a vain man to bear."

The first number of the *Female Tatler* appeared on July 8, 1709, and No. 111, apparently the last, is dated March 31, 1710. This paper was issued by Thomas Baker, but with No. 19 another periodical with the same title appeared, "printed for A. Baldwin." The two papers attacked each other, and the world in general, and the original *Female Tatler* was presented as a nuisance by the Grand Jury at the Old Bailey. The paper was by "Mrs. Crackenthorpe, a Lady that knows everything," and the first number was, after the example of the *Tatler,* given away gratis. After the fifty-first number the periodical was "written by a Society of Ladies." The *British Apollo* maintained constant warfare with Thomas Baker, and what it says must be taken with great reservation.[1] The first number of *Titt for Tatt* was published under the name of "Jo: Partridge, Esq.," on March 2, 1709[–10]. As an opening for these "dilucidations" the author announced the death of his old friend and dear brother, Bickerstaff; but there is no evidence to show that his own papers extended to more than five numbers. The *Whisperer* was first published on October 11, 1709, by "Mrs. Jenny Distaff, half-sister to Isaac Bickerstaff, Esq." She is represented as being dissatisfied with the person designed for her husband, and determined to set up for herself. The *Gazette-à-la-Mode, or Tom Brown's Ghost,* was published on May 12, 1709; it is doubtful whether either this paper or the *Whisperer* ever reached a second number. Of the *New Atalantis,* the *Examiner,* and the *Annotations upon the Tatler* enough has been already said. No copy of a *Retattler,* if Addison is to be taken as referring to a periodical paper of that name, appears now to exist; and the word "condoled" refers, as we have seen,

[1] For remarks on "the Tatler's ape," see especially vol. ii. of the *British Apollo,* Nos. 45, 47–53, 55, 60, 61. In *The History of the London Clubs, or the Citizen's Pastime,* 1709, p. 8, attributed to Ward, there is mention of a Female Tattling Club in Clare Market.

to a pamphlet called "A condoling Letter to the Tatler." There were other papers issued besides those mentioned by Addison; as, for example, the *Tory Tatler*[1] (No. 1, November 27, 1710); the *Northern Tatler*[2] (April 1, 1710); the *Tattling Harlot* (two quarto leaves; No. 1, August 22, 1709); and *Serious Thoughts* (No. 2, August 15 to 17, 1710). The *Silent Monitor* (January 18, 1711) and the *Growler* (January 27, 1711) appeared after the cessation of the *Tatler*. The *Visions of Sir Heister Ryley* was a modest quarto periodical, following in Bickerstaff's footsteps, which first appeared on August 21, 1710, and reached to eighty numbers. *The Tatler, By Donald MacStaff of the North,* was published at Edinburgh on January 10, 1711, and extended to thirty numbers.[3]

The last number of Steele's *Tatler* appeared on January 2, 1711; but on Thursday, January 4, a spurious paper, with the number 272, was published by John Baker, "at the Black Boy in Paternoster Row." This paper commenced with a complimentary "Character of Mr. Steele, alias Isaac Bickerstaff, Esq.;" the new writer would endeavour to excel by pursuing his steps; and it concluded with an advertisement: "Whereas the Mercuries and Hawkers did use to call on Mr. Morphew for the Tatler, they are now desired to alarm Mr. Baker, who has promised to deliver them out at 5 in the morning, his neighbours having consented thereto, rather than be without it." No. 273 was by "Isaac Bickerstaff, J^{r}." On January 6, however, another spurious paper appeared, sold by John Morphew, and purporting to be Nos. 272, 273

[1] This paper appeared three days a week. No. 13, "Sold by J. Baker," was published on December 27 (*Post Boy*, December 26 to 28, 1710).

[2] Printed, according to Timperley's *Encyclopedia*, by John Reid, for Samuel Colvil, Edinburgh, and published on Mondays and Fridays.

[3] I have Nos. 5 to 24 of this periodical, as well as a folio leaf, "The Humble Address of Donald M'Staff of the North, in name of the M'Staffs there, to Isaac Bickerstaff, Censor of Great Britain." London printed, and Edinburgh reprinted, 1710[-11]. Donald had a sister, Mary MacStaff, and in all things closely followed Bickerstaff; calling himself, by the way, Censor of Great Britain. MacStaff's *Tatler* was by Robert Hepburn of Bearford, who was only twenty-one when he wrote it. He was, says Lord Woodhouselee (*Memoirs of Lord Kames*, 2nd edition, Edinburgh, 1814, i. 228), a man of vigorous powers, but he gave offence by describing known characters. He studied civil law in Holland, became a member of the Faculty of Advocates, 1712, and died soon afterwards.

of the original issue, with a letter from Charles Lillie, and the note that "this paper, which was not published on Thursday last, is now, upon better thoughts, resolved to be continued as usual." In No. 276 (January 13) of this series Baker was denounced for stating that he was Isaac Bickerstaff.[1] "This paper is continued to be sold by John Morphew, as formerly." No. 1 of a *Tatler*, sold by A. Baldwin, appeared on this same day, January 13, with the statement that the *Tatler* had been omitted for some time, by the neglect of those who had the care of it, in the absence of Isaac Bickerstaff, Esq., and several spurious papers had appeared; Bickerstaff therefore now declared that he had no intention to discontinue his paper, which would be published every Tuesday and Saturday. This was the first number of William Harrison's *Tatler*.

We have already seen that Swift intended to make Harrison's fortune. On the 11th January he told Esther Johnson that others had suggested to Harrison a new *Tatler*, and that he had encouraged him, had made the necessary arrangements

[1] The name Bickerstaff was, of course, introduced into the titles of many forgotten pamphlets of the time, to attract notice. One of these was called "Bickerstaff's Æsop: or, the Humours of the Times, digested into Fables. . . . Price 1s." (*Daily Courant*, January 28, 1710, and *Works of the Learned*, 1709); and another, "British Visions, or Isaac Bickerstaff, Sen., being Twelve new Prophecies for the year 1711," "Printed first in the North, and now in London, 1711." In the *Review* for April 21, 1711 (vol. viii. No. 12), Defoe says he found this little book at Newcastle, as he came last up from Scotland; it was sold for but twopence; but it was a "not much known book." The prophecy that the Dauphin would die in March had come to pass, and so had the prophecy that Partridge would die and be buried by a certain day; should, then, the other prophecies in the book not be considered? In No. 14 Defoe says that he saw the book in MS. in November last; and that since he spoke of it several pirated editions had appeared. The only true copy was sold by J. Baker, publisher of the *Review*. Was Defoe more closely connected with this little book than appears on the surface? There was also a "Bickerstaff's Almanack . . . for the year 1710. . . . By Isaac Bickerstaff, Esq: Student in Astrology, Commentator on the Occult Sciences, and One of the Eighth Order of Poets of the Cities of London and Westminster," 1710. This book contains a testimonial of the death of Mr. Partridge, signed Jeremy Wagstaff, and dated from Staff Hall in Staffordshire, September 3, 1709 (see *Works of the Learned*, November 1709). A small tract, "Isaac Bickerstaff's Letter to the Tongue-loosed Doctor," was published in 1713; another, "The famous prophesie of the White King and the Dead Man, explain'd to the present times. . . . By Isaac Bickerstaffe, Esq. London, J. Morphew," is without date. "Bickerstaff's Coffeehouse," a good-customed house in Great Russell Street, near the Piazza, Covent Garden, was advertised as To Let in the *Daily Courant* in 1712.

with a printer, and had corrected Harrison's "trash." The scheme was Mr. St. John's and his, but he doubted whether Harrison would succeed. Two days later the new paper came out. "There is not much in it, but I hope he will mend. You must understand that, upon Steele's leaving off, there were two or three scrub *Tatlers* came out, and one of them holds on still, and to-day it advertised against Harrison's; and so there must be disputes which are genuine, like the strops for razors. I am afraid the little toad has not the true vein for it." On the 15th he gave Harrison hints for another *Tatler;* "the jackanapes wants a right taste: I doubt he will not do." This proved to be the case, in spite of all Swift's efforts, and although Congreve, then nearly blind and just recovering from a severe fit of the gout, wrote a paper for Harrison at Swift's request. Harrison quarrelled with the printer with whom Swift had made arrangements, and resorted to John Morphew and Charles Lillie, the publishers of the original *Tatler*, after inserting a humble petition from those persons in his seventh number. The printer with whom Harrison disagreed was Swift's own cousin, Dryden Leach, but after hearing his relative's complaints, the Doctor got rid of him and ordered his servant to deny him ever after. Swift remained a true friend to Harrison, and before his *Tatler* had to be given up[1] took steps to obtain for him the post of Secretary at The Hague.[2] Harrison's papers were afterwards reprinted as a fifth volume to the collected edition of the *Tatler*. In No. 28 Swift alluded to Steele under the name Hilario, and spoke of "his natural wit, his lively turn of humour, and great penetration into human nature."

[1] The last number (No. 52) appeared on May 19, 1711.

[2] "Since I writ this a gentleman tells me that Mr. Harrison says he's recommended to you for your Secretary. So I went to Mr. L[ewis] and he tells me he hears so; and that 'tis Mr. St. John recommends him to you, for your own private secretary. He is the man that writs the *Tattler* since Steel left it of, he's a very good Scholar and was some time tutor to the Duke of Queensboroughs children and of late brought into his office" (Peter Wentworth to Lord Raby, March 20, 1711; *Wentworth Papers*, 188, 191). Harrison died in February 1713, "very much lamented by all that knew him here. His brother Poets bury'd him, as Mr. Addison, Mr. Philips, and Dr. Swift" (*Ib.* 319–20). Swift wrote, "No loss ever grieved me so much" (*Journal*, February 13 and 14, 1713).

Gay, in a few lines in his *Present State of Wit*, has admirably dealt with the papers alluded to in this section. The expiration of Bickerstaff's Lucubrations, he says, immediately produced whole swarms of little satirical scribblers. "One of these authors called himself *The Growler;* and assured us, that, to make amends for Mr. Steele's silence, he was resolved to *growl* at us weekly, as long as we should think fit to give him any encouragement. Another gentleman, with more modesty, called his paper *The Whisperer.* And a third, to please the ladies, christened his *The Tell-Tale.* At the same time came out several *Tatlers;* each of which, with equal truth and wit, assured us that he was the genuine Isaac Bickerstaff. . . . Some of our wits were for forming themselves into a club, headed by one Mr. Harrison, and trying how they could 'shoot in this bow of Ulysses'; but soon found that this sort of writing requires so fine and particular a manner of thinking, with so exact a knowledge of the world, as must make them utterly despair of success. They seemed indeed at first to think, that what was only the garnish of the former *Tatlers* was that which recommended them, and not those substantial entertainments which they everywhere abound in. Accordingly they were continually talking of their Maid, Night-cap, Spectacles, and Charles Lillie. However, there were now and then some faint endeavours at humour, and sparks of wit; which the Town, for want of better entertainment, was content to hunt after, through an heap of impertinences; but even those are at present become wholly invisible, and quite swallowed up in the blaze of the *Spectator.*" Steele is said to have spoken of his imitators as holding the censorship in commission.

We have only three or four notes of Steele's for the whole of the winter of 1710-11, and beyond a proposal to go with his wife to see their son Dick at Lambeth they contain nothing of special interest. There is also a fragment written by Mrs. Steele, apparently in October, in which she gives a recipe for the teeth, and adds, "I shall be glad to hear what part Mrs. Oakley has in what my Aunt Oakley [1] has left her brother who is dead. Moll Pugh gives you her service. She knows not

[1] See pedigree, p. 172. Lady Steele's grandmother was a Miss Oakley.

how she has disobliged, that you do so *Madam* her. She is very busy with the still, and other matters."

Of Steele's personal history during the months of January and February 1711 there is very little to tell. In several places in his *Journal* for this period Swift dwells upon his separation from Addison and Steele, respecting which his mind was evidently not quite at ease. On the 14th January he met Addison at the coffee-house, and talked coldly awhile with him. "All our friendship and dearness are off: we are civil acquaintances, talk words, of course, of when we shall meet, and that is all." They had not dined together anywhere for six weeks. "Is it not odd? But I think he has used me ill; and I have used him too well, at least his friend Steele." On the 3rd February, however, Swift dined at Addison's. "We are grown common acquaintance; yet what have not I done for his friend Steele? Mr. Harley reproached me the last time I saw him, that to please me he would be reconciled to Steele, and had promised and appointed to see him, and that Steele never came. . . . I have represented Addison himself so to the ministry, that they think and talk in his favour, though they hated him before. Well; he is now in my debt, and there is an end; and I never had the least obligation to him, and there is another end." On the 6th March, Swift repeated that all his friendship with Addison was over; and on the 7th he gravely wrote: "Yes, I do read the *Examiner*, and they are written very finely, as you judge. I do not think they are too severe on the duke; they only tax him of avarice, and his avarice has ruined us. You may count upon all things in them to be true. The author has said, it is not Prior; but perhaps it may be Atterbury." On March 5, two days before this was written, the twenty-third number of the *Medley* appeared. The first portion of it was by Steele, and it was directed against the "slanderous and reproachful libels" of the *Examiner*.

The *Tatlers* were published in collected form in four volumes; a subscription edition in 8vo, and a popular edition in 12mo. The dedication of the fourth volume to Lord Halifax is dated April 7, 1711. Title-pages, dated 1710 and 1711 respectively, were sold to be bound with sets of the original folio numbers, to make two volumes, as well as indexes, dedications, and preface. A fine engraving was also published as a frontispiece. "The Effigies of Isaac Bickerstaff Esq[re], Writer of the Tatler. Engraven on a folio page, with proper Emblems, and may be bound up with them; engraven and sold by John Sturt, in Golden Lion Court, Aldersgate Street, and most Printsellers. Price 6[d]."[1] The engraving is marked "B. Lens sen[r] delineavit;" it represents a man in a wide hat and loose gown, with long curls, and his finger placed on his forehead, sitting at a writing-desk, with books. A pack of cards, dice, and two broken swords are on the ground, where a dog and cat are playing. A familiar spirit (? Pacolet) is bringing in a letter. Bickerstaff is represented as a clerical-looking person, thin and hollow-cheeked. The picture does not seem to have been meant for a likeness of any one in particular.

Hilary term, 1711, did not pass without an action against Steele for debt. Richard Steele, of the parish of St. Martin-in-the-Fields, was summoned by Thomas Gibbs, from whom he has borrowed, on the 1st January 1711, at Westminster, £270, to be paid when required. As he now refused to pay, Gibbs instituted these proceedings, and claimed £10 damages. Steele's counsel, William Battell, made no answer, and judg-

[1] Published on July 18, 1710 (*Post Man*, July 15 to 18, 1710). There is a copy of this engraving in the fine copy of the *Tatler* in the Grenville Library, 916. A similar portrait appeared on a very rare folio broadside, *The Three Champions*, printed on one side only, "For J. Baker," in or about 1710. There is a copy in the Lambeth Palace Library, 66.A.2 (95), and another in the Print Room in the British Museum. On the upper part of this sheet are three heads, "The British Censor, Isaac Bickerstaff Esq[r]"; and "The British Libellers," "Y[e] Review," and "Y[e] Observator"; and below are verses about these "three brethren in iniquity":—

> "Let Whigs but have their will, they'd quickly all
> Th' Apostles' writings vote apochryphal,
> That square not with their interest, and instead,
> Milton's and Hoadley's to the Canon add.
> But oh, that Isaac that romantic 'Squire,
> Should prostitute the sciences for hire!
> Question that Right the Queen by birth receives,
> When She th' Ingrate both place and pension gives!
> That one that's thought a cunning man should sneak
> To a wrong interest when his all's at stake!"

The Whigs, this writer concludes, made Britain's Censor their tool, conscious that their Defoes and Ridpaths—"that have the pillory disgraced and may the gallows"—exposed the cause to contempt.

ment was therefore given for the plaintiff, with 50s. damages.[1] Mr. Gibbs, as appears from the following notes, was a butcher :—

FROM MR. ASHURST,[2]
Jan. 21st, 1711.[3]

DEAR PRUE

I stay dinner here but shall come home as soon as I have dined.

In the mean time I desire you would order Michaell to carry the enclosed to Mr. Gibbs's Lodgings, and bid Him afterwards be in the way to wait for Me.

Yr Obliged Husband RICHARD STEELE.

Jan: 22d, 1711.

DEAR PRUE

Give me till ten of Clock tomorrow without dunning for your payments, for Diggle[4] insists upon paying Butcher Gibbs and settling two or three things, before my domestick comes.

Yours RICHARD STEELE.

[1] Common Pleas, Judgment Roll. Hilary, 9 Anne, 385.

[2] Mr. Ashurst was godfather to Steele's son, Eugene, who was christened in April 1712.

[3] Nichols, in printing this and the following letter, altered the "1711" to "1711–12," doubtless because of the allusions to Mr. Ashurst and Diggle. The alteration may be correct, but in making it Nichols was not aware of the action decided in Gibbs's favour at the commencement of 1711. The original letters are placed with those of 1711 in the volume in the British Museum. Steele generally gave the double date when there might be ambiguity.

[4] A friend of whom we shall hear again in 1712.

BOOK FIFTH.

"THE SPECTATOR" AND "THE GUARDIAN."

1711–1713. ÆT. 38–41.

I.—"THE SPECTATOR."
II.—SWIFT, POPE, AND THE WORTLEY MONTAGUES.
III.—PEACE NEGOTIATIONS. MONEY DIFFICULTIES.
IV.—"THE GUARDIAN."

I.

"THE SPECTATOR."

1711–12. ÆT. 38–40.

THE first number of the *Spectator* appeared on the 1st March 1711,[1] with the announcement, "To be continued every day," and the paper was issued without intermission until the 6th December 1712, when No. 555, the last of the original series, was published. Addison afterwards revived the paper for a time in 1714, but in that continuation Steele had no share. The *Spectator*, like the *Tatler*, consisted of a single folio sheet; the first fifteen numbers bore the inscription, "Printed for Sam. Buckley, at the Dolphin in Little Britain; and sold by A. Baldwin in Warwick Lane," with the addition, from the second number, "where Advertisements are taken in;" but from the sixteenth number there was added after these words, in consequence of a letter from Charles Lillie asking for the office, "and also by Charles Lillie, Perfumer, at the Corner of Beaufort-Buildings in the Strand."[2] Tonson's name was added from No. 499. Machinery such as had hardly been used at all in the *Tatler* was introduced at the very beginning in the *Spectator*. Addison wrote the first number, which contains a

[1] "This day is published, A paper entitled *The Spectator;* which will be continued every day. Printed for Samuel Buckley at the Dolphin in Little Britain, and sold by A. Baldwin in Warwick Lane." (*Daily Courant*, March 1, 1711.)

[2] Lillie's name was, no doubt accidentally, omitted in No. 17. Besides the inscription at the bottom of the paper, there was often a note stating where sets of the back numbers could be obtained, and the increase in the names of the shops mentioned shows the continual growth in the sale. The note in the 29th number contains six names; the 39th, seven; the 69th, eight; the 125th, nine; the 135th, ten; the 145th, eleven; and the 221st, twelve.

light sketch of the Spectator himself. This "looker-on" had shown remarkable gravity and silence as a child, and whilst at school and college. A thirst for knowledge led him to travel after his father's death; but he had passed his latter years in London, where he was frequently to be seen in public places, though there were not above half-a-dozen of his select friends that knew him. He now resolved, however, although he never opened his lips but in his own club, to publish a sheet full of thoughts every morning, for the benefit of his contemporaries. In No. 2 Steele described the club where, as the Spectator had said, the plan of the work, as all other matters of importance, were laid and concerted.[1] The first of the Society was a gentleman of Worcestershire, of ancient descent, and a baronet, Sir Roger de Coverley. Besides Sir Roger the paper contains sketches of the Templar; the Merchant, Sir Andrew Freeport; the Soldier, Captain Sentry; the Fine Gentleman, Will Honeycomb; and the Clergyman. Several of these characters hardly ever come to the front in the subsequent working-out of the original plan. The Clergyman and the Templar are never conspicuous; Sir Andrew Freeport makes sensible remarks on trade and thrift, and on giving alms to beggars,[2] but he has not any very distinct personality in papers subsequent to the second number. Captain Sentry, "a man of good sense but dry conversation,"[3] appears hardly more frequently; and even Will Honeycomb, the fine gentleman about town, who, after pursuing every belle for thirty years, marries a farmer's daughter when he is sixty, occupies comparatively little space. Sir Roger de Coverley alone retains a prominent place in the paper, and the development of his character we owe chiefly to Addison. But Steele drew the first sketch, and wrote several papers containing touches worthy of comparison with Addison's best efforts. I need only particularise Steele's description of Sir Roger's love for the perverse widow.[4] We have no evidence as

[1] See, too, No. 34, where Addison points out that all classes of his readers might feel that they were represented in the club by one or other of its members.

[2] Nos. 174, 232 (by Hughes or Henry Martyn).

[3] No. 197 (by Budgell); Nos. 34, 350, 517, 544.

[4] No. 113; see, too, Nos. 107, 109, 118, 174, all by Steele. No. 410, in which Sir Roger is exhibited in an equivocal position, was probably by Tickell,

to the manner in which Addison and Steele arranged the work between them except that of Tickell, who says that "the plan of the *Spectator*, as far as regards the feigned person of the author, and of the several characters that compose his Club, was projected in concert with Sir Richard Steele," and he accordingly printed No. 2, which was by Steele, in his edition of Addison's Works, in order to render subsequent papers more intelligible. "As for the distinct papers," he adds, "they were never or seldom shewn to each other by their respective authors; who fully answered the promise they had made, and far outwent the expectation they had raised, of pursuing their labour in the same spirit and strength with which it was begun."

There have been many foolish efforts to find originals in real life for the various members of the club. Thus Sir Roger de Coverley has been identified with a Sir John Packington, a Tory knight of Worcestershire, and Will Honeycomb with a Colonel Cleland. In a similar way Sir Andrew Freeport has been said to be taken from Mr. H. Martyn, and Captain Sentry from Colonel Magnus Kempenfelt. The perverse widow, too, has been identified with Mrs. Katherine Bovey, to whom Steele afterwards dedicated the second volume of his *Ladies' Library*. As to these surmises, it is enough to say that Tickell, Addison's intimate friend, looked upon the whole of the characters as feigned,[1] and that the writers themselves said that everything had been rejected "that might create uneasiness in the minds of particular persons." "When I place an imaginary name at the head of a character, I examine every syllable and letter of it, that it may not bear any resemblance to one that is real. I know very well the value which every man sets upon his reputation, and how painful it is to be exposed to the mirth and derision of the public, and should therefore scorn to divert my reader at the expense of any private man."[2]

The *Spectator* has remained to this day, as Steele hoped, the most lasting monument of his friendship with Addison. In No. 555 Steele wrote, with his usual noble generosity, of "the

though Steele, as editor, apologised for the passage in a later paper (No. 544). The original conception of Sir Roger's character was modified in several respects by Addison in subsequent papers.

[1] Preface to Addison's Works, 1721.

[2] No. 262.

gentleman of whose assistance I formerly boasted in the Preface and concluding leaf of my *Tatlers*. I am indeed much more proud of his long-continued friendship, than I should be of the fame of being thought the author of any writings which he himself is capable of producing. I remember when I finished the 'Tender Husband,' I told him there was nothing I so ardently wished, as that we might some time or other publish a work written by us both, which should bear the name of *The Monument*, in memory of our friendship." It was of this friendship that Addison wrote in a verse of his well-known hymn, which was first printed in No. 453:—

> "Thy bounteous hand with worldly bliss
> Has made my cup run o'er,
> And in a kind and faithful friend
> Has doubled all my store."

In No. 532 Steele said: "I claim to myself the merit of having extorted excellent productions from a person of the greatest abilities, who would not have let them appear by any other means; to have animated a few young gentlemen into worthy pursuits, who will be a glory to our age; and at all times, and by all possible means in my power, undermined the interests of ignorance, vice and folly, and attempted to substitute in their stead learning, piety and good sense."

Addison was certainly at his best in the *Spectator*. He wrote 274 out of the 555 numbers, while Steele contributed 236, leaving only 45 for Budgell, Hughes, Pope, and other occasional contributors. Addison had, indeed, been little more than an occasional contributor to the *Tatler*, and although some of his articles in that periodical take rank among his finest work, yet it was only in the *Spectator* that he found opportunity to show fully all his powers. Steele, on the other hand, was at his best in the *Tatler*, in which there is a certain sense of freedom and freshness which we can hardly expect to find always in its more stately successor. Yet, as Forster says in comparing Steele's work in the *Spectator* with that in the *Tatler*, "there was the same inexpressible charm in the matter, the same inexhaustible variety in the form; and upon all the keen exposure of vice or the pleasant laugh at folly, as prominent

1712. ÆTAT 40.

From Meadows' Engraving of the Portrait by Richardson.

in the life-like little story as in the criticism of an actor or a play, making attractive the gravest themes to the unthinking, and recommending the lightest fancies to the most grave, there was still the old and ineffaceable impress of good-nature and humanity—the soul of a sincere man shining out through it all." After what has been said of the *Tatler*, it is not necessary to examine here in detail the various numbers of the *Spectator* written by Steele; I will only mention a few, to most of which special reference has been made by other writers, as examples of Steele's powers. Such, for instance, are the accounts of the death of Estcourt (No. 468) and of Stephen Clay (No. 133); the stories of Inkle and Yarico, and of Brunetta and Phillis[1] (Nos. 11 and 80); and the criticism of Etherege's "Sir Foppling Flutter," accounted a pattern of genteel comedy, but in reality "a perfect contradiction to good manners, good sense, and common honesty" (No. 65); and of Beaumont and Fletcher's "Scornful Lady" (No. 270): "It is so mean a thing to gratify a loose age with a scandalous representation of what is reputable among men, that is to say what is sacred, that no beauty, no excellence in an author ought to atone for it; nay, such excellence is an aggravation of his guilt, and an argument that he errs against the conviction of his own understanding and conscience." Or take No. 66, on female education: "The true art in this case is, to make the mind and body improve together; and if possible, to make gesture follow thought, and not let thought be employed upon gesture;" or

[1] Mr. Darnell Davis has pointed out that the original of the story of Brunetta and Phillis is to be found in a letter from Captain Walduck, who resided in Barbados, to Mr. James Petiver, Apothecary to the Chartreuse, who no doubt told the story to Steele. Captain Walduck's letter is now in the British Museum, Sloane MS. 2302 (*The Spectator's Essays Relating to the West Indies*, Demerara, 1885, pp. 8–11). Leigh Hunt remarked of Steele's stories that they "are just such stories as a man might tell over his wine to a party of friends. . . . Steele, indeed, may be said to have always talked rather than written; and hence the beauties as well as defects of his style." And he goes on: "If there were no worse men in the world than Steele, what a planet we should have of it! Steele knew his own foibles as well as any man. He regretted, and made amends for them, and left posterity a name for which they have reason to thank and love him. Posterity thanks Addison too; but it can hardly be said to love him, even by the help of the good old knight, Sir Roger, whom Steele invented for him. Perhaps they would have loved him more, had he too confessed his faults" (*A Book for a Corner*, 1849, ii. 39–42).

No. 152, on the fear of death; or No. 153, on youth and age; or No. 192, on parents and children; or No. 157, on flogging in schools: "A great or good mind must necessarily be the worse for such indignities; and it is a sad change to lose of its virtue for the improvement of its knowledge." Look, again, at what he says of Raffaelle's cartoons[1] (No. 226); of comic actors (No. 370); of servants (Nos. 88, 96, 107); of short-faced and ordinary people (Nos. 4 and 17); of affectation, envy, and many other faults (Nos. 19, 38, 82, 438, &c.); of the man of wit and pleasure (No. 151); of the "portable quality of good humour" (No. 100): "No one can repeat anything that Varilas has ever said that deserves repetition; but the man has that innate goodness of temper, that he is welcome to everybody, because every man thinks he is so to him. He does not seem to contribute anything to the mirth of the company; and yet upon reflection you find it all happened by his being there." In another paper (No. 75) the false ideas as to what constitutes a fine gentleman are discussed. "When a gentleman speaks coarsely, he has dressed himself clean to no purpose; the clothing of our minds certainly ought to be regarded before that of our bodies." In No. 490, upon marriage, Steele says: "I have very long entertained an ambition to make the word Wife the most agreeable and delightful name in Nature;" and in No. 486 he maintains that a man of the town should be as infamous a character as a woman of the town. A contemporary writer, speaking of the periodicals started by Steele, said: "This was laying the axe to the root of vice and immorality. All the pulpit discourses of a year scarce produced half the good as flowed from the *Spectator* of a day. They who were tired and lulled to sleep by a long and laboured harangue, or terrified at the appearance of large and weighty volumes, could cheerfully attend to a single half-sheet, where they found the images of virtue so lively and amiable, where vice was so agreeably ridiculed, that it grew painful to no man to part with his beloved follies; nor was he easy till

[1] Hazlitt says: "I prefer Steele's occasional selection of beautiful poetical passages, without any affectation of analysing their beauties, to Addison's finer-spun theories. The best criticism in the *Spectator*, that on the Cartoons of Raphael, of which Mr. Fuseli has availed himself with great spirit in his Lectures, is by Steele" (*English Comic Writers*—"On the Periodical Essayists").

he had practised those qualities which charmed so much in speculation." [1]

Of the great favour with which the *Spectator* was received there is abundant evidence. I may, in the first place, quote once more from Gay's valuable tract, *The Present State of Wit*, published in May 1711. Gay, it will be seen, was sufficiently a party man to speak of "the better part of the nation," meaning the Tories, when expressing a hope that Steele would not be led into the imprudence of lashing out into party, and thus render his wit no longer a common good. And yet Swift thought Gay's tract was written by a Whig.

"You may remember I told you before, that one cause assigned for the laying down of the *Tatler* was want of matter; and, indeed, this was the prevailing opinion in town, when we were surprised all at once by a paper called *The Spectator*, which was promised to be continued every day, and was written in so excellent a style, with so nice a judgment, and such a noble profusion of wit and humour, that it was not difficult to determine it could come from no other hands but those which had penned the *Lucubrations*. This immediately alarmed those gentlemen who (as it is said Mr. Steele phrases it) had *the censorship in commission*. They found the new *Spectator* come on like a torrent, and swept away all before him; they despaired

[1] "An Essay sacred to the memory of Sir Richard Steele," *British Journal, or the Censor*, September 13, 1729. Another writer, Mr. Newcome, described, in his *Bibliotheca, a Poem*, 1712, some of the good accomplished by Steele and his fellow-workers. The whole poem is to be found in Nichols' *Select Collection*, iii. 19-74:—

> "Improving youth and hoary age,
> Are bettered by thy matchless page;
> And what no mortal could devise,
> Women, by reading thee, grow wise."

Where divines and philosophers had failed Steele had succeeded.

> "Taught by those rules thy pen instils,
> Nobly to conquer human ills;
> A week is now enough to pine,
> When puking lap-dog cannot dine;
> While grief as real swells her eyes
> When spouse, as when her parrot, dies."

The fop, too, no longer measured merit by perfume, and confessed that virtue had no regard for dress. The widow no more cursed the tedious year; and ladies aspired "to write correct, and spell."

ever to equal him in wit, humour, or learning (which had been their true and certain way of opposing him), and therefore rather chose to fall on the author, and to call out for help to all good Christians, by assuring them again and again that they were the first, original, true, and undisputed Isaac Bickerstaff.

"Meanwhile the *Spectator*, whom we regard as our shelter from that flood of false wit and impertinence which was breaking in upon us, is in every one's hand, and a constant topic for our morning conversation at tea-tables and coffee-houses.[1] We had at first, indeed, no manner of notion how a diurnal paper could be continued in the spirit and style of our present *Spectators;* but, to our no small surprise, we find them still rising upon us, and can only wonder from whence so prodigious a run of wit and learning can proceed; since some of our best judges seem to think that they have hitherto, in general, outshone the Squire's first *Tatlers*. Most people fancy, from their frequency, that they must be composed by a Society; I, withall, assign the first place to Mr. Steele and his Friend.

"I have often thought that the conjunction of those two great geniuses (who seem to stand in a class by themselves, so high above all our other wits) resembles that of two famous statesmen[2] in a late reign, whose characters are very well expressed in their two mottoes, viz., *Prodesse quam conspici*, and *Otium cum dignitate*. Accordingly the first was continually at work behind the curtain; drew up and prepared all these schemes and designs which the latter still drove on; and stood out exposed to the world, to receive its praises or censures.

"Meantime, all our unbiassed well-wishers to learning are in hopes that the known temper and prudence of one of these gentlemen will hinder the other from ever lashing out into

[1] This was what Addison wished: "I shall be ambitious to have it said of me that I have brought philosophy out of closets and libraries, schools and colleges, to dwell in clubs and assemblies, at the tea-tables and in coffee-houses" (No. 10). The writers of the *Spectator* aimed at no special class or party, but at the wide circle of readers, men and women, who form the majority of the nation.

[2] Lord Somers and the Earl of Halifax.

party,[1] and rendering that wit, which is at present a common good, odious and ungrateful to the better part of the nation. If this piece of imprudence does not spoil so excellent a paper, I propose to myself the highest satisfaction in reading it with you over a dish of tea, every morning next winter."

Swift wrote to Esther Johnson on the 16th March: "Have you seen the *Spectator* yet, a paper that comes out every day? It is written by Mr. Steele, who seems to have gathered new life, and have a new fund of wit; it is in the same nature as his *Tatlers*, and they have all of them had something pretty. I believe Addison and he club." On the 28th April he repeated that the *Spectator* was written by Steele with Addison's help; "it is often very pretty." Defoe frequently spoke in his *Review* in friendly terms of the *Spectator*, though he could not always agree with the views expressed on some subjects. "There is not a man in this nation," he says in one place, "that pays a greater veneration to the writings of the inimitable *Spectator* than the author of the *Review;* and that not only for his learning and wit, but especially for his applying that learning and wit to the true ends for which they are given, viz., the establishing virtue in, and the shaming vice out of the world."[2]

[1] In No. 50 Addison laughed at the party feud, when he made the Indian kings who had recently visited England describe what different accounts of things were given them by the two men appointed by the Queen to attend them. The one said that this island was infested with a monstrous kind of animals in the shape of men called Whigs, who would probably knock the Indians down for being kings, if they met with them; while the other talked much of a kind of animal called a Tory, as great a monster as the Whig, and who would treat the Indians as ill for being foreigners. These two creatures engaged, it was said, when they met, as naturally as the elephant and the rhinoceros. But as the Indian kings saw none of either of these species, they were apt to believe that their guides had deceived them with misrepresentations and fictions. In another paper (No. 57) Addison pointed out to his female readers that nothing was worse for the face than party zeal.

[2] *The Review*, vol. viii., No. 82, Oct. 2, 1711. See, too, Nos. 4, 65, 131, 153–5 and 159 of the same volume. In No. 40 (December 3, 1712) of the very rare continuation of *The Review* which Defoe published in 1712–13, he said that a small portion of the paper would be reserved to moralise upon such subjects as came in his way. "Not that I propose to put in for a *Spectator*, mistake me not, good folk, no, I understand the person whose province that is; and who, with so just applause, has carried it on, and my own station too, as also the mighty charity of the day, as to censure, better than to expose myself so far."

We have already seen with what interest the arrival of the *Tatlers* and *Spectators* was looked forward to throughout the country. In Perthshire, we are told, when "the gentlemen met after church on Sunday to discuss the news of the week, the *Spectators* were read as regularly as the *Journal*."[1] When the *Spectator* was drawing to a close, Addison expressed the gratification he felt at finding some of the most outlying parts of the kingdom alarmed at the discontinuance of the paper. One correspondent at Berwick, with whose letter he was well pleased, after comparing the work of the *Spectator* with the weeding of a great garden, remarked that it was not sufficient to weed once for all, and afterwards to give over, but that the work must be continued daily, or the same spots of ground which are cleared for a while will, in a little time, be overrun as much as ever.[2] There are several allusions in the *Spectator* itself to the circulation to which it attained. In No. 10 Addison says that there were already 3000 copies distributed every day: "So that if I allow twenty readers to every paper, which I look upon as a modest computation, I may reckon about threescore thousand disciples in London and Westminster." Although the *Spectator* was much read at tea-parties (Nos. 158, 296), yet there would hardly be an average of twenty readers to each copy.[3] On July 23 Addison wrote: "My bookseller tells me, the demand for these my papers increases daily," and on December 31 he repeated, "I find that the demand of my papers has increased every month since their first appearance in the world." On the 1st August 1712 St. John's Stamp Act came into force, by which a halfpenny stamp was imposed upon all newspapers and periodical sheets. This attempt to suppress free expression of opinion succeeded to some extent; many of the papers of the day ceased to exist. The *Spectator* continued as before, but the price was raised from one penny to twopence. In announcing this alteration Addison took the opportunity of remarking upon the friendly reception accorded

[1] *Addisoniana*, ii. 8, 9. [2] No. 553.

[3] Ricken has fully discussed this question in his "Bemerkungen über Anlage und Erfolg der Wichtigsten Zeitschriften Steele's und den Einfluss Addison's auf die Entwicklung derselben" (Elberfeld). Defoe calculated that there were in 1711 above 200,000 single papers published every week in the nation (*Review*, vol. vii., Preface).

to the paper by the most distinguished persons of all conditions, parties, and professions. "I have endeavoured to make nothing ridiculous that is not in some measure criminal" (No. 445). Swift wrote to Esther Johnson, five days later: "Do you know that all Grub Street is dead and gone last week? . . . The *Observator* is fallen; the *Medleys* are jumbled together with the *Flying Post;* the *Examiner* is deadly sick; the *Spectator* keeps up and doubles its price: I know not how long it will last." The circulation of the *Spectator* fell when the price was raised, and some persons, including "the ingenious T. W.,"[1] complained that as the tax was only a halfpenny, the price ought not to have been raised to more than three-halfpence (No. 488). One correspondent, however, advised that the price should be made sixpence, and was good enough to promise that he would himself engage for above a hundred of his acquaintance to take in the paper at that price! Addison suggested that if his readers would make some slight retrenchment in their ordinary expenditure they could easily make up the halfpenny a day; or if they would not do this, they could buy the papers in the lump, when republished. "My bookseller has now about ten thousand of the Third and Fourth Volumes, which he is ready to publish, having already disposed of as large an edition both of the First and Second Volume." On the 11th November a pocket edition of the third and fourth volumes was published,[2] and when the paper came to an end on the 6th December the collected edition of the three remaining volumes was in the press. In this last number Steele also says: "An edition of the former volumes of *Spectators* of above nine thousand each book is already sold off, and the tax on each half-sheet has brought into the Stamp Office one week with another above £20 a week arising from this single paper, notwithstanding it at first reduced it to less than half the number that was usually printed before this tax was laid." A payment of over £20 a week for stamp duty represents a daily circulation of more than 1600 copies, or 10,000 a week, from the 1st August to the 6th December 1712, and the daily circulation before the 1st August would

[1] Perhaps Thomas Walker, Master of the Charterhouse School. See p. 28.
[2] No. 533, advertisement.

therefore be, according to Steele's statement, nearly 4000.[1] These figures, as Forster says, might be multiplied by six to give a corresponding popularity in our day.

The writers for the *Spectator* signed their respective papers with certain initials, which were partly explained by Steele in the last number. Addison's papers are marked with a C, an L, an I, or an O, that is, by any letter in the name of the Muse Clio. Budgell used the letter X. Steele's papers were marked either with an R or a T: with R up to No. 91; with T, and occasionally R, until No. 134; after that T always. Tickell, however, appears to have occasionally used the letter T. In spite of Steele's plain statement, it has, with misplaced ingenuity, been suggested, and often repeated, that Addison signed C when writing at Chelsea, L when in London, I when in Ireland, and O when at the Office. Equally absurd is the theory that L was attached to papers formed from the materials in the letter-box. Many papers with this letter affixed do not consist of such materials, and Addison says that though he often made use of letters sent to him, yet many things published in the form of letters were in reality of his own composition.[2] In another paper (No. 221) he laughs at the efforts made to assign meanings to the various initials affixed to the papers, and tells the story of the philo-

[1] Addison, as we have seen, says that the sale reached 3000 a few days after the paper was started, and that it steadily increased. Dr. Fleetwood, whose famous Preface was printed in the *Spectator* for May 1, 1712, says in a letter to the Bishop of Salisbury, dated June 17, 1712, that the daily issue of the paper was 14,000 (Pope's *Literary Correspondence*, 1736, iv. 107). Nichols suggested that the "0" in "20*l*.," the amount paid for stamp duty, should perhaps be read as a "9." It is true that in the folio issue the figure is badly printed, but it could hardly be an imperfect 9; and the "20" is printed quite clearly in the collected octavo edition. It is interesting to note from the circulation of the *Times* in its early years what a circulation of 3000 or 4000 meant in the last century. The first number of the *Times*, under that title at least, appeared on January 1, 1788, and in 1794 the circulation was upwards of 4300 a day. In April 1794 the price was raised to 4½d., owing to a new tax on paper. The sale was between 4000 and 5000 in April 1797, when the price was raised to 6d., owing to Pitt's additional stamp of 1½d. on each paper. The number of copies printed in November and December 1798 was never on any day below 3000, and fluctuated between that number and 3350 (*Times* for February 7, 1794, April 28, 1797, and January 1, 1799, quoted in Ashton's *Eighteenth Century Waifs*, pp. 213–225).

[2] Nos. 271, 542.

sopher who, when asked by an acquaintance to let him know what it was he covered so carefully with his cloak, answered, "I cover it on purpose that you should not know." The notion that the R and T which Steele used were meant to distinguish between original and transcribed papers is disproved by the fact that Steele finally abandoned the use of the letter R when only a quarter of the work had appeared.

The first annotated edition of the *Spectator* was published by Nichols in 1789, the notes being, as was stated in speaking of the *Tatler*, by Bishop Percy and Dr. Calder. Dr. Percy had edited two volumes for R. Tonson in 1764, but the death of the bookseller stopped the work for a time. Bisset and Chalmers, in subsequent editions bearing their names, added little except some general introductory remarks, but they considerably increased the number of misprints and corruptions that had crept into the text. In 1868 Professor Henry Morley produced a very useful edition in one volume, with many fresh notes and a text showing at a glance how the papers read when first issued from day to day, and what modifications were introduced when the numbers were reprinted in book form. The type used in Professor Morley's edition was necessarily small, but the book has since been reprinted in three volumes, with larger type.

Laudis amore tumes? sunt certa piacula quæ Te
Ter pure lecto poterunt recreare libello: Hor:

Fac-simile of entry, in Steele's writing, on a leaf of Addison's Note-Book.[1]

---

[1] This MS. Note-Book, which contains portions of essays afterwards used in the *Spectator*, was reprinted by Mr. J. Dykes Campbell in 1864, and a long controversy ensued as to its genuineness and as to the handwriting. I have seen the original book, and there can be no doubt respecting its genuineness; but it is not clear by whom the bulk of the book was written. Many additions and alterations on the left-hand pages seem certainly to be in Addison's writing. There are also passages in a third hand. Of all these Mr. Campbell gave fac-similes; but at the beginning of the paper on Fame the lines here reproduced occur, in a hand different from all the others, and which I believe to be Steele's. The reader can to some extent judge for himself by comparing the fac-simile with those of undoubted specimens of Steele's writing given in these volumes.

II.

SWIFT, POPE, AND THE WORTLEY MONTAGUES.

1711–12. ÆT. 39.

THE first letter that we have of Steele's written after the commencement of the *Spectator* is addressed to his friend, Mr Joseph Keally, of Kilkenny, asking his good offices on behalf of John Bateman, who administered to Henry Gascoigne's property in 1707. From a second letter, written in July, it will be seen that Mr. Keally was able to render Bateman the aid that Steele asked for.

April 2, 1711.

SIR,

The bearer hereof, Mr. John Bateman, is the nearest of blood to my uncle Gascoigne; to whose bounty I owe a liberal education. He has a demand upon my Lord Longford, as administrator to my said uncle, together with some other debts which lie out in Ireland. I earnestly recommend his affairs to your favour and patronage; and desire you would stand by him, and appear for him, in order to his obtaining speedy justice. He is of himself an helpless; and your goodness herein will be the highest obligation, to, Sir,

Your most obedient and most humble servant,

RICH. STEELE.

July 26, 1711.[1]

SIR,

Happening to be now at Mr. Addison's lodgings, and talking of you (which we often do with great affection), I recollected that I had not yet thanked you for your great kindness to Mr. Bateman. The poor man acknowledges he should have made nothing of his journey

[1] This letter is taken from Berkeley's *Literary Correspondence*, p. 400, where it is printed more fully than in Nichols' edition of Steele's *Correspondence*.

without your assistance; for which you will ever have the blessings of his numerous family. You have laid an infinite obligation upon me in it.

I am, with great truth, your most affectionate and most humble servant, RICH. STEELE.

My most humble service to Mr. Thomas Vesey, who, I am sorry to hear, mistakes me.

In this Easter term judgment was given against Steele in an action for debt. Hezekiah Benson was attorney for Richard Steele, of the parish of St. James, Westminster, Esq., and Jacob Harrison was attorney for the complainants. In Hilary term last past William Stroud and Anne his wife, who was executrix of John Williams, deceased, brought their bill against Steele, in the custody of the Marshal of the Marshalsea, the effect of which was that on the 20th May 1708, in the parish of St. Clement Danes, Steele had bound himself by a duly sealed document, which was produced in court, to pay the sum of £200 to Williams or his executors when required. But he had not paid, and refused to do so, and the Strouds now claimed £30 damages. On Wednesday next after the Quindene of Easter (18th April 1711), the case came on for judgment, and as Steele made no defence, it was ordered that the complainants should recover the debt, with 36s. damages.[1]

In the following term there was another action, brought by Nicholas Jonquel Lepine against Richard Steele, Esq., administrator of all and singular the goods and chattels, rights and credits of Robert Ford, deceased. In his bill, brought in in Easter term, Lepine said that Robert Ford, in his lifetime, on the 1st May, 4 Anne [1705], owed him, at Westminster, £150 for tailoring done by him for Ford at his request; also for divers materials provided for the said work, and for money paid for Ford's use. Ford promised to pay the money, and afterwards, on the same date, in consideration of other tailoring done for him before that time, and for divers other materials used, promised to pay what was right; Lepine therefore said he ought to have another £150, of which Ford had notice. But Ford did

[1] Queen's Bench Judgment Roll, 10 Anne, Easter, 183.

not pay in his lifetime, and Steele, although asked to do so on the 1st August, refused. Lepine claimed, therefore, £200 damages. On the 4th June the complainant appeared, but Steele neither came nor said anything; and the sheriff was ordered to ascertain what damages Lepine had sustained.[1] This case affords us evidence that Robert Ford visited London; but the date mentioned is evidently incorrect, because his sister, Mrs. Steele, administered to his property in March 1705, and he could not, therefore, be incurring debts in May. The whole amount of the debt was of course, as has been explained in other cases, £150.

Swift's *Journal* contains little that concerns us during the spring of 1711. On March 16 Swift wrote that he never saw Addison and Steele: "I plainly told Mr. Harley and Mr. St. John, ten days ago, before my Lord Keeper and Lord Rivers, that I had been foolish enough to spend my credit with them in favour of Addison and Steele; but that I would engage and promise never to say one word in their behalf, having been used so ill for what I had already done." On the 24th he wrote: "Have you yet seen any of the *Spectators?*" and on the 11th April: "Henley would fain engage me to go with Steele and Rowe, &c., to an invitation at Sir William Read's. Surely you have heard of him. He has been a mountebank, and is the Queen's oculist; he makes admirable punch, and treats you in gold vessels. But I am engaged and will not go, neither indeed am I fond of the jaunt." A week later he wrote that letters should be sent to Erasmus Lewis, for he never went to the coffee-house, and they would grudge to take in his letters. Little Harrison was to go on the 20th to the secretaryship Swift had got him at The Hague, and St. John gave him fifty guineas for his charges. "Am not I a good friend?" On the 28th April he protested that he thought the *Medley* very fine, and the *Examiner* a wretched thing. Steele's *Spectator* was often very pretty. "Yesterday it was made of a noble hint I gave him long ago for his *Tatlers,* about an Indian supposed to write his Travels into England. I repent he ever had it. I intended to have written a book on that subject. I believe he has spent it all

[2] Queen's Bench Judgment Roll, Trinity, 10 Anne, 571.

on one paper, and all the under-hints there are mine too; but I never see him or Addison." On the 14th May he mentioned Trapp's *A Character of the Present Set of Whigs*, "a very scurvy piece" which he had looked over at the request of Mr. Secretary. "Dr. Freind was with me, and pulled out a two-penny pamphlet just published, called *The State of Wit*, giving a character of all the papers that have come out of late. The author seems to be a Whig; yet he speaks very highly of a paper called *The Examiner*, and says the supposed author of it is Dr. Swift. But above all things he praises the *Tatlers* and *Spectators;* and I believe Steele and Addison were privy to the printing of it. Thus is one treated by these impudent dogs." On the 29th, after informing his correspondents that he had that day called upon the secretary and the Duke and Duchess of Ormond, he asked, "Pr'ythee, do not you observe how strangely I have changed my company and manner of living? I never go to a Coffee-house; you hear no more of Addison, Steele, Henley, Lady Lucy, Mrs. Finch, Lord Somers, Lord Halifax, &c. I think I have altered for the better." On the 7th June he hinted that he was about to cease to write the *Examiner;* he prophesied they would be trash for the future. "Observe whether the change be discovered in Dublin, only for your own curiosity, that is all." On the 22nd he remarked that it was plain the hand was changed. Swift continued, however, to help the Government in every way possible by pamphlets and lampoons, which he either wrote or superintended. He had interceded with the Lord Treasurer on behalf of Congreve, with success; "so I have made a worthy man easy, and that is a good day's work. I am proposing to my Lord to erect a society or academy for correcting and settling our language, that we may not perpetually be changing as we do. . . . I design to write a letter to the Lord Treasurer with the proposals of it, and publish it; and so I told my Lord, and he approves it."

There are a few letters, written in June, from Steele to his wife, who was then sometimes staying at her mother's lodgings in Bromley Street, Holborn—"last door, left hand"—but they are of no special importance. One dated June 20 was printed *verbatim* in the *Spectator* (No. 142), a few weeks later, with the date June 23, 1711. Another note contains allusions to Mr. Glanville[1] and Sir Harry Furnese, the rich alderman.[2] On the 29th June Swift wrote: "Steele has had the assurance to write to me, that I would engage my Lord Treasurer to keep a friend of his in an employment: I believe I told you how he and Addison served me for my good offices in Steele's behalf; and I promised Lord Treasurer never to speak for either of them again." Next day Philips, the pastoral poet, wrote asking Swift to get him a certain employment from the Lord Treasurer. "I have now had almost all the Whig poets my solicitors;[3] and I have been useful to Congreve, Steele, and Harrison;" but Swift would do nothing for Philips, who was more a puppy than ever; moreover, he would not trouble the Lord Treasurer "unless upon some very extraordinary occasion." On the 3rd July he met Mrs. Manley at Lord Peterborough's; she wanted to get some reward for her services in the cause, in writing her *Atalantis*, and her prosecution, &c., upon it. "I seconded her, and hope they will do something for the poor woman."[4] Mrs. Manley succeeded Swift as writer of the *Examiner;* only two years before he had violently attacked her in the *Tatler*. On the 26th July Swift again met Addison and Steele. "Mr. Addison and I have at last met again. I dined with him and

[1] See p. 331 below.

[2] He died in 1712. Swift wrote of this Sir Harry Furnese, or Furnasse, in the *Examiner*, No. 40: "I know a citizen who adds or alters a letter in his name with every plumb he acquires; he now wants only the change of a vowel to be allied to a sovereign prince in Italy; and that, perhaps, he may contrive to be done by a slip of the graver on his tomb-stone."

[3] Years afterwards Swift wrote: "He [Lord Oxford] knows how often I pressed him in favour of Mr. Addison, Mr. Rowe, Mr. Congreve, and Mr. Steele, . . . I remember it was in those times a usual subject of raillery towards me among the ministers, that I never came to them without a Whig in my sleeve. . . . I frequently conversed with Mr. Addison and the others I named (except Mr. Steele) during all my Lord Oxford's ministry" (Swift to Pope, January 10, 1720–21). And again: "You may remember that, on Mr. Addison's desire, I applied to my Lord Treasurer Oxford in favour of Mr. Steele, and his lordship gave me a gentle rebuke, which cured me for ever" (Swift to Alderman Barber, March 9, 1737–8).

[4] Six months later Swift wrote: "Poor Mrs. Manley, the author, is very ill of a dropsy and sore leg; the printer tells me he is afraid she cannot live long. I am heartily sorry for her; she has very generous principles for one of her sort, and a great deal of good sense and invention: she is about forty, very homely, and very fat" (*Journal*, January 28, 1712).

Steele to-day at young Jacob Tonson's." The Tonsons wanted Swift to intercede to prevent the printing of the *Gazette* being taken away from them, but Swift told them it was too late. "Mr. Addison and I talked as usual, and as if we had seen one another yesterday; and Steele and I were very easy, although I writ him lately a biting letter, in answer to one of his, where he desired me to recommend a friend of his to Lord Treasurer." After this there is no mention of Steele of any importance in the *Journal* for some months.

In June Steele seems to have made the acquaintance of Alexander Pope, then in his twenty-third year. On the 18th June Pope wrote to Caryll: "I've not yet had the honour of a letter from Mr. Steel," and there can be little doubt that Pope owed his introduction to Steele to Caryll, an old friend whose acquaintance Steele probably made, as we have seen, while he was secretary to Lord Cutts. This is the first letter from Steele to Pope that has come down to us.

July 26, 1711.

SIR,

I writ to you the other day, and hope you have received my letter. This is for the same end, to know whether you are at leisure to help Mr. Clayton, that is Me, to some words for music against winter. Yr answer to me at Will's will be a great favour to, Sir,

Yr most obedient, humble servant,

RICH. STEELE.[1]

In April Steele had written to Hughes that Mr. Clayton and he would be glad if Hughes would alter Dryden's "Alexander's Feast" for music, preserving as many of Dryden's words and verses as possible. Hughes made the alterations desired, but sent a long criticism of Clayton's music, trusting to Steele's good sense for the use he would make of it. "I should not, you may be sure, give you or myself this trouble, but that I do not know how far it may concern your interest to be rightly informed." In December a letter was printed in the *Spectator* (No. 258), giving particulars of the concerts at Clayton's house in York

[1] Homer MSS.

Buildings.[1] Pope undertook, somewhat unwillingly, to do what Steele asked. On August 2 he wrote to Caryll: "I have two letters from Mr. Steele, the subject of which is to persuade me to write a musical interlude, to be set next winter by Clayton, whose interest he espouses with great zeal. His expression is, Pray oblige Mr. Clayton, that is me, so far as, &c. The desire I have to gratify Mr. Steele has made me consent to his request, though it is a task that otherwise I am not very fond of." In the *Spectator* for December 20 (No. 253) Addison wrote very flatteringly of Pope's *Art of Criticism*, advertised in No. 65 (May 15) as published that day, calling it "a masterpiece in its kind." Thereupon Pope sent an elaborately polite letter to Steele,[2] dated December 30, 1711. "I have passed part of this Xmas with some honest country gentlemen, who have wit enough to be good-natured, but no manner of relish for criticism or polite writing, as you may easily conclude when I tell you they never read the Spectator. This was the reason I did not see that of the 20th till yesterday at my return home, wherein, tho' it be the highest satisfaction to find oneself commended by a person whom all the world commends, yet I am not more obliged to you for that than for your candour and frankness in acquainting me with the error I have been guilty of in speaking too freely

[1] Possibly the following note relates to some musical entertainment of Clayton's (Bodleian Library, Rawl. MSS. C. 743. 18).

Sepbr. 28th, 1711.

DEAR SR,

Be pleased to underwrite the names of the Boys and the places to enquire for them.

Yr Humble Servt
RICHD STEELE.

. . . . Newman.

Among the same MSS. (Rawl. MSS. C. 743. 21) is a copy of an unsigned letter to Henry Newman from a resident at Whitehaven, Oct. 30, 1713. "The Englishman writes so Heroically that I hope he wil do good, if anything can in such an Age. I wonder neither the Engl. M. nor Fl. P. writes pretty fully about the invasion of the Right of the City of Dublin who are not allowed to choose their Mayor or Sheriffs, unless they wil elect such as are pointed out to them."

[2] Miss Aikin found this letter among Addison's papers, and concluded that it was written to him. It has no address, but Pope did not yet know Addison, and, moreover Steele's letter which follows is evidently a reply to this letter of Pope's.

of my brother moderns." He was himself aware of enough faults in his book to make him very humble; but the *Spectator* had been so lavish in praise "that I almost hope—not to call in question your judgment in the piece—that it was some particular partial inclination to the author which carried you so far. This would please me more than I can express, for I should in good earnest be fonder of your friendship than the world's applause." Steele, after apparently handing this letter over to Addison, answered that the paper to which Pope referred was not his, but was by one whom he would introduce to Pope.

Jan. 20, 1711[-12].

DEAR SIR,

I have received y[r] very kind letter. That part of it which is grounded upon y[r] belief that I have much affection and friendship for you, I receive with great pleasure. That which acknowledges the honour done to y[r] Essay, I have no pretence to. The paper was written by one whom I will make you acquainted with, which is the best return I can make to you for y[r] favour to, Sir,

Y[r] most obliged humble servant,

RICH. STEELE.

Here we must leave Pope for a short time, and turn back to other matters.

The following interesting account of the *Tatlers*, from Tonson, evidently belongs to the autumn of 1711. Among other things it proves that the price of the collected edition, on royal paper, was £1 a volume, and on medium paper ten shillings. The letter and account, all very neatly written by Tonson himself, are addressed to "Richard Steele, Esq[r]."[1]

S[R]

You have Inclosed, my Account of the Tatlers, w[ch] I have endeavoured to make as plain as I can. besides this, I am to pay Nutt 107[l] 10[s] the 16th of next Month for the last parcell delivered to Lillie. I have sent a 1st and 2[d] Vol by the bearer for M[r] Aislabie, & Gen[ll] Farringdons Books will be ready tomorrow[2] morning.

[1] Blenheim MSS.

[2] "Monday morning," cancelled.

Mr Scott wou'd be glad to talk with you about his affair; I sent you the copy of his first paper by my boy on Wednesday.

Sr I am

Yr humble Servant

Fryday. JACOB TONSON.

It appears by the account that I owe Nutt 17l 12s 0d besides the 33l 0s 0d due from you, which sume I am accountable to Nutt for. You will be pleased to allow me that sume upon Account, & I will answer it to Nutt.

This was the account:—

Books Recd. from Mr Nutt. Viz—

1711		ll	s	d
Apr. 27.	1 Medium 1 & 2	01	00	00
May 22.	1 Royal 2nd Voll	01	00	00
29.	1 Medium 1 & 2	01	00	00
Apr. 27.	5 Royal 3 & 4 .	10	00	00
May 1.	1 Do. . .	02	00	00
3.	1 Do. . .	02	00	00
12.	1 Do. . .	02	00	00
22.	1 3rd & 24th Royal	03	00	00
29.	1 Medium 3 & 4	01	00	00
June 4.	25 Royal 3 & 4	50	00	00
,,	12 Medium 3, 4	12	00	00
Augt 25.	1 Royal 1 & 2 .	02	00	00
		87	00	00
		26	08	00
		60	12	00

By Mr Steel	33 : 00 : 00	
By Self .	17 : 12 : 00	
By Books left	10 : 00 : 00	
	60 : 12 : 00	60 : 12 : 00

July 20, 1711. Paid Mr Nutt	25 : 08 : 0
Mr Nutt: 1 Med: 3, 4	1 : 00 : 0
	26 : 08 : 0
Paid by Delivery of ye Books by Mr Steels Order—viz.	
D. Queensbery. Royal 3d 4th	2 : 00 : 0
Sr. A. Cairns. Do .	2 : 00 : 0
Lady Clargis. Do .	2 : 00 : 0
Ld Plymouth. Do .	2 : 00 : 0
Mr Ferrers. Do .	2 : 00 : 0
Ld Cholmly—5 Do . .	10 : 00 : 0
Col. Smith. Dr Garth, M.	1 : 00 : 0
Mr Gay 1 Complt Royal .	4 : 00 : 0
E. Holderness. Roy. 3. 4. .	2 : 00 : 0
Gen. Farringdon. Do .	2 : 00 : 0
Mr Aislabie. Do 1 & 2 .	2 : 00 : 0
1 Imperfect . . .	2 : 00 : 0
	33 : 00 : 0
left 3 Roy. 3d & 4th . .	6 : 00 : 0
left 4 Mod. 3d & 4th .	4 : 00 : 0
	10 : 00 : 0

The following notes are in Steele's writing :—

To Mr Tonson.

156 Large		124 . 16 . 00
145 Small		72 . 10 . 00
		197 . 6 . 00
Recd of Lillie	20 . 0 . 0	
Glanvill [1]	61 . 5 . 6	
Subscript	86 . 0 . 0	
	167 : 5 : 6	
Wants	30 . 0 . 0	
Diggle [2]	20 . 0 . 0	

Besides on acct of ye four Vols

Nutt	55 . 0 . 0	
Note Diggle	30 . 0 . 0	
Books	33 . 0 . 0	
On acct of cash	36 . 15 . 10	of this 36
	154 : 15 : 10	charged against me at Mr Buckleys 20.

This is partly explained by another paper, also by Steele :—

Mr Tonson
to
Mr Steele
For Spectators.

Dr	l : s : d	Cretr	
By receipt from Lillie .	20 : 00 : 00	156 Large Spectators at sixteen shillings the Sett	124 : 16 : 00
By Mr Glanville . .	61 : 00 : 00		
By Subscribers to Him .	86 : 00 : 00	145 small at 10s sett .	72 : 10 : 0
	167 : 00 : 00	Paid to Mr Diggle [3] .	20 : 00 : 00
	247 : 06 : 00		217 : 06 : 00
	167 : 00 : 00		
	080 : 06 : 00		

For the Tattlers.

By Note to Nutt . .	55 : 00 : 00
By Note to Mr Diggle .	33 : 00 : 00

[1] See p. 326. [2] See p. 305, 351.

[3] Followed by the line, "By note payable to Mr Diggle, 30 : 00 : 00," erased.

There are several allusions to Steele in 1711 in the correspondence of Edward Wortley Montague and Lady Mary Pierrepont, who became his wife in August 1712. Wortley Montague was godfather to Steele's eldest child, Elizabeth, in 1709, and he was cousin to Charles Montague, Earl of Halifax, who was in close intercourse with Steele and Addison. In two letters written in 1710 to her future husband, Lady Mary Wortley Montague, to give her the name by which she is best known, alludes to passages in Steele's plays, and she was on terms of intimacy with Mrs. Steele. In a letter to Lady Mary, of which the conjectural date is 3rd March 1711, Mr. Wortley Montague says: "Now you have been so free before Mrs. St. [Steele], you may call upon her, or send for her, tomorrow or next day. Let her dine with you, or go to visit shops, Hyde Park, or other diversions. You may bring her home; I can be in the house, reading, as I often am, though the master is abroad. If you will have her visit you first, I will get her to go tomorrow." The second volume of the *Tatler* had been, it will be remembered, dedicated to Wortley Montague, and there is evidence among the Wortley MSS., in the shape of original sketches of essays which may be found in the *Tatler*, that he was in the habit of supplying Addison and Steele with hints for papers.[1] On the 21st July 1711 Addison wrote to Wortley Montague sending a copy of that day's *Spectator* (No. 123), with which he was well pleased, and asking his friend's opinion of the story of Eudoxus and Leontine. "Dick Steele and I often remember you," says Addison at the end. In October, Mr. Montague wrote thus to Addison:[2]—

WORTLEY, 8 Oct. 1711.

DEAR S^R^

I intend to set out this week for Durham, & to return hither about 3 weeks hence. I can scarce hope you will be for a long

[1] *Letters and Works of Lady M. W. Montagu*, 1861; Memoir by W. Moy Thomas.

[2] The original of this letter, endorsed "To Mr Addison, 8 Oct. 1711," is in Mr. Alfred Morrison's collection. It was printed, but inaccurately, in *Addisoniana*, i. 240, and it has been erroneously described as Lady M. W. Montague's; but the contents show it to be by Mr. Montague. It is, moreover, dated from Wortley, and Lady Mary was not married until 1712. There is another letter in

journey at this season; but if you shoud like a Country Life so well, I will stay here till January to attend you, & perhaps longer. There is a house within two miles of this Place, which I am sure woud please you, as well as any in these parts. I design to lodge there for the advantage of shooting when I come back from Durham, but if you shoud not like it, I can find another: least this climate shoud not suit with you, I dare say nothing in praise of it; unless you think I speak well of it, in telling you I grow fat, and am very easy. It woud however agree with me much better, if you were in it. My most humble service to Mr Steel. he knows I shoud have invited him often, had he bin at liberty to come.

It is not clear what there was to prevent Steele visiting at Wortley, unless it was his duties as editor of the *Spectator*. On the 27th October 1714 Lady Mary wrote to her not specially brilliant husband, "I wish you would learn of Mr. Steele to write to your wife." Many years afterwards, in 1755, in a letter to her daughter, the Countess of Bute, upon the death of Henry Fielding, her second cousin, Lady Mary wrote: "There was a great similitude between his character and that of Sir Richard Steele. He had the advantage both in learning, and, in my opinion, genius: they both agreed in wanting money in spite of all their friends, and would have wanted it, if their hereditary lands had been as extensive as their imagination; yet each of them was so formed for happiness, it is a pity he was not immortal."

Mr. Morrison's possession, addressed to Addison, and dated Wortley, 28th July 1711, in reply to Addison's of the 21st, in which Mr. Wortley Montague says: "Notwithstanding your Disappointments I had much rather be in your Circumstances than my own. The Strength of your constitution woud make you happier than all who are not equal to you in that." He alludes to the *Spectator* sent him by Addison, whom he invites to Wortley. In two months he will be going to Newcastle. "You told me you should like it. If you do not, perhaps we may contrive how you may pass your time here."

III.

PEACE NEGOTIATIONS. MONEY DIFFICULTIES.

1711–12. ÆT. 39–40.

HARLEY had been made Earl of Oxford and Lord Treasurer after the attempt made upon his life by Guiscard, a French refugee,[1] and in the summer of 1711 the negotiations, open and secret, for a peace with France were carried on with renewed energy. At the same time a portion at least of the Tory party, including, probably, the Earl of Oxford himself, were scheming for a restoration of the Stuarts. Prior was sent to Paris, and the negotiations conducted by him led to the drawing up, in London, on September 27th, of eight preliminary articles. Louis acknowledged Anne and the Protestant succession; Dunkirk was to be demolished, a fair equivalent being given; a new treaty of peace was to be made; England was to have Gibraltar, Minorca, and Newfoundland; and the Assiento was transferred by Spain from France to England. Holland and Austria were angry at these arrangements, but were compelled to agree, and a conference was appointed to be held at Utrecht. In the meantime Marlborough had taken Bouchain, but had not been able to carry out his plans further. Upon his return to England he joined himself to the Whigs, who had formed a coalition with some of the Tories, under Nottingham. These allies succeeded in defeating the Government by eight votes in the House of Lords in December, upon an amendment to the Address, but in the Commons the Government had a large majority. To pre-

1 "This day is published, The Spectator's Address to the Whigs, on the occasion of the Stabbing Mr. Harley. Printed in the year 1711. Price 2d." (*Post-Boy*, March 17, 1710–11.)

vent another adverse vote in the House of Lords twelve new peers were created, and the report of a Commission which had been appointed to examine into the public accounts enabled the Government to get rid of Marlborough, who was deprived of all his offices. His well-known avarice gave colour to the charges brought against him, but the explanations and excuses which he furnished were really not inadequate. The Queen declared in Council, on the 30th December, her determination to dismiss the Duke, and on the following day she sent him a letter, written in her own hand, signifying her royal pleasure to resume all the employments she had entrusted him with. Steele immediately published, on the 4th January,[1] a quarto pamphlet, *The Englishman's Thanks to the Duke of Marlborough*, in the form of a letter to the Duke, dated January 1, 1711[-12], and signed "Scoto-Britannus," expressing in the warmest terms his admiration for the great general, whose fame would never die. Steele afterwards acknowledged this tract by printing it in the volume of his *Political Writings* published in 1715.[2]

The fourth volume of the *Spectator* was afterwards dedicated to Marlborough in terms showing the heartiest admiration of the Duke's private as well as public character. Steele and Addison did not desert him because he was fallen from power and was in broken health; but the Tory writers, headed by Swift with his *Fable of Midas*,[3] did not hesitate to attack him in

[1] *Daily Courant*, January 4, 1712.

[2] The writer of the *Examiner* for January 10, 1711[-12], thought from the style of this pamphlet, and the manifest thefts from his own unlucky plays, that an old sour critic—Dennis—was the author, although the tract was "very fairly printed in large characters," and avoided, in outward circumstances, all appearance of Grub Street. This called forth a furious rejoinder from Dennis: "To the Examiner, upon his wise paper of the Tenth of January." Dennis called the Examiner the vilest and most contemptible of all dogs, and an insipid libeller; an ecclesiastical Jack-pudding, whose first published work (the allusion is to Swift's *Tale of a Tub*) was written with a design to banter all Christianity. The tract was not his, said Dennis, but he would not be ashamed to commend the greatest man upon earth, when the Examiner was neither afraid nor ashamed to calumniate him.

[3] This, like other political poems by Swift, was printed, after the fashion of the lowest productions of Grub Street, on a single folio leaf, without printer's name, for ready circulation in the streets. Among the broadsides in my possession are, besides the *Fable of Midas*, verses directed against Lord Nottingham, who had led the party hostile to the Government in the House

the most bitter and unscrupulous spirit. Swift was at this period assisting the Tories by his pen in many ways. His object was to prepare the public for a peace upon such terms as France would grant rather than endanger the existence of the Tory Government, but not such as the course of the war justified them in expecting. In September 1711 he issued the account of Prior's visit to Paris—*A New Journey to Paris*—"a formal, grave lie, from the beginning to the end;" on the first day, September 11, one thouand copies were sold, and five hundred more were ready on the second.[1] Two days later he met Addison and Pastoral Philips, and supped with them at Addison's lodgings: "We were very good company, and I yet know no man half so agreeable to me as he is." On the 10th October he says: "I have sent, and caused to be sent, three pamphlets out in a fortnight. I will ply the rogues warm; and whenever anything of theirs makes a noise, it shall have an answer." A rogue who wrote the *Protestant Post-Boy* should have a squeeze extraordinary: "He says that an ambitious tantivy, missing of his high hopes of preferment in Ireland, is come over to vent his spleen on the late ministry, &c. I'll 'tantivy' him with a vengeance." Yet there was a certain hankering after old friends. On November 18 he wrote to Esther Johnson: "Do you read the *Speetators?* I never do; they never come in my way: I go to no coffee-houses. They say abundance of them are very pretty; they are going to be printed in small volumes; I'll bring them over with me."[2] Mrs. Anne Long, of whose death a month later Swift spoke very feelingly, wrote to him on the 18th November: "I have a

of Lords. It is a pity that Swift condescended to write such things as "An excellent new Song, showing the intended Speech of a famous Orator against Peace," and "Toland's Invitation to Dismal to dine with the Calves-Head Club." Swift himself speaks of these and others as "Grub Street papers." (*Journal*, July 17, 1712.)

[1] *Journal*, September 11 and 12, 1711.

[2] In his *Proposal for Correcting, Improving, and Ascertaining the English Tongue*, published in May 1712, Swift remarked that he had already, about a year ago, communicated to the public his thoughts upon the subject, "by the hands of an ingenious gentleman, who for a long time did thrice a week divert or instruct the Kingdom by his papers; and is supposed to pursue the same design at present, under the title of *Spectator*. This author, who hath tried the force and compass of our language with so much success, agrees entirely with me in most of my sentiments relating to it."

shelf pretty well filled at home, but want a Miscellany Mr. Steele put out that year. Miss Hessey [Vanhomrigh] promised it me, but has forgot it; I fancy you have interest enough with him to get it for me." Mrs. Long, once a beauty and a toast of the Kit Cat Club, got into debt, and retired into Norfolk.

It was the custom on the 17th November, the anniversary of Queen Elizabeth's accession, for the citizens to parade the streets in procession with effigies of the Pope, cardinals, and others, the effigy of his holiness being eventually burnt as an expression of detestation of the Romish Church. The Whigs were determined, it was said, that the show of 1711 should be very imposing, and the Pope, devil, and the rest were to be made to resemble the members of the Government. It was to be arranged, said Tory writers, that Whig noblemen, and Marlborough himself, were to take part in this demonstration, and that the houses of Oxford and others were to be wrecked. The Spectator, too, "who ought to be but a looker-on, was to have been an assistant, that, seeing London in a flame, he might have opportunity to paint after the life, and remark the behaviour of the people in the ruin of their country, so to have made a *diverting Spectator*."[1] The Government made these lying reports the excuse for seizing all the images and other paraphernalia that were to have been used in the procession. Swift admits in his *Journal* that the images were worth less than forty pounds, and not a thousand, as he had said, and that the devil was not like the Lord Treasurer; yet he did not hesitate to "put an under-strapper upon writing a twopenny pamphlet"—*A true Relation of the several facts and circumstances of the intended Riot and Tumult*, &c. —full of the most outrageous lies that were being spread about for party purposes. "The pamphlet war grows fiercer than ever," wrote Peter Wentworth to Lord Raby; grave people

[1] Addison afterwards alluded to this passage when he described Sir Roger de Coverley asking with unusual seriousness, "'Tell me truly, don't you think Sir Andrew had a hand in the Pope's Procession?'—but without giving me time to answer him, 'Well, well,' says he, 'I know you are a wary man, and do not care to talk of public matters'" (No. 269). Peter Wentworth wrote to Lord Raby on the 25th November: "There has been information that the Duke of Montague, Edgecomb, and Steel were to be at the head of the Mob that was to have made this procession; if so, I know nobody has more reason to be thankful 'twas prevented" (*Wentworth Papers*, p. 212).

thought that unless a remedy was found to moderate it, it would be of ill consequence.[1] On the 27th November the *Conduct of the Allies* was published; on the 1st December a second edition was issued; on the 3rd December the third edition; and on the 5th December a fourth edition was being printed. The sequel of this tract was called *Some Remarks on the Barrier Treaty.* On the 6th December the *Examiner* was revived, after being in abeyance since July; the new series was written chiefly by Oldisworth. "I have got an underspur-leather to write an Examiner again, and the secretary and I will now and then send hints; but we would have it a little upon the Grub Street, to be a match for their writers." In this form the paper was continued for two and a half years longer. When the first series was reprinted in a small volume it went off but slowly. "The printer over-printed himself by at least a thousand; so soon out of fashion are party papers, however so well writ."[2] On the 15th December Swift was alarmed at the position of the ministry: "I look upon them as certainly ruined, and God knows what may be the consequences." He had already pitched upon a place to which he would retire for some months; he did not wish to be in the way at the commencement of the ferment, "for they lay all things on me, even some I have never read." The fears turned out to be groundless, and the Ministry maintained its position.

On the 8th February Swift asked his correspondents whether the *Conduct of the Allies* was liked in Ireland. "I don't care whether they do or no; but the resolutions printed t'other day in the votes are almost quotations from it; and would never have passed, if that book had not been written. I will not meddle with the Spectator, let him fair-sex it to the world's end."

Steele's third child was born in March, and was named after Prince Eugene, Marlborough's friend and colleague. Lady Steele left the following memorandum: "My son Eugene was born the 4th of March 1712, on a Tuesday, half an hour after ten at night. He was christened the 2nd of April; the gossips

[1] *Wentworth Papers*, p. 215; November 27, 1711.
[2] *Journal*, March 25, 1712.

Mr. Warner, Mr. Ashurst, and my Mother in person." Eugene was baptized at St. Andrew's, Holborn, and the entry in the Registers of that church shows that Steele was still called "Captain," and that he was staying at this time in Brownlow Street, Holborn:—"1712 April 2. Eugene, son of Capt. Richard Steele & Mary. Brownlow street." Of Mr. Ashurst we have already heard. The following and other letters show that he was engaged in money transactions with Steele. Later in the year, a Benjamin Ashurst had to bring an action to recover £3000 which Steele had borrowed; but perhaps he was not the same person as the Mr. Ashurst of whom we are now speaking.

DEAREST WIFE,

Ashurst is just gone. He says he thinks himself sure of 2500*l.*, and bids me be of comfort. I have sent to Mr. Brodrick,[1] to give me some covers to Mr. John Scurlock [2] at Carmarthen, South Wales.

I am charmed with your letter to Cousin.

Kiss Bess and Dick for me,

RICH^D STEELE.[3]

From a document in the Forster Collection at South Kensington, it appears that Steele borrowed money from Mr. Warner, the other godfather.

June 5th 1712.

On the 20th instant I promise to pay to Mr. John Warner or Order the sum̃ of one hundred pounds for value received by me.

RICHARD STEELE.

£100 : 00 : 00

In March 1712, Ambrose Philips's *Distressed Mother*, taken from Racine's *Andromaque*, was published, with a "Prologue, written by Mr. Steele. Spoken by Mr. Wilks." Steele had

[1] Thomas Brodrick, Esq., of Wandsworth, was elected M.P. for Stockbridge, with Steele, on the 25th August 1713. He was appointed Comptroller for Accounts of the Army, April 1708, and he held this post until June 1711. In May 1709 he was Controller of the Salt (Luttrell's *Diary*; Pointer's *Chronological History*, 592, 692). Under William III. he had been one of the Privy Council in Ireland, and member for Cork. He was one of George the First's Privy Council, and died in 1730. His son, Allan, was the first Lord Midleton.

[2] Mrs. Steele's uncle.

[3] From a copy, not in Steele's writing.

already devoted No. 290 of the *Spectator* to praise of the play, and Addison, in No. 335, had described Sir Roger de Coverley's visit to the theatre to see this "excellent piece." No. 338, for March 28, the day upon which the play was published, contained a letter criticising the comic epilogue to the tragedy. This epilogue was printed as by Budgell, but there is a tradition that Addison was the real author, but ordered it to be given to Budgell in order to help him in his efforts to obtain a place. In any case, Budgell defended the Epilogue in No. 341 of the *Spectator*. Steele's Prologue was serious enough, containing as it does a discussion of the dramatic unities, which Shakespeare had dared to set aside in *The Tempest* and elsewhere.

PROLOGUE TO "THE DISTRESSED MOTHER."

Since fancy of itself is loose and vain,
The wise by rules that airy power restrain;
They think those writers mad, who at their ease
Convey this house and audience where they please;
Who Nature's stated distances confound,
And make this spot all soils the sun goes round:
'Tis nothing, when a fancied scene's in view,
To skip from Covent Garden to Peru.
But Shakespeare's self transgressed; and shall each elf,
Each pigmy genius, quote great Shakespeare's self!
What critic dares prescribe what's just and fit,
Or mark out limits for such boundless wit!
Shakespeare could travel through earth, sea and air,
And point out all the powers and wonders there;
In barren deserts he makes Nature smile,
And gives us feasts in his Enchanted Isle.
Our Author does his feeble force confess,
Nor dares pretend such merit to transgress;
Does not such shining gifts of genius share,
And therefore makes propriety his care.

Andromache—If in our Author's lines,
As in the great original, she shines,
Nothing but from barbarity she fears.
Attend with silence; you'll applaud with tears.

A week after this Prologue was printed Steele wrote a hasty note to Ambrose Philips, from which it appears that Mrs. Scurlock was then in London, and very ill.[1]

Ap. 6th, 1712.

DEAR Sr

My Mother in law is so extremely ill that it would be the greatest indecency imaginable for me to leave Her, and she desires the Contrary.

Yr obliged

Humble Servant

RICHARD STEELE.

Pray make my excuse

I am under concern that

desire you to pardon Hast—

Easter was late in 1712, so that it would be in May that judgment was given by Thomas Lord Trevor, Baron of Bromham, in an action for debt brought against Steele—late of the parish of St. James, Westminster—by Stephen Stretch, who was doubtless a relative of the Mr. Stretch who was the former husband of Steele's first wife. Stephen Stretch, by Thomas Prowse, his attorney, stated that on the 1st December 1710, at Westminster, Steele by a certain bond acknowledged himself bound to him in the sum of £580; but he had not paid, and refused to pay, whereupon Stretch claimed £40 damages. Steele was defended by John Bowley, his attorney, who, however, was not informed of any answer to be made, or of anything else to be said. Judgment was therefore given for Stretch, with 50s. damages.[2] The money was not, however, paid, and the case again came before the Court in Trinity term, 1713, when the Sheriff was commanded to make it known to Steele that he should be there in fifteen days from Trinity Day to show cause why Stretch should not have execution against him of his debt, and damages according to the form of the recovery. But Steele, although solemnly requested, did not come, and it

[1] The original of this letter is in Mr. A. Morrison's possession; it is endorsed on the back, "To Mr. Philips."

[2] Common Pleas Judgment Roll, 11 Anne, Easter, 453.

was therefore ordered that Stretch should have execution against him of his debt and damages, by Steele's default.[1]

This will be a suitable place to mention the well-known tradition of the execution put in by Addison to recover money which he had lent to Steele. The exact date of this occurrence is not known, but it was probably in 1711 or 1712. Steele had on a former occasion borrowed £1000 of Addison, which he repaid in August 1708.[2] The further loan of which we are now speaking is probably referred to in this letter, which is undated.

PRUE,

Addison's money you will have tomorrow noon. I have but Eighteen shillings, but have very many reasons to be in good humour, except you are angry with me.

If you can pay the Woman for coles, you [may] have it from Nutt in the morning.

Y[r] Obedient Husband
Lover Servant and Paramour RICH[D] STEELE.

Johnson, who says that the story was "known to all who are acquainted with the literary history of that period," tells us that Steele, "whose imprudence of generosity, or vanity of profusion," kept him always necessitous, borrowed £100 of his friend, who, growing impatient of delay, reclaimed his loan by an execution. "Steele felt with great sensibility the obduracy of his creditor, but with emotions of sorrow rather than of anger." Sir John Hawkins says that this story was communicated to Johnson in his hearing by a person of unquestionable veracity —Burke, according to Malone—who had it, as he told them, from Lady Dorothea Primrose, who was said to have been well acquainted with Steele. Croker, by the way, doubted whether Lady Dorothea could have been old enough at this time to have known Steele personally; but she died in 1768, and it is admitted that she may then have been 65, so that she would be 21 before Steele retired from London. Hawkins adds that the account was confirmed to him by Dr. Stinton, who heard it from Hooke, author of the Roman History, and he from Pope.

[1] Common Pleas Judgment Roll, 12 Anne, Trinity, 1832.

[2] See p. 219.

Johnson, when questioned by Malone as to his authority, said he had the story from Savage, who mentioned that Steele narrated it to him with tears in his eyes. As Steele had quarrelled with Savage, this alone could not be held to be sufficient evidence, but the facts generally were confirmed to Johnson by Benjamin Victor, who had them from Wilks, Steele's colleague at Drury Lane. Macaulay, who could not agree with Miss Aikin in rejecting the tale—"few private transactions which took place a hundred and twenty years ago are proved by stronger evidence than this"—defended Addison's conduct, by a graphic account of how Addison, moved by a pathetic letter from his friend imploring help in his great need, determined to deny himself in order to send the money; and how, when he called on Steele next day, he found scores of ladies and gentlemen assembled, and the table groaning under wines and sweetmeats. "Is it strange," says Macaulay, after drawing this imaginary picture, "that a man whose kindness is thus abused, should send sheriff's officers to reclaim what is due to him?" The most trustworthy account is that told by Benjamin Victor to Garrick in a letter written in 1762. He says that he had his relation first from Wilks, but that afterwards, in 1725, he had a full confirmation of it from Steele's own lips. According to Victor's letter, Steele borrowed £1000 of Addison—Johnson says £100—on the house at Hampton-Wick and its furniture, giving bond and judgment for the repayment of the money at the end of twelve months. On the forfeiture of the bond Addison's attorney proceeded to execution, the house and furniture being sold, and the surplus sent to Steele, with a "genteel" letter, "stating the friendly reason of this extraordinary proceeding, viz., to awaken him, if possible, from a lethargy that must end in his inevitable ruin." Steele, adds Victor, "told me it was literally true, and that he received it as he believed it was meant by his friend, to do him service."[1] Dr. Thomas Sheridan considered that the execution was simply put in to screen Steele's goods from other creditors; but in the

[1] Victor's *Original Letters*, &c., 1776, i. 328-9. Johnson remarked that if Addison had merely wished to give Steele a lesson he might have afterwards returned the money, which it is not pretended he did.

face of Victor's narrative this suggestion can hardly be accepted. The affair seems to have caused no interruption in the friendship between Steele and Addison, though there may have been, as Dr. Birch says, "a few little bickerings on economical occasions." Nichols suggested that when Steele said, in 1708, that he had *paid* Addison his £1000, he meant that he had given Addison a bond upon the house at Hampton-Wick, as security for the payment of it in, say, a twelvemonth; possibly Addison might wait for three or four years before he put in his execution. This, however, is rather a forced reading of Steele's letter. I shall only add that I have found no trace in the records of the law-courts of any action for debt brought by Addison against Steele.

In June 1712 Steele was living in retirement at a cottage on Haverstock Hill, where Sir Charles Sedley had died a few years earlier. This house, of which engravings will be found in Drake's *Essays on the Tatler*, &c., in Smith's *Historical and Literary Curiosities*, and elsewhere, was opposite the house now numbered 94 Haverstock Hill.[1] It was pulled down in 1867, but several places in the neighbourhood yet bear Steele's name. Nichols feared that solitude was resorted to for pecuniary reasons, but this is a superfluous surmise. The cottage was simply taken, no doubt, for change of air during the summer months. The members of the Kit Cat Club used to call for Steele on their way to the Upper Flask at Hampstead, an inn close to the heath, which still exists as a private house. It was thither that "Clarissa" fled, and there George Steevens afterwards lived and died. There the Club met on summer evenings, and we catch a glimpse of the gathering of noblemen and wits in a note from Steele to Philips written about this time: "If you please to come to Mr. Edgecomb's in Marlborough-street he will wait on you in His Chaise to Hampstead. I ride with the Duke of Montague."[2]

On June 1 Steele wrote to Pope from his "solitude," with reference to the *Messiah*, which had been published in the

[1] Hutton's *Literary Landmarks of London*, 1885; *Old and New London*, v. 491–4.

[2] The original, endorsed to Mr. Philips, is in Mr. A. Morrison's collection.

Spectator (No. 378) a fortnight earlier, with an introductory note by Steele stating that the poem was "written by a great genius, a friend of mine, in the country, who is not ashamed to employ his wit in the praise of his Maker."[1]

June 1, 1712.

Sir,

I am at a solitude, an house between Hampstead and London, wherein Sir Charles Sedley died. This circumstance set me a-thinking and ruminating upon the employments in which men of wit exercise themselves. It was said of Sir Charles, who breathed his last in this room,

> "Sedley has that prevailing gentle art,
> Which can with a resistless charm impart
> The loosest wishes to the chastest heart;
> Raise such a conflict, kindle such a fire
> Between declining virtue and desire,
> Till the poor vanquish'd maid dissolves away,
> In dreams all night, in sighs and tears all day."

This was an happy talent to a man of the town; but, I dare say, without presuming to make uncharitable conjectures on the author's present condition, he would rather have had it said of him that he prayed,

> "Oh thou my voice inspire,
> Who touch'd Isaiah's hallow'd lips with fire!"

I have turned to every verse and chapter, and think you have preserved the sublime heavenly spirit throughout the whole, especially at—"Hark a glad voice"—and—"The lamb with wolves shall graze."

There is but one line[2] which I think below the original:

> "He wipes the tears for ever from our eyes."

You have expressed it with a good and pious, but not so exalted and poetical a spirit as the prophet, "The Lord God will wipe away tears

[1] Preceding writers, apparently not noticing the date of No. 378 of the *Spectator*, have spoken as if this letter of June 1 was written before the *Messiah* was published, instead of after.

[2] "In consequence of this objection this line was altered thus:

> 'From every eye he wipes off every tear.'

I own I cannot forbear thinking that this repetition of the word *every* is a quaint and pretty modernism, unsuited to the subject."—*Warton.* The altered reading was given in the collected 8vo edition of the *Spectator*.

from off all faces." If you agree with me in this, alter it by way of paraphrase or otherwise, that, when it comes into a volume, it may be amended.

Your poem is already better than the Pollio.

I am yours, &c. RICH. STEELE.

On the 18th June, Pope answered, or is supposed to have answered, in a letter beginning, "You have obliged me with a very kind letter, by which I find you shift the scene of your life from the town to the country, and enjoy that mixed state which wise men both delight in and are qualified for." The rest of the letter is composed of trite remarks from various philosophers upon solitude and upon life in general.[1] On the 15th July he sent Steele another essay in the form of a letter upon sickness and health, life and death. A few weeks later Steele wrote this note to Mr. Caryll:[2]—

Aug. 27, 1712.

DEAR S^R^

Upon occasion of seeing yours to Mr Tonson I repeat my acknowledgm^ts^ for the Veneson you sent me. Itt was eaten in company whome you would like and itt did great honōr to

S^r^

Y^r^ most obed^t^ humble Servant,

RICHARD STEELE.

Mr Addison gives his
Ser^se^ to Mr Pope.

We must now turn to one of the very few allusions to Steele at this period in Swift's *Journal*. Under date 1st July, Swift wrote: "Steele was arrested the other day for making a lottery, directly against Act of Parliament. He is now under prosecution; but they think it will be dropped, out of pity. I believe he will very soon lose his employment, for he has been mighty impertinent of late in his Spectators; and I will never offer a word in his behalf." The impertinence here referred to was, perhaps, the publishing in the paper for May 21 (No. 384) of

[1] The conclusion, relating to what Plutarch "just now told me," appeared in the 1727 edition in a letter to Cromwell of the 18th March 1708, but in the 1735 edition it was omitted from that letter.

[2] Caryll Papers, Add. MS. 28618, f. 85 b.

the Preface to Dr. Fleetwood's *Four Sermons*, a Preface which had been ordered to be burnt by the House of Commons. Swift may also have been alluding to the fact that the several volumes of the collected edition of the *Spectator* were dedicated to eminent Whig statesmen,[1] the fourth, in particular, to the Duke of Marlborough, and the fifth to the Earl of Wharton, the late Lord Lieutenant, against whom Swift had, in his most bitter style, brought the gravest charges. But the first part of this entry from the *Journal* is of more importance. Steele seems to have got into some trouble at this time, but it does not appear that he was arrested, and Swift probably was only repeating an inaccurate rumour. It will be seen that the arrest is alleged to have occurred "the other day." On the 24th June a letter signed by Steele was inserted in the *Spectator* after one of Addison's essays on the Pleasures of the Imagination. Steele there describes in somewhat vague terms a new design, "of which I am partly author," for "getting money." It was called the Multiplication Table, and was to be worked indirectly in connection with the State Lottery. Receipts were to be given for half-guineas received, which would entitle the fortunate bearer to certain sums in the Table, "as is set forth at large in the Proposals printed the 23rd instant." Every one that had half-a-guinea was put into a possibility of gaining, from that small sum, an easy fortune. This is all we are told of the scheme.[2] But on this same 24th June the Act against illicit lotteries came into operation, and four days later, on the 28th June, the following advertisement appeared in the *Spectator*: "Whereas the Proposal called the Multiplication Table is under an information from the Attorney-General, in humble submission and duty to Her Majesty the said undertaking is laid down and attendance is this day given at the last house on the left hand in Ship Yard in Bartholomew Lane in order to repay such sums as have been paid into the said Table without deduction."

[1] The first volume was dedicated to Lord Somers, the second to Lord Halifax, the third to Mr. Henry Boyle, the fourth to the Duke of Marlborough, the fifth to Lord Wharton, the sixth to Lord Sunderland, and the seventh to Mr. Methuen.

[2] Perhaps Addison was referring to this plan of Steele's when he makes the Guardian (No. 107) speak of his "refinements upon lotteries, and insurances."

On the same day Steele wrote to his wife that all was safe and well. He had looked forward to great results following from his plan, but, in some way or other not explained, he considered that his disappointment had produced one good, namely, a certainty of his keeping his Commissionership in the Stamp Office.

In July Steele seems to have taken a house on the east side of Bloomsbury Square. It is of this that he speaks in the first of the following letters.

July 15th, 1712.

DEAR PRUE

I thank you for your Kind Billet. The nurse shall have money this Week. I saw your Son Dick but He is a Peevish Chit. You cannot conceive How pleased I am that I shall have the prettyest house to receive the Prettyest Woman who is the Darling of

RICHARD STEELE.

July 24th, 1712.

DEAR CREATURE

All you desire shall be done. I begg of You to Compose your self for nothing else can [make] happy one that doats on You so much that He cannot hide it tho' He Heartily wishes He could.

Yrs Unchangeably

RICHARD STEELE.

From the next letter it appears that Steele was visiting Lord Halifax at Hampton Court. The letters which follow are without date, and are placed here conjecturally.

Thursday Noon,
Sepbr 17th, 1712.
HAMPTON-COURT.

DEAREST WIFE

The finest Women in nature should not detain Me an hour from You, but You must sometimes suffer the Rivalship of the Wisest Men. Ld Hallifax and Sommers leave this place after dinner and I go to Watford to speake with the Sollicitor Generall[1] and from thence come directly to Bloomsbury-Square.

Yrs faithfully RICHARD STEELE.

[1] Sir Robert Raymond; afterwards, in succession, Attorney-General, a Serjeant-at-Law, Chief-Justice of the King's Bench, and a Commissioner of the Great Seal.

Dear Wife

It is an Unspeakable trouble to me that I ever let fall a passionate word in return for any impatience you show about the provision I make for you. I am indeed. I take all the pains imaginable and love you better than toungue can expresse.

Yrs faithfully, Richard Steele.

My Dear

The coachmen were so very dear that I have taken places in the Stage-Coach, where We are to be exactly half hour after one. Pray Give my Duty to my Mother and excuse that I can't come to receive Her commands. Put money in your Pockett. Give necessary Orders for the House to be in readinesse against Our return.

Yrs Ever Richd Steele.

On the 8th August Steele wrote to his mother-in-law, inviting her to his new house. We have heard something before of the "little frowardnesses" of his wife, which prevented her always being on good terms with her mother. From the expression, "the renewal of my employments in my favour," it would almost seem as if Steele held at that time some other post besides his Commissionership.

August 8th, 1712,
Bloomsbury-Square.

Dear Madam

Ever since I had the honour to be of your family My heart has yearned to Exert my self in a particular manner towards you, and to make your life easy and happy. The uneasinesses of my fortune have hitherto made it impracticable to me, and some little frowardnesses of Prue have also been an Hindrance to it. But I thank God matters are now settled after such a manner, and the renewall of my Employments in my favour has enabled me to invite you hither, where you shall be attended with Plenty Chearfulnesse and Quiet. I shall wait on you to talk further on this subject, and if you are averse to it nothing shall be taken ill by,

Madam,
Yr Most Obedient Son &
Most Humble Servant Richard Steele.

The settlement of Steele's affairs was not of so satisfactory a nature as would appear from this letter; for only three days before it was written he had borrowed £3000 from Mr. Ashurst.

In September and October he wrote three interesting letters to Mrs. Scurlock about the provision which she might be expected to make for her grandchildren. In the second of these letters, it will be seen, he remarked that he had had no fortune with his wife, but that they were now living in the handsomest manner, supported only by his industry. "The main of the estate is wholly in you, and that part which is my wife's I shall, I doubt not, find her ready to settle in the manner my friend will acquaint you."

HAMPTON-COURT,
Sep^br 27th, 1712.

HONOURED MADAM

The encrease[1] of my family and reflection upon what vast sums of money I have lett slip through my hands since I have had opportunityes of mending my fortune in the world, have made me very anxious for the future. I understand there has been some discourse between my Wife and your self upon this Subject, but if there has any thing past too eager, I beseech You to attribute it to a Laudable tendernesse for a numerous family. All that I intend by it is to know what foundation I may think I am upon with relation to posterity, which are Your offspring as well as mine. I ask nothing of you, but by the Blessing of God will add to the Estate in the family, as well as provide for my Younger Children, with as much haste as honour and integrity will permit. I only want to know for the encouragement of my industrey in so Great a Work how all things stand now to a farthing. I am very much above any distasts to any one you may affect, but shall ever be ready to Serve to my utmost any one that you are inclined to do for or favour. I send this before me,[2] as a preface to a discourse of this kind when I have the Honour to See You, and am with great truth,

Madam,
Y^r Most Obliged
& Most Humble Servant, RICHARD STEELE.

Oct^br 25th, 1712,
BLOOMSBURY-SQUARE.

DEAR MOTHER

I give you this to lay before You in the humblest manner what I think reasonable should be done in favour of me and mine.

[1] Eugene, Steele's third child, was born in March 1712.

[2] "because" erased.

You are well acquainted that I have had no fortune with your daughter, that I have struggled through Great difficulties for our Maintenance, that We live now in the handsomest manner, supported only by my Industrey. I say, Madam, when you consider all this, and add to it, that My posterity is Yours also you will be, I doubt not, inclined that Your estate should passe to them, I not having any veiw nor making the least request of any support from You during your life. The Gentleman[1] who brings this will inform You in what manner I desire this may be effected. He is a Sensible and Good man and I hope you will be prevailed upon to do me the reasonable favour I ask you by His interposition between Us. This provision made for my Poor Children will make me meet all the Changes and chances of this life with Chearfulnesse and Alacrity, for want of which I have many melancholy reflexions. The main of the estate is wholly in You and that part which is my Wife's I shall, I doubt not, find her ready to Settle in the manner my freind will acquaint You.

I am, Dear Madam,

Yr Most Obedient Son &

Most Humble Servant,

RICHARD STEELE.

Octbr 31st, 1712.

DEAR MOTHER

As soon as I had left You this afternoon I went to Mr. Diggle, my freind whome I sent to you in my behalfe about the Settlement. I find the whole is in You and that the part which descends to Prue is Covered by assignments for Debts you have paid so that I have nothing to do but to prevail upon You. Please to put the anxiety of a Father of a numerous family in your thoughts and you will pardon my importunity to preserve them from Want. When You have been thus kind to my poor Children who descend from You I can think of adding to their fortune with some alacrity, but to have the matter to do wholly myself makes it so Great a Labour that I am dispirited from beginning it. I do not desire any consideration of me my self, But I beseech God to put it in your heart to make a Certainty for them. I am in hopes in your cool thoughts you will approve of what I ask, which will ease the Loaded Heart of,

Madam,

Yr Most Obliged Son &

Most Humble Servant

RICHARD STEELE.

[1] Mr Diggle. See pp. 305, 331.

At the end of October came actions for debt in the Court of Queen's Bench which explain the loaded heart of which Steele here speaks. The first action was brought by Benjamin Ashurst, against Richard Steele, of the parish of St. Giles-in-the-Fields, Esq., for the recovery of a debt of £3000. Ashurst said that Steele had, on the 5th August last, in the parish of St. Clement Danes, by a certain bond sealed by him, acknowledged himself bound to him in the sum of £600, parcel of the said £3000, to be paid when requested; and that on the same day Steele gave him three other bonds for £600, £800, and £1000 respectively, parcels and residue of the said £3000; but he had not repaid the money, and refused to do so, to the damage of Ashurst of £100. Steele appeared by James Tully, his attorney, but when the complainant prayed that he should answer his plea, Steele said nothing in bar, and judgment was therefore given against him, with 53s. for the damages Ashurst had sustained.[1]

Another action was brought by Edward Vernon, who complained that on the 22nd July last, at Westminster, Steele made a certain note in his own handwriting, commonly called a "promissory note," whereby he promised to pay to Vernon £24 upon the 25th August then next following, for value received, by reason whereof Steele became bound to pay the said money. But he had not paid, although Vernon requested him to pay on the 20th August, at Westminster, and he still refused. Vernon therefore claimed £30 damages. Steele appeared by his attorney, Thomas Bateman, and upon Vernon praying that answer should be made to the plea, a day, Friday next after the Quindene of St. Martin, was given to Steele; but he did not come, neither did his attorney say anything in bar. Judgment was therefore given for Vernon, but as the Court did not know what damages he had sustained, the Sheriff was commanded to find out the amount.[2]

On the 4th October Steele wrote the following letter, a draft of which is among the Blenheim papers. It was probably addressed to Mr. Compton, the Paymaster to Her Majesty's

[1] Queen's Bench Judgment Roll, 11 Anne, Mich., 57.
[2] Ibid., 75.

Pensioners, and seems to relate to the pension Steele received as Gentleman Waiter to the late Prince George. Perhaps the favour Mr. Compton did him, mentioned in the letter of the 7th May 1709, already printed, consisted in advancing a portion of the pension before it was due. Mr. Godfrey was evidently an official in Mr. Compton's office.

Octbr 4th, 1712.

SR

I begg the favour of you to direct Mr Godfrey to accommodate me with sixty pounds in the same manner that you were pleased to [1] order him once before in behalf of,

Sr

Yr Most obliged and
Most Obedient Humble Sernt.

The following document relates to the same matter:[2]—

November 18th, 1712.

Left then in Mr Warren's hands an Assignment of my Sallary at Mr Compton's office of the net sum of seventy-three pounds eleven shillings and nine pence, on which Mr Warren this day lent me fifty pounds. RICHARD STEELE.

Mem: ye assignt above menc'oned I left wth Mr. Godfry att Mr. Compton's office, 20th Mch 1712. J. W.

Sad to relate, Steele was, on this same 18th November, conscious that he had drunk too much, and was looking forward with some apprehension to his wife's reproaches.

November 18th, 1712.

DEAR PRUE

I am come from a committee where I have [been] Charman, and drank too much. I have the head Ach and should be glad you would come to Me in Good Humour, which would always banish any uneasinesse of temper from, Dear Prue,

Yr Fond Fool of a Husband R. S.

In November 1712 Addison and Steele assigned to Samuel Buckley a half-share in the four volumes of the *Spectator* already

[1] "Do me the same favour," cancelled.
[2] *Gent. Mag.*, 1856, vol. xlv. pp. 266–7.

published, and in three not yet out. Buckley paid £575. This is the deed of assignment.[1]

Whereas there is already printed Four Volumes of the Spectators which Include from Number one to Number Three hundred Twenty one: and Whereas there is two Volumes more now printing which will take in from Number Three hundred Twenty one to to (*sic*) Number four hundred & eighty or thereabouts Which will make Six Volumes and Whereas it is intended by the authors whose names are hereinafter mens̃oned to continue writing the said Spectator to the end of this present month of November which will make a Seventh Volume.

Now know all men by these presents that Joseph Addison of St. James Westminster Esq[r] and Richard Steele of St. Giles's in the fields Esq[r] for and in consideration of the Sum̃e of Five hundred Seventy and five pounds to them or one of them in hand paid by Samuel Buckley of London printer and Bookseller the Receipt whereof they the said Joseph Addison and Richard Steele doe hereby respectively acknowledge They the said Joseph Addison and Richard Steele Have and each and either of them Hath Granted Bargained Sold Assigned Transferred and Sett over and by these presents They the said Joseph Addison and Richard Steele and each and either of them doth Grant Bargain Sell Assign Transfer and Sett over unto the said Samuel Buckley his Executors Administrators and Assigns All that their full and Sole right and Title of in and to one Moiety or full half Share of the Copys of all and every the above mens̃oned Seven Volumes of Spectators which said Moiety or full half Share to remain unto the said Samuel Buckley his heirs and and Assigns for Ever In Wittness whereof The said Joseph Addison and Richard Steele have hereunto Sett their hands & Seals this Tenth day of November Anno Dom: 1712.

Witnesses RICHARD THWAITES JOSEPH ADDISON (L.S).
DAVID VERDON RICHARD STEELE (L.S).
at the Fountain tavern in the Strand.

Two years later, on the 13th October 1714, Buckley reassigned this half-share in the *Spectators* to Jacob Tonson, jun., stationer, for £500.

We now come to some further correspondence with Pope.

[1] Add. MS. 21110. A copy, or draft, of this deed is in Mr. A. Morrison's collection.

This is not the place to discuss the whole complicated story of the methods resorted to by Pope to bring about, for the gratification of the vanity which accompanied his physical weaknesses, the publication of his correspondence with the famous persons of the time. What chiefly concerns us is the fact that certain of the letters purporting to have been written to Addison and Steele were in reality concocted from letters which Pope had written at various times to his friend John Caryll. In 1712 Pope wrote to Caryll, asking for the return of his letters; and in 1726 he requested that Caryll would return any that he had retained, for fear they should fall into Curll's hands. But this time Caryll did not respond, and for two years their correspondence fell off. Caryll then complained, and in 1729 Pope replied that he could not write to people unless they would return his letters every year. Caryll gave way, and on the 8th April 1729 Pope acknowledged the receipt of the letters. But Caryll copied most of the letters before he returned them, and this he continued to do until July 1735. In the meantime the publication of Pope's correspondence was delayed, because Caryll, although weak and old, might have exposed the fabrications which were about to be put forth; but his death, in April 1736, removed this difficulty. Pope's frauds were, however, to be exposed more than a century later. The copies that Caryll had kept of letters he received from Pope, Steele, and others fell into the late Mr. Dilke's hands, and are now in the British Museum; and they bring home to Pope one of the most extraordinary of the acts of duplicity of which he was guilty.[1]

In No. 523 of the *Spectator* (October 30, 1712) Addison wrote in praise of the Miscellany edited by "that ingenious gentleman," Mr. Pope. Four days later a letter from Pope, with some lines upon the story of Cephalus and Procris, was printed in the *Spectator*, and in the number for November 10 there was another letter from Pope, about the verses spoken by the Emperor Adrian on his death-bed. This letter was subsequently repub-

[1] "Pope in the Darkness mining like a Mole,
Forged on Himself, as from Himself he stole,
And what for Caryll once he feigned to feel,
Transferred, in Letters never sent, to Steele!"
(Lang's *Letters to Dead Authors*.)

lished in 1735 with the date November 7, 1712, and accompanied by a metrical version of Adrian's lines. On November 12 Steele wrote to Pope, who had sent him the *Temple of Fame*, praising the poem, about which he would write again when Addison had seen it, and asking his assistance in a design to be opened a month or two hence, with the aid of the few who were like Pope. This was the *Guardian*, which it thus appears was being planned some time before the *Spectator* came to an end. The following was Pope's reply :—

Nov. 16, 1712.

You oblige me by the indulgence you have shewn to the poem I sent you, but will oblige me much more by the kind severity I hope for from you. No errors are so trivial but they deserve to be mended. But, since you say you see nothing that may be called a fault, can you but think it so, that I have confined the attendance of guardian spirits to Heaven's favourites only ?[1] I could point you to several: but it is my business to be informed of those faults I do not know; and as for those I do, not to talk of them, but to correct them. You speak of that poem in a style I neither merit, nor expect; but, I assure you, if you freely mark or dash out, I shall look upon your blots to be its greatest beauties; I mean, if Mr. Addison and yourself should like it in the whole; otherwise the trouble of correction is what I would not take; for I was really so diffident of it as to let it lie by me these two years, just as you now see it. I am afraid of nothing so much as to impose any thing on the world which is unworthy of its acceptance.

As to the last period of your letter, I shall be very ready and glad to contribute to any design that tends to the advantage of mankind, which, I am sure, all yours do. I wish I had but as much capacity as leisure, for I am perfectly idle (a sign I have not much capacity).

If you will entertain the best opinion of me, be pleased to think me your friend. Assure Mr. Addison of my most faithful service; of every one's esteem he must be assured already.

I am your, &c. A. POPE.

On the 29th November, apparently after some conversation with Steele on the subject, Pope wrote another polite letter; but the letter, as we have it, is really taken from one written to Caryll, dated "Binfield." Pope professed to be sorry that his name had been affixed to the notion about Addison's verses in

[1] This is not now to be found in the poem.

the *Spectator*. If he had contemplated its publication, he would have written with more diffidence. On the 4th December Steele replied, asking Pope for "an ode as of a cheerful dying spirit; that is to say, the Emperor Adrian's 'animula vagula,' put into two or three stanzas for music." Pope, according to a letter purporting to have been written immediately afterwards, sent what was desired—*The Dying Christian to his Soul*—"just warm from the brain." The "&c." after "Sappho" stands for Thomas Flatman, who published *Songs and Poems* in 1674, and who had made a version of Adrian's lines, from which an enemy might plausibly suggest that Pope had borrowed to some extent.

Dec. . . . 1712.

I do not send you word I will do, but have already done the thing you desire of me. You have it (as Cowley calls it) just warm from the brain. It came to me the first moment I waked this morning: yet, you will see, it was not so absolutely inspiration, but that I had in my head not only the verses of Adrian, but the fine fragment of Sappho, &c.

This all seems clear enough. Steele asked for the poem only two days before the *Spectator* came to an end, so that the verses could not have reached him in time for insertion in that paper. The lines did not appear in the *Guardian*, but that paper was not commenced until three months later. The poem was, in fact, first published years afterwards in Lintot's edition of Pope's Works. But the proof of Pope's deception is to be found in a letter which he sent to Caryll on the 12th June 1713. In that letter Pope gave three versions of the lines, "of three different hands." "I desire your opinion of these verses, and which are best written." The third version is:—

"Vital spark of heavenly flame!
Dost thou quit this mortal frame?" &c.

This version first appeared anonymously in 1730, in Lewis's Miscellany. We are therefore driven to the conclusion that the improved version, which Pope pretended was sent to Steele in December 1712, was not written when he wrote to Caryll in June 1713, or even in 1730. Moreover, as Mr. Dilke remarked,[1]

[1] *Papers of a Critic*, 1875, vol. i. 245–8.

if the ode had been made public in any way before June 1713, Caryll would have heard of it, which it is evident from Pope's letter that he had not, and this affords further evidence that the ode had not been sent to Steele, for Caryll was a friend of Steele's as well as of Pope's.

There is nothing to show what determined Steele and Addison in bringing the *Spectator* to a close in December 1712. All we know is, that the decision was not one taken suddenly. On the 12th November Steele told Pope that he had a new design—the *Guardian*—which he proposed to open in a month or two; and in the agreement with Buckley of the 10th November it is stated that it was proposed to continue the *Spectator* to the end of November. The members of the Club were gradually disposed of; and a new Club was to be formed, where the Spectator would alter his character and be loquacious. The ceremony of opening the Spectator's mouth was to be on the 25th March next. The date, however, might be altered, but of this public notice would be given.[1]

[1] Nos. 550, 553, by Addison.

IV.

"THE GUARDIAN."

1713. ÆT. 40–41.

In January 1713 George Berkeley, afterwards Bishop of Cloyne, but then a young man of eight-and-twenty, came to London from Trinity College, Dublin. Berkeley was already known by his *New Theory of Vision*, published in 1709, and the *Treatise concerning the Principles of Human Knowledge*, 1710, and he brought with him from Ireland a new book, *Three Dialogues between Hylas and Philonous*, which was published in May 1713. But his object in coming to London was "to make acquaintance with men of merit, rather than to engage the interests of those in power." He found Steele ready to welcome him on his arrival, and Swift, another countryman, was soon numbered among his friends. Berkeley's opinions of those with whom he came in contact are expressed in his correspondence with Sir John Perceval, afterwards Earl of Egmont,[1] and these letters give us many interesting particulars about Steele. On the 26th January, Berkeley wrote: "In a fortnight after I left Dublin I arrived here, having made easy journeys and staid some time at Chester. . . . The first news I had upon my coming to town was that Mr. Steel did me the honour to desire to be acquainted with me; upon which I have been to see him; he is confin'd with the Gout, and

[1] Sir John Perceval, a member of the Irish House of Commons, was raised to the Irish peerage in 1715 as Lord Perceval, and in 1733 was made Earl of Egmont. In 1732 he obtained a charter to colonise Georgia; and in 1748 he died, aged sixty. The letters of Berkeley here given are taken from copies in Sir John Perceval's letter-books, to which the Earl of Egmont kindly gave me access.

is, as I am informed, writing a Play, since he gave over the Spectators. This gentleman is extreamly civil and obliging, and I propose no small satisfaction in the conversation of him and his ingenious friends, w^ch^, as an encouragement he tells me, are to be met with at his House." The next letter, dated February 23, contains some important information: "Mr. Addison and Mr. Steele (and, so far as I can find, the rest of that party) seem extremely persuaded there is a design for bringing in the Pretender. They think everything looks that way, and particularly three of the best Papist officers . . . being now all in London. . . . I must desire you will not quote me for this, not caring to be thought the spreader of such news. But I tell this to my Lady, Mrs. Parker, and y^r^ self, that you may take proper measures against that time. The value you have always shown for the Spectators makes me think it neither impertinent nor unwelcome news to tell you that by his mother-in-law's death he is come into an estate of 500*l.* a year; the same day his wife was brought to bed of a son. Before she lay down the poor man told me he was in great pain and put to a thousand little shifts to conceal his mother's desperate illness from her. The tender concern he showed on that occasion and what I have observed in another good friend of mine makes me imagine the best men are always the best husbands. I told Mr. Steele if he neglects to resume his writings the world will look on it as the effect of his growing rich; but he says this addition to his fortune will rather encourage him to exert himself more than ever; and I am the apter to believe him because there appears in his natural temper, something very generous and a great benevolence to mankind. One instance of it is his kind and friendly behaviour to me (even tho' he has heard I am a Tory). I have dined frequently at his house in Bloomsbury Square, wch is handsome, and neatly furnished. His table, servants, coach and everything is very gentile, and in appearance above his fortune before this new acquisition. His conversation is very chearful, and abounds with wit and good sense. Somebody (I know not who) has given him my Treatise of the Principles of Human Knowledge, and that was the ground of his inclination to my acquaintance. For my part, I should reckon it a sufficient recompence of my pains in writing it, that it gave me some share in the friendship of so worthy a man."

From this letter we learn that Mrs. Steele's mother died at the end of January or early in February, and that Steele thereupon came into £500 a year. Mrs. Steele administered to the property of her mother, "late of St. Andrew's, Holborn," on the 20th March.[1] We also learn that about the time of Mrs. Scurlock's death another child was born to Steele. Berkeley says it was a son, but probably he was mistaken, the child really being Steele's daughter Mary, who we know was born in this year, 1713. It is, however, just possible that the child to which Berkeley refers was a boy, who died young, and of whom no trace has been preserved, and that the daughter Mary was born at the end of the same year. Mrs. Steele's approaching confinement is referred to in a letter from Steele to Caryll, at the close of December, declining an invitation to visit Ladyholt.[2]

Dec. 23, 1712, BLOOMSBURY SQUARE.

S^R^

I am honourd with your kind invitation to Ladyholt for wch I give you my most hearty thanks. My Wife expects to lye in this next month, and I'm honour'd with the duty of one of the Nurses, wch is a Post that obliges me to Residence. I wish all happinesse to you and your Family, and am with affection and respect

S^r^

Y^r^ most obedient and
most humble Servant
RICHARD STEELE.

On the 7th March, Berkeley wrote: "You will soon hear of Mr. Steel under the character of the Guardian; he designs his paper shall come out every day as the Spectator. He is likewise projecting a noble entertainment for persons of a refined taste. It is chiefly to consist of the finest pieces of eloquence translated from the Greek and Latin authors; they will be accompanied by the best musick suited to raise those passions that are suited to the occasion. Pieces of poetry too will be there recited.

[1] In the warrant Mrs. Scurlock is said to have been dead "ad annum elaps!"

[2] Caryll Papers, Add. MS. 28618, f. 85 b.

These informations I have from Mr. Steel himself. I have seen the place designed for these performances. It is in York Buildings, and he has been at no small expense to embellish it with all imaginable decorations. It is the finest chamber I have seen, and will contain seats for a select company of two [hundred] persons of the best quality and taste who are to be subscribers. I had last night a very ingenious new poem upon Windsor Forest[1] given me by the author, Mr. Pope. The gentleman is a Papist, but a man of excellent wit and learning, and one of those Mr. Steel mentions in his last paper as having writ some of the Spectator." Of Steele's scheme for "a noble entertainment for persons of refined taste"—a description which we may well believe that Berkeley had from Steele himself—we shall hear again under the name of the "Censorium." In the meantime, the first number of the *Guardian* was published on the 12th March.

The periodicals issued since the commencement of the *Spectator* can be disposed of in a few words.[2] In 1711 there were the *Miscellany*, the *Surprize*, the *Hermit*, the *Inquisitor* (the aim of which was announced to be the exposure of vice at masquerades and elsewhere, but not of persons, which gives opportunity for praise of the *Spectator*), the *Pilgrim*, the *Restorer* (which was to restore peace and friendship; it was by Francis Hoffman), and the *Free Thinker*. In 1712 there were the *Historian*, the *Rhapsody*, the *Plain Dealer*, the *Useful Intelligencer* for promoting trade, several *Medleys*, and the *Rambler*, a title which Johnson afterwards bestowed on a much more distinguished periodical. In January 1713 appeared the *Britain*, a political paper, and in March the *Monitor*. Of some of the above papers only single numbers have survived, and none of them are of any consequence. Some periodicals published on the Continent are of much more importance, and show the widespread influence of Steele and Addison's work. The first of

[1] "This day is published, Windsor-Forest. To the Right Honourable George Lord Landsdown. By Mr. Pope, price 1s. Printed for Barnard Lintott" (*Post-Boy*, March 5 to 7, 1712–13). "Mr. Pope has published a fine poem, called Windsor Forest. Read it" (Swift's *Journal*, March 9, 1713).

[2] See Harl. MS. 5958; *Notes and Queries*, 3rd Series, ix. 53, 72, 92; Timperley's *Encyclopedia of Literary and Typographical Anecdote*.

these papers was *Le Misanthrope*, by Justus Van Effen, a member of the Royal Society of London, which was commenced in May 1711 and continued until December 1712. In the Notice to the Reader prefixed to the collected edition published at the Hague in 1712–13, Effen referred to one of the finest geniuses of the time who started two years before in England the *Tatler*, with which all the world was charmed. There was hardly a family in London, he said, where the *Tatler* was not taken in regularly, to read in the morning while drinking tea, for the instruction both of young and old; and he was assured that from twelve to fifteen thousand copies were sold every time. The *Spectator*, published daily, was meeting with equal success. Effen was one of the translators of *Robinson Crusoe* in 1720, and he afterwards wrote *Le Nouveau Spectateur Français*, the *Hollansche Spectator*, and other periodicals. The *Discurse der Mahler*,[1] by Bodmer and others, appeared in 1721, and Gottsched's *Vernünftigen Tadlerinnen* in 1725.

The *Guardian* was published daily, and extended to 175 numbers, the last of which appeared on the 1st October. Addison, occupied with the preparation of *Cato* for the stage, took little part in the earlier numbers of the *Guardian*, but afterwards he was a frequent contributor. Pope, Berkeley, and Tickell all assisted Steele with excellent papers,[2] Berkeley, we are told, receiving a guinea and a dinner in return for each paper contributed by him. Budgell, Hughes, and others also helped, but Steele himself wrote 82 out of the total of 175 papers. In a Notice to the Reader, in the collected edition,[3] there is the usual hearty acknowledgment of Addison's aid.

[1] See "Der Spectator als Quelle der 'Discurse der Maler,'" by Theodor Vetter, Frauenfeld, 1887. In the "Chronick der Gesellschaft der Mahler, 1721–1722," edited by the same writer (1887), and which forms a part of the "Bibliothek älterer Schriftwerke der deutschen Schweiz," there is a long letter to "M. le Spectateur," dated October 1721, and signed "Les Peintres," about the popularity of Steele's papers in Germany and Switzerland, and their indebtedness to him.

[2] "But you must know, Sir, that this arduous undertaking is not carried on by *Teague* alone, but by a Triple League" (John Dennis to * * * * Esq.; upon the first publishing the Guardians.—*Original Letters*, ii. 286).

[3] The first volume was dedicated to Lieutenant-General Cadogan, and the second to Mr. Pulteney, afterwards Lord Bath.

"All those papers which are distinguished by the mark of an hand were written by a gentleman who has obliged the world with productions too sublime to admit that the author of them should receive any addition to his reputation from such loose occasional thoughts as make up these little treatises. For which reason his name shall be concealed." It is unfortunate that Addison did not take a more active share in the production of the *Guardian* in its earlier days, for Steele and Addison were at their best when working in conjunction. Pope wrote to Caryll on the 23rd June: "I wholly agree with you in your opinion of the Guardian in general, only I must do Mr. Steele the justice to assure you those he writes himself are equal to any he has wrote. The great difference is caused by the want of Mr. Addison's assistance, who writes as seldom as I do,—one a month or so."

The Guardian was a certain Mr. Nestor Ironside, and his relations with the various members of the Lizard family, who are introduced to us by Steele in Nos. 2, 5, and 6, form the machinery used throughout the periodical. The main purpose of the work was, "to protect the modest, the industrious; to celebrate the wise, the valiant; to encourage the good, the pious; to confront the impudent, the idle; to contemn the vain, the cowardly; and to disappoint the wicked and profane." It aimed at the advancement of the conversation of gentlemen, the improvement of ladies, the wealth of traders, and the encouragement of artificers.[1] After speaking, in No. 21, of the aid rendered by Raphael's paintings to the cause of religion, Steele says: "It is with this view that I presume upon subjects of this kind, and men may take up this paper, and be catched by an admonition under the disguise of a diversion." Everything published on a Saturday, as was the case during the greater part of the career of the *Spectator*, bore some relation to the duties of the following day. "It is an unspeakable pleasure to me, that I have lived to see the time when I can observe such a law to myself, and yet turn my discourse upon what is done at the play-house. I am sure the reader knows I am going to mention the tragedy of Cato."[2] There is the same variety of

[1] No. 1. [2] No. 33.

X

The following letter is full of Imagination and in a Fabulous manner
~~setts forth the alliance between se-~~
~~verall good and Bad~~ setts forth a ~~the~~
Connexion between things, and alliance
between Persons that are very distant
and remote to common Eyes. I think
I know the hand ~~and [illegible] no prefer~~
~~to any other~~ to be that of a very ingenious man, and shall ~~therefore~~ ~~[illegible]~~
~~it the entrance~~ give it the reader
without further preface.

To the Guardian

Sr,

Fac-simile of draft of introductory remarks by Steele to a letter by Thomas Parnell, in the *Guardian*, No. 66 (Blenheim MSS.).

topics discussed in the *Guardian* as in its predecessors, and as in the earlier papers, here too Steele expressed opinions on many subjects which were far in advance of the time. In No. 34 he gave another excellent character of a fine gentleman,—"a man completely qualified as well for the service and good as for the ornament and delight of society." In No. 61, by Pope, the writer plainly showed his opinion of sanguinary sports, and in particular hunting, great as were the authority and custom which supported the diversion. In No. 98, while announcing the erection of a Lion's Head at Button's Coffee-house, into whose mouth letters and papers for the *Guardian* could be conveyed,[1] Addison reviewed the course of periodical writing, and said that above a hundred authors, some of them writers of great eminence in other paths, had endeavoured after Bickerstaff and Nestor Ironside's way of writing, but that none of them had hit upon the art; though several had acquitted themselves well in single papers.

In the first number of the *Guardian* Steele observed that parties were too violent to make it possible to pass them by without observation; but that as to these matters he would be impartial, though he could not be neuter. "I am, with relation to the government of the church, a tory, with regard to the state, a whig. . . . I am past all the regards of this life, and have nothing to manage with any person or party, but to deliver myself as becomes an old man with one foot in the grave, and one who thinks he is passing to eternity." But before the close of April, when the paper had reached its fortieth number, Steele was drawn into a quarrel with the *Examiner*, and the contest was continued in subsequent papers. Of all this we shall have to speak more fully hereafter; here it need only be said that whatever the justice of the cause, the introduction of politics was the ruin of the *Guardian*, a periodical which, so far as it went, contained work in no way unworthy of being placed by the side of Steele's contributions to the *Tatler* or *Spectator*.

[1] See Nos. 71, 114, &c. Particulars of the subsequent history of the Lion's Head will be found in *Notices and Extracts relating to the Lion's Head*, by Charles Richardson, Esq., 1828.

BOOK SIXTH.

POLITICS. STEELE AS ENGLISHMAN.

1713. ÆT. 41.

I.

"CATO." MRS. STEELE'S PROPERTY.

1713. ÆT. 41.

About the time that the *Guardian* was commenced Steele published, in broadside form, *A Letter to Sir Miles Wharton, concerning Occasional Peers*, dated March 5, 1712–13. Sir Miles, or Michael Wharton,[1] was amongst those who declined a peerage when, at the beginning of 1712, twelve new peers were created in order to secure to the Government a majority in the House of Lords against the combination formed between Lord Nottingham and the Whigs. In March 1713 there was a report that six more peers were to be created, and Steele wrote to show how injuriously such an action affected the Queen, the House of Lords, and the whole people. He suggested that a peer should be disabled from voting until three years after the date of his patent. "It is amazing that such care should be taken to prohibit an occasional Conformist from being a Constable, and nobody takes it in his head to prevent an occasional Lord from being a Judge, nay, a Legislator." This piece was issued under the assumed name of Francis Hicks, but was included in the volume of his political works which Steele published in 1715. We learn from a pamphlet called *Reflections on a paper lately printed, entitled, A Letter to Sir Miles Wharton. Addressed to the Guardian and Examiner*, intended as a reply to

[1] In March 1688–9 Sir Michael Wharton was appointed a Commissioner for the Admiralty. In May 1691 the Lord Carmarthen, who had been left chief Minister when William III. went abroad in the preceding December, turned out Sir Michael Wharton and some others, who were Whiggishly inclined (*Luttrell's Diary*, i. 507, ii. 230, vi. 709; Pointer, 358).

Steele, that the *Letter* was "industriously handed about, with the character that its reasons are unanswerable." [1]

The following interesting letter of Berkeley's to Sir John Perceval is valuable on account of the remarks upon Steele and Addison, and upon their relations with Swift. In the references to the Lord Treasurer we have one more proof that Steele was able to obtain access to the Earl of Oxford without Swift's intervention.

LONDON, March 27, 171⅔.

D[R] S[R]

I receiv'd your letter about three days since. Your opinion of Mr. Steele I take to be very just, and am persuaded a man of his Discernment and insight into men will know how to value an acquaintance so much to be courted as that you design to honour him with. His wit, natural good sense, generous sentiments, and enterprising genius, with a peculiar delicacy and easiness of writing, seem those qualities which distinguish Mr. Steele. Mr. Addison has the same talents in a high degree, and is likewise a great philosopher, having applied himself to the speculative studies more than any of the wits that I know.

After what I have formerly told you of the apprehensions those Gentlemen had, I think myself obliged to let you know that they are now all over,—Mr. Steele having told me that he now imagines my Lord Treasurer has no design of bringing in the Pretender, and that in case he had, he is persuaded he could never perform it; and this morning I breakfasted with Mr. Addison at Dr. Swift's lodgings. His coming in while I was there, and the good temper he shewed was construed by me as a sign of an approaching coalition of parties. Mr. Addison [? Steele] being more earnest in the Whig cause than Mr. Steele [? Addison] (the former having quitted an employment rather than hold it under the Tories, which by a little compliance he might have done), and there having passed a coldness, if not a direct breach between those two gentlemen and Dr. Swift on the score of politicks. Dr. Swift's witt is admired by both of them, and indeed by his greatest enemies, and if I were not afraid of disobliging my lady and Mrs. Parker, I should tell you that I think him one of the best natured and agreeable men in the world. Mr. Steele's entertainment at York Buildings only waits the finishing of two pictures, the one

[1] This writer said that Steele would "certainly find the armour of his integrity too weak to protect him against the laws." "Tho' this gentleman will not die with the laws, yet he is in a very fair way to die by them."

of Truth, the other of Eloquence, which are designed as part of the ornaments of the place where it is to be. He tells me he had some discourse with the Lord Treasurer relating to it, and talks as if he would engage my Lord Treasurer in his project, designing that it shall comprehend both Whigs and Tories. A play of Mr Steele's which was expected, he has now put off till next winter. But Cato, a most noble play of Mr. Addison, and the only one he writ, is to be acted in Easter week. The town is full of expectation of it, the Boxes being already bespoke, and he designing to give all the Benefit away among the Actors in proportion to their performing. I would send you the Guardians, and two very fine poems, one[1] of them being writ by an Irish Clergyman, Dr. Parnell, if you would direct me how. My humble service to my Lady and Mrs. Parker.

Your most humble Servnt

G. Berkeley.

On the 28th, the day after this letter was written, Swift had a mighty levee. "I deny myself to everybody, except about half a dozen, and they were all here, and Mr. Addison was one." On the 1st April Swift wrote: "I prevailed on Lord Bolingbroke to invite Mr. Addison to dine with him on Good Friday [April 3]. I suppose we shall be mighty mannerly. Addison is to have a play on Friday in Easter week: 'tis a tragedy, called Cato; I saw it unfinished some years ago. Did I tell you that Steele has begun a new daily paper called the Guardian? They say good for nothing. I have not seen it." On the 3rd, accordingly, Addison, Swift, and others dined with Lord Bolingbroke. "We were very civil, but yet, when we grew warm, we talked in a friendly manner of party." The peace had been signed by all the Ministers at Utrecht, except those of the Emperor; "so that now the great work is in effect done, and I believe it will appear a most excellent peace for Europe, particularly for England."

Cibber says that in 1703 he had the pleasure of reading privately with Steele the first four Acts of *Cato*, which was all of it that was then written. Steele was delighted at the pleasure Cibber showed in the piece, but said that he doubted if

[1] The *Hermit*, which Pope described as "very good." Swift wrote: "Parnell's poem is mightily esteemed; but poetry sells ill" (*Journal*, 27th March 1713).

Addison would ever have courage enough to let the play—written for his own amusement in leisure hours in Italy—stand the censure of an English audience. Steele himself was concerned at this poetical diffidence, and exclaimed, "Good God! what a part would Betterton make of Cato!" But Betterton passed away, and it fell to Booth's lot to make his fortune by the play when it was acted, after Addison, yielding to the importunities of his friends, who thought the state of parties made it "a proper time to animate the public with the sentiments of Cato," had hastily finished it. The fifth act, according to Steele, was written in less than a week.[1] On Easter Monday, the 6th April, Swift and half-a-score others stood on the stage to see the rehearsal of the piece; and in the evening, finding the Lord Treasurer away from home, Swift went back and dined privately with Addison. *Cato* was not acted publicly until Tuesday the 14th April.[2] The Prologue, by Pope, and the Epilogue, by Garth, were both printed in the *Guardian* (No. 33). The play was published on the 27th April.[3] First among the verses to the author, subsequently prefixed to it, were these of Steele's:—

> While you the fierce divided Britons awe,
> And *Cato*, with an equal virtue, draw,
> While envy is itself in wonder lost,
> And factions strive who shall applaud you most;
> Forgive the fond ambition of a friend,
> Who hopes himself, not you, to recommend;
> And joins the applause which all the learned bestow
> On one, to whom a perfect work they owe.
> To my light scenes I once inscribed your name,[4]
> And impotently strove to borrow fame:
> Soon will that die which adds thy name to mine;
> Let me, then, live, joined to a work of thine.

Much has been written of the famous first performance of *Cato*, of how Steele undertook to fill the house, and of how the repre-

[1] Dedication to Congreve, prefixed to the second edition of the *Drummer*.

[2] *Daily Courant*, April 14, 1713.

[3] *Guardian*, No. 40, Advertisement. "N.B.—There are a small number printed on a fine paper."

[4] Dedication of the *Tender Husband* to Addison.

sentatives of both parties applied to themselves and applauded the sentiments of the piece.[1] Here it will be enough to add one touch from the point of view of the author's box, taken from a letter written by Berkeley on the 16th: "On Tuesday last Cato was acted the first time. I was present with Mr. Addison and two or three more friends in a side box where we had a table and two or three flasks of Burgundy and Champagne, with which the author (who is a very sober man) thought it necessary to support his spirits, . . . and indeed it was a pleasant refreshment to us all between the acts." On the 12th Swift wrote: "I went to court to-day, on purpose to present Mr. Berkeley, one of your fellows of Dublin College, to Lord Berkeley of Stratton. That Mr. Berkeley is a very ingenious man and great philosopher, and I have mentioned him to all the ministers, and have given them some of his writings; and I will favour him as much as I can. This I think I am bound to, in honour and conscience, to use all my little credit towards helping forward men of worth in the world." Swift rendered real aid in this case, for in November he procured for Berkeley the chaplaincy and secretaryship to Lord Peterborough, who was then going as envoy to Sicily.

We have seen that Steele came into an estate worth £500 a year upon his mother-in-law's death. On the 16th March 171$\frac{2}{3}$ Mr. Morgan Davies, who appears to have acted as a sort of agent for Steele in Wales, wrote to Steele from "Heryford" about leases and other matters relating to the Welsh property. The original of this letter is in Mrs. Wills' possession.

I rec^{d} yo^{rs} of the 6th And am very Much oblig^{d} to yor Lady for the great favour you mension^{d} therein: Hopeing that I shall not only make you the fairest an^{sw} as to what is past, but shall if you & yor Lady thinks me Capable serve you according to the trust that shall be reposed in me.

[1] The *Examiner*, which was annoyed at the Whigs thinking there was anything on their side in the tragedy, said that on the first night a crowd of silly people "were drawn up under the leading of the renowned Ironside, and appointed to clap at his signals. . . . The Spectator never appeared in public with a worse grace. I remember Mr. Bickerstaff at the Playhouse, and with what a modest, decent gravity he behaved himself: Hence he was so well supported in his decline, and so heartily pitied at his death."

I delivered yours to Mr Newsham, and for y^{r} satisfaction I have inclosed his Answer und^{r} his owne hand, as you may the bett^{r} give me your directions therein.

I hope in a little time for to draw up yor an^{sw} whereby you may finde the value of yor Estate, and how all things are. I have sev^{ll} Count^{r} parts of Leases deliv^{d} me by Mrs Scurlock wch shall be delivered w^{n} sha^{l} fitt.

I shall be glad to hear w^{n} you intend for the Country.

A draft answer to this letter is among the Blenheim MSS.

March 21st, 171$\frac{2}{3}$,
BLOOMSBURY-SQUARE.

S^{R}

I have received yours of the 16th instant, with Mr Newsham's enclosed. I think he offers nothing to satisfaction. Be pleased to let him know that I think it no suitable return to the kind offer of forbearance I make to Him, that he will neither give up the land nor give Security for what is past. The first is in his power, tho He says the latter is not. Common Fame gives Lady Ann Vaughan to the Marquis of Winchester Son to the Duke of Bolton.[1] When we meet which will be, God willing, in the beginning of May, You will be able to advise me upon all matters relating to the neighbourhood, and the estate it self. I desire you would send me the date of the leases in your hands and for what time they are respectively given.

Probably about this time the question as to the settlement of the property was under consideration. Of this we obtain a glimpse from a somewhat petulant letter written by Mrs. Steele to her husband, now first printed. The paper, unfortunately, does not bear any date.[2]

MR STEELE

Tho in ye first Article of my proposall I seem to provide for futurity on Earth, yet I have many reasons to belive I sh'ant be long

[1] Lady Anne, daughter and heiress of John Vaughan, Earl of Carbery, duly married Charles, Marquis of Winchester, who became third Duke of Bolton in 1722. This was the nobleman who married, as his second wife, Miss Fenton, the actress who distinguished herself in the part of Polly Peacham in Gay's *Beggar's Opera*. He had three illegitimate sons by Miss Fenton, but as the first wife did not die, Miss Fenton had to wait many years before she could be made Duchess of Bolton. As the Duke had no legitimate issue by either wife, the title passed to his brother.

[2] The original of this letter is in the possession of Miss Mills.

a disturbance to you in y^{s} being therefore am resolv'd to show my inclination to Live Easie wth you ye time it may please God wee are together: As y^{u} reckon'd y^{u} Cleer'd y^{r} Concience by a publick demand of a settlement upon y^{r} Children: so I think I cleere mine by ye offer I now make in behalf of them wch differs but in one Article from what you proposed w^{n} Mrs Bynns &c: was present y^{t} is the power I reserve to my self of disposing of three thousand pounds by Will where I shall think fitt; this (wth submistion) I Insist upon without the least guilt of those mean or vicious reasons y^{u} wou'd insinuate, since providence has enabled me to behave my self as a Christian as well as a Rationall Creature in relation to you I hope he won't forsake me so far to permitt my acting Contrary to both these Characters, to punish my self, but I intend not to Enter into Argument least (in passion) I may be answar'd as severly in writing as I have been by Speech, I'm fix'd that if y^{u} Calmly Consider of this, & have any good opinion of, or kindness for mee, I shall have, only a letter of Aprobation in Answar to these, if I am so unhappy as to have no place in y^{r} best thoughts or affections, I must make my Self as Easie as I can, wth the bare sattisfaction of a good Concience which I trust in God will not be in the power of any thing to take from me

Who am Dear S^{r}, in all things reasonable
Y^{r} Obedient Wife

M. S.

What follows is on the fly-leaf of the letter:—

The following I call hints how to settle my Estate not yet knowing ye proper form, so desire to have no advantage taken of my ignorance, & expect to be allowed to amend w^{t} I may hereafter reckon Errors to my meaning.

Mr Steele & my Self to make over ye whole Estate to Trustees, for ye uses following, so securely y^{t} Mr Steele's debts present or futur may not touch it, to enable me by ye power of the trustees to receive it, till, by Examining my accounts they find I Act Contrary to the interest of the Children.

The Settlement.

First ye whole secured to me for my Life wth ye power of Leasing &c: as tis at present, by way of Joynter.

Then upon ye Eldest Son & heirs Male of Mr Steele & self to commence at the expiration of my Life, wth reserve of three thousand pounds for me to dispose of as I shall think fitt by Will made Either now or hereafter.

With charge of fifty pounds a year for each younger Child, during ye time of their Lives (to commence at the Expiration of my Life) as each of them dies to return to the Estate.

Perhaps the note of the 28th March given below was the letter of approbation which Mrs. Steele says she expected to receive from her husband. The letter immediately following relates to the same or some similar episode. What more was done as to the settlement of the property we do not know; there is no trace of any will having been made by Steele's "obedient wife,"—"in all things reasonable."

March 28th, 1713.

DEAR PRUE

I will do every thing you desire your own way.

Y^rs Ever RICHARD STEELE.

DEAR PRUE

I inclose to You y^r letter and think it needless to make any other answer than what is a very True one to y^r own Knowledge. I never deny'd You any thing in my power to give or do. When I had not money I have given promises to keep up y^r Spirits and keep you in good humour. I do not pretend to reply to the severe things you say to Me, because I never did nor ever will mean any thing but pleasing You, therefore, I hope you will continue to Love

Y^r Affectionate & Obedient Husband
RICHARD STEELE.

Steele seems to have been on sufficiently friendly terms with his wife when the next letters were written.

Ap. 22^d, 1713.

DEAR PRUE

I have met with Doggett[1] and We shall fall into a discourse which will turn to account. I shall dine with Him at some Eating

[1] Thomas Doggett, an author and an actor, who had, not long before the date of this letter, thrown up in disgust his office of joint-manager of Drury Lane Theatre, which he had some time held with Wilks and Cibber. By his frugality he secured a sufficient competence to retire from the hurry of business whilst in the height of his reputation. In political principles, to use the

House. If you will be exactly at five at Button's[1] We will go together to the Park or elsewhere and be with you all night, if you condescend to take me out of my Truckle-bed.

Y^rs^ Faithfully RICHARD STEELE.

May 5th, 1713, 9 in the Morning.

DEAR PRUE

I have sent Will to get a place in the Coach for your new Maid, and am going out to visit the Company I invited to Hampton-Court, to Know their resolution. Y^r^ Maid may be always with the Children. If the appointment holds, Ile send Will also this afternoon with further directions. I value a person you are fond of too much to ride late in the Evening therefore shall sett out my self early in the morning tomorrow.

Y^r^ Obedient Husband RICHARD STEELE.

words of Steele, he was "a Whig up to the head and ears;" and so strictly was he attached to the House of Hanover, that he never let slip any occasion that presented itself of demonstrating his sentiments in that respect. The year after George I. came to the throne, Doggett gave a waterman's coat and silver badge to be rowed for by six watermen on the 1st day of August, being the anniversary of the accession; and at his death bequeathed a certain sum of money, the interest of which was to be appropriated annually, for ever, to the purchase of a like coat and badge, to be rowed for in honour of the day. The ceremony continues to be annually performed; the claimants setting out on a signal given at that time of the tide when the current is strongest against them, and rowing from the Old Swan, near London Bridge, to the White Swan at Chelsea. [Nichols.

[1] The coffee-house in Russell Street, Covent Garden.

II.

ELECTION TO PARLIAMENT.

1713. ÆT. 41.

IN April Steele became more deeply involved in political controversies. In December the writer of the *Examiner* had stated that he was concerned with things, and not persons, but that as these were so closely connected he could not always avoid touching upon the latter. He would not, however, follow "those abominable precedents for scandal and calumny" to be found in the writings of the other party. In the number issued on April 24 he showed how far he would carry out in practice the principle of avoiding personalities. Lord Nottingham had been for some time constantly attacked by the Tory writers, especially under the name of "Dismal," because he had allied himself to the Whigs. Oldisworth, who was now conducting the *Examiner*, extended the attack to Lord Nottingham's daughter, Lady Charlotte Finch, afterwards Duchess of Somerset. "Thus," he said, "to instance in one of their late converts, no sooner was Dismal among the Whigs, and confirmed past retrieving, but Lady Char—te is taken knotting in St. James's Chapel, during Divine service, in the immediate presence both of God and Her Majesty, who were affronted together, that the family might appear to be entirely come over. I spare the beauty for the sake of her birth; but certainly there was no occasion for so public a proof, that her fingers are more dexterous in tying a knot than her father's brains in perplexing the Government." Steele's wrath was kindled at this miserable attack, for party purposes, upon the young lady, and in the *Guardian* for April 28 (No. 41) he warmly defended Lord Nottingham, and expressed in eloquent terms the indignation which every man of sense and honour must feel at the outrage on Lady Charlotte Finch. "Every man that hopes for a virtuous woman to his wife, that would defend his child, or protect his mistress, ought to receive this insolence as done to himself." "When due regard is not had to the honour of women," he added, "all human society is assaulted." The Examiner retorted by reminding the Guardian of personalities in the *Tatler*, but at the same time made some sort of apology for the attack on the lady. On the 12th May Steele replied in a letter bearing his own signature, published in the *Guardian* (No. 53). In the *Tatler* he had not, he said, fixed odious images on persons, but on vices; he had no occasion to draw people, whose actions he thought hurtful to his country, under feigned names. "I have wanted and abounded, and I neither fear poverty nor desire riches; if that be true, why should I be afraid, whenever I see occasion to examine the conduct of any of my fellow-subjects?" As regards the reports respecting the authorship of the *Examiner*, he said it was nothing to him whether the Examiner wrote against him in the character of "an estranged friend or an exasperated mistress;" by which epithets Steele meant, of course, to indicate Swift and Mrs. Manley.

On the day after this letter appeared in the *Guardian*, Swift wrote to Addison, complaining bitterly of Steele's conduct.

May 13, 1713.

SIR,

I was told yesterday, by several persons, that Mr. Steele had reflected upon me in his Guardian; which I could hardly believe, until, sending for the paper of the day, I found he had, in several parts of it, insinuated with the utmost malice, that I was author of the Examiner; and abused me in the grossest manner he could possibly invent, and set his name to what he had written. Now, Sir, if I am not author of the Examiner, how will Mr. Steele be able to defend himself from the imputation of the highest degree of baseness, ingratitude, and injustice? Is he so ignorant of my temper, and of my style? Has he never heard that the author of the Examiner (to whom I am altogether a stranger[1]) did, a month or two ago, vindicate me

[1] This is confirmed by Swift's *Journal* for March 12, 1713: "The chancellor of the exchequer sent the author of the *Examiner* twenty guineas. He is an ingenious fellow, but the most confounded coxcomb in the world, so that I dare not let him see me, nor am acquainted with him."

from having any concern in it?[1] Should not Mr. Steele have first expostulated with me as a friend? Have I deserved this usage from Mr. Steele, who knows very well that my Lord Treasurer has kept him in his employment upon my intreaty and intercession?

My Lord Chancellor[2] and Lord Bolingbroke will be witnesses how I was reproached by my Lord Treasurer, upon the ill returns Mr. Steele made to his Lordship's indulgence, &c. JON. SWIFT.

Addison seems to have simply sent on this letter to Steele, who replied on the 19th, candidly admitting that he still believed Swift to be an accomplice of the Examiner, and that he did not attach so much value to Swift's intervention on his behalf as Swift himself appeared to do. The letter ends with congratulations on Swift's preferment to the Deanery of St. Patrick's. This was certainly meant in all honestness, but it would only annoy Swift, who was bitterly disappointed at not having some better position given him. The Queen, however, had been implacable, and Swift had been obliged at length to accept the Dublin deanery, which he looked upon as banishment.

May 19, 1713.

SIR,

Mr. Addison shewed me your letter, wherein you mention me. They laugh at you, if they make you believe your interposition has kept me thus long in my office. If you have spoken in my behalf at any time, I am glad I have always treated you with respect: though I believe you an accomplice of the Examiner. In the letter you are angry at, you see I have no reason for being so merciful to him, but out of regard to the imputation you lie under. You do not in direct terms say you are not concerned with him; but make it an argument of your innocence, that the Examiner has declared you have nothing to do with him. I believe I could prevail upon the Guardian to say there was a mistake in putting my name in his paper; but the English would laugh at us, should we argue in so Irish a manner.

I am heartily glad of your being made Dean of St. Patrick's.

I am, Sir,

Your most obedient humble servant,

RICHARD STEELE.

[1] On February 9 the writer of the *Examiner* spoke of the efforts made to discover the author of the paper, and on March 23, while proud that such a mistake could be made, he declared that the gentleman charged with writing the paper was clear of that imputation.

[2] Harcourt.

Swift replied in a long and powerful letter, of which the original is imperfect. In it he repeated his assertions as to what he had done in Steele's behalf and as to the authorship of the *Examiner*, adding that before he gave up troubling about such things, he often struck out reflections upon Steele from papers that were brought to him.

Sir,

I may probably know better, when they are disposed. . . . The case was thus: I did, with the utmost application, and desiring to lay all my credit upon it, desire Mr. Harley (as he then was called) to shew you mercy. He said he would, and wholly upon my account: that he would appoint you a day to see him: that he would not expect you should quit any friend or principle. Some days after, he told me, he had appointed you a day, and you had not kept it; upon which he reproached me, as engaging for more than I could answer; and advised me to more caution another time. I told him, and desired my Lord Chancellor and Lord Bolingbroke to be witnesses, that I would never speak for or against you as long as I lived; only I would, and that it was still my opinion, you should have mercy till you gave farther provocations. This is the history of what you think fit to call, in the spirit of insulting, "their laughing at me:" and you may do it securely; for, by the most inhuman dealings, you have wholly put it out of my power, as a Christian, to do you the least ill office. Next I desire to know, whether the greatest services ever done by one man to another, may not have the same turn as properly applied to them? And, once more, suppose they did laugh at me, I ask whether my inclinations to serve you merit to be rewarded by the vilest treatment, whether they succeeded or no? If your interpretation were true, I was laughed at only for your sake; which, I think, is going pretty far to serve a friend. As to the letter I complain of, I appeal to your most partial friends, whether you ought not either to have asked, or written to me, or desired to have been informed by a third hand, whether I were any way concerned in writing the Examiner? And, if I had shuffled, or answered indirectly, or affirmed, or said, I would not give you satisfaction; you might then have wreaked your revenge with some colour of justice. I have several times assured Mr. Addison, and fifty others, that I had not the least hand in writing any of those papers; and that I had never exchanged one syllable with the supposed author in my life, that I can remember, nor even seen him above twice, and that in mixed company, in a place where he came to pay his attendance. One thing more I must observe to you, that, a year or two ago, when some printers used to bring me their papers in manuscript, I absolutely forbid them to give any hints against Mr. Addison and you, and some others; and have frequently struck out reflections upon you in particular, and should (I believe) have done it still, if I had not wholly left off troubling myself about those kind of things.

I protest, I never saw any thing more liable to exception, than every part is of the letter you were pleased to write me. You plead, that I do not, in mine to Mr. Addison, in direct terms, say I am not concerned with the Examiner. And is that an excuse for the most savage injuries in the world a week before? How far you can prevail with the Guardian, I shall not trouble myself to enquire; and am more concerned how you will clear your own honour and conscience than my reputation. I shall hardly lose one friend by what you. . . . I know not any . . . laugh at me for any . . . absurdity of yours. There are solecisms in morals as well as in languages; and to which of the virtues you will reconcile your conduct to me, is past my imagination. Be pleased to put these questions to yourself: 'If Dr. Swift be entirely innocent of what I accuse him, how shall I be able to make him satisfaction? and how do I know but he may be entirely innocent? If he was laughed at only because he solicited for me, is that sufficient reason for me to say the vilest things of him in print, under my hand, without any provocation? And how do I know but he may be in the right, when he says I was kept in my employment at his interposition? If he never once reflected on me the least in any paper, and hath hindered many others from doing it, how can I justify myself, for endeavouring in mine to ruin his credit as a Christian and a clergyman?'[1]

I am, Sir,

Your most obedient humble servant,

JON. SWIFT.

The *Examiner* of May 22 contained a long criticism of the *Guardian* for May 12, which was not without point. The few

[1] This is an allusion to the passage in the *Guardian*, No. 41, where Steele, after quoting what the *Examiner* said about Lady Charlotte Finch knotting "in the immediate presence of God and her majesty," remarked, "It is very visible which of those powers (that he has put together) he is the more fearful of offending." Steele also called the *Examiner* a miscreant; but in No. 53 of the *Guardian* he expressed his sorrow for having used this word, which "I think signifies an unbeliever."

words preceding Steele's letter in the *Guardian* were obviously open to attack. "It is not my business to enquire how fond Mr. Steele may be of his own company, how much he will leave to his children, or whether he will be turned out or no; a circumstance that mankind ought to be as indifferent to as himself, 'who knows how to want and to abound,' or if he pleases, 'to abound and to want,' with that decency, which has furnished so considerable and diverting a part of his private history." Further on Steele is blamed for what he insinuated about Mrs. Manley, for the weakness of the excuse made for having called the Examiner a miscreant, for the personalities in the *Tatler*, and for the open defiance of the Ministry. Steele's reply was published in the *Guardian* for the following day (No. 63). The answer to Swift's letter is interesting, but did not help matters forward. Steele thought that the statement in the *Examiner* that Addison had "bridled him in point of party" must have emanated from Swift.

BLOOMSBURY, May 26, 1713.

SIR,

I have received yours, and find it is impossible for a man to judge in his own case. For an allusion to you, as one under the imputation of helping the Examiner, and owning I was restrained out of respect to you, you tell Addison, under your hand, you think me the vilest of mankind, and bid him tell me so. I am obliged to you for any kind things said in my behalf to the Treasurer; and assure you, when you were in Ireland, you were the constant subject of my talk to men in power at that time. As to the vilest of mankind, it would be a glorious world if I were: for I would not conceal my thoughts in favour of an injured man, though all the powers on earth gainsaid it, to be made the first man in the nation. This position, I know, will ever obstruct my way in the world; and I have conquered my desires accordingly. I have resolved to content myself with what I can get by my own industry, and the improvement of a small estate, without being anxious whether I am ever in a Court again or not. I do assure you, I do not speak this calmly, after the ill usage in your letter to Addison, out of terror of your wit, or my Lord Treasurer's power; but pure kindness to the agreeable qualities I once so passionately delighted in in you.

You know, I know nobody but one that talked after you could tell

"Addison had bridled me in point of party." This was ill hinted, both with relation to him, and,

Sir,

Your most obedient humble servant,

RICH. STEELE.

Next day Swift closed the correspondence. He was, he said, leaving for Ireland, and might never see Steele again. He explicitly denied the last charge made against him.

May 27, 1713.

SIR,

The reason I give you the trouble of this reply to your letter, is because I am going in a very few days to Ireland: and although I intended to return towards winter, yet it may happen, from the common accidents of life, that I may never see you again.

In your yesterday's letter, you are pleased to take the complaining side, and think it hard I should write to Mr. Addison as I did, only for an allusion. This allusion was only calling a clergyman of some little distinction an infidel; a clergyman, who was your friend, who always loved you, who had endeavoured at least to serve you; and who, whenever he did write any thing, made it sacred to himself never to fling out the least hint against you.

One thing you are pleased to fix on me, as what you are sure of; that the Examiner had talked after me, when he said, "Mr. Addison had bridled you in point of party." I do not read one in six of those papers, nor ever knew he had such a passage; and I am so ignorant of this, that I cannot tell what it means: whether, that Mr. Addison kept you close to a party, or that he hindered you from writing about party. I never talked or writ to that author[1] in my life; so that he could not have learned it from me. And, in short, I solemnly affirm, that, with relation to every friend I have, I am as innocent as it is possible for a human creature to be. And, whether you believe me or not, I think, with submission, you ought to act as if you believed me, till you have demonstration to the contrary. I have all the Ministry to be my witnesses, that there is hardly a man of wit of the adverse party, whom I have not been so bold as to recommend often and with earnestness to them; for I think principles at present are quite out of the case, and that we dispute wholly about persons.[2] In

[1] *I.e.*, the writer of the *Examiner*.

[2] Steele says, "I thought it was the shortest way to impartiality, to put myself beyond farther hopes or fears, by declaring myself at a time when the dispute is not about persons and parties, but things and causes" (*Tatler*, No. 193).

these last you and I differ; but in the other, I think, we agree: for I have in print professed myself in politics to be what we formerly called a Whig.

As to the great man[1] whose defence you undertake; though I do not think so well of him as you do, yet I have been the cause of preventing five hundred hard things being said against him.

I am sensible I have talked too much when myself is the subject: therefore I conclude with sincere wishes for your health and prosperity, and am, Sir,

Your, &c.

JON. SWIFT.

You cannot but remember, that, in the only thing I ever published with my name, I took care to celebrate you as much as I could,[2] and in as handsome a manner as I could, though it was in a letter to the present Lord Treasurer.

On the 1st June, Swift left London to take up his duties in Dublin. Every writer upon Steele or Swift must regret that Swift's last weeks in England were embittered by controversy, but the question as to who was in fault will probably always be answered in different ways according to the bias of the writer. I agree entirely with what Mr. Dobson has said upon the matter. The quarrels of old friends are notorious for their bitterness; every real or fancied affront or grievance is magnified by a comparison with the past, and a consciousness that the fault does not all rest with the other side often adds to the feeling of soreness. Each sees, too, in what is said by the other, allusions to things which would not have been known had there not previously been such confidential relations between hem. We cannot wonder that Steele found it difficult to believe that Swift had no connection with the *Examiner*. His name was constantly joined to the paper, and if he was not personally acquainted with the writer, we have his own admission that he assisted that writer with hints at least as recently as January.[3] The active part which Swift had taken in the

[1] The Duke of Marlborough.

[2] In his *Proposal for Correcting the English Tongue.*

[3] "I gave the Examiner a hint about this prorogation, and to praise the queen for her tenderness to the Dutch, in giving them still more time to submit" (*Journal to Stella*, January 15, 1713). These hints were duly used in the *Examiner* published on the following day: "Her Majesty is all goodness and

war of pamphlets was, too, notorious, and his complaint that Steele ought to have known by the style that certain papers were not his loses any point it might have had when we remember that Swift wrote in the most various of manners, sometimes only "two degrees above Grub Street," as he himself puts it.

The *Examiner* urged that Steele should be deprived of his office, and there were reports that the commission was already passing without his name in it. Steele had, however, decided to resign his office, in order that he might enter Parliament, and on the 4th June he announced his intention in a characteristic letter to Lord Oxford. Of this important letter there are two rough drafts among the Blenheim MSS., and it is interesting to compare them with the letter as it was ultimately written. The first draft is as follows; the notes show the principal alterations made while writing it.

STAMP-OFFICE, May 23d
1713.

MY LORD

I should be wanting to my self[1] if I did not give your Lord ship some account of my self, who having the honour of sitting at this board, under your direction, have uttered expressions[2] in the Guardian which I cannot but suppose would be something unacceptable to you.

I do assure you I have the greatest abhorrence imaginable of being serviceable to the opinions or prejudices of Party, and it is wholly indifferent to me with regard to my private, on whome favour[3] is bestowed, but shall always, with great deference follow it with all my good Wishes and Services, when that obsequiousnesse[4] is consistent with the Welfare of my Countrey, and the Honour due to persons who have eminently and faithfully served it.[5]

tenderness to her people and her Allies. . . . She has now prorogued the best Parliament that ever assembled in her reign, and respited her own glory, and the wishes, prayers and wants of her people, only to give some of her Allies an opportunity to think of the returns they owe her, and try if there be such a thing as gratitude, justice, or humanity in Europe," &c.

[1] The words first written were, "I begg the fa"; these were then cancelled, and "I should want sense of Decency" substituted; finally this was altered as shown in the text.

[2] "delivered my" first written.

[3] "the Royall favour" first written.

[4] "when I think it" first written.

[5] "who have served it with fidelity and success" first written.

The Examiner in this last particular has given so great Offence that I could not, without valuing what consequences it[1] may have upon my own affairs, endeavoured [*sic*] to obviate the Force of his detraction[2] from the Duke of Marlborough and others of the late Ministrey. It is possible I have in doing this spoken with less Reverence[3] of the present. Would it not diminish the good opinion of any Impartiall man, to see gentlemen who have the Administration of the greatest Empire in the world, ungenrously suffer a Writer[4] with an Air of being in their interests and Confidence traduce all who have been in power before them? Losse of Office and favour is misfortune enough to those who are affected with the enjoyments[5] of glory and Riches without the aggravation of being loaden with Calumnies and reproaches?[6]

I hope I have kept within bounds of my Duty in Gainsaying such unworthy treatment of great men in the Examiner and demanding of those in authority to animadvert upon Him for it. Thus far I thought fit to say in Justification of my behaviour as I am a Commissioner Here, but separate from that Quality, I cannot accuse my self of any thing liable to Exception in what I have said. I have done it[7] from no other motive in nature but the Love of Truth; But, my Lord, this is not the matter[8] for which I principally tooke the liberty of Writing to you. The cheif cause of this addresse was in the Humblest manner to thank you for the favour of assuring me I should be in the next commission for the management of these Duties, and to desire I may be left out. I tell your Lordship frankly my reason[9] for this, is that I hope to be in the ensuing Parliament, of which Honour a Commissioner, Here, is incapable. Whatever Turn or colour my life is to take you will find me, instead of what may be insinuated to you, in all points wherein I do not beleive you too enterprising, to my utmost instrumentall to any Just and great designs, Which you shall

[1] "let it have what consequences it will" first written.

[2] "Calumni" first written.

[3] "spoken without much veneration for the present; If it be so I am sure without Irreverently" first written.

[4] "permit a Writer in a way declarative of their approbation and connivance traduce" first written.

[5] "applause" first written.

[6] The ensuing words, which originally followed here, were cancelled: "This is one of the greatest causes of Exception which I have had against publick management."

[7] "with an Heart void of any motive" originally written.

[8] "whole matter" originally written.

[9] "design" first written.

undertake for the good of Your Countrey.[1] I begg pardon that I speake as a man of moderate desires and without much hope[2] or fear, and with the reserve of differing where We may dissent in what is for the good of our Countrey. I sincerely wish you all prosperity and am,

My Lord,
Yr Lordship's Most Obedient
and Most Humble Servant
RICHARD STEELE.

This first draft was, it will be seen, entirely recast before the letter was finally written. On the 4th June a second draft was prepared, and on the same day the letter was despatched. The following is the letter itself, with notes showing the principal points in which it differed from the second draft.[3]

June 4th, 1713,
BLOOMSBURY SQUARE.

MY LORD

I presume to give your Lordship this trouble to acquaint you that[4] having an Ambition to Serve in the ensuing Parliament I humbly desire your Lordship will please to accept of my resignation of my[5] office as Commissioner of the Stamp-Revenue. I should have done this sooner, but that I heard the Commission was passing without my name in it, and I would not be guilty of the Arrogance of resigning what[6] I could not hold. But having heard this, since, contradicted, I am obliged to give it up, as with all Humility I do by this present Writing. Give me Leave to say something on this occa-

1 "With that reserve I sincerely wish you all prosperity and am" originally written.

2 "strong hopes" originally written.

3 The original of this letter is in the Lansdowne MSS., 1236, in the British Museum. In some points the letter as printed in the *Apology* in 1714 follows this second and unsigned draft where the draft and the signed letter differ.

4 "I have an inclination to be chosen in the ensuing," "having resolved, if I can," written successively in the draft and obliterated.

5 "Commission in the Stamp-office" in draft. The following words are cancelled in the draft: "I desire to have my name omitted in the ensuing commission for managing the Stamp Revenue. Whatever may have been insinuated to your Lordship, you will find, if I should succeed in my design of going into Parliament, me very far from a man inclined to be dissatisfyed with."

6 "what I knew I could not hold" in draft. The following words in the letter, down to "occasion," are not in the draft.

sion as to my late conduct with relation to those in former power,[1] and to assure your Lordship, that whatever I have done, said or writ has proceeded from no other motive, but the Love of, what I think, Truth. For merely as to my own affairs I could not wish any man in the administration of the publick[2] rather than yourself who favour[3] those who become your dependants with a greater liberality of Heart, than any man I have ever before observed. When I had the honour of a short conversation with you, you were pleased not only to signifie to me that I should remain in this Office, but to add that if I would name to you one of more value which would be more commodious to me, you would favour me in it.[4] I am going out of any particular dependance on your Lordship,[5] and will tell you with the freedome of an indifferent man, that it is impossible for any one who thinks and has any publick[6] Spirit,[7] not to tremble at seeing His Countrey in its present circumstances, in the hands of so daring a Genius as yours. If incidents should arise that should place your own safety, and (what Ambitious men call) Greatnesse, in a ballance against the publick[8] Good, our All depends upon your choice under such a temptation. You have my Hearty[9] prayers to Heaven to[10] avert all such dangers from you.[11] I thank your Lordship for the distinction you[12] have at sundry times showed me, and wish you with yr Countrey's Safety all Happinesse and prosperity. Share, my Lord, your good fortune with whome you will. While[13] it lasts you will want no Freinds, but if an Adverse day happens[14] to you, and I live to see it, you will find I think myself obliged to be your Freind and your Advocate. This is talking in a strange Dialect[15] from a Private man[16]

[1] "with relation to the late men in power, whatever," &c., in draft.

[2] "in power" altered to "in the administration" in draft.

[3] "favour your dependants" in draft.

[4] The following words were in the draft, but were obliterated: "I have My Lord no more reason to be against you than Brutus had to kill Caesar."

[5] "out of your dependance" in draft.

[6] "independant" obliterated.

[7] "for a thinking man who loves His Countrey" first written in draft, but obliterated.

[8] "Generall" in draft.

[9] "and fervent" in draft.

[10] "direct your Heart aright and" in draft, but cancelled.

[11] "and I solemnly swear to you that if it lay in my power to do you any Service" in draft, but obliterated.

[12] "for the regard and distinction which you" in draft.

[13] "and while" in draft.

[14] "ever happens" in draft.

[15] "language" obliterated.

[16] "from such a one" in draft, but cancelled.

to the first of a nation, but to desire only a little exalts a man's condition to a levell with those who want a great deal. But I begg your Lordship's pardon and am, with great respect,

My Lord,
Y^r^ Lordshipp's[1] most obedient and
most humble Servant
RICHARD STEELE.

Notwithstanding this application Steele's name was included in the Commission appointed on the 12th June, but on the 30th July Steele wrote to the Earl of Oxford, asking that his surrender of his position at the Stamp Office might be made good. The letter is endorsed "Mr Steel may make a Surrend^r^."[2]

July 30, 1713,
BLOOMSBURY-SQUARE.

MY LORD

I trouble your Lordship with this to signifie to you, that with all Humility I entreat your Lordship a new Commission of the Stamp-Office may be issued, and my name left out of the Patent, or that in any other way your Lordship shall think fitt this my Surrender to her Majesty, as to my part of the said Commission, may be made and deemed good.

I am, my Lord,
Y^r^ Lordships most Obedient
and most Humble Servant
RICHARD STEELE.

About the same time Steele resigned his pension as servant to the late Prince George, and was therefore able to repel the charge brought against him that he was receiving a salary from those whom he attacked.[3] During June he wrote, or edited, most of the *Guardians*, but from the 1st July to the 7th August the paper seems to have been left entirely to Addison, with occasional assistance from other writers. Steele's correspond-

[1] Here the draft ends.

[2] Treasury Papers, Public Record Office, vol. 163, No. 27. Steele's successor was Charles Vivian, Esq., who was appointed at the beginning of January 1714 (Patent Rolls, 4th Part, 12 Anne, 19; 3rd Part, 12 Anne 4. Pointer, ii. 736; *Post-Boy*, January 7 to 9, 1713–14).

[3] *Importance of Dunkirk Considered.* Benjamin Victor (*Original Letters*, &c., i. 347–351) says that when Steele resigned his employment he had received but two quarters' salary.

ence during this summer does not throw any very material light upon his more private life. Towards the end of May, John Scurlock, Mrs. Steele's uncle, wrote to Steele about the Pibur estate,[1] and from the latter portion of the letter it would appear that Steele had some idea of going down to Wales at this time.

May 25, 1713.

DEAR SIR,

I am informed that you have been threatened in the purchase and possession of Pibur (an estate of 80*l.* a-year). Give me leave to assure you, that you are not in any manner of danger; and that Pibur does not lie on the same footing with the rest of Browne's estate; but much prior to that. My father was well advised when he bought it; therefore you may be easy: it is about 60 years ago.

I am impatient to know the certainty of yours and your lady's coming to the country. Pray give my service to her; and be pleased to let me know when or what week you intend to set out for Wales; and you will thereby very much oblige, good Sir,

Your affectionate kinsman,
and humble servant, whilst
JOHN SCURLOCK.[2]

Steele's letters to his wife are of the usual kind, and contain obscure allusions to the Barbados property, and to a meeting with certain Whig Lords, arranged by Addison. "Since the death of my poor Mother, I find a growing melancholy increase upon me; but hope for every happiness in you."[3]

In June judgment was given in the only action for debt

[1] See pp. 172, and 201 note.

[2] Directed "For Richard Steele, esq. at his house in Bloomsbury-square, London."

[3] Who Mr. Christopher Philips was who is mentioned in the following note, which was in the possession of the late Mr. A. Preston, does not appear. Mr. Warner may be the same as the Mr. Warner who was godfather to Eugene Steele.

July 25th, 1713.

SR

Pray pay to Mr. Christopher Philips twenty guinneas for, Sr,

Your Most Humble Servant,
RICHARD STEELE.

To Mr Warner & Snow.

which appears to have been brought against Steele in 1713. The complainant was Edward Minshull, Esq., the Mr. Minshull whom Steele not long afterwards consulted in writing the *Crisis*. In the bill brought before the Court of Queen's Bench in June, Mr. Minshull stated that on the 1st of that month, in the parish of St. Clement Danes, he had accommodated Steele with the sum of £250, to be paid when required. But the money had not been paid, and damages of £20 were claimed. Steele's attorney, James Tully, did not answer the plea, and judgment was therefore given for the complainant, with 63s. for damages which he had sustained.[1]

The peace concluded at Utrecht on the 31st March was proclaimed on the 5th May, and on the 1st July the Duc d'Aumont, the French ambassador, made his public entry into London. Upon the occasion of his last visit to England, in January, he had been cheered by the mob as long as he threw money broadcast; but afterwards, when the fancy of the crowd had veered round, his house was burnt under suspicious circumstances, and he had to be accommodated in Somerset House, with a double guard. But now he was brought in Her Majesty's barges from Gravesend to the Tower, and thence driven in great state to Somerset House, the place appointed for his entertainment. The procession included thirty of the ambassador's footmen, walking two by two; four Swissers, twelve pages, &c., on horseback; the ambassador, in the Queen's state coach; a second Queen's coach; five of the ambassador's coaches drawn by eight horses each, with four others drawn by six; and a numerous train of coaches of the nobility, Ministers, and others, of six horses each. To view this pageant Steele took his wife to Mr. Hoole's, a stationer, next door to Ludgate Church. The ambassador's liveries were magnificent, and the pages and others all had white feathers in their hats. The streets and houses along the route were much crowded, and the Duc d'Aumont

[1] Queen's Bench Judgment Roll, 12 Anne. Trinity, 47. In 1713–15, "Edward Minshull, Esq., of St. James's, Westminster, heretofore of Stoke, Co. Chester," was involved in Chancery suits against his sister Dorothy and members of their mother's family about property left by their father (Chancery Pleadings, Woodford, 1714–58, No. 960, Minshull *v.* Mackworth, and No. 1175, Minshull *v.* Minshull).

threw handfuls of money among the people in all the streets through which he passed.

The ninth Article of the Treaty of Utrecht said that "the most Christian King shall take care that all the fortifications of the City of Dunkirk be razed, that the harbour be filled up, and that the sluices or moles which serve to cleanse the harbour be levelled, and that at the said King's own expense, within the space of five months after the conditions of peace are concluded and signed; that is to say, the fortifications towards the sea within the space of two months, and those towards the land, together with the said banks, within three months; on this express condition also, that the said fortification, harbour, moles or sluices be never repaired again. All which shall not however be begun to be ruined, till after everything is put into his Christian Majesty's hands which is to be given him instead thereof, or as an equivalent." It was currently reported that the Ministry intended to ignore this and other Articles in the Treaty. On the 3rd June the Commons addressed the Queen, asking what was the equivalent the French King was to have for Dunkirk, and on the 20th the Queen sent a message, that in pursuance of the treaties between France and this country and the States, the equivalent to be given for the demolition of Dunkirk was already in the hands of his most Christian Majesty.

Naturally many members were dissatisfied with this answer. On the 4th July the Duc d'Aumont, who just a year before had been Governor of Dunkirk when that town was, by order of Lewis the Fourteenth, given up to the English under Brigadier Hill, had a public audience of the Queen at St. James's; and about the same time M. Tugghe, the Deputy from the Dunkirk magistrates, presented to the Queen an address or memorial, praying that the harbour and port of the town might be spared. Bolingbroke replied that the Queen beheld with sorrow the damages which the inhabitants of the town would sustain by the demolition of its ramparts and harbour; but that she did not think it convenient to make any alteration in a thing agreed upon and determined by a treaty. M. Tugghe then presented a second address to the Queen, praying that the moles and dykes which formed and kept up the harbour alone might be preserved, in order that the people might not be deprived of their subsistence. This address was printed and circulated widely among the people,[1] by express authority of an agent of the Ministers, according to Toland; by the Whigs, according to Swift; and it was at this stage that Steele intervened, and published in the *Guardian* for the 7th August (No. 128) a strong protest against the memorial, which he considered was so daring and traitorous that he did not care what misinterpretation he suffered by exposing it.[2] In the letter, which forms the greater part of this number of the *Guardian*, Steele dwelt upon the fact that the Queen had not pronounced sentence against Dunkirk, but that the French King had agreed by treaty that the town and harbour should be demolished; and he added, and this he repeated thrice, that "the British nation expects the demolition of Dunkirk."

This outspoken declaration of course brought down upon Steele's head all the abuse of which Tory writers were capable. On the 14th August[3] appeared a pamphlet called *The Honour and Prerogative of the Queen's Majesty Vindicated and Defended against the Unexampled Insolence of the Author of the Guardian: In a Letter from a Country Whig to Mr. Steele.* The writer of this tract—said at the time to be Mrs. Manley[4]—commenced by remarking that among his neighbours in the country it had been the habit, when political discussion grew too warm, for some of the party to say, "Adjourn your debate till you have more temper; come, let us read the *Guardian;*" and so the storm would be allayed, though they knew very well that the greatest part of the wit and humour in the paper was not

[1] "July 30. Yesterday a paper was given gratis about the streets, intitled A most humble Address or Memorial," &c. (*Flying Post*, July 28 to 30, 1713).

[2] In a letter to Lord Macclesfield, of the 6th June 1716, William Moore, the lawyer who suggested to Steele the publication of the *Crisis*, said that he went to Steele with the Memorial of the Sieur Tugghe, showed it to Steele, and then sat down and wrote with him the *Guardian* about Dunkirk. Moore added that he wrote several of the *Englishmen*, and asked Lord Macclesfield to recommend him for a Commissionership of Forfeited Estates (Somerville's *History of Great Britain during the Reign of Queen Anne*, 1798, pp. 653–55).

[3] *Examiner*, August 10 to 14, 1713; Advertisement.

[4] Boyer's *Political State*, September 1713, p. 140.

Steele's, and that he was not always an exemplification of the morals he recommended. But all this harmony had now been destroyed by the paper of the 7th August; the Tories said, "See how the villain treats the best of sovereigns, the best mistress to him, whose bread he has eaten, and who has kept him from a gaol!" The Queen was addressed just as an imperious planter of Barbados would speak to a negro slave. Orders had been given, said this writer, that the *Guardian* was never more to be received into the town; and he concluded by urging that Steele should let the honest people of Stockbridge know how the gentleman they were asked to choose as their representative had treated the Queen, in "justice to your country, which you have shown great inclination to serve in other cases," "though I know your election is necessary to you, to protect you from your just debts, which you are or might be able enough to pay."

On the day after this pamphlet was published Steele went to Stockbridge, Hants, and on the 25th August was duly elected member for that borough,[1] which had been possessed of a charter since 1692. One account of the place said that the number of voters was about seventy; "the population chiefly consists of cobblers. It's a very wet town, and the voters are wet too. The ordinary price of a vote is £60, but better times may come."[2] Seventy-one votes seem to have been given when Steele was elected.[3] Gay wrote, in his *Journey to Exeter*:—

"Sutton we quit, and leave her spacious town,
And with the setting sun reach Stockbridge town.
Sad melancholy every visage wears:
What, no Election come in seven long years!
Of all our race of mayors shall Snow alone
Be by Sir Richard's dedication known,

[1] *Return of Members of Parliament*, Part ii., 1878. There is a well-known anecdote of the way in which Steele gained the interest of the women at this election. The story is told, with variations, in a letter from Lord Perceval to Charles Dering, dated March 27, 1722, in the Earl of Egmont's collection.

[2] "*Stock* at the *Bridge* formerly was at an hundred, is now near 500. We are informed that Mr. Nestor, alias Birmingham Iron-side, designs to make a Guardian upon the Nature and Usefulness of Bribery" (*Post-Boy*, September 3 to 5, 1713).

[3] *Guardian*, September 23, 1713.

No more her streets with tides of ale shall float,
Nor cobblers live for seven years on a vote!"

And Defoe, in his *Tour through the whole Island of Great Britain*, says: "Returning to Winchester we struck up North West and came to Stockbridge, a poor sorry borough town, noted for its corruption in electing Members of Parliament, two of whom it returns." From all which it is evident that even in those days Stockbridge enjoyed a specially bad name. On the 31st August Pope wrote to Caryll: "Mr. Steele, you know, has carried his election, though it is said a petition will be lodged against him, and he is of that opinion himself. Some people say, that passage in Scripture may be applied to him upon the resignation of his place, 'I have left all and have followed you;' but whether or no 'his reward will therefore be great' is hard to determine. I made him my compliments in wishing he might become a pensioner."[1]

[1] Steele was only indirectly concerned in the relations existing between Pope and Addison at this time; it will be enough to say here that Pope had seized the opportunity afforded by a bitter attack made by Dennis upon *Cato* to publish a very coarse piece, called *Dr. Norris's Account Concerning the Strange and Deplorable Frenzy of John Dennis*. The sole object of this pamphlet was to revenge himself for what Dennis had said of Pope's own poems; in fact, as Pope himself put it in a letter to Addison, dated July 20, 1713—a letter, by the way, concocted from one written to Caryll on November 19, 1712—it was published "not in defence of you, but in contempt of him." Addison saw at once the cause of Pope's zeal, and commissioned Steele to write to Lintot, the publisher of Dennis's remarks on *Cato*.

Aug. 4, 1713.

MR. LINTOT,

Mr. Addison desired me to tell you, that he wholly disapproves the manner of treating Mr. Dennis, in a little pamphlet by way of Dr. Norris's Account. When he thinks fit to take notice of Mr. Dennis's objections to his writings, he will do it in a way Mr. Dennis shall have no just reason to complain of. But when the papers above mentioned were offered to be communicated to him, he said he could not, either in honour or conscience, be privy to such a treatment, and was sorry to hear of it.

I am, Sir,

Your very humble servant,

RICH. STEELE.

Lintot gave this letter to Dennis, who printed it in 1729. In 1728 Dennis stated that it was Pope himself who, jealous of the success of *Cato*, went to Lintot and persuaded him to engage Dennis to write an attack upon Addison,

On the 21st August the *Examiner*, in the course of a paper about ambition, and its offspring ingratitude, remarked that no more flagrant example of the latter had gone unpunished than the way in which the Guardian—a subject, a servant under a salary, and favoured in spite of past ill behaviour with a considerable employment in the government—had treated the Queen. The very name and memory of this contemptible wretch should be trampled under foot; and yet his conduct had made him dearer than ever to the Whigs, who were endeavouring to get him chosen for Parliament, so that he might "obtain the honour, as another of their haughty leaders has already done, *of being expelled the House.*" Thus early did coming events cast their shadows before them. In the next number the *Examiner* asked why Dunkirk should be demolished *just now*, as the Guardian insolently demanded in his "seditious libel." On the 12th September another Tory pamphlet appeared: *Reasons Concerning the Immediate Demolishing of Dunkirk: Being a Serious Enquiry into the State and Condition of that Affair.* The author of this somewhat lengthy work, in which the whole question is gravely argued, said that the writer in the *Guardian* who told the Government that the British nation expected Dunkirk should be immediately demolished, was guilty of insolence, falsehood, sedition, and absurdity; but that as this man, who was thought to be a gentleman, promised himself to be a Member of Parliament, that honourable House would no doubt do justice in the case when he came before them. Here again, it will be seen, was an intimation of how it was proposed by the Tories to deal with Steele in the House of Commons. On the 13th, too, the day

and Pope did not deny this charge. It is, moreover, to be remembered that on the 17th October 1713 Pope had disclaimed the authorship of *Dr. Norris's Account*, in a letter to Caryll, and this in spite of what is said in the fabricated letter to Addison of July 20, 1713, a letter which Pope republished in the acknowledged 1737 edition of his Correspondence, with a note that the defence of Addison which he wrote was this very "Narrative." It was upon the strength, chiefly, of the letter to Caryll of October 1713 that Mr. Dilke thought Pope did not write *Dr. Norris's Account*, and suggested that Steele was the author. Dennis and Cromwell were both old antagonists of his, and Cromwell is satirised in the "Narrative" (*Papers of a Critic*, i. 100–104, 253–265; but cf. *Athenæum*, May 15, 1858).

after this pamphlet appeared, Peter Wentworth wrote to his brother: "I hear of a bite that is design'd the Guardian Steele, who as he thought had resign'd his place before he stood for a member; but it seems he has not, for the Commission is not alter'd, nor will not be till after he's turn'd out of the house, and then may be he may have leave to resign."[1] As a matter of fact, Steele's successor at the Stamp Office was appointed some weeks before Parliament met. On the 18th September the *Examiner* remarked that he answered those Whig writers who would push him into an engagement with the *Guardian:* "I design to meddle with my match."

In the meantime Steele had been defended in several pamphlets, and among them in one written by John Toland in reply to the "pick-thank pamphlet," by a "mercenary wretch," entitled *Reasons Concerning the Immediate Demolishing of Dunkirk.* The nature of Toland's pamphlet is sufficiently explained in the title, *Dunkirk or Dover:* "Or, The Queen's Honour, the Nation's Safety, the Liberties of Europe, and the Peace of the World, all at stake till that Fort and Port be totally Demolished by the French." There was also a folio half-sheet entitled, *A Letter to the Guardian about Dunkirk,*[2] with which Steele seems to have been much pleased. The writer of this Letter wondered how it would please the Town to say that the nation did *not* now *expect* that Dunkirk should be demolished. The use of words was wonderfully changed, and no one should be surprised at hearing that to Expect signified to fire a blunderbuss at several great Lords, nay, even to commit high treason; Demolishing may signify keeping, and Five Months may signify Five Years, or longer if convenient. The borough of Stockbridge was to be congratulated on its member; the nation expected that he should be zealous for her religion, for her honour and for her trade. "Let your friend come out but as honest as

[1] *Wentworth Papers*, 354.

[2] A copy of this piece is bound in at the end of vol. ii. of the Newspapers for 1713 in the Burney collection at the British Museum. Steele was also defended in pieces reprinted in *Letters and Poems on Political Subjects. Written by a hearty Whig*, 1716, pp. 2, 6. In one letter it is stated that a very fine "polianto," "to be seen at Mrs. Eager's, an eminent florist at the Star and Garter in Greenwich," had been named the *Captain Steele.*

he goes in, and I can wish no better to him, or Stockbridge, or my country." On the 7th September Colonels Armstrong and Clayton, who had been appointed Commissioners to see the fortifications of Dunkirk demolished and razed, set out for that place, and on the 26th the demolition was commenced. On the 14th September Addison said in the *Guardian* that he wrote with fear and trembling ever since the Examiner in his little pamphlet had found treason in the word "expect." "But I shall, for the future, leave my friend to manage the controversy in a separate work, being unwilling to fill with disputes a paper which was undertaken purely out of good will to my countrymen." Accordingly, on the 22nd September, Steele published, as a quarto pamphlet, *The Importance of Dunkirk Considered: In Defence of the Guardian of August the 7th*, 1713. *In a Letter to the Bailiff of Stockbridge;* and on the following day printed a letter in the *Guardian*, explaining why he addressed the work to the Bailiff of Stockbridge, "who allowed that fifty was a greater number than one and twenty, and returned me accordingly to serve for that borough." He added that he had turned the scurrilous things said against him to his advantage by quoting them at large, and so swelling the volume to the price of a shilling.

In his pamphlet Steele printed M. Tugghe's Memorial, and answered its arguments in full; and he also quoted extracts from the various pamphlets on both sides, to which we have already referred, and did not omit to clear himself of the charge of ingratitude, by declaring that he had resigned his office and pension before writing the letter to the *Guardian*. He was no enemy to the prerogative: "These writers shall treat me as they think fit, as I am their brother-scribbler; but I shall not be so unconcerned when they attack me as an honest man." It was said that a man of so small a fortune as he must have secret views or supports, or he would not have left his employments and lost a crowd of well-wishers to subject himself to the hatred of many who had before had a partiality towards him; to which Steele replied that he had particular views, and was animated in his conduct by charity. "Great qualifications are not praises to the possessor, but from the application of them. . . . He is but a poor creature who cannot bear being odious in the service of virtue. Riches and honours can administer to the heart no pleasure like what an honest man feels when he is contending for the interests of his country and the civil rights of his fellow-subjects. . . . The highest pleasure of the human soul consists in this charity, and there is no way of making it so diffusive as by contending for liberty. . . . When a man has deeply planted such a sentiment as this for the rule of his conduct, the pursuits of avarice and ambition will become as contemptible as the sports of children." He knew that prostituted pens would entertain one who pretended to remove the prejudice which Englishman has against Englishman, and to reconcile wounded brethren, with a recital of his own faults and infirmities; but for this he was well prepared. "It is the disgrace of literature that there are such instruments, and to good government that they are suffered." These pamphleteers attacked even friends if they did not act with as sincere a prejudice as themselves. And so, with warm praise of the Queen—who, however, was compelled to act by the information of others—the pamphlet closed.

III.

"THE ENGLISHMAN."

1713. ÆT. 41.

THE immediate replies to the *Importance of Dunkirk Considered* do not call for any detailed notice. The *Examiner*, which was full of the matter, said that Steele had obliged his party with a very awkward pamphleteer, in the room of an excellent droll, and then attacked "the impious Toland," "once the butt of the *Tatler*, but now in high favour with Mr. Steele." A lengthy paper concludes: "I know of no person yet named for the *Examiner* to whom Mr. Steele is not obliged, as a wit; or who has not tried to reform both his morals and politics." This and subsequent passages were soon to be discussed by Steele in a new periodical. Berkeley wrote to Sir John Perceval, on the 2nd October: "Mr. Steele having laid down his employment because (as he says) he wou'd not be obliged to those to whom he could not be gratefull, has of late turned his hand towards politicks, and published a Pamphlet in relation to Dunkirk, w[ch] you may perhaps have seen by this time." On the 24th September, *A Second Whig Letter from Will. Prynn to Nestor Ironside, Esq.*, seems to have been published.[1] There was also *Another Letter from a Country Whig to Richard Steele, Esq.*;

[1] *Post-Boy*, September 22 to 24, 1713. Another pamphlet, advertised in the *Post-Boy* for October 8 to 10, was called "The Importance of Penknives considered. In a letter to the Bayliff of Ipswich, occasioned by the fragments of Count Guiscard, as also an anatomical discourse, wherein some mistakes of the modern anatomists are corrected; and the throat and ears are proved to be situate in the same place, being the Sequel to the Letter, Written for his own private use, and now published for the benefit of the public. By a Barrister of the Inner Temple."

on his Defence of his Guardian, August the 7th, which is dated September 25, but which was not published, according to the *Post-Boy,* until November 17. It contains sneers at the Dedication to the Bailiff of Stockbridge, who knew nothing of the subject, but who would perhaps now return Steele *gratis* if he should lose his seat upon the petition lodged against him. The borough would choose Lewis Baboon himself if his Louis d'ors outweighed Steele's guineas, in spite of this Epistle. He had eaten the Queen's bread for many years, "and that too whilst he wanted it." "All the world knows he served at first (if not as a caddee) as a subaltern in the Guards for bread."

Questions arising out of the Treaty of Commerce were discussed during this summer by two periodicals, the *Mercator,* to which Defoe was the principal contributor, and the *British Merchant,* by Henry Martyn. It is interesting to notice the tone in which Defoe referred to Steele, even when opposing his views. In the *Mercator* for September 26 to 29 Defoe wrote: "To carry on this war more successfully than they have yet been able to do, they have chosen a new General. The Guardian is now entered into the dispute; and who shall be able to stand before the Guardian? . . . The Guardian has so many better talents that it can be no detracting from him to say that the knowledge of trade was not of the number of his acquisitions. . . . The Mercator thinks he does the Guardian all possible honour in this, that he leaves the little barking world to triumph in their own mistakes, and to fancy themselves conqueror, when another paper would annihilate the very being of all they had to say; that he may join issue with a man whose sense and good manners qualify him to be a match for any man, provided his cause be good, and who it is hoped will handsomely yield a cause up if it be otherwise." Defoe then proceeded to argue, in the three following numbers, against certain things maintained in No. 170 of the *Guardian.* It is to be regretted that Addison, in his contribution to the discussion, a pamphlet called *The Trial and Conviction of Count Tariff,* adopted a very different style. He classed the *Mercator* and *Examiner* together, hinted at the fear occasioned by the word

Pillory, and called the Mercator "a false, shuffling, prevaricating rascal."

On the 1st October No. 175 of the *Guardian* appeared, without any indication that it was to be the last, but so it was. Steele felt fettered by the plan of the work, and thought it better to start a new paper, in which politics could be freely discussed. Accordingly the first number of the *Englishman, Being the Sequel of the Guardian*, appeared on the 6th October, published by Buckley. Pope wrote that the true reason why Steele laid down the *Guardian* was a quarrel with J. Tonson, its publisher. "He stood engaged to his bookseller in articles of penalty for all the Guardians; and by desisting two days, and altering the title of the paper to that of the Englishman, was quit of the obligation, these papers being printed for Buckley."[1] It is to be presumed that Pope learned this from Tonson, who was his own publisher, but nevertheless we are not convinced of the accuracy of the statement. It has been pointed out that the agreement with Tonson must have been very loosely worded if it could be so easily evaded. Two days before the last number of the *Guardian* appeared Steele wrote to his wife that he had "settled all things to great satisfaction," and

[1] This passage occurs in a letter to Addison—to whom it would have been manifestly absurd to have sent as information what is told in it—which, from its position in the series, is represented as having been written after November 2, 1713. In reality this letter is compiled from three addressed to Caryll, two in June and one in October, and as first published this concoction mentioned the *Guardian* as if it were still going on, at the same time that the termination of that periodical was described. Pope therefore omitted, in the quarto edition, the paragraph quoted in the text; but this alteration only led to new contradictions, for what followed was thus made to refer to the *Guardian*, a paper which had, as a matter of fact, been discontinued before this portion of the letter was really written to Caryll on the 17th October—instead of the *Englishman*, to which allusion was in reality made. This was the passage (Pope had said that he had been rebuked by violent Tories for writing with Steele): "As to his taking a more politic turn, I cannot any way enter into that secret, nor have I been let into it, any more than into the rest of his politics. Tho' 'tis said, he will take into these papers also several subjects of the politer kind, as before: but I assure you, as to myself, I have quite done with them for the future. The little I have done, and the great respect I bear Mr. Steele as a man of wit, has rendered me a suspected Whig to some of the violent; but as old Dryden said before me, ''tis not the violent I design to please.'"

that if she would send the coach he would come to her, to take the air and talk further.

The *Englishman* appeared three days a week,[1] and reached to fifty-seven numbers, of which the last was published as a quarto pamphlet. It was chiefly concerned with political matters, sometimes in the form of discourses on the constitution, on passive obedience, on the Protestant succession; sometimes in the more definite form of replies to the *Examiner;* and it cannot be denied that as a whole it is dry reading. But there are various passages of more general interest, of which the most noteworthy is the account of Alexander Selkirk in No. 26. In No. 21 a correspondent described the pleasure he found in country drives in his chaise, and in No. 34 Steele wrote pleasantly of a recent visit to Oxford. From this and other passages of an autobiographical kind quotations have already been made. There is evidence that Steele received assistance from others in conducting the paper;[2] and apart from this, especially when we take into account the large number of letters printed, there could be little doubt that he did not write the whole himself.

In the first number we are told how Nestor Ironside, in handing over his goods to the Englishman, his successor, said it was not "now a time to improve the taste of men by the reflections and railleries of poets and philosophers, but to awaken their understanding by laying before them the present state of the world like a man of experience and a patriot: It is a jest to throw away our care in providing for the palate, where the whole body is in danger of death." It was this feeling that was the real cause of the change from the *Guardian* to the *Englishman*, in which there were to be no fetters to prevent the discussion of what Steele now felt to be vital questions. But he did not think discourses on polite learning at all digressive from the main design, "which is, to collect all I can for the improvement of our public spirit." It was the

[1] "This day is published, The Englishman. Being the Sequel of the Guardian. No. 1. To be published every Tuesday, Thursday and Saturday. Price 2d" (*Daily Courant*, October 6, 1713).

[2] Page 394, note 2.

misfortune of the time that people thought it as easy to be critics as politicians. In the last number Steele says: "That which moved in me an indignation not to be suppressed was the licentious abuse of great and good men who had served their country with honour and success. I thought what favour I had obtained by being the author of an instructive way of representing the manners of men, and describing vices and virtues in a style that might fall in with their ordinary entertainments, could not be more worthily employed, improved, or lost, than in defence of such men and of the constitution itself, which they had supported."

About this time Steele seems to have contemplated starting another periodical, to be called *The Scavenger*, or some such name. The following draft of the opening number is among the Blenheim papers.

Many years ago it was thought a True saying that a good name is better than precious ointment but indeed things by reason of contending parties are at present brought to that Height that a man does not know what to beleive, or where to have any body that is talking to Him. Now observing that there are so many flim-flams spread abroad that People do not know how to give credit to their nearest relations I have undertaken this paper, and have given it the name as above, to signifie y[t] as the man who comes once a Week to clear the streets of filth, I shall take upon me the office of removing Scandall, at whosever door it is laid, without regard to anything but the Truth. It is said that good Wine needs no bush, Therefore I shall depend upon the matter rather than the Stile of my writings. But I am to let the world understand a little after what manner I shall pursue this labour. It is therefore to be observed that the Great Nuisances in the morall World are occasioned by the News Writer and other publick papers which come out every day. The greatest man in England at present for this sort of writing is M[r] Able Roper who some people say, is author of the Post Boy. He is but an inconsiderable man to look at. His Height four foot three inches; of late He is very fashionable in His Cloaths. His nose is short, his eyes are sleepy, His face is round, His Head much like the Spectators as to the outward form of it. He smoakes tobacco, and drinks in a morning at any of the Tippling places near White Hall when a mail comes in. He is not a fool tho he has more cunning than understanding. But that the World is full of Wonders, one would be amazed how He should be so much talked of as He is. I shall take this man and all his works away with me at once;[1] But in the same Cart I would if I could find Him out remove also the Examiner who is as much a Knave as the other is a fool. These two Authors take upon them to use passengers as they please and smut their faces at such a rate that they make devils of them. My plan therefore is to have my eye more particularly on these Gentlemen and carry to the Hillocks of dirt and cinders behind Grubstreet their works as fast as they come out and shall begin with their two last.

On the 6th October, immediately after the cessation of the *Guardian*, Hughes wrote to Addison suggesting the establishment of a paper to be called the *Register*, which was to give the proceedings of a supposed society of learned men, partly in dialogue. Steele's *Englishman*, he said, was "written with great boldness and spirit, and shows that his thoughts are at present entirely on politics. Some of his friends are in pain about him, and are concerned that a paper should be discontinued, which might have been generally entertaining without engaging in party matters." Addison answered, on the 12th, that he could not at present write for the proposed new paper, as he required rest to lay in fuel; and Hughes abandoned his design. But Sir Richard Blackmore, who had prompted Hughes in writing to Addison, determined to make the experiment, and he accordingly started the *Lay Monk* on the 16th November, with the assistance of Hughes. This periodical, which met with no great success, lasted until February 1714, when the numbers were collected into a volume, under the title of *The Lay Monastery*. While declining to assist Hughes, Addison added: "In the meantime I should be glad if you would set such a project on foot, for I know nobody else capable of succeeding in it, and turning it to the good of mankind, since my friend has laid it down. I am in a thousand troubles for poor Dick, and wish that his zeal for the public may not be ruinous to himself; but he has sent me word, that he is determined to go on, and that any advice I can give him, in this particular, will have no weight with him."

[1] "for he has nothing that can be preserved with any safety to the," cancelled.

Pope said that "Addison used to blame his dear friend Steele for being too much of a party man;" but Addison must have admired the courage of his friend, who had the same cause at heart as himself, but was prepared to risk more for it.

Swift's stay in Ireland had been short, for Oxford and Bolingbroke had broken out into open quarrel, and Swift was summoned to England in the hope that he could effect a reconciliation. One of the first things he did upon his return was to produce a pamphlet against Steele, which is one of the cleverest and one of the most rancorous of his works. *The Importance of the Guardian Considered, in a Second Letter to the Bailiff of Stockbridge. By a Friend of Mr. St—le,* was published at the end of October.[1] In the Preface Swift said he would enter very little into the subject Steele pretended to treat, but would consider his pamphlet partly as a critic and partly as a commentator; "which, I think, 'is to treat him only as my brother-scribbler,' according to the permission he has graciously allowed me." Certainly Swift carried out this plan; there is little in the pamphlet about Dunkirk, and a great deal about Steele. He began by saying that the *Importance of Dunkirk* was chiefly taken up in showing the importance of Mr. Steele; he would therefore aim at setting this gentleman's importance in a clearer light, but without running into his early history, "because I owe him no malice." Then came the following passage, from which, and from others that follow, it may be judged how far Swift wrote without malice. "He hath no invention, nor is master of a tolerable style;[2] his chief talent is humour, which he sometimes discovers both in writing and discourse; for after the first bottle he is no disagreeable companion. I never knew him taxed with ill-nature, which hath made me wonder how ingratitude came to be his prevailing vice; and I am apt to think it proceeds more from some unaccountable sort of instinct than premeditation. Being the most imprudent man alive, he never follows the advice of his friends, but is wholly at the

[1] *Post-Boy*, October 29 to 31, 1713.

[2] On this point it is interesting to compare what Swift wrote in his *Proposal for Correcting the English Tongue*, in 1712. There Steele is spoken of as the ingenious author of the *Tatler* and *Spectator*, "who hath tried the force and compass of our language with so much success." See p. 336, note 2.

mercy of fools or knaves, or hurried away by his own caprice; by which he hath committed more absurdities in economy, friendship, love, duty, good manners, politics, religion, and writing, than ever fell to one man's share." The *Tatler*, "by contribution of his ingenious friends," obtained a great reputation, which it maintained until Steele published virulent libels against Harley. Then follows the account of Steele's appointment as Gazetteer and of his loss of that post, which has already been given. The charge of ingratitude, says Swift, had clearly broken down, for Steele "had already received his salary, and spent his money, and consequently the bread was eaten at least a week before he would offer to insult his Prince." Steele said he quitted his employments to render himself more useful as a member of Parliament. Swift would add some other motives. First, Steele thought it impossible that the ministry would let him keep his place much longer, after the part he had acted; secondly, he said publicly that he was ashamed to be obliged any longer to the Lord Treasurer, whom he had used so ill; thirdly, he "appeals for protection to you, Mr. Bailiff, from *others* of your *denomination*, who would have carried him *somewhere else*, if you had not relieved him by your *habeas corpus* to St. Stephen's Chapel;" and, fourthly, he found that the ministry was near expiring, and stripped off, therefore, the very garments spotted with the flesh, so as to be wholly regenerate against the return of his old masters. The first of these reasons given by Swift is, of course, directly contradicted by what Steele said in his letter to Lord Oxford in June. Of the *Englishman* Swift wrote: "Mr. Steele publishes every day a penny paper, to be read in coffee-houses, and get him a little money. This, by a figure of speech, he calls 'laying things before the ministry,' who seem at present a little too busy to regard such memorials; and, I dare say, never saw his paper, unless he sent it by the penny post." A little further on he says: "What Bailiff would venture to arrest Mr. Steele, now he has the honour to be your representative? And what Bailiff ever scrupled it before?" "How did he acquire these abilities of directing in the councils of Princes? Was it from **publishing** *Tatlers* and *Spectators*, and writing now and then a *Guardian?* Was it from his being a soldier, alchemist, gazetteer, commissioner of stampt papers, or gentleman-usher?" No; but every man, he said, had a right to lay "before the Queen and ministry" in print his views of their faults, and to point out dangers which he could certainly see, but which the ministers did not. "Mr. Steele, who, from some few sprinklings of rudimental literature, proceeded a gentleman of the Horse Guards, thence by several degrees to be an ensign and an alchemist, where he was wholly conversant with the lower part of mankind, thinks he 'knows the world' as well as the Prime Minister; and, upon the strength of that knowledge, will needs direct her Majesty in the weightiest matters of government." "As for the importance of Dunkirk, and when it shall be demolished, or whether it shall be demolished or not, neither he nor you nor I have anything to do in the matter. Let us all say what we please, her Majesty will think herself the best judge, and her ministers the best advisers; . . . and it is not altogether impossible that there may be some few reasons of State which have not been yet communicated to Mr. Steele."

So ends Swift's pamphlet. I have quoted from it at some length, because it represents well what was said by many unknown and weaker writers, whose attacks were not so damaging because they wrote less coolly and in a coarser style. But such pieces served their purpose, no doubt, among those for whom they were written, and Swift himself certainly gave hints, if nothing more, towards the composition of some of them. Colley Cibber laughed at the manner in which, while Steele wrote the *Tatler*, persons of all classes and ages were his friends, "and thought their tea in a morning had not its taste without him," and yet in a moment, when Steele's sense of duty caused him to take upon himself the restless office of a patriot, one half of the nation denied that he had either wit, sense, or genius, and in order to maintain this in the face of his writings, gave the chief merit of them to another great author, his nearest friend.[1]

In the *Post-Boy* for October 10 to 13 it was announced that

[1] Dedication to *Ximena*, 1719.

"there is in the press, and will be published next Term, A dialogue between Jacob Broad and the late Nestor Ironside, in relation to Building; the first plainly proves that in some cases it's lawful to untile a house; and the other proves that in other cases it's as lawful to get into it, provided he pays the Bayliff." Whether this production ever really saw the light does not appear, but from the fact that Jacob Broad was a well-known bailiff[1] we may guess what form this attack upon Steele would take. In the middle of October[2] a pamphlet appeared with the title, *A Dialogue between A and B*, "Containing some remarks upon Mr. Steele's Letter to the Englishman." The author, after discussing Steele's letter about the *Examiner* in the first number of the *Englishman*, remarked that anger often leads to frenzy, and that madness runs in the blood. "Therefore, if there's any man that is in the first place a great wit, in the next place has had the misfortune of a fine woman of his family to grow distracted, and moreover finds that anger leads him the same way," should he not be very cautious amidst misfortunes which threatened to end not, as some had thought formerly, in a Gaol, but in Bedlam? Here we apparently have another allusion to Steele's sister Katherine.

A little later a much better-known pamphlet was published, under the title, *The Character of Richard St—le, Esq.; With some Remarks;* by "Toby, Abel's Kinsman; or, according to Mr. Calamy, A. F. & N. In a Letter to his Godfather." This tract appeared on the 12th November; on the 14th the *Post-Boy* announced that 1000 copies had been struck off, and that a second edition was ready; on the 19th the public was warned against a spurious edition by R. Marthard, near Fleet Street, which was abridged, and had a forlorn portrait on wood; and on the 28th the *Post-Boy* said that as the *London Gazette* had stated that it was not doubted but that Steele would write an answer to the *Character*, Mr. Toby defied him to answer it; and added that the said Mr. Toby was collecting some choice

[1] Broad died in 1721. Some particulars about him will be found in *The Comical and Tragical History of the Lives and Adventures of the most noted Bayliffs in and about London and Westminster, . . . and particularly, the Lives of Jacob Broad and Jack Faringdon*, by Captain Alexander Smith, 1723.

[2] *Post-Boy*, October 15 to 17, 1713.

materials concerning the recent history of Mr. Steele, "which, if he does not mend his manners, may be communicated in due course to the surprise of the whole world." In the same paper for the 3rd December there were sneers at philosophers and philosophers' stones, and on the 8th a third edition of the *Character* was announced, together with the warning, "Beware of counterfeits, for there are many." The fourth edition was issued on the 18th March 1714, the day upon which Steele was expelled the House of Commons.

Of the contents of this widely circulated pamphlet it is not necessary to say much. Steele had lately, the writer states, had a Welsh estate left him by his wife's mother, and beginning to look upon himself as a considerable person in land as well as sense, he was told by the minor poets at Button's that if he was in the Senate he had all the qualifications necessary for a minister of State. He was the more ready to listen to this advice because if he got into the House he could not be arrested; and above all there "was a pension from the party,[1] double the income of the Stamp-Office at present, and in hand, for speaking in the House." The only thing that perplexed him at Stockbridge was a demand for the payment of a £300 bond, which lessened the sum he carried down. As regards the question of Dunkirk, "the person of M. Tugghe was obscure, if not feigned, his memorial inconsiderable, if not written by Mr. St—le." Yet this was the man who published the *Tatlers* and *Spectators*, who was believed to be one of the most accomplished gentlemen in the world, who talked like an oracle, and had all the gay, the delicate, the humorous, at his command. No one had so good an opinion of his veracity as to believe him in trifles and matters of the least importance. His debts were the effect of his luxury, vanity, and ambition, not of accident or misfortune. Spendthrifts and projectors of any sort are pernicious. Where was the public spirit of a man who could be bribed to recommend a barber, a buffoon, or a perfumer to the world? Where is his disinterest who votes for more than double an equivalent of

[1] Steele refers to this "groundless suspicion" at the close of the last number of the *Englishman*.

the Stamp-Office? The best thing Steele could do would be to retire into Wales and live upon his estate; he might thus keep his circumstances within bounds, and when his head was purged of politics he might now and then revisit and divert the Town by publishing the works of his friends. If he persisted in his purpose he would ere long be in gaol, or in Bedlam. "It would have been as much a crime, but a little while since, to have spoke against him, as now it is to speak for him." Toby's letter, which is dated from Will's Coffee-house, October 27, concludes with remarks upon the advertisements of Steele's forthcoming Treatise in favour of the Hanover Succession. In a postscript there are remarks on the *Importance of Dunkirk Considered*, such as the following: "A man of liberal education, according to Mr. St—le's acceptation of that word, is, one of mean parentage, who was bred at school till he could almost construe Latin, and has since improved himself in the knowledge of the world by riding in the Guards, by conversing with porters, carmen, foot-soldiers, players, bullies, bawds, pimps, and whores of all sorts and sizes; who has been arrested for the maintenance of his bastards, and afterwards printed a *Proposal* that the public should take care of them; one who has no invention, no judgment, no style, no politics, no gratitude, and no honesty." Although "Dr. W—k—r so often flogged our author when he was at school, for false grammar," he continued to affront Lilly almost in every word.

Such was the pamphlet of which the authorship has been so much discussed.[1] To take, in the first place, the names given on the title-page, Abel Roper was a scurrilous printer and bookseller, who conducted the Tory *Post-Boy*. He had a nephew "Toby," or Edward King, son of Thomas King, a farrier of Coventry, and Ruth Roper, Abel's sister. This blinking boy came to London and helped his uncle in his business. These and other particulars are to be found in a pamphlet published in 1726, which seems to have escaped the notice of writers upon the subject; it is called "Some Memoirs of the Life of Abel, Toby's Uncle. By Dr. Andrew

[1] Dilke's *Papers of a Critic*, i. 366–82; *Notes and Queries*, 3rd Series, i. 381, ii. 131, 253; 6th Series, x. 223.

Tripe. To which is added the Phyz of his Nephew Toby, curiously engraved on Copper: As also his Life and Character." The author says that the *Character of Richard St—le, Esq.*, was not by Toby, who knew nothing of politics; "the real author (as I am informed by Mr. Butler, the bookseller, in Holborn) was Dr. Wagstaff, Physician to St. Bartholomew's Hospital, a very facetious and pleasant gentleman; who was likewise author of that excellent piece, called 'A Comment upon the History of Tom Thumb.'" But when Toby was asked whether he wrote the *Character* he would shake his head, squint, and say nothing. Further on we are told how Toby, reading a tract about the Great Rebellion, found in the Journals of the Rebels a Resolution, dated 8th January 1648, in which the name Steele—the William Steele who was afterwards Lord Chancellor of Ireland—was mentioned as counsel; Toby said he hoped this was no relation of Sir Richard Steele, "for tho' I have lately taken upon me to give the character of that gentleman, I have a better opinion of him than to think him descended from one that could plead against Majesty." Sir Christopher Hales, who is stated to have been present, said he knew nothing of the matter.

So much for Toby. Who, then, was Dr. Wagstaff, here said to be the author of the *Character?* In June 1706, William Wagstaffe, Gent., of Lincoln College, Oxford, published "Ramilies, a Poem."[1] He had taken his degree of B.A. in 1704, was M.A. in 1707, and B. and D.M. in 1714. At the close of 1720 he was appointed physician to St. Bartholomew's Hospital;[2] in 1722 he published a tract on inoculation; and he died in May 1725. In the following year appeared a volume, entitled *Miscellaneous Works of Dr. William Wagstaffe*, together with a Life substantially correct, and, as a frontispiece, a portrait of "Mr. Toby," a person with a spotted complexion and a squint, identical with that prefixed to the original issue of the *Character of Richard St—le, Esq.;* and used also in the *Memoirs of the Life of Abel, Toby's Uncle.*[3] This curious volume

[1] *Works of the Learned*, June 1706, p. 382.

[2] *Historical Register*, 1721.

[3] Granger said that he had seen Vander Gucht's print of Roper and his man

contains, among other things, reprints of *A Comment upon the History of Tom Thumb*,[1] written in ridicule of Addison's papers upon "Chevy Chase" in the *Spectator;* the *Story of the St. A——n's Ghost;*[2] the *Plain Dealer*, which had been published as a periodical in 1712, and in which Steele was often attacked under the name of Dick Hotspur; *A Letter from the Facetious Dr. Andrew Tripe, at Bath, to his Loving Brother the Profound Greshamite;*[3] and the fourth edition of the *Character of Richard St—le, Esq.* The author of the Life prefixed to this volume apologises for the *Character*, "because it seems to bear too hard upon a gentleman of known parts and abilities, though of contrary principles to the Doctor," who, when the thing was written, did not even know Steele by sight.

Who, then, wrote the *Character* and the other things in this volume? Mr. Crossley thought they were really by Wagstaffe, but was not able to bring forward any other literary works by the Doctor. Mr. Solly, however, subsequently pointed out that Wagstaffe had written the poem "Ramilies." Scott assumed that Wagstaffe was an "under-spur leather" of Swift's, and some of the papers in the volume of "Works" certainly seem to be Swift's. Mr. Dilke thought that Swift himself wrote the *Character*. The tract implies personal knowledge of Steele, and a feeling of personal wrong; in *Gulliveriana* it seems to be attributed to Swift, and Steele himself appears to have thought Swift the author.[4] Swift afterwards published his own *Polite Conversation*, under the name of "Simon Wagstaffe,"[5] and he had some years before made use of the name "Tripe" in his poem

Toby, with warts on his face, inscribed "Dr. Wagstaff," in manuscript, but that he was afterwards assured by Vander Gucht that Toby was not designed for Wagstaffe (Noble's *Continuation of Granger*, 1806, ii. 310–11). These effigies of Abel and Toby, "from the original at Will's," were published in March 1713 (*Flying Post*, March 10 and 14, 1712–13).

[1] Mr. Crossley possessed a copy of the first edition of this pamphlet (1711), with the words "By Mr. Wagstaff" on the title-page in contemporary writing.

[2] Swift speaks equivocally of the authorship of this tract in his *Journal*, February 22, 1712.

[3] See vol. ii. page 10.

[4] *Englishman*, No. 57.

[5] Oldisworth, too, published his *Annotations on the Tatler*, 1710, under the name of Walter Wagstaff, Esq.

The Swan Tripe Club. Pope, in the "Testimonies of Authors," prefixed to the *Dunciad*, spoke of the Dr. Andrew Tripe pamphlet as "one Mr. Wagstaff's," evidently a person of some obscurity. All this, however, even if we grant that the volume of "Works" was probably by various authors, and was merely palmed off upon the lately deceased Dr. Wagstaffe, does not prove that Swift was author of the *Character*. He may or may not have had a hand in it, but there were many who would know enough of Steele's private affairs to enable them to introduce such personal allusions as are to be found in the tract. These scandalous tales would no doubt be the common talk of the town, and could be gathered together and served up by any unscrupulous writer. The argument that this tract was surely beneath Swift cannot, on the other hand, count for much when we remember that he was not above writing, and admitting that he wrote, articles for the *Post-Boy*, "as malicious as possible, and very proper for Abel Roper, the printer of it."[1]

A few words will be sufficient for the other pamphlets published in this year. On the 8th December[2] appeared a quarto pamphlet, with the date 1714, called *John Tutchin's Ghost to Richard St—le, Esq.; Discovering something omitted by Mr. Toby.* This tract, partly in verse, describes Steele's decease as essayist, and reappearance as *Englishman* and successor to Tutchin. He had, "with the greatest justice, gained himself the applause of the best part of mankind, as well as the admiration of the fair sex, who were grown such constant readers of his paper, that you should scarce find a lady dressing, or drinking tea in a morning with her friend, but Mr. St—le's paper made up the best part of the entertainment." How deplorable, then, was the catastrophe which had befallen him! At the end of the tract are advertisements of imaginary forthcoming books against Steele,[3] the last of which announcements

[1] *Journal*, November 17, 1712.

[2] *Post-Boy*, December 5 to 8, 1713.

[3] For example, "Complete Sets of those Tatlers, Spectators and Guardians, that came abroad in Mr. St—l's name, of which he was only the publisher; whereby the world may see how indifferent a figure the crow makes when the gay birds have the fine feathers returned, which they stuck in his cap."—"Letters Amorous and Gallant, in the most polite style, from the wisest

contains allusions to the Preface to a poetical tract which had been published on the 1st December, with the title, *An Original Canto of Spencer:* Designed as part of his Fairy Queen, but never printed. Now made publick. By *Nestor Ironside, Esq.*[1] This tract, as well as *Another Canto*, &c., was by Samuel Croxall, one of whose poems appeared shortly afterwards in Steele's *Poëtical Miscellanies*, and another in the second edition of that collection. The *Examiner* for December 14 to 18 attacked the *Original Canto*, a political allegory very popular among the Whigs, on the assumption that Steele was the author. On the 23rd December Croxall published *The Examiner Examin'd. In a Letter to the Englishman: Occasioned by the Examiner of Friday, December* 18, 1713. *Upon the Canto of Spencer.*[2] This pamphlet reached a second edition before the close of the year, but it contains nothing that calls for remark.

The first of the following letters relates to the subscription for the *Crisis*, which had been announced in the *Englishman*:—

BLOOMSBURY.[3]

DEAR PRUE,

I have, on second thoughts, resolved to go to the Club, and ask for a subscription myself; and, with as gay an air as I can, lay before them that I take it to be their constitution to do it, as I am labouring in the common cause. I will be at home early. Pray do you resolve to be beautiful, as I do to be cheerful.

Yours ever, RICHARD STEELE.

It frets my proud heart to do this, but it must be.

Mr. Hopkins spoke to me to-day to go with my Lord Godolphin to Putney. I stayed only to finish my papers, and am gone thither in haste.

Yours ever, R: S:

I shall now learn all that[4]

S—tor of B——n to the Fidler's wife of S—kbridge; with her answers."—"The Irishman, containing the pleasant History of the Family of Ironsides, from the time of Sidrophel the ballad-singer, in the reign of Henry the Fourth, to Nestor Ironside the Gypsy, in the time of Charles the Second. This work being designed to be published in fragments, three times a week: the first, which will come out the day Mr. S—le sits in the H—use, after the S—kbridge petition is heard, will relate," &c.

[1] *Daily Courant*, December 1, 1713. A second edition was advertised as "just published" in the same paper for December 3rd. See *Notes and Queries*, 6th Series, xi. 515.

[2] *Daily Courant*, December 23, 1713.

[3] Afterwards erased.

[4] The paper is here cut.

DEAR PRUE,

If you and Mrs. Edwards can make use of these tickets which were given Me I shall be glad, If not send them back, and I will give them to other people for I will not go my self to any publick diversion except you are of the assembly.

Y^rs ever RICHARD STEELE.

BLOOMESBURY-SQUARE,
December 24th, 1713.

DEAR PRUE

I dine with Lord Hallifax and shall be at home half hour after six.

For Thee I dye for Thee I Languish

RICHARD STEELE.

From the *Englishman* for the 26th December it appears that Steele had been suffering from an attack of gout. We are there told how he was ushered into the room by Mr. Button, on his crutches, and consoled by the company as regards the calumnies published against him during his indisposition. But he turned off the discourse, and told them how on his way there the people, incommoded by the chairmen, and seeing a fat fellow in a vehicle, cried out, "Lazy booby, marry come up, carrying would become him better than being carried;" but when he met a gentleman and explained that he was lame, the gentleman's sourness turned to a smile. It would be as easy, Steele added, to answer the other reproaches brought against him as that of laziness on his journey thither.

There is an amusing place-hunting letter among the Blenheim MSS. from the Bailiff of Stockbridge to the member for the borough, who had brought notoriety upon the town and its bailiff by publishing the *Importance of Dunkirk Considered*, in the form of a letter to the Worshipful Mr. John Snow.

HON^D S^R

A Particular ffriend of yo^rs and Mine has been with me to desire me to write this to yor Hon^r to desire ye favour of you to put him in a Method which way he may get a friend into some small post in ye Stamp office, he knowing that you have been one of y^e

Masters of it thought you to be a proper person to Advize what Method to take and whom to aplie to for such a favour and if there be any of y[e] pence required by those that are in power to hasten such a favour it shall not be wanting pray S[r] doe me and my friend y[e] favour as to send me an Answer as soon as you cann conveniently to advize him w[t] to do in this Case And in soe doeing you'l oblige S[r]

Y[r] Most Obedient Most
humble Serv[t] to Comm[d]
JOHN SNOW.

STOCKBRIDGE
Decem[br] y[e] 21st, 1713.

I shall have occasion to draw a bill of five pounds odd money payable to M[r] Reynoldson, when brought to you I begg y[e] favour of you to pay it.

At the close of the year[1] Steele published a volume of *Poetical Miscellanies,* "consisting of Original Poems and Translations By the best Hands," but, in accordance with the usual practice, the book bore the date 1714 on the title-page; a second and enlarged edition appeared in 1727. Contributions to the volume had been invited in an advertisement in the *Guardian* for the 8th May. The collection opened with Pope's *Wife of Bath,* and included verses by Parnell, Tickell, Philips, Gay, Eusden, Budgell, Young, Harrison, and others. Steele's own contributions, so far as we know, consisted only of the lines to Congreve on the *Way of the World*, and of the *Procession*, both of which had been printed many years before. Nichols surmised that some of the numerous anonymous pieces were by Steele. Steele also wrote a very laudatory Dedication to Congreve, in which he bestowed especial praise upon Congreve's poem *Doris*, "my favourite."[2] But he chose rather, as one that had passed many happy hours with him, to celebrate his friend's easy condescension of mind, and command of a pleasant

[1] Published "this day" (*Englishman*, No. 37, December 29); published "this day" (*Daily Courant*, December 31, 1713). The book was announced as to be published "in a few days" in the *Englishman*, No. 31, December 15.

[2] Cf. *Spectator*, No. 422.

imagination, which gave him "the uncommon praise of a man of wit, always to please, and never to offend. No one, after a joyful evening, can reflect upon an expression of Mr. Congreve's that dwells upon him with pain."

END OF VOL. I.